Coursebook to accompany

ECONOMICS
Private and Public Choice

Sixth Edition

A.H. Studenmund
Occidental College

Richard L. Stroup
Montana State University

James D. Gwartney
Florida State University

The Dryden Press
Harcourt Brace Jovanovich College Publishers
Fort Worth   Philadelphia   San Diego   New York   Orlando   Austin   San Antonio
Toronto   Montreal   London   Sydney   Tokyo

Address for Editorial Correspondence
The Dryden Press, 301 Commerce Street, Suite 3700, Fort Worth, TX 76102

Address for Orders
The Dryden Press, 6277 Sea Harbor Drive, Orlando, FL 32887
1-800-782-4479, or 1-800-433-0001 (in Florida)

ISBN: 0-15-518924-7

Printed in the United States of America

2 3 4 5 6 7 8 9 0 1   054   9 8 7 6 5 4 3 2 1

The Dryden Press
Harcourt Brace Jovanovich

Preface

We are often asked why we call this book a *Coursebook* rather than a "study guide." We use the title *Coursebook* because we feel that this volume goes well beyond the typical study guide in at least three ways:

1. *Critical Analysis*   We stress questions that require in-depth economic reasoning. Most of these more analytical questions force students to come up with their *own* answers rather than passively choosing between a group of prepared alternatives.

2. *Readings and Debates*   We include short and interesting readings by a broad spectrum of economists. For example, we have paired opposing viewpoints on given topics into a series of debates. These debates not only provide material for classroom discussion, they also allow students to develop their own opinions on the issues. In this edition, we've added two interesting crossword puzzles.

3. *Explained Answers with References to Pages in the Text*   For about half the questions, we include explanations of *why* a particular answer is correct. We also provide a page reference to the section in the text that explains the topic in more detail.

In writing this *Coursebook*, we have attempted to strike a balance between economic reasoning and mechanics. Often, a supplementary workbook is little more than a set of mechanical exercises. Such exercises lack substance and meaning for the student who has not yet acquired a firm foundation in the economic way of thinking. Our teaching experience has shown that stressing real-world situations, presenting actual data, providing selected short readings, and explaining why particular answers are correct — as we have done in the *Coursebook* — illuminate the power and utility of economic reasoning.

The *Coursebook* has been structured to maximize the student's comprehension of the concepts presented in each chapter of *Economics: Private and Public Choice*, Sixth Edition. Like the main text, the *Coursebook* contains 34 chapters; each chapter is divided into several sections that combine the instruction of economic principles, as covered in the text, with mechanical exercises.

The first section of each chapter is composed of approximately 14 true-false questions. Although this section has a realistic flavor, mechanics are emphasized. "Problems and Projects," the second section, emphasizes both mechanics and economic reasoning. This section contains some case-study-type problems as well as some questions that ask students to review basic concepts. The third section, "Learning the Mechanics – Multiple Choice," contains multiple-choice questions of the type familiar to most students. Many questions are sufficiently difficult to challenge even knowledgeable students. Questions posed in the fourth section, "The Economic Way of Thinking – Multiple Choice," often utilize actual data to emphasize economic reasoning. Some items test the student's ability to distinguish between sound logic and economic nonsense; others ask the student to devise the proper policy for reaching a given set of economic goals. To answer these "complex application"-type questions, the student must be able to apply principles to realistic situations. For students unaccustomed to critical thinking, these questions will be difficult; yet they present a challenge far more stimulating than exercises that test rote learning. Finally, each chapter contains discussion questions that are intended to provoke further speculation on economic issues.

More than merely a workbook, the *Coursebook* serves as a reader, presenting a "Perspectives in Economics" section in almost every chapter. These articles are readable and engaging, will reinforce the classroom presentation of economic lessons, and will expand on important concepts discussed in the text. Some articles offer an historical perspective, clearly stating the views of such renowned economists as Milton Friedman or Walter Heller. Other readings give students the opportunity to read firsthand the ideas of newer voices such as Sam Bowles or Robert Crandall. Following each selection are questions asking the student to evaluate the position of the author. Is the reasoning sound? Is it opinionated? Does empirical evidence support the author's contention? This feature of the *Coursebook* again highlights the usefulness of economics in our everyday lives.

A popular item for students is a series of "Current Debates in Economics," paired readings that express opposing viewpoints on such topics as "Should We Raise the Minimum Wage?" and "Should We Have a Market Economy?" These debates will force students to come to grips with differences in opinion among economists and to form their own views on the issues. In addition, classes can stage formal "debates," allowing some or all of the students to develop their argumentation and oral presentation skills.

The Sixth Edition marks the first time we've included crossword puzzles, one each on macroeconomics and microeconomics, in the *Coursebook*. These puzzles, which originally appeared in *The Margin*, provide a relaxing and interesting way for students to review economic definitions and concepts.

Answers to virtually every question are provided in the "Answer Key" at the back of the *Coursebook*. The Answer Key also contains two unique features that will make the questions significantly more useful for student learning. First, all the multiple-choice answers are followed by an explanation of why that particular answer is correct. In addition, we refer the student to the page(s) where the subject of the question is discussed in *Economics: Private and Public Choice*. In this way, a student who does not get the correct answer the first time can get an explanation of the correct answer. If that explanation is not convincing, then the student can refer to the corresponding page in the text. Students who take the time to master these questions – and who understand the rationale behind each answer – should do very well in introductory economics classes.

The Sixth Edition of the *Coursebook* has been blessed by the contributions of two talented individuals who were not previously involved with this project. Professor Jane Rossetti of Occidental College created a number of new and challenging multiple choice questions based on interesting data or realistic market situations. Rauna Sinkewitsch, a senior economics major at Occidental, provided feedback on the book from a student's point of view and helped with the task of updating data and preparing copy for publication. Others to whom we owe a debt of gratitude include Margie Rogers of Harcourt Brace Jovanovich, Paul Stewart and Tim Westmoreland of The Dryden Press, Suzanne Tregarthen of *The Margin*, and, especially, Jaynie Miller Studenmund. To these folks and everyone else involved in the Sixth Edition, we offer our heartfelt thanks.

A. H. Studenmund
Richard L. Stroup
James D. Gwartney

Contents

Contents in Brief

Chapter Number in Principles of Economics

1

The Economic Approach

TRUE OR FALSE

T F

1. According to economic theory, if there is an increase in the benefit derived from an activity, individuals will be more likely to choose that activity.

2. Leisure is not an economic good.

3. If human action were not influenced by changes in cost and benefits, economics would not have any predictive value.

4. Only the actions of selfish men are influenced by economic incentives.

5. Economic activity often has secondary effects that are not initially observable.

6. Economic theory cannot be tested because it involves human decision-makers.

7. One's use of time involves economic choice.

8. Economists utilize empirical evidence from the real world in order to test the validity of economic theory.

9. Positive economic statements involve value judgments about how the world "should be."

10. Scientific methodology can be used to test normative economic statements.

11. The following is a positive economic statement: "An increase in the price of butter will lead to a reduction in the quantity of butter purchased by consumers."

12. If public education is freely provided to the consumer, it will not qualify as a scarce or economic good.

13. Economics is based on the principle that changes in economic incentives cause human decision-makers to alter their courses of action.

14. Economic analysis applies only to those choices that relate to the production or consumption of physical goods.

15. A person's well-being is dependent only on the consumption of material goods.

1

PROBLEMS AND PROJECTS

1. For each question below, use the indicated guidepost from the text to help you answer the question and explain your answer:
   a. Guidepost 1: Do "full scholarships" make education free?
   b. Guidepost 2: According to federal and state laws, Exxon was responsible for a complete cleanup of its 1989 Alaskan oil spill. Should economizing behavior have played a role in the cleanup?
   c. Guidepost 3: Suppose a sudden increase in the quality of television increased the value of leisure time to the average citizen. Would this be likely to cause a decline in the proportion of citizens who vote?
   d. Guidepost 4: Halfway through your economics course, you consider dropping the course because of its heavy workload. What should you base your decision on, the total workload of the course or the remaining workload?
   e. Guidepost 5: Should the Food and Drug Administration require that all new drugs for AIDS be exhaustively tested for safety and effectiveness before approving their use?
   f. Guidepost 6: When the U.S. signed a deal to sell a large volume of grain to the Soviet Union in 1973, do you think the initial impact was to raise or lower the price of U.S. beef?
   g. Guidepost 7: Many Superbowl ticketholders end up reselling their tickets, sometimes for over $1,000 each. Who benefits from this "scalping," the ticket buyers, the ticket sellers, both or neither?
   h. Guidepost 8: Does it make sense to assume that firms try to maximize their profits even though firm owners often deny that profit maximizing is their primary goal?

2. Exhibit 1 shows the relationship between gas consumption of a new Chevrolet and the number of miles traveled.

Exhibit 1

Total distance traveled (miles)	Amount of gasoline consumed (gallons)
0	0
75	5
150	10
225	15
300	20
375	25
450	30

a. Graph the relationship between miles traveled and gas consumption in the space provided. Measure miles traveled on the horizontal axis (x axis) and gasoline consumption on the vertical axis (y axis). Label the graph clearly.

b. Is gasoline consumption related positively or negatively to distance traveled?

c. How many miles can be traveled on a gallon of gas? What is the slope of the distance traveled-gasoline consumption line ("curve")?

(graph for question 2)

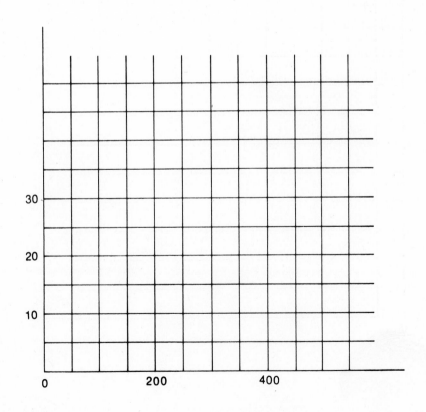

3. Height and weight are usually related. Exhibit 2 presents data for a sample of men. The average weight for men of different heights is shown.

Exhibit 2

Number of men in class	Height of individual (inches)	Mean weight (pounds)
20	70	160
23	71	168
17	72	176
18	73	182
14	74	186

a. Graph the height-weight relationship, plotting height on the horizontal axis and weight on the vertical axis. Be sure to label both axes.

b. What is the slope of the line ("curve") between 70 and 71 inches? Between 73 and 74 inches?

(graph for question 3)

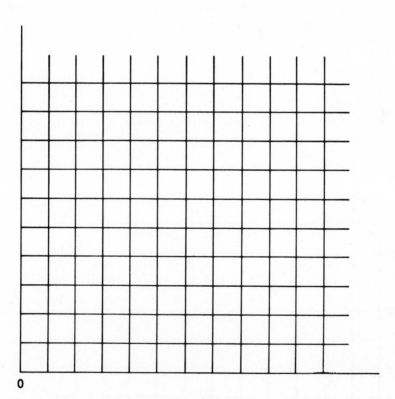

0

4. Exhibit 3 presents data on national income and personal consumption expenditures for the period from 1985 to 1990.

Exhibit 3

Year	Disposable personal income (in billions)	Personal consumption expenditures (in billions)
1985	$2839	$2629
1986	3013	2797
1987	3195	3009
1988	3479	3238
1989	3726	3450
1990	3946	3658

Source: *Economic Report of the President 1991, p. 316.*

a. Graph the relationship in the space provided. Plot disposable income on the horizontal axis and consumption expenditures on the vertical axis. Be sure to label both axes.
b. Is the relationship between disposable income and consumption expenditures positive or negative?
c. Between 1985 and 1986, by how much did income increase? By how much did consumption increase? What was the slope of the consumption-income relationship during this time period?
d. Calculate the slope of the consumption-income relationship between 1989 and 1990. Is the slope of the relationship constant from year to year?

(graph for question 4)

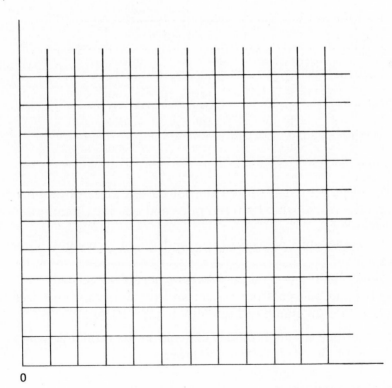

0

5. Each of the following statements ignores or violates one of the eight guideposts to economic thinking discussed in the text. In each case, identify the guidepost and explain how it has been violated.

    a. Before voting in an important election, each voter should learn as much as possible about the issues involved.

    b. Reducing the prices of necessities would clearly benefit the poor. Therefore, the government should pass laws (price controls) requiring producers of necessities to sell at low prices.

    c. One way to lower the costs associated with the armed services would be to have a military draft with low pay for those who are required to serve.

    d. Since I get the same satisfaction from reading a book, seeing a movie, or hearing a concert, it makes no difference to me which one I do.

    e. Since criminal activity is associated more with the poor than with the rich, the poor must have lower moral standards than the rich.

    f. I recently heard that some people are hiring others to do their shopping for them. It sure is silly to hire someone to do something you can clearly do for yourself.

    g. If hamburgers and pizza-by-the-slice cost the same and you like pizza more than you like hamburgers, you would always rather have another slice of pizza than another hamburger.

6. Exhibit 4 shows how the quantity of melons bought by consumers depends on the price of melons and on average consumer income.

Exhibit 4

Price (cents per pound)	Quantity bought (thousands of tons per year) for average income of	
	$10,000/year	$15,000/year
1.5	1500	1690
1.6	1420	1600
1.7	1350	1510
1.8	1280	1430
1.9	1210	1370
2.0	1170	1310

    a. On a piece of graph paper (if you do not have a piece of graph paper, draw your own) graph the relationship between price and quantity bought if income is $10,000. Label this curve D_1.

    b. Graph the relationship between price and quantity bought if income is $15,000. Label this curve D_2.

    c. Are price and quantity bought positively or negatively related?

    d. If price is fixed at 1.7 cents per pound and consumer income rises from $10,000 to $15,000 per year, how much will quantity bought change?

7. The text discusses three common pitfalls to avoid in the economic way of thinking:

    (1) Violation of the *ceteris paribus* condition
    (2) Association is not causation
    (3) Fallacy of composition

Indicate which pitfall applies to each of the following statements. Briefly explain each case.
- a. Since everyone who buys a lottery ticket hopes to win the lottery prize, the perfect lottery would make everyone a winner.
- b. Since low-income families tend to be larger than average, low-income parents must be particularly fond of children compared to the average parent.
- c. In recent years, drug abuse has increased despite increased drug enforcement efforts, so it is pretty clear that drug enforcement efforts have been ineffective.

LEARNING THE MECHANICS – MULTIPLE CHOICE

1. Which of the following is a normative economic statement?
   - a. An increase in taxes will take some purchasing power away from the consumers.
   - b. Unemployment will decline if taxes are reduced.
   - c. Higher butter prices will cause consumers to purchase more butter.
   - d. Taxes should be raised because the federal budget needs to be balanced.

2. "A nation as wealthy as the United States need not concern itself with further increases in wealth. Government policy must concentrate now on a more equitable distribution of income." This statement is
   - a. definitely true.
   - b. an objective statement about economic policy.
   - c. a normative statement about economic policy.
   - d. a testable hypothesis.

3. When an economist states that a good is scarce, she means that
   - a. production cannot expand the availability of the good.
   - b. there is a shortage or insufficient amount of the good at the existing price.
   - c. desire for the good exceeds the amount that is freely available from nature.
   - d. people would want to purchase more of the good at any price.

4. Which of the following is a positive economic statement?
   - a. The price of gasoline is too high.
   - b. The sales tax on food should be repealed.
   - c. An increase in the corporate income tax will lead to a higher rate of unemployment.
   - d. The present tax structure is not fair to the poor.

5. "The national debt is too large. The government must stop spending so much and start thinking about the resources they are depleting." This statement is
   - a. a normative statement about economic policy.
   - b. an objective statement about economic policy.
   - c. a testable hypothesis.
   - d. a conclusion supported by economic theory.

6. Which of the following is *not* a guidepost to clear economic thinking?
   - a. The value of a good is subjective.
   - b. Scarce goods have a cost.
   - c. Incentives matter.
   - d. Goods are scarce for the poor but not for the rich.

7. Which of the following is the best example of a positive economic statement?
   - a. U.S. energy consumption must be reduced this year.
   - b. The government should redistribute income in favor of the middle-income recipients.
   - c. The market demand for gasoline increases as consumer income expands.
   - d. Automobile firms should lower the price of cars.

8. Within the context of economics, the statement "There are no free lunches" refers to which of the following?
    a. Individuals must always pay for the lunch that they consume.
    b. Production of a good requires the use of scarce resources regardless of whether it is supplied free to the consumers.
    c. Restaurant owners act in their own interest.
    d. Economic man is selfish; therefore, he will not provide anything free for others.

9. A good economist will
    a. think much like an ecologist, recognizing the secondary effects of an action as well as the direct effects.
    b. ignore secondary effects, since in an economy such effects seldom matter.
    c. recognize that, almost always, secondary effects just reinforce the direct effects of a policy action.
    d. analyze the secondary effects of an action, so long as they occur at about the same time as the direct effects.

10. Which of the following is *not* an example of an economic resource?
    a. Human skills
    b. A water buffalo
    c. An atomic reactor
    d. All of the above *are* (or can be) economic resources.

11. "If I grow more oranges, I will make more money; similarly, if the aggregate output of oranges increases, the earnings of orange growers will expand." This statement is a clear example of
    a. a normative viewpoint.
    b. the role of incentives and the economic way of thinking.
    c. the fallacy of composition.
    d. economizing behavior by decision-makers.

Questions 12 through 14 refer to the following data:

Function Y		Function Z	
Q	P	Q	P
5	$10	5	$120
10	20	10	95
15	30	15	75
20	40	20	60
25	50	25	50
30	60	30	41
35	70	35	35

12. From the data above, we know that
    a. function Y is linear but function Z is not.
    b. function Z is linear but function Y is not.
    c. both function Y and function Z are linear.
    d. neither function Y nor function Z are linear.

13. From the data above, we know that the slope of function Y between Q = 20 and Q = 25 is
    a. -0.5.
    b. -2.0.
    c. 0.5.
    d. 2.0.

14. From the data above, we know that function Y and function Z intersect (cross each other) at
    a. Q = 35.
    b. Q = 25.
    c. an indeterminate point.
    d. the two functions do not intersect.

THE ECONOMIC WAY OF THINKING – MULTIPLE CHOICE

1. The basic difference between macroeconomics and microeconomics is that
    a. macroeconomics looks at how people make choices, and microeconomics looks at why they make those choices.
    b. macroeconomics is concerned with economic policy, and microeconomics is concerned with economic theory.
    c. macroeconomics focuses on the aggregate economy, whereas microeconomics focuses on small components of that economy.
    d. macroeconomics is associated with the fallacy of composition, whereas microeconomics has little to do with the fallacy of composition.

2. Which of the following is the best example of "economizing behavior" on the part of a student whose only objective in economics is to get an A in the course?
    a. taking the optional final exam to improve her grade even though an A in economics is already a certainty
    b. spending the economics lecture hour studying for an exam in another class because she is already assured of an A in economics
    c. doing outside readings in economics which will not be beneficial for the examination
    d. spending time reading the text and attending classes even though the teacher informed the student that her present grade, a B, could not possibly change

3. Which of the following actions is consistent with the basic economic postulate (the guidepost that incentives matter)?
    a. Consumers buy fewer potatoes because the price of potatoes declines.
    b. A politician votes against a proposal because most of her constituents are strongly in favor of it.
    c. Fewer students attend lectures in the introductory economics courses because class participation counts 40 percent of their grade.
    d. Farmers produce less barley because barley prices have declined.

4. Whenever the word "should" is included in an economist's analysis, we know that
    a. the economist is more likely to be engaged in positive economic reasoning than in normative.
    b. the economist knows what is best for us.
    c. the economist is more likely to be engaged in normative economics than in positive.
    d. the economist knows more about economics and is in a position to tell us what to do.

5. Positive economics differs from normative economics in that
    a. positive economics deals with how people react to changes in benefits, whereas normative economics deals with how people react to changes in costs.
    b. positive economic statements are, in principle, empirically testable; normative statements are not.
    c. positive economic statements tell us what we should be doing; normative economics tells us what we should have done.
    d. normative economic statements are theoretical, whereas positive statements focus on the application of the theory.

6. The basic economic postulate concerns human decisions about the allocation of
   a. leisure and work.
   b. food and clothing.
   c. studying and dating time.
   d. all of the above.

7. The basic economic postulate implies that, other things constant, the amount of cheating on an economics exam would
   a. decline as the probability of getting caught increased.
   b. not be influenced by economic incentives if students were basically honest.
   c. increase if the penalty for cheating were made more severe.
   d. not be influenced by economic incentives, since human actions involving morality and fairness cannot be altered.

8. "The price of food usually rises when there is an increase in the general level of prices. High food prices cause inflation." this statement best illustrates fallacious reasoning stemming from
   a. the fallacy of composition.
   b. failure to recognize that association is not causation.
   c. failure to consider the secondary effects of an action.
   d. wishful thinking on the part of the spokesperson.

9. **(I)** A luxury automobile is a scarce good. **(II)** Elementary public schooling in the United States is a scarce good.
   a. I is true, II is false.
   b. I is false, II is true.
   c. Both I and II are false.
   d. Both I and II are true.

10. The best test of an economic theory is
    a. the congruence of its assumptions with reality.
    b. its ability to yield predictions that are consistent with real-world events.
    c. its possibility of being subjected to controlled experiments.
    d. the agreement by a majority of economists that the theory is correct.

11. Economics assumes that decision-makers
    a. always act rationally and act only when they have full information.
    b. base their evaluations on psychic factors, leaving out the utility derived from economic goods.
    c. maximize their utility, insofar as utility indicates the pleasure derived from material goods.
    d. seek to choose those options that will best advance their objectives.

12. The central message of Adam Smith was that the production and wealth of a nation would be magnified if
    a. individuals were left free to act in their own interest.
    b. a central planning agency were established to ensure that labor and capital were allocated efficiently.
    c. the central government provided free education and training to workers.
    d. employers were more humanitarian toward workers and employees more concerned about the importance of efficiency in production.

13. Suppose that the Bush administration cancelled a highway building project after $3 billion already had been spent on it. If the administration expected that the total value of the highways to society would be $25 billion, then:
    a. the cancellation would have made economic sense only if the remaining cost of the project exceeded $25 billion.
    b. the cancellation would have made economic sense only if the remaining cost of the project exceeded $22 billion.
    c. the cancellation would have made economic sense only if the remaining cost of the project exceeded $28 billion.
    d. the cancellation could not possibly make sense since $3 billion had already been spent on the project.

14. Positive economics is most useful in addressing which of the following pollution issues?
    a. How much pollution people ought to be willing to tolerate.
    b. The most cost-effective methods for achieving a targeted amount of pollution reduction.
    c. Who ought to be charged to finance a targeted amount of pollution reduction.
    d. None of the above; they are all normative issues.

THE ECONOMIC WAY OF THINKING – DISCUSSION QUESTIONS

1. What is scientific methodology? How does the methodology differ for economics compared to a laboratory science? For a laboratory science, experimental results must be replicable before they are accepted. How, if at all, can this standard be applied to research in economics?

2. List three things that you appreciate having and that are not scarce. List three things that are commonplace but still scarce. How did you decide whether an item was scarce or not?

3. "Economics is of limited relevance. Most people will not be directly involved in management or the production of material goods. Neither will they put much money in the stock market. Understanding the economic approach will be of limited value to the typical student." Do you agree or disagree with this view? Be honest. Explain your reasoning.

4. "A tax increase is necessary if we want inflation to subside. Higher taxes will reduce the amount of money available to the consumer, causing his spending to decline. A tax increase is the most reasonable policy alternative at this time." Indicate the positive and normative aspects of these three statements.

5. "Under our plan, health care in the United States will now be free. No citizen will be denied medical care because of inability to pay. The program will be funded by increasing the employer's tax on the wages of his employees."
    a. Will health care be free? If so, why? If not, who do you think will end up paying for it?
    b. Will the total amount of health care consumption rise or fall? Do you consider this change in health care consumption desirable or not? Explain.

6. Consider the following scenario: Mark and Janet get married; Janet acquires medical training while Mark supports the family and pays Janet's educational expenses; Mark and Janet get divorced with no physical assets to divide up. Consider the following reaction: "Janet leaves with the only jewels of the marriage. Mark deserves compensation." What are the positive and normative aspects of this reaction? Do you agree or not? Why?

PERSPECTIVES IN ECONOMICS

On Economic Ignorance
By Irving Kristol

[Reprinted with permission from
NYU Business, Spring 1986.]

As one looks back at the history of the human race, one is appalled at the human misery that can be attributed to sheer economic ignorance. It would be no exaggeration to say that, if it could be given a quantitative measure, this misery might outrank that caused by warfare. Whole populations have been devastated by the economic ignorance of their rulers; whole civilizations have deteriorated and crumbled. To take an easy and relatively modern example: Spain in the 16th century was one of the richest and most powerful nations in Europe. For the next three centuries, it slid ineluctably downhill, becoming one of Europe's most impoverished countries. The only reason for its decline was that Spain's ruling elites were possessed of an invincible ignorance of elementary economics.

Today, whole continents — Africa and Latin America, most notably — are being pushed to ruination by that same seemingly invincible ignorance. There is no reason why the people of Argentina should not be as affluent as the people of Canada — the two countries are almost twins from an economic standpoint. Nor is there a reason why the people who live in Nigeria should be so much poorer than the people (white *and* black) who live in South Africa.

There is a puzzle here. Economic activity has been around almost as long as the human race itself, and one would have thought ruling elites would have benefitted from accumulated experience and wisdom. Moreover, while these elites, being human, are likely to make occasional egregious errors in policy, they are rarely self-destructive in the sense of wishing to persist over long periods in policies that are clearly counterproductive. Except in economics, that is, where such persistence is quite common.

The puzzle is especially exasperating at this time. After all, Adam Smith's *Wealth of Nations* which distills the economic experience of mankind into plain, readable English, was published over two centuries ago. A 20-page précis of the book would suffice for anyone interested in grasping the fundamentals of an economic policy that leads to growth. Watching the downright economic silliness that prevails in so many countries, one finds oneself wondering: Since we really do know better, why does such silliness persist?

The answer, I suggest, is in two parts. First, it turns out to be less easy to grasp the fundamentals of elementary economics than one might think. Second, while no government likes the idea of presiding over a declining economy, there are many governments that have other priorities. And these two issues are closely related.

Anyone who has tried to teach elementary economics knows that students are quick to grasp the principles — and almost as quick to forget them. This is because those principles, though clear and simple, are often counterintuitive. It's like trying to understand Einstein's Special Theory of Relativity. It's not hard — I myself have learned to understand it at least a dozen times. The trouble is that, having learned it, I then forget it.

Any economics teacher who touches on the topic of rent control or wage and price controls can attest that something of the same sort happens. Students promptly perceive that the adverse, unanticipated consequences — unanticipated by the economically ignorant, that is — of such controls soon overwhelm the immediate benefits. But for them to remember the essence of what they have learned, they have to have developed the intellectual habit of looking for second-order and third-order consequences. And such a habit is not easily acquired. It involves intellectual formation — a cast of mind — not just learning a few principles by rote. One has to learn to "think economically."

To think economically with any degree of consistency, one has to be motivated. There is rarely an immediate "payoff" to an individual in thinking economically about a matter of public policy — indeed, the benefits to an individual may be most tangible when that policy makes no economic sense. (Just think of all the people who do benefit from rent control!) In short, the habit of thinking economically must be an integral part of the national culture, the sort of thing one does almost instinctively.

In most Western democracies, this process of integration has occurred, at least to some extent. No democratic government can proceed with a policy of economic nonsense without also provoking controversy — and that's about as much as one can reasonably hope for. But in large areas of the world, the national cultures have little but contempt for the "economic way of thinking" even while the people are promised the fruits (affluence, mobility and modern conveniences) that only respect for such an intellectual formation can, in fact, deliver.

In a way, this is easily explained. Historically, most national cultures have regarded money-making, the pursuit of wealth, and the market arrangements that make both possible, as necessary evils at best. They distract from the "higher things" in life — religious piety, military valor, ideological rectitude, imperial aspirations. Any civilized person would have to agree that there is indeed something "higher" (most of the time, anyhow) than the pursuit of wealth. Still, most people, practically everywhere and at every time, do wish to participate in economic growth. Their problem is that they don't know how to think and act to achieve it and their governments either share their ignorance or are willing to impose their own priorities.

To put it another way: for any national culture to be economically rational, it must have a large "bourgeois" component, i.e., it must be sympathetic (or at least not antipathetic) to the mundane aspirations of ordinary men and women, as distinct from "higher" aspirations. Unfortunately, such a culture then incites hostility among its intellectual elites. But that is another story.

Discussion

1. What is Kristol's main point? Do you agree with him? Why or why not?

2. Do you really believe that to "think economically" is different from any other kind of thinking? Why or why not? In particular, how would you characterize the economic way of thinking? [Hint: refer to the eight guideposts to economic thinking.]

3. Kristol suggests it is "less easy to grasp the fundamentals of elementary economics than one might think." Such an opinion is similar to a common complaint from beginning students that runs something like "Economics seems so logical when I read it in the book, but when it comes time to apply it myself, I have more trouble." What reasons can you give for economics seeming easier to learn than it actually is? What can *you* do in your studies of economics to make sure that you *do* learn the material?

2
Some Tools of the Economist

T F

☐ ☐ 1. The opportunity cost of washing your car is the discomfort and drudgery associated with the task.

☐ ☐ 2. Time is not a component of opportunity cost.

☐ ☐ 3. If you are an avid football fan, the opportunity cost of going for a drive while the Super Bowl game is on television would probably be high.

☐ ☐ 4. The law of comparative advantage helps explain why fathers often have their 12-year-old sons mow the lawn even though the fathers could do it more rapidly.

☐ ☐ 5. It would usually be economical for a lawyer to do her own typing if she could type better than her secretary.

☐ ☐ 6. The economic way of thinking suggests that an individual should consider only monetary cost when making consumption decisions.

☐ ☐ 7. A rainy day often reduces the opportunity cost of a farmer's going to town.

☐ ☐ 8. A country such as the United States, which has an abundance of fertile grain-growing land but little land suitable for raising sugarcane, can gain by exporting wheat to other countries and buying sugar from them.

☐ ☐ 9. The principle of comparative advantage causes both individuals and nations to specialize in the production of those things for which they have the greatest relative advantage.

☐ ☐ 10. According to the principle of comparative advantage, it would never make economic sense for a young doctor to be a professional ice skater.

☐ ☐ 11. All economies must make decisions about what to produce, how to produce it, and to whom to distribute the goods produced.

PROBLEMS AND PROJECTS

1. Sam and Larry jointly operate a shop. They specialize in the production of tables and chairs. Their respective production possibilities schedules are presented in Exhibit 1.

    ### Exhibit 1

Sam's weekly production possibilities		Larry's weekly production possibilities	
Tables	Chairs	Tables	Chairs
5	0	4	0
4	2	3	1
3	4	2	2
2	6	1	3
1	8	0	4
0	10		

    a. In terms of chairs, what is Sam's opportunity cost of producing a table? What is Larry's?
    b. On average, they sell three times as many chairs as tables. Thus, Sam currently produces two tables and six chairs, while Larry produces one table and three chairs. Total production is three tables and nine chairs. Is this the maximum joint output that Sam and Larry could produce? If not, how could total output be expanded?

2. Exhibit 2 presents the annual production possibilities schedules for two typical farmers — one in California, the other in Kansas. Currently, the California farmer is producing 200 bushels of oranges and 600 bushels of wheat. The Kansas farmer is producing 100 and 400 bushels of oranges and wheat, respectively. Thus, the total output of the two farmers is 300 bushels of oranges and 1000 bushels of wheat.

    ### Exhibit 2

California Farmer		Kansas Farmer	
Oranges (bushels)	Wheat (bushels)	Oranges (bushels)	Wheat (bushels)
0	1000	0	800
100	800	50	600
200	600	100	400
300	400	150	200
400	200	200	0
500	0		

a. The California farmer is able to produce more oranges and wheat than his Kansas counterpart, so he has an absolute advantage in the production of both goods. Does this mean that gains from trade are impossible? (*Hint*: Ignore transportation costs throughout this question).

b. Suppose both want to consume their initial amounts of wheat – 600 bushels for the Californian and 400 for the Kansan. The Kansan decides to specialize in wheat production (800 bushels). Setting aside 400 bushels of wheat for herself, she offers to trade 400 bushels of wheat to the Californian for 150 bushels of oranges. Would the Kansan gain from this transaction? What consumption combination would she end up with?

c. Could the Californian gain if he increased his orange production to 400 and then traded the 150 bushels to the Kansan for the 400 bushels of wheat? If so, by how much (be specific) would the Californian gain compared to his original situation? What will happen to the total output of this two-farmer economy if these production changes and trades take place? (Be specific)

d. Are *both* farmers made better off by the specialization and trade described in parts b and c? Explain why such gains from trade are or are not possible. (*Hint*: Begin by calculating opportunity costs.)

3. The following questions relate to the constant hours of work required for production specified in Exhibit 3:

   a. Calculate each country's opportunity cost of producing one ton of coffee (in terms of tobacco) and one ton of tobacco (in terms of coffee).

   b. Which country has a comparative advantage in (is the relatively efficient producer of) coffee? Why? Which country has a comparative advantage in tobacco? Why?

   c. Which country should specialize in coffee production? Why?

   d. Which country, if either, has an absolute advantage in the production of both goods? Explain your answer.

Exhibit 3

	Hours of work required per ton of	
	Coffee	*Tobacco*
United States	15	45
Brazil	25	50

4. Exhibit 4 shows the production possibilities curve for growing wheat and corn.

Exhibit 4

Corn (millions of bushels)

a. Are resources efficiently employed at point *A*? At point *B*? At point *D*?

b. At point *A*, how much wheat is being produced? How much corn?

c. To increase corn production from *A* to *B*, how much wheat must be sacrificed? What is the opportunity cost of one bushel of corn when production moves from point *A* to *B*?

d. What is the opportunity cost of one bushel of corn when production moves from point *B* to *C*?

5. Exhibit 5 presents information regarding expenses for childbirth and the first year of child care for the Pastor family. The primary-care parent quits his/her job for the first year of the child's life. As a fringe benefit, the employer of the spouse of the primary-care parent covers all of the child's medical expenses.

Exhibit 5

Medical expenses	$ 2,000
Direct expenses (food and clothing, for example)	
50 percent purchased by family, 50 percent gifts	2,000
Before-tax income of primary-care parent	15,600
After-tax income of primary-care parent	12,000

   a. What is the cost to the family of the child for the first year?

   b. What is the cost to society (which includes the family) of the child for the first year?

   c. If this were the case for the typical American family, what do you think would happen to the U.S. birthrate if the cost to the family became equal to society's cost?

6. The division of labor enhances the value that citizens contribute to an economy. Each of the five statements below is a potential answer to a question about the division of labor; read them before going on.

  (1) According to the laws of physics, matter is never created or destroyed, it is only rearranged. Manufacturing reshapes matter; distribution relocates it. Both activities, done wisely, rearrange matter in a way that increases its value.

  (2) Deciding which activities to undertake and how to undertake them are risky and costly activities.

  (3) "You measure the worth of a ballplayer by how many fannies he puts in the seats." (George Steinbrenner, former baseball team owner).

  (4) For jobs which are not inherently pleasant, groups of workers left on their own may not accomplish much.

  (5) Lots of activities generate value without being exchanged in the marketplace.

Now read each of the questions below and indicate in the blank space to the left of the question the number of the statement above that best answers the question:

  ____ a. How can a baseball pitcher like Roger Clemens or Frank Viola ever be worth over $4 million a year?

  ____ b. Why not buy direct more often and cut out the wasteful middleman?

  ____ c. Why do so many house spouses just "sit at home" instead of going out and getting a "real" job?

  ____ d. Why don't we encourage more labor-managed firms so we can eliminate unproductive jobs, like shift leaders and supervisors?

  ____ e. Why do firm owners get all the profits, instead of just getting a wage like anybody else?

7. Exhibit 6 contains a production possibility curve for consumption (C) and investment (I) goods for a country. Output is measured in millions.

Exhibit 6

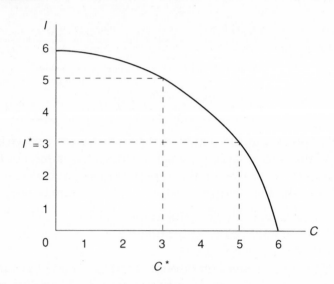

C*   indicates the economy's subsistence level of consumption good C.

I*   indicates the amount of the investment good I necessary to replace capital equipment that wears out each year. If investment falls short of I*, the economy's production possibilities curve will shrink from its present position. If investment exceeds I*, the economy's production possibilities curve will expand.

   a. What will be the consumption/investment good production point(s) if
     (1) it wants to grow as rapidly as possible without starving its citizens?
     (2) it wants to enjoy as much consumption as possible without reducing its future production capabilities?
     (3) it wants to produce at least C* and I* simultaneously.
   b. Suppose that a severe long-term drought forces the country's production possibilities curve to shift inward until the point (C = 3, I = 3) is on that curve. How does this shift change your answer to part a of this question?

LEARNING THE MECHANICS – MULTIPLE CHOICE

1. The opportunity cost to the United States of placing a man on the moon was
   a. the loss of government revenues that were allocated to the moon shot.
   b. the money prices paid to all factors of production involved in the space program.
   c. the loss of utility from the highest valued bundle of products that had to be foregone because of the moon shot.
   d. less than zero, since the long-run benefits of the project will be greater than the cost.

2. When Benjamin Franklin wrote, "Remember that time is money!" he understood
   a. the principle of substitution.
   b. the law of comparative advantage.
   c. the concept of opportunity cost.
   d. the Protestant ethic.

3. The opportunity cost of building a new civic auditorium in your town would be
   a. the money cost of the structure.
   b. the necessary increase in tax revenues to finance the building.
   c. the highest valued bundle of other goods and services that must be foregone because of the auditorium construction.
   d. the enjoyment that must be foregone because the capacity of the current structure prevents many people from attending athletic and community events.

4. Which of the following best describes the implications of the law of comparative advantage? If each person sells goods for which he or she has the greatest comparative advantage in production and buys those for which his or her comparative advantage is least, then the
   a. total output available to each person can be expanded by specialization and exchange.
   b. total output can be expanded, although some individuals will be net "losers."
   c. buyers of goods will gain at the expense of sellers.
   d. total output will increase if, and only if, persons with a comparative advantage also have an absolute advantage, relative to their trading partners.

5. When comparative advantage exists, then
   a. voluntary exchange is likely to occur independent of government action.
   b. economists must inform the public that exchange will improve the general welfare before trade will occur.
   c. trade will occur until the weakest of the parties finds it impossible to continue trading.
   d. exchange can make one trader better off, but only at the expense of the other.

6. Which of the following is *not* one of the basic economic questions that all economies must answer?
   a. What will be produced?
   b. To whom will the goods produced be allocated?
   c. What is the highest opportunity cost method of producing each good?
   d. How will goods be produced?

7. Private property rights give owners a chance to act selfishly, but they also make owners responsible and accountable for their actions. As a result, when deciding on the wisest use of their resources, property owners are likely to
   a. always disregard the wishes of others.
   b. disregard the wishes of others to the extent that accountability for misuse of the property is not enforced.
   c. be concerned about the wishes of others whether or not accountability is enforced.
   d. lose revenue when the wishes of others are taken into consideration.

Use the following information to answer questions 8-10. Exhibit 7 outlines the production possibilities of Italia and Slavia for food and clothing.

Exhibit 7

Italia		Slavia	
Food	*Clothing*	*Food*	*Clothing*
0	8	0	32
2	6	2	24
4	4	4	16
6	2	6	8
8	0	8	0

8. What is the opportunity cost of producing one unit of clothing in Slavia?
   a. One unit of food
   b. Two units of food
   c. One-twelfth unit of food
   d. One-fourth unit of food

9. Which of the following is true?
   a. Italia has a comparative advantage in the production of both goods.
   b. Slavia is the high opportunity cost producer of clothing.
   c. Slavia has a comparative advantage in the production of food.
   d. Italia is the low opportunity cost producer of food.

10. The law of comparative advantage suggests that
    a. both countries would gain if Slavia traded food for Italia clothing.
    b. neither country would gain from trade even if the transportation costs for the products were zero.
    c. both countries would gain if Italia traded food for Slavia clothing.
    d. Slavia would not gain from trade because it has an absolute advantage in the production of both goods.

11. When resources are being used wastefully
    a. the production possibilities curve shifts inward.
    b. the production possibilities curve shifts outward.
    c. the economy is operating at a point inside its production possibilities constraint.
    d. the economy is operating at a point outside its production possibilities constraint.

12. The production possibilities curve
    a. assumes that technology is increasing at a constant, long-run rate.
    b. assumes that all individuals have equal incomes.
    c. is normally convex (bowed in) to the origin over its entire range.
    d. assumes that the level of technology is constant.

13. Which of the following is a transaction cost?
    a. The price of a ticket to a concert
    b. The price of food eaten before the concert
    c. Time spent buying the ticket
    d. Time spent driving to the concert

14. Transaction costs
    a. can be reduced by gathering more information about many possible alternative exchanges.
    b. can be reduced by consulting people who specialize in providing information about alternative exchanges.
    c. cannot be reduced by forming consumer cooperatives.
    d. cannot be reduced at all; they are fixed by law.

15. Private property rights exist when property rights are
    a. exclusively controlled by one owner.
    b. transferable to others.
    c. both a and b.
    d. neither a nor b.

THE ECONOMIC WAY OF THINKING – MULTIPLE CHOICE

1. Any economy that fails to realize all its potential gains stemming from the domestic division of labor (specialization) is
    a. operating outside its production possibilities curve.
    b. operating inside its production possibilities curve.
    c. operating on its production possibilities curve but in an inefficient manner.
    d. operating on its production possibilities curve and therefore need not be concerned about comparative advantage.

2. Suppose that the production possibilities of Robinson Crusoe and Friday are as follows:

Which of the following would maximize the consumption alternatives available to Crusoe and Friday?
    a. Crusoe should specialize in the production of good x and Friday should specialize in the production of good y, but there should be no trade allowed.
    b. Crusoe should specialize in the production of good x and Friday should specialize in the production of good y and trade should occur.
    c. Crusoe should specialize in the production of good y and Friday should specialize in the production of good x and trade should occur.
    d. This is a special case. Both individuals should strive for self-sufficiency, since this maximizes output.

3. When an economy is operating efficiently, the production of more of one commodity will result in the production of less of some other commodity because
    a. all resources are specialized and only imperfectly mobile.
    b. resources are limited (i.e., scarce) and efficiency implies that all are in use.
    c. the structure of demand is fixed at any given time.
    d. material wants are insatiable.

4. "Since I am going to start school soon, I will have to quit my current job." This statement most clearly reflects
    a. the law of comparative advantage.
    b. the principle of opportunity cost.
    c. gains for technology.
    d. a decision that is inconsistent with economizing behavior.

5. "Now that John washes all the dishes and I mow the lawn, we can finish in two-thirds the time it took when we shared both functions." This statement most clearly reflects
    a. the law of comparative advantage.
    b. gains from capital formation.
    c. gains from technology.
    d. choices that are inconsistent with economizing behavior.

6. "If I didn't have a date tonight, I would save $10 and spend the evening playing tennis."
   The opportunity cost of the date is
   a. $10.
   b. $10 plus the foregoing of a night of tennis.
   c. dependent upon how pleasant a time one has on the date.
   d. the foregoing of a night of tennis.

7. Use the diagram below to answer the following questions.

Points *A* and *B* indicate the current levels of consumption and investment for two different economies. Other things constant, which of the two economies is likely to grow more rapidly?
   a. *A*
   b. *B*
   c. They can be expected to grow at the same rate.
   d. Uncertain, since the growth rate is not influenced by the factors indicated in this hypothetical example.

8. Dr. Jones, a dentist, is choosing between driving and flying from Florida to Montana for her vacation. If Jones drove, she would have to close her office three days earlier than if she flew. Her expected income (after taxes) from her practice is $80 per day. Jones's preferences are such that she would rather drive: She would stand to gain $50 worth of nonpecuniary (non-monetary) benefits if she drove and saw the beautiful countryside. If Jones was a rational decision-maker, she would drive if the price differential (air cost minus driving) was greater than
   a. $50.
   b. $80.
   c. $130.
   d. $190.

9. According to the law of comparative advantage
   a. each producer should strive toward self-sufficiency in order to maximize the total production of the economy.
   b. each product should be produced by the lowest opportunity cost producer in order to maximize output.
   c. one should never compare one's abilities with those of another; in doing so production time is lost.
   d. each product should be produced by the individual who can produce more of that product than any other individual.

10. "The economic wealth of this country was built primarily by some individuals profiting from a transaction, whereas others were harmed by that transaction." This statement indicates that the spokesman
    a. fails to comprehend the mutual gains resulting from specialization and exchange.
    b. fails to comprehend the fallacy of composition.
    c. fails to understand the significance of the production possibilities constraint.
    d. utilizes the economic way of thinking. The statement is essentially correct.

11. Which of the following is most likely to occur under a system of clearly defined and enforced private property rights?
    a. Resource owners will tend to abuse resources and use them selfishly.
    b. Resource owners will fail to conserve vital resources for the future even if they expect their scarcity to increase.
    c. Resource owners will ignore the wishes of others, including others who would like to use the resource that is privately owned.
    d. Resource owners will consider the wishes of others, including potential future purchasers, when they decide how to employ privately owned resources.

12. Which of the following is a disadvantage that may arise when individuals specialize in the production of those things for which they are the low opportunity cost producer?
    a. When individuals specialize in production, they have little incentive to trade for other commodities that they may also enjoy.
    b. Specialization does not allow individuals to enjoy the benefits of learning by doing; that is, repetition prevents individuals from developing more efficient methods of production.
    c. A worker may become bored with performing the same monotonous task over a period of time.
    d. Individuals have little incentive to utilize their particular talents.

    Questions 13-15 refer to Exhibit 8 below:

Exhibit 8

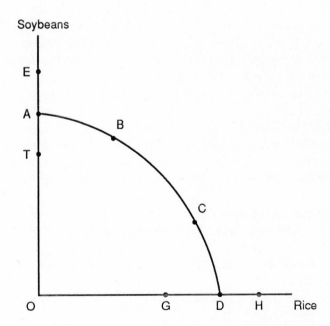

13. The diagram in Exhibit 8 indicates Japan's production possibilities for rice and soybeans. Given the exhibit, Japan's opportunity cost of producing more soybeans, in terms of rice
    a. increases from D to A.
    b. decreases from D to A.
    c. does not change from D to A.
    d. is impossible to determine from the information given.

14. Suppose Japan experiences a long-term water drought that reduces its ability to produce all agricultural goods. The new Japanese production possibilities frontier will most closely resemble a curve connecting
    a. T and G.
    b. T and D.
    c. E and H.
    d. A and H.

15. Suppose Japan invents new improved soybean seeds that cost the same as the old ones but allow more beans to be grown with the same amount of other inputs as the older seeds. If nothing else has changed, the new Japanese production possibilities frontier will most closely resemble a curve connecting
    a. E and G.
    b. A and G.
    c. E and D.
    d. A and H.

THE ECONOMIC WAY OF THINKING – DISCUSSION QUESTIONS

1. As an individual, you will ultimately take part in determining how your economy answers its three basic economic decisions. What will help you choose what *you* should produce, how *you* should produce it, and *for whom* you should produce it? Are these answers at all interrelated?

2. "In the progress of the division of labor, the employment to the . . . great body of the people comes to be confined to a few very simple operations, frequently to one or two . . . The man whose whole life is spent in performing a few simple operations . . . becomes as stupid and ignorant as it is possible for a human creature to become." – Adam Smith, *The Wealth of Nations*.
    a. Smith seems to be saying that specialization carries with it a loss in utility due to monotony and alienation. Do you agree? Why or why not?
    b. If it is true that specialization increases productivity but also increases worker boredom, how do we decide the extent to which we should specialize?
    c. Smith's comments were made in the context of the production specialization as it was known in the 18th century. How applicable is his analysis to today's "high-tech" world? Why?
    d. Smith felt that education was the best remedy for this problem associated with the division of labor. Do you agree? Why or why not?

3. Consider the cost to you of this economics course.
   a. About how much money did you spend on tuition and books for this course? When did you incur these costs?
   b. What is the cost of actually attending the class once you've paid your tuition and purchased your books?
   c. Use your answer to part b to comment on the following quote (heard at a Southern California liberal arts college with fairly high tuition): "I could earn $15 if I worked during today's economics class, but tuition averages out to $20 per lecture, so I can't afford to go. If only I went to UCLA, where tuition is lower, I could skip class and earn the money." Do you agree or disagree? Explain your answer.

4. Explain why it is often efficient for faculty members with training in computer programming to hire student programmers to do their computer work.

5. Consider the following quote by a lawyer who knows something about economics: "It doesn't make sense for me to care for my own lawn when my opportunity cost is $80 per hour."
   a. Do you agree with the lawyer's view? Explain.
   b. Would you be surprised to find this lawyer's lawn exquisitely maintained? Explain.

6. After a class discussion of how Capitalist and Socialist nations approach their three economizing decisions, your friend says: "I'm a capitalist on questions one and two but a socialist on question three." What does your friend mean? Why do you think she feels that way? Could such a system ever work? Why or why not?

PERSPECTIVES IN ECONOMICS

Unfair Competition With The Sun
By Frédéric Bastiat

[From Frédéric Bastiat, "Petition of the Manufacturers of Candles, Wax-Lights, Lamps, Candlesticks, Street Lamps, Snuffers, Extinguishers, and of the Producers of Oil, Tallow, Resin, Alcohol, and, Generally, of Everything Connected with Lighting." To messieurs the members of the Chamber of Deputies.]

Gentlemen, – You are on the right road. You reject abstract theories, and have little consideration for cheapness and plenty. Your chief care is the interest of the producer. You desire to protect him from foreign competition, and reserve the *national market for national industry.*

We are suffering from the intolerable competition of a foreign rival, placed, it would seem, in a condition so far superior to ours for the production of light that he absolutely *inundates* our *national market* with it at a price fabulously reduced. The moment he shows himself our trade leaves us – all consumers apply to him; and a branch of native industry, having countless ramifications, is all at once rendered completely stagnant. This rival, who is no other than the sun, wages war to the knife against us, and we suspect that he has been raised up by *perfidious Albion* (a good policy as times go); inasmuch as he displays towards that haughty island a circumspection with which he dispenses in our case.

What we pray for is, that it may please you to pass a law ordering the shutting up of all windows, skylights, dormer-windows, outside and inside shutters, curtains, blinds, bull's-eyes, in a word, of all openings, holes, chinks, clefts, and fissures, by or through which the light of the sun has been in use to enter houses, to the prejudice of the meritorious manufactures with which we flatter ourselves we have accommodated our country – a country, which, in gratitude, ought not abandon us now to a strife so unequal.

We trust, Gentlemen, that you will not regard this our request as a satire, or refuse it without at least previously hearing the reasons which we have to urge in its support.

And, first, if you shut up as much as possible all access to natural light, and create a demand for artificial light, which of our French manufacturers will not be encouraged by it?

We foresee your objections, Gentlemen, but we know that you can oppose to us none but such as you have picked up from the effete works of the partisans of Free Trade. We defy you to utter a single word against us which will not instantly rebound against yourselves and your entire policy.

You will tell us that, if we gain by the protection which we seek, the country will lose by it, because the consumer must bear the loss.

We answer:

You have ceased to have any right to invoke the interest of the consumer for, whenever his interest is found opposed to that of the producer, you sacrifice the latter. You have done so for the purpose of encouraging workers and those who seek employment. For the same reason you should do so again.

You have yourselves obviated this objection. When you are told that the consumer is interested in the free importation of iron, coal, corn, textile fabrics – yes, you reply, but the producer is interested in their exclusion. Well, be it so; if consumers are interested in the free admission of natural light, the producers of artificial light are equally interested in its prohibition.

If you urge that the light of the sun is a gratuitous gift of nature, and that to reject such gifts is to reject wealth itself under pretense of encouraging the means of acquiring it, we would caution you against giving a death-blow to your own policy. Remember that hitherto you have always repelled foreign products, *because* they approximate more nearly than home products to the character of gratuitous gifts.

Nature and human labour co-operate in various proportions (depending on countries and climates) in the production of commodities. The part which nature executes is very gratuitous; it is the part executed by human labour which constitutes value, and is paid for.

If a Lisbon orange sells for half the price of a Paris orange, it is because natural, and consequently gratuitous, heat does for the one what artificial, and therefore expensive, heat must do for the other.

When an orange comes to us from Portugal, we may conclude that it is furnished in part gratuitously, in part for an onerous consideration; in other words, it comes to us at *half-price* as compared with those of Paris.

Now, it is precisely the *gratuitous half* (pardon the word) which we contend should be excluded. You say, How can national labour sustain competition with foreign labour, when the former has all the work to do, and the latter only does one-half, the sun supplying the remainder. But if this *half*, being *gratuitous*, determines you to exclude competition, how should the *whole*, being *gratuitous*, induce you to admit competition? If you were consistent, you would, while excluding as hurtful to native industry what is half gratuitous, exclude a *fortiori* and with double zeal, that which is altogether gratuitous.

One more, when products such as coal, iron, corn, or textile fabrics are sent us from abroad, and we can acquire them with less labour than if we made them ourselves, the difference is a free gift conferred upon us. The gift is more or less considerable in proportion as the difference is more or less great. It amounts to a quarter, a half, or three-quarters of the value of the product, when the foreigner only asks us for three-fourths, a half or a quarter of the price we should otherwise pay. It is as perfect and complete as it can be, when the donor (like the sun is furnishing us with light) asks us for nothing. The question, and we ask it formally, is this: Do you desire for our country the benefit of gratuitous consumption, or the pretended advantages of onerous production?

Make your choice, but be logical; for as long as you exclude as you do, coal, iron, corn, foreign fabrics, in proportion as their price approximates to zero what inconsistency it would be to admit the light of the sun, the price of which is already at zero during the entire day!

Discussion

1. What does the Bastiat reading have to do with this chapter? (*Hint*: the text states that the law of comparative advantage applies to nations as well as to individuals.) Does comparative advantage mean that *all* trade is good? Explain your answer.

2. Do you think that individuals or industries ever need protection from competition? If so, how would we decide whether an industry (like the lighting industry or the automobile industry) deserves to be protected from competition?

3. What arguments would you, as an economist, use before a congressional hearing on a bill to accomplish what Bastiat suggests? How would you deal with the political problems involved?

3
Supply, Demand, and the Market Process

TRUE OR FALSE

	T	F

T F

☐ ☐   1. Consumers will purchase less beef at higher prices than at lower prices if other factors remain the same.

☐ ☐   2. If the price of bananas increased, consumers would substitute oranges, apples, ice cream, and other related commodities for bananas.

☐ ☐   3. The law of supply reflects the willingness of producers to expand output in response to an increase in the price of a product.

☐ ☐   4. Excess demand in the market will cause the price of a product to decline.

☐ ☐   5. An increase in demand for wheat would cause price to rise and producers to expand output.

☐ ☐   6. A reduction in the supply of fertilizer relative to its demand would cause the price of fertilizer to decline.

☐ ☐   7. Payments to input suppliers provide them with an incentive to acquire skills that are valuable in the production process.

☐ ☐   8. The market price is in short-run equilibrium when suppliers are willing to supply only the amount demanded by consumers at the current price.

☐ ☐   9. When a market is in long-run equilibrium, the opportunity cost of supplying the product will be equal to the product's market price.

☐ ☐ 10. Three factors that will *each* cause the supply curve for Napa county wine to shift to the left include a drought in Napa county, higher wages for Napa county grape pickers, and higher prices for Napa county wine.

☐ ☐ 11. If the government fixed the price of farm products above the competitive equilibrium, consumer demand would increase.

☐ ☐ 12. An increase in the price of inputs used in the construction industry would cause housing prices to rise and the demand for housing to decline.

PROBLEMS AND PROJECTS

1. Exhibit 1 presents hypothetical supply-and-demand schedules for shoes in a local market area.

Exhibit 1

Price (1)	Initial quantity demanded (2)	Quantity supplied (3)	New quantity demanded (4)
$ 6	270	120	320
9	230	170	280
12	200	200	250
15	170	220	220
18	130	250	180
21	90	300	140

a. Graph the initial demand (column 2) on the chart below.
b. What is the initial equilibrium price?
c. The region experiences a boom and consumer income increases, causing an increase in demand. The new demand schedule is indicated in column 4. Graph the new schedule.
d. What is the new equilibrium price?
e. Suppose the price of shoes is fixed by law at $9; draw in this fixed price on your diagram. Describe the market for shoes at the initial demand level. Describe the market for shoes at the increased demand level. What has happened?

2. As indicated by Exhibit 2, the initial demand for soybeans was D_1. The supply was S.
   a. What was the initial market-clearing price? Quantity sold?
   b. Soybeans have a high protein content and are a substitute for meat. Higher meat prices caused the demand for soybeans to increase to D_2. What is the new equilibrium price? Quantity sold?
   c. Wheat is also a substitute for soybeans. What will happen in the wheat market if the price of soybeans changes, as in part b? Illustrate your answer with a graph.

Exhibit 2

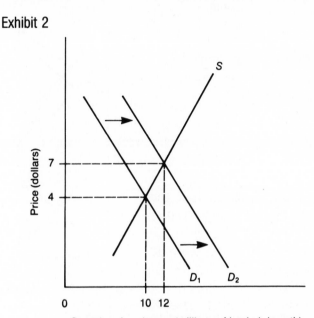

Quantity of soybeans (millions of bushels/month)

3. The pricing system sends out signals that influence the decisions of producers and consumers. Understanding the secondary effects of a change in market conditions is essential if one is to understand how a market system works. For example, what impact did the substantially higher fuel (e.g., gasoline, fuel oil) prices of the mid-1970s have on
   a. the demand for large cars? small cars?
   b. the relative demand for steel and aluminum by the auto industry?
   c. the demand for home swimming pools relative to cross-country driving vacations?
   d. employment conditions in the automobile industry?
   e. the farmer's cost of producing wheat?
   f. the demand for solar heating units and the incentive to produce them?
   g. the demand for home insulation?
   h. the incentive to speed up the development of the Alaskan pipeline during the mid-1970s?
   i. the incentive to undertake research on the development of low-pollution, coal-generated electricity?
   j. the supply of petroleum-derived fertilizers?
   k. the supply of non-petroleum-derived fertilizers?
   l. the short-run price of firewood?

4. Use the diagrams below to indicate the changes in demand (D), supply (S), equilibrium price (P) and equilibrium quantity (Q) in response to the events described to the left of the diagrams. First show in the diagrams how supply and/or demand shift in response to the event, and then fill in the table to the right of the diagrams using + to indicate increase, − to indicate decrease and 0 to indicate no change. If an effect cannot be determined show this by using?. As an example, the first question has been answered.

Market	Events	Diagrams	D	S	P	Q
a. Automobiles	Price of gasoline rises; cost of producing autos rises.		−	−	?	−
b. Oranges	Frost destroys half the Florida orange crop.					
c. Butter	There is an increase in the supply of margarine.					
d. Lumber	Lower interest rates cause a housing construction boom; lumber jacks' wages fall significantly.					
e. Wine	The cost of growing grapes falls; consumer income decreases					

5. Exhibit 3 below shows the market for rental housing in Limitville, a small, fictitious town on the California coast. The curve labeled D is the demand for rental housing, S_{sp} is the *short-run* supply curve, and S_{lr} is the *long-run* supply curve.

Exhibit 3

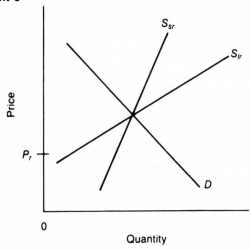

a. Indicate in the diagram the equilibrium price and quantity for rental housing in Limitville.
b. If the Limitville Municipal Council decided to limit rentals charged by landlords, to P_r, what would happen to the quantity of rental housing demanded?
c. In the short run, what is the quantity of rental housing supplied in Limitville at the price P_r? In the diagram, indicate the excess demand ("shortage") of rentals in the short run.

d. Now indicate the excess demand in the long run. Suggest reasons why the reduction in quantity supplied would be greater in the long run than in the short run.
e. At the controlled price of rentals, P_r, is price fully performing its rationing function? What sorts of *non*-price rationing mechanisms might be used to ration rentals?

6. Consider the information about the market for corn contained in Exhibit 4. (Quantities are in billions of bushels.)

Exhibit 4

Quantity demanded	Price per bushel	Quantity supplied
3.0	2.65	3.9
3.1	2.50	3.7
3.2	2.35	3.5
3.3	2.20	3.3
3.4	2.05	3.1
3.5	1.90	2.9
3.6	1.75	2.7
3.7	1.60	2.5

P

2.50

2.20

1.90

1.60

O   2.0   2.5   3.0   3.5   4.0 Q

a. Diagram an initial equilibrium in the market for corn. What is the equilibrium price and quantity?

Now suppose the U.S. government imposes a price floor for corn at a price of $2.50 per bushel. The government buys up and stockpiles the corn surplus that results from the price floor.

b. Depict the price floor in your diagram from part a. What are quantities produced, consumed, and stockpiled?

c. What is the value of the total dollar receipts of corn farmers? The total spending on corn products by consumers? By taxpayers?

Some have proposed that a better way of supporting corn prices would be to replace the price floor with a target price at the same price level. Farmers would base their production decisions on the target price but would dump their entire output on the market for whatever price consumers would pay for it. The government would then give farmers a "deficiency payment" equal to the difference between the target price and the market price.

d. Indicate in your diagram the market price and the size of the deficiency payment under this target price policy. What would be the market price? The size of the deficiency payment?

e. Comparing the target price option to the price floor policy:
   (1) Do the total receipts of farmers (and therefore the total spending of consumers and taxpayers combined) rise, fall, or remain the same?
   (2) Does the quantity of corn consumed by the public rise, fall, or remain the same? Which policy do you prefer? Explain briefly.

7. Consider the following passage from *Business Week* magazine:

"Says Irvin Elkin, president of the Associated Milk Producers Inc. 'Major cuts in [dairy] support prices run the risk of driving many dairy farm families out of business, which would mean higher milk prices.'" What is probably correct about Elkin's assertion? What is incorrect? Support both answers.

LEARNING THE MECHANICS – MULTIPLE CHOICE

1. If the price of tickets to the World Series were below the competitive equilibrium price, then
   a. the quantity supplied would be greater than the quantity demanded.
   b. the demand for World Series tickets must be elastic.
   c. there would be no transactions between buyers and sellers of the tickets.
   d. the number of persons seeking to obtain tickets to World Series games would be greater than the number of available tickets.

2. Which of the following would cause the price of wheat to rise?
   a. A decrease in the price of corn, a substitute for wheat
   b. An increase in the price of soybeans, a substitute for wheat
   c. A decrease in the price of fertilizer
   d. A diet craze among Americans that decreases their demand for bread products

3. A demand curve gives the relationship between price and quantity demanded, *other things constant.* These "other things" include all of the following except
   a. consumer preferences.
   b. income.
   c. the price of the commodity.
   d. the price of substitute goods.

4. If cigars and cigarettes are substitute goods, an increase in the price of cigars would result in
   a. an increase in the sales of cigarettes.
   b. a decrease in the price of cigarettes.
   c. a decrease in the sales of cigarettes.
   d. an increase in the sales of cigars.

5. If the price of a bushel of wheat is fixed (say, by government price regulations) *above* its market equilibrium price, the most likely result would be
   a. an increase in the quantity of wheat demanded.
   b. a decrease in the quantity of wheat supplied in the short run.
   c. a decrease in the incentive to expand the future supply of wheat.
   d. a surplus of wheat.

6. Which of the following would be most likely to cause the demand for Miller beer to increase?
   a. An increase in the price of Budweiser beer
   b. A decrease in consumer income
   c. A decrease in the price of the barley used to make Miller beer
   d. An increase in the price of pretzels, eaten with beer

7. The demand curve for a commodity indicates the maximum amount the consumer would be willing to pay for each unit of the good. What will be the effect of an increase in the price the consumer must pay for the product?
   a. There will be a decrease in the quantity demanded.
   b. The entire demand curve will shift to the right.
   c. There will be no effect, since the maximum amount the consumer would be willing to pay stays the same.
   d. The consumer's demand will decrease.

8. All other things constant, a decrease in bus, train, and airplane fares will
   a. shift the demand curve for automobiles to the left.
   b. cause a movement along the demand curve for automobiles.
   c. shift the demand curve for automobiles to the right.
   d. have no impact on the demand curve for automobiles.

9. In the absence of government intervention, the pricing system would ration gasoline to those individuals and firms
   a. who were able and willing to pay the highest price.
   b. who had the highest income.
   c. who lived the farthest from their place of work.
   d. who owned automobiles that used the most gas.

10. If the market price is above the equilibrium price, there will be a tendency for price to fall, causing
    a. quantity demanded to fall and quantity supplied to rise.
    b. quantity demanded to rise and quantity supplied to fall.
    c. both quantity demanded and quantity supplied to fall.
    d. both quantity demanded and quantity supplied to rise.

11. Quotas restricting imports of Japanese automobiles will have what effects on the supply of and demand for *domestically* made automobiles?
    a. cause demand and supply to increase
    b. cause demand and quantity supplied to increase
    c. cause supply and quantity demanded to increase
    d. cause demand to increase and supply to decrease

12. Alfred Marshall helped develop the concepts of "long run" and "short run." Which of the following is the most accurate description of the distinction between the two?
    a. The short run is a time period of less than three months, whereas the long run covers time periods of more than seven months.
    b. The long run is a time period of sufficient length for decision-makers to make adjustments that are too costly (or impossible) to make in the short run.
    c. The long run is a time period of sufficient length for producers to develop new technologies, whereas in the short run, technology is constant.
    d. The long run is a marathon, whereas the short run is more like the hundred-yard dash.

13. The tendency for capital investment in each market to move toward a uniform or normal rate of return is called the
    a. uniform market law of supply.
    b. uniform market law of demand.
    c. capital investment equilibrium principle.
    d. rate-of-return equalization principle.

14. Under competitive conditions, market prices
    a. are always in long-run equilibrium.
    b. can be determined only after a detailed study of supply and demand conditions has been made.
    c. are incapable of coordinating the actions of buyers and sellers.
    d. generally bring the self-interest of individual consumers and producers into harmony with the general welfare, resulting in economic efficiency.

THE ECONOMIC WAY OF THINKING – MULTIPLE CHOICE

1. If the quantity demanded is greater than the quantity supplied, the pricing system (through the invisible hand) will respond by:
    a. lowering the product price and therefore the profits of the firms responsible for not producing enough.
    b. raising the product price and producer profits.
    c. lowering product price, but increasing producer profits.
    d. raising product price, but lowering producer profits.

2. "If gasoline were taxed, the price of gasoline would rise. Consequently, the demand for gasoline would fall, causing the price to fall to the original level. Therefore the tax would not be effective." This statement
    a. is essentially correct.
    b. is incorrect – after the demand falls, the price would fall, but to some level higher than the original level.
    c. is incorrect – demand and quantity demanded are confused.
    d. is incorrect – the tax would be effective even if the price fell to the original level, since the demand for gasoline dropped (which was the primary purpose of the tax).

3. Which of the following was a result of the increased prices of gasoline and petroleum-related products in early 1979?
    a. The demand for small cars expanded.
    b. The incentive to use more oil for heating increased.
    c. Tourism in south Florida increased relative to 1977-1978.
    d. The demand for used Cadillacs and Lincoln Continentals increased.

4. About two-thirds of the private rental housing in New York City is subject to rent control. The rent control price is usually set below the market equilibrium price. Economic theory suggests that this rent control price would
    a. increase landlords' profits.
    b. cause many rental units to be abandoned or poorly kept up by landlords.
    c. result in a surplus of rental units in the near future.
    d. reduce housing discrimination against minorities.

5. With a price ceiling *above* the equilibrium price,
    a. quantity demanded would exceed quantity supplied.
    b. quantity supplied would exceed quantity demanded.
    c. the market would be in equilibrium.
    d. the equilibrium price would be expected to fall over time.

6. "The price of wheat rose sharply because (a) the drought reduced the yield per acre, and (b) millers sought to stockpile wheat to protect themselves from future price increases that would occur if the drought were to continue." This quotation suggests that the price rise was caused by
    a. an increase in demand and a movement along the supply curve.
    b. an increase in supply and a movement along the demand curve.
    c. an increase in both demand and supply.
    d. a reduction in supply and a short-run increase in demand.

7. "The winds of the recent hurricanes in Florida are bringing financial gain to California citrus growers. Because of the extensive damage to the Florida citrus crop, California citrus products are commanding their highest prices ever." Which of the following statements best explains the economics of this quotation?
    a. The supply of Florida oranges has decreased, causing their price to increase and the demand for the substitute California oranges also to increase.
    b. The supply of Florida oranges has decreased, causing the supply of California oranges to increase and their prices to rise.
    c. The demand for Florida oranges has been reduced by the hurricane, causing a greater demand for the California oranges and an increase in their price.
    d. The demand for Florida oranges has been reduced, causing their prices to fall and thereby increasing the demand for the substitute California oranges.

8. Which of the following is an example of one of the basic questions being solved with the price mechanism?
    a. What to produce is decided by a central planning board, and the decisions on what prices to charge are passed down to the retailers.
    b. How to produce is decided only after negotiation with union leaders.
    c. What to produce is decided when consumers who want more of a good bid up the price of that good, attracting more production.
    d. For whom to produce is decided by setting up a rationing program and charging a fair price to all consumers.

9. All of the following would affect the supply of automobiles except one. Which would *not* affect the supply of automobiles?
    a. Higher prices for steel and other resources used in the production of automobiles
    b. A successful physical fitness plan encouraging all Americans to walk to their destinations
    c. A technological improvement reducing the production costs of automobiles
    d. Increased wages for the members of the United Auto Workers

10. Per capita expenditures for physicians' services increased from $31.45 in 1960 and $47.70 in 1966, an increase of 35 percent in dollars of constant purchasing power. Most of this change occurred in price, rather than in quantity of services delivered. Economic theory would suggest that the observed data could best be explained as
    a. an increase in supply, but little change in demand.
    b. a decrease in both supply and demand.
    c. an increase in demand, while supply remained relatively constant.
    d. a sharp increase in both supply and demand.

The following background will help answer questions 11 through 14.

In the U.S. today, it's difficult to find affordable, dependable, and responsible day care for children of working parents. For simplicity, let's assume that the day-care market has two halves. One half is made up of day-care centers, both privately and publically funded. The other half is made up of "at home providers," principally nannies. Some of the nannies are illegal immigrants who have no other job opportunities, while others have special visa status with the INS (Immigration and Naturalization Service). Further assume that equilibrium in the day-care center market is at $140 per week and that equilibrium in the nanny market is $120 a week. Finally, suppose that the INS cracks down on illegal aliens and restricts the number of special "nanny visas."

11. After the crackdown, you'd expect the new equilibrium price in the nanny market to be
    a. less than $120 a week.
    b. still $120 a week.
    c. more than $120 a week.
    d. equal to the equilibrium price in the day-care market.

12. The price and quantity changes caused by the crackdown in the nanny market could most easily be confused with price and quantity changes resulting from
    a. the establishment of free, national day care.
    b. a marked increase in the desire and ability of parents to stay at home with their children.
    c. the closing of all federally funded day-care centers.
    d. an increase in the legal job opportunities available in the U.S. for people with local experience as nannies.

13. After the crackdown, you'd expect the new equilibrium price in the day-care market to be
    a. unchanged.
    b. less than $140 a week.
    c. greater than $140 a week.
    d. equal to the equilibrium price in the nanny market.

14. Suppose that Congress passes a law that fixes prices at $140 per week for day-care centers and $120 per week for nannies. If the INS does not change its crackdown policy, the Congressional act would
    a. restore the nanny market to its original equilibrium.
    b. cause a shortage (excess demand) in the nanny market.
    c. cause a surplus (excess supply) in the nanny market.
    d. have an indeterminate effect on the nanny market.

THE ECONOMIC WAY OF THINKING – DISCUSSION QUESTIONS

1. Air traffic congestion is a major problem at the municipal airports of many major cities. Some economists have suggested that charging a higher usage price, particularly during peak traffic periods (8-10 A.M. and 5-10 P.M.), would improve the situation. What impact would the higher fees have on the
   a. scheduling of flights?
   b. number of landings and takeoffs during heavy traffic periods?
   c. fuel wastage and other costs of circling the airport?
   d. number of small private planes using major airports?

2. Consider the following statement: "Campus parking permits and meters are inefficient and unfair. Campus parking should be free, with parking spaces allocated on a first-come, first-served basis."
   a. Is "free" parking more efficient than permit or meter parking?
   b. With "free" parking, who, if anyone, gains? Who loses?
   c. Would you favor "free" parking on your campus? Why or why not?

3. Consider the choice between "rationing by price" (with prices flexible) and "rationing by waiting" (with prices fixed).
   a. What type of waste occurs with rationing by waiting?
   b. Suppose there is a surge in the demand for butter. Which rationing system provides butter producers with better information and incentives? Explain.

4. Explain what is wrong with the following reasoning: "When meat prices rise due to a decrease in the supply of meat, the demand for meat decreases, so meat prices end up falling."
   a. Suppose a price is temporarily above its equilibrium level. How do you think producers figure out that the price is in fact "too high"? Explain how a lower price causes both production and consumption adjustments that help to correct the situation.
   b. Suppose a price is temporarily below its equilibrium level. How do you think producers figure out that the price is in fact "too low"? Explain how a higher price causes both production and consumption adjustments that help to correct the situation.

5. People often use the term "demand" when they actually mean "quantity demanded"; the same is true of "supply" and "quantity supplied."
   a. What causes a change in quantity demanded but not a change in demand?
   b. What absurd condition is implied by the following statement: "The supply of oil is expected to exceed demand by 1995."
   c. How can you rephrase the statement of part b so that it makes economic sense?

6. In an effort to control rising prices during the 1970s, many governments adopted price controls, fixing prices (and wages) for extended periods of time and thereby causing shortages of some goods and surpluses of others. Respond to the following statement: "Shortages are a disadvantage of price controls, but surpluses are an offsetting advantage."

7. How would a prolonged drought in the Midwest affect each of the following?
   a. Water prices in the Midwest
   b. Farmland prices in the Midwest
   c. Farmland prices in other parts of the country
   d. Fertilizer prices
   e. Manufacturing wages in the Midwest

CURRENT DEBATES IN ECONOMICS

Debate Number One: Should We Raise the Minimum Wage?
Yes, We Should Raise the Minimum Wage:

A Living Wage
A *Los Angeles Times* editorial

[Reprinted with permission from the *Los Angeles Times*,
October 14, 1986, page 4, Part II.]

It used to be that the minimum wage provided more than just gas money for middle-class teenagers. Back when it was $1.60 an hour, in 1967, a 40-hour work week at minimum wage brought home enough to support a family of three. Now, at $3.35, it is scarcely enough to keep one worker out of poverty. The working poor will keep working themselves deeper into poverty as long as the minimum wage is stagnant.

Congress established the minimum wage in 1935 to prevent workers from savagely undercutting each other during the Depression. In doing so, it sought to guarantee a decent – a minimum – standard of living for all workers. Until this decade the minimum wage did that, equaling about half of the average private industry wage. But the wage floor that Congress built has sunk into the depths of neglect. Today's minimum wage is only 38% of the average private industry wage, its lowest point by that measure since 1949. Its buying power has dropped 25% since 1981, when Congress last raised it. It was inadequate then, a cruel joke now.

About 8 million individuals now work at or near the minimum wage. A worker clocking a 40-hour week 50 weeks a year at minimum wage earns $6,964. For an individual not heading a family, that's just above the official poverty line, generously drawn at $5,600. Try living on it. Worse, try supporting a family. The minimum wage is dismally deficient for any worker who has to support someone else. The income, for example, of a family of three headed by a minimum wage worker is $1,700 under the poverty line – 20% less than it takes to live decently. Minimum wage earners are not just well-to-do teens; indeed employers in some cities and suburbs cannot find anyone to work at that wage. Almost half of minimum wage workers are 25 years or older, and one of every four is a head of household. In 1984, 2.1 million people worked full-time year round, but they and their families remained in poverty, including 1.2 million heads of households.

Most states, like California, prop up the working poor with programs such as Medicaid, food stamps and AFDC. These usually do not, nor were they designed to, lift a family out of poverty. They just make poverty less miserable.

In some states, workers forfeit their benefits once they take a job. That, of course, destroys the incentive for welfare recipients to take a job that pays less than welfare, as in most circumstances minimum wage jobs do. Thus it is expensive and self-defeating to keep the minimum wage so low. Taxpayers are subsidizing the wages of the working poor, making up for what employers ought to be paying.

After five years of inaction, Congress should lift the minimum wage to at least $4.35 an hour, which would be equivalent to its traditional level of half the average private industry wage. If raised gradually, it wouldn't squeeze employers who have to pay more. A better minimum wage won't stoke inflation; there are simply too few who work at it. It might result in fewer jobs, but any loss should be more than offset by higher earnings. And those stung would most likely be youths, not adults. Raising the minimum wage would cut welfare expenses, restore the purchasing power of the working poor, and most important, lift many of them from the throes of poverty.

Economics aside, the decision to raise the minimum wage is a moral one. It is unnecessary and unconscionable for persons to work and be poor. The term, *working poor*, should be an oxymoron. Right now, it's not. Congress can change that.

No, We Should Not Raise the Minimum Wage:

Minimum-Wage Politicking
By *Robert J. Samuelson*

[Reprinted with permission from *Newsweek*,
July 11, 1988. Abridged.]

Some of you may think that raising the minimum wage is a long-overdue way of helping the poor. Please discard this outdated idea. Increasing the minimum wage is misguided social policy, even if it seems the fair thing to do.

Popular wisdom is understandable and well meaning. The current minimum – $3.35 an hour – hasn't been raised since 1981. By 1987 it stood at only 37% percent of average hourly earnings. It hasn't been that far below the average wage rate since 1949. This seems monstrously indecent. Workers stuck in minimum-wage jobs are being progressively impoverished. Their pay is about $7,000 a year. That's less than two-thirds of the government's official poverty floor for a family of four. It's a dismaying picture. It's also thoroughly misleading.

The profile of minimum-wage workers simply doesn't fit the popular stereotype. Consider:

- Most aren't from poor families. About 70 percent come from families with incomes at least 50 percent above the poverty line, according to a study by the Congressional Budget Office. Only 19 percent come from families below the poverty line.
- Most minimum-wage jobs aren't held by heads of families. About two-thirds are held by young (24 and under) and single workers. About a third are teenagers. The typical minimum-wage worker is a teenager from a non-poor family working as a waiter or waitress. A third of all minimum-wage jobs are in restaurants.
- Most workers don't get stuck in full-time minimum-wage jobs; indeed, two-thirds of minimum-wage jobs are part time. Some jobs permanently pay the minimum, but they have high turnover. Other jobs may start at the minimum, but companies quickly give raises to employees they want to keep. Since 1980 the proportion of workers receiving the minimum has fallen from about 11 to 4 percent.

Government policies shouldn't be based on stereotypes that are demonstrably false. Legislation passed by the House Education and Labor Committee would raise the minimum wage about 51 percent, to $5.05, by 1992. Enacting this sort of increase to help the minority of workers who fit the stereotype — heads of families with full-time jobs — is self-defeating. It would raise unemployment and inflation in return for, at most, a tiny reduction in poverty.

When government mandates higher labor costs, someone has to pay them. Companies are likely to raise prices and fire (or not hire) the least productive workers. After reviewing the available studies, economists Frederick Furlong and Marc Charney of the Federal Reserve Bank of San Francisco concluded that the present proposal would raise inflation at least a quarter of a percentage point and result in the loss of 100,000 to 300,000 jobs. "The increase in unemployment would be among lower-wage workers, the group that the minimum-wage law is supposed to help," they write.

Supporters of a higher minimum dismiss these side effects as trivial. For instance, they point out that the extra joblessness would add only 0.1 to 0.3 percentage points to the unemployment rate. This argument is absurd. It justifies bad legislation as long as the bad effects are small, as Rep. Richard Armey, Republican of Texas, says. "Why not raise [the minimum] to $10 or $20 an hour?" he asks. "The adverse effect of the minimum wage is perfectly obvious when we imagine it inflated to $10 an hour . . . At $5.05 the effects on employment are not quite so blindingly apparent. Instead of millions of workers being laid off, there will only be a mere few hundred thousand."

Tough choices: There are better ways of helping the working poor. Rep. Thomas E. Petri, Republican of Wisconsin, suggests improving the earned-income tax credit, which goes to working parents with low incomes. The maximum credit is now $874. Because most of these workers don't owe income taxes, the credit is refundable. It's a direct payment that covers their social-security taxes and a bit more. But today's credit doesn't vary according to family size. Petri would provide bigger credits for larger families, up to $2,500 for four children. This approach wouldn't raise prices, wouldn't deter hiring and would direct benefits to those in need.

It's not a partisan idea. An early advocate was economist Robert Reischauer of the Brookings Institution, a Democrat. Privately, some Democratic congressmen concede it's a good concept. But the Democratic congressional leadership clings to the minimum wage out of habit and expediency. It's superficially popular. One recent Gallup poll showed 77 percent of Americans support a higher minimum. It's also heavily favored by organized labor, a major Democratic constituency. Finally, it doesn't add to the budget deficit. By contrast, Petri's proposal would cut tax revenues about $2 billion. Doing it right would mean raising someone else's taxes or cutting some spending.

There's no taste for such tough choices. Even raising the minimum wage is harder than it seems. The dilemma is basic: the larger the increase, the greater the economic damage; the smaller the increase, the more it's a gesture.

A lot of intricate legislative maneuvering lies ahead. It should be fascinating. But be assured that it doesn't have much to do with the poor. It's over political symbolism. Raising the minimum wage involves the worst kind of backdoor spending and feel-good politics: people can say they're helping the poor when they're really not.

Holding a Debate

Many students will benefit from and will enjoy participating in a debate on this topic either in class or in an informal study group. After completing both readings and possibly doing some additional research (for example, see pages 624-627 of the text), get three to four volunteers for each side of the debate, choose a moderator if your instructor is not available, and devote about a half an hour to opening statements, rebuttals, and summaries. Good luck!

Discussion

1. If you read both articles, see if you can explain the following paradox. Most politicians, including both major party candidates in the 1988 presidential campaign, are in favor of increasing the minimum wage, and yet most economists, including economists from almost every political and cultural background, think that the minimum wage hurts many of those it is intended to help. How can you explain this difference in opinion?

2. If you read the *Los Angeles Times* editorial, do you agree with the normative judgment in the last paragraph? Explain, Is the phrase "working poor" an oxymoron? (What *is* an oxymoron?)

3. If you read the Samuelson article, do you see any potential problems with his suggestion that we improve the earned-income tax credit instead of increasing the minimum wage? Which do you think will cost more? Which do you think will help the poor more? Explain.

4
Supply and Demand for the Public Sector

TRUE OR FALSE

T F

1. When production of a good results in externalities that impose a cost on secondary parties, the output level of the good often exceeds the socially ideal amount.

2. The total social cost of an action includes the costs to the voluntary participants and any costs imposed on secondary parties.

3. Any commodity provided by the public sector is defined as a public good.

4. It is often difficult to exclude nonpaying citizens from receiving the benefits of a public good.

5. When an activity imposes spillover costs on secondary parties, a government tax policy that would reduce the level of the activity could improve economic efficiency.

6. Well-organized special interest groups may be able to use the political process for their own gain even though the action results in a net social loss.

7. A policy that provides immediate, readily identified benefits at the expense of a cost that is in the future and difficult to identify tends to be very attractive to a legislator seeking to enhance his or her chances of winning an election.

8. Spillover costs often result from the production of steel when the air is used for purposes of waste disposal.

9. The public sector produces nothing and therefore contributes nothing to the improvement of resource allocation.

10. Although income distribution may not be ideal, the voluntary exchange mechanism will always lead to the socially efficient allocation of resources.

11. National defense is an example of a public good.

PROBLEMS AND PROJECTS

1. Indicate which of the following goods is a private good (P), a public good (PG), or has characteristics of both (B). Explain your answer in each case.

    a. A measles shot _____

    _____

    b. A fireworks display _____

    _____

    c. National defense _____

    _____

    d. Neckties _____

    _____

    e. A television program _____

    _____

    f. A filet mignon steak _____

    _____

    g. A taxicab _____

    _____

    h. A rose garden _____

    _____

    i. A flood control project _____

    _____

    j. A poem _____

    _____

2. Consider the supply and demand for public-sector action, and decide whether each of the following illustrates
    (1) rent-seeking behavior by private parties,
    (2) vote-seeking behavior by elected officials, or
    (3) the rational ignorance effect

    ____ a. Members of Congress have resisted curbing the lobbying activities of political action coalitions (PACs).

    ____ b. Election results are often distorted by poorly informed voters and low voter turnouts.

    ____ c. Liquor wholesalers in most states have lobbied for state laws that compel retailers to buy their liquor supplies only from the nearest available wholesaler, instead of shopping around.

    ____ d. A majority of voters support protectionism against imports even though such protectionism cost consumers over $80 billion in 1988.

3. Exhibit 1 illustrates what the world demand for petroleum might look like in the short run. The supply curve (S) represents the world supply of petroleum if petroleum suppliers behave competitively.

Exhibit 1

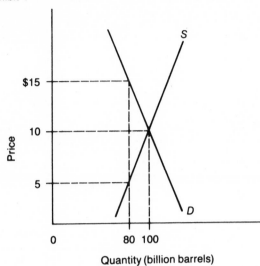

Quantity (billion barrels)

a. What would be the long-run, competitive equilibrium price and quantity of petroleum? Show these in the diagram.
b. At competitive equilibrium, calculate the total revenues earned by petroleum suppliers. (Remember that total revenue is price times quantity sold.)
c. Suppose now that petroleum suppliers agree to restrict the quantity they sell to 80 billion barrels. Draw in the supply curve. What price would they charge? What would total revenue be?

d. If only 80 billion barrels were sold, what is the value (in dollars) of the consumers' valuation of the last barrel produced and sold? Is this consumer valuation of the last unit larger or smaller than the producers' opportunity cost of producing that last unit? Is this an efficient or an inefficient outcome for society?
e. Could government policy have helped avoid this problem? How?

4. Exhibit 2 shows the supply and demand schedules for pulp paper in Academia, a hypothetical country.

Exhibit 2

Price (per ton)	Quantity (ton/year)	
	Demanded	Supplied
$150	1000	7000
140	2000	6000
130	3000	5000
120	4000	4000
110	5000	3000
100	6000	2000

a. On a piece of graph paper, plot the demand and supply curves and show the equilibrium price and quantity for pulp paper in Academia.
b. Suppose that the production of pulp paper results in external pollution costs of $20 per ton produced. In your diagram, show a supply curve that would include these external costs. What are the "ideal" (efficient) price and output for pulp paper? Show these in your diagram.

5. Exhibit 3 below depicts the market for baseball teams, with the total number of teams on the horizontal axis and the price of each team (in millions of dollars) on the vertical axis.

Exhibit 3

Quantity demanded	Price	Quantity supplied
17	68	35
20	62	32
23	56	29
26	50	26
29	44	23
32	38	20
35	32	17

a. Diagram the supply and demand curves and determine the values of the free market equilibrium price and quantity.

Some have argued that a baseball team generates external benefits for a city by increasing the city's morale and pride and bringing in extra tourist revenue.

b. Suppose that the value of these external benefits turns out to be $24 million per team. Use your diagram from part a to depict these externalities. What is the efficient total number of baseball teams?

c. What type of policy could a city government use to attract a baseball team?

d. Suppose that there really are no external benefits associated with baseball teams. What theory described in the text suggests that the policies you described in part c might get adopted anyway?

LEARNING THE MECHANICS – MULTIPLE CHOICE

1. All but one of the following public sector actions will help to provide an economic environment that can facilitate the attainment of gains from market exchange. Which one *reduces* the efficiency of the market process?
   a. Promoting competitive markets
   b. Protecting persons from fraud
   c. Providing a stable monetary framework
   d. Protecting consumers by fixing prices below equilibrium

2. Competition among producers is important because it
   a. serves to protect the consumer by providing him with alternatives to the prices offered by any single seller.
   b. serves to protect the producer, assuring her of at least a fair rate of return.
   c. means that the market will always meet the social conditions of ideal economic efficiency.
   d. always leads to prices that reflect the total social cost of producing each good.

3. Ideal public sector action can potentially improve economic efficiency
   a. because political decision-makers are generally concerned with problems associated with income distribution.
   b. if the government sets prices above equilibrium for commodities in a competitive market and below equilibrium for commodities in monopolistic markets.
   c. when spillover or external effects cause market inefficiency.
   d. because of the rational ignorance effect.

4. An action that imposes spillover costs on a secondary party results in
   a. voluntary exchange.
   b. public sector action.
   c. involuntary exchange.
   d. market adjustments that lead to the ideal social outcome.

5. It is difficult for the market process to provide public goods because
   a. they must be produced by government.
   b. it will be difficult to get potential consumers to pay for such goods since there is not a direct link between payment for and receipt of the good.
   c. consumers do not really want public goods, even though such goods are best for them.
   d. individual consumers will fail to gain from the production of goods that benefit the general public.

6. When there is no interference with the market mechanism
   a. the market will under-allocate resources to the production of goods with external costs.
   b. the market will over-allocate resources to the production of goods with external benefits.
   c. the cost to society from production will be greater than the private cost to producers when external costs are present.
   d. the output of public goods will generally exceed the optimal level of output.

7. Public sector action
   a. promotes economic efficiency except when self-interest leads to political corruption.
   b. sometimes improves efficiency and sometimes generates inefficiency, since proposals that help win elections are not necessarily efficient.
   c. generally leads to economic inefficiency because the public sector is bureaucratic in nature, and bureaucrats are lazy.
   d. promotes economic efficiency when collective decisions are made democratically.

8. All of the following are true about the market and public sectors *except*
   a. competitive behavior is present in both sectors.
   b. the public sector utilizes the price mechanism more than the private sector.
   c. the public sector can break the individual consumption-payment link more easily than can the private sector.
   d. there is more free choice for individual consumers in the private sector than in the public sector.

9. Which of the following is *not* true of the concept of economic efficiency?
   a. Economic efficiency defines the ideal income distribution.
   b. An economically efficient solution occurs when all exchanges that will lead to an improvement in the well-being of individuals have been undertaken.
   c. The largest possible benefit is obtained from a given level of cost.
   d. Each good is produced at the lowest possible cost.

10. Simply stated, the rational ignorance effect explains why
    a. consumers are rational but not very intelligent.
    b. voters are rational but not very intelligent.
    c. voters are intelligent to remain rational.
    d. rational voters remain ignorant.

11. Despite many differences, the market and public sectors are *similar* in which one of the following respects?
    a. In both sectors, income (or power) is distributed on the basis of the same criterion.
    b. Consumers in the market sector and voters in the public sector are equally well informed.
    c. Voluntary exchange, rather than compulsion, is characteristic of both sectors.
    d. It will be costly to use scarce goods, whether through the private or the public sector.

12. Which of the following activities is *least* likely to give rise to external costs or benefits?
    a. Spraying to control mosquitos in your backyard
    b. Driving one's car during rush hour
    c. Inoculating your children during a flu epidemic
    d. Watching fewer movies on television

13. Which of the following is the best example of rent-seeking?
    a. A lobbying organization that has no position on rent control makes contributions to politicians who favor rent control.
    b. A steel company makes contributions to politicians who favor lowering taxes on steel.
    c. A politician convinces colleagues of the advantages of renting an apartment rather than buying a home while in Washington, D.C.
    d. A diaper manufacturer hires only those employees who favor lower taxes on diapers.

THE ECONOMIC WAY OF THINKING – MULTIPLE CHOICE

1. Driving your automobile in Los Angeles during the rush hour causes externalities because
   a. it adds to congestion and pollution from auto exhaust, reducing the welfare of others.
   b. gasoline is scarce and you must pay for it.
   c. gasoline is a public good.
   d. your actions will benefit others even though you will be unable to charge them for the service.

2. In the absence of government action, the private market probably would not produce as much national defense as citizens desire because
   a. individual citizens do not receive personal benefits from national defense.
   b. private firms do not like to produce goods with public good characteristics.
   c. it would be difficult for private firms to charge for national defense since it cannot usually be withheld from nonpaying customers.
   d. national defense benefits a country but not its citizens.

3. If economic efficiency is the criterion, which of the following is the most important justification for the government, rather than private enterprise, providing certain economic goods and services?
    a. The government can provide political goods free of charge.
    b. The government can redistribute incomes such that the poverty problem is mitigated.
    c. A private market cannot eliminate the misallocation that results from the rational ignorance of consumers.
    d. A private market does not provide a way to sell certain "public goods" because the benefits derived cannot be limited to those persons who pay for them.

4. Apart from income distribution, criteria of ideal economic efficiency require that **(I)** all trading in which both buyers and sellers can gain take place; **(II)** no trading take place for which the social cost (including any cost imposed on nonconsenting parties) exceeds the social benefit derived from the exchange.
    a. Both I and II are true.
    b. Neither I nor II is true.
    c. I is true, II is false.
    d. II is true, I is false.

5. Under a market system, individuals normally pay for a particular good; when goods are allocated through the public sector,
    a. an individual "pays" the approximate value of the government service through taxes.
    b. the individual does not pay – nor does anyone else – since the government simply prints money to finance the service.
    c. although the individual consumer often does not pay, costs are incurred that must be covered by someone (or some group).
    d. payment is avoided since the production of the services is not for profit.

    The following quotation relates to questions 6 and 7.
    > "The ideal policy, from the viewpoint of the state, is one with identifiable beneficiaries, each of whom is helped appreciably, at the cost of many unidentifiable persons, none of whom is hurt very much" – George Stigler, *A Dialogue on the Proper Economic Role of the State.*

6. This statement is probably
    a. incorrect, because voters are well informed on a wide range of political issues.
    b. incorrect, because the political process dilutes the influence of special interest groups, since like other citizens, their members have only one vote.
    c. correct, because the well-informed voter will favor policies that cater to the views of small groups of people.
    d. correct, because voters who have a strong personal interest in an issue will tend to support candidates who cater to their views, whereas most other voters ignore the issue.

7. Which of the following groups does the above quotation suggest would have the most influence on public sector action?
   a. Taxpayers
   b. Nonunion laborers
   c. Special interest groups
   d. Consumers

8. Which of the following "goods" is the best example of a pure public good?
   a. Interstate highways
   b. Clean air
   c. Cultural centers
   d. Public education

9. An action that improves economic efficiency is one
   a. that does not involve any discrimination.
   b. for which the sum of the net benefits to those who favor the action is less than the sum of the net costs imposed on those who oppose the action.
   c. for which the sum of the net benefits to those who gain from the action is greater than the sum of the net costs to those who lose.
   d. that results in a majority of the people benefiting from the action.

10. If there are no spillover effects, voluntary exchange results in **(I)** an expected net gain for all participants in the transaction, **(II)** a social benefit that exceeds the social cost.
    a. Both I and II are true.
    b. Neither I nor II is true.
    c. I is true, II is false.
    d. II is true, I is false.

11. Special interest issues may lead to economic inefficiency since
    a. special interest groups consist, in general, of individuals who are less worthy than the general populace.
    b. politicians are members of special interest groups.
    c. individual voters are irrational in not obtaining information on special interest issues.
    d. the political process is likely to give undue weight to special interest groups, even though contrary action may be more efficient.

12. Economists use the term *short-sightedness effect* to describe which one of the following phenomena?
    a. Politicians tend to support actions that have immediate and easily recognized current benefits.
    b. Individuals are apt to spend their income on goods that bring immediate personal benefits.
    c. Voters elect politicians on the basis of campaign promises, regardless of what they may do once they are in office.
    d. Politicians support the programs of special interest groups in order to get elected; however, special interest support may be detrimental later, costing politicians popularity after the programs are implemented.

13. In the absence of government intervention, goods with external costs tend to be
    a. overproduced and overconsumed.
    b. overproduced and underconsumed.
    c. underproduced and overconsumed.
    d. underproduced and underconsumed.

THE ECONOMIC WAY OF THINKING – DISCUSSION QUESTIONS

1. What are the two conditions for economic efficiency? Provide a specific example for each of four reasons why unregulated markets might fail to be efficient. Give three reasons why government intervention might promote inefficiency.

2. Respond to the following statement: "In the private sector, it's one vote per dollar. In the public sector it's one vote per citizen. Lobbying can be useful in bridging this gap between dollar votes and ballot votes: it can promote efficiency by offsetting the tendency of the political process toward a tyranny of the majority."

3. For some public goods it is feasible to withhold the benefits from those who don't contribute to the costs of production; for other public goods it is not feasible. List some examples of both types of public goods. Which type is more commonly provided by the private sector? Why?

4. Do you find the public choice theory of political behavior convincing? What do you see as its strengths? Its weaknesses? Do you think most politicians are motivated by personal self-interest? Cite evidence in support of your answer.

5. Why are well-organized special interest groups likely to be politically powerful? Why will vote-seeking political entrepreneurs have an incentive to cater to their views?

6. List as many goods as you can think of that have substantial public good characteristics that are provided by the private sector. Try weather forecasts and television signals for starters.

7. Chapter 2 introduced the concept of transaction costs. How do transaction costs help to explain why there is more (and more effective) lobbying by special interest groups than by the general public?

PERSPECTIVES IN ECONOMICS

New Buzzword, Old Philosophy
A Mobil advertisement

[From the *Los Angeles Times*,
February 18, 1986, p. 4.
Reprinted with the permission of the
Mobil Corporation. ©1986 Mobil Corporation.]

The "mixed economy," that marriage of public and private enterprise so widely hailed in the 1960s, has lost some of its pizzazz these days. The buzzword of the '80s is privatization, and it's firing the imagination of countries the world over – Capitalist, Socialist and Communist alike.

In Europe, for example, the British government has sold more than a dozen state-owned companies – some of the giants of its aerospace, communications, energy, tourism and trucking industries – and shifted more than 400,000 workers from public to private payrolls. Similar moves are taking place in France, Germany, Italy, Spain and Sweden.

In Asia, Japan is divesting the government railway, airline and telephone systems. South Korea is selling off banks and heavy industry. Less developed nations like Bangladesh and Pakistan are returning nationalized jute, textile, rice and flour mills to their former owners.

The economic momentum has even spread to the communist world. The Cuban government is selling state-owned houses to tenants. More than 10 million self-employed capitalists operate restaurants, street stalls, repair shops and other small enterprises in China. And in rural areas, farmers are prospering by selling surplus produce in the cities, and keeping the proceeds. Entrepreneurs in Hungary bid for the right to run their own businesses, and the system is catching on in other Eastern European nations.

Why the interest in privatization? Mostly because it works. Especially in the Communist lands, privatization has tended to raise the standard of living.

Not surprisingly, privatization is becoming popular in America, too. Prompted by the need to cut the deficit, the Reagan administration is seeking to cut costs by turning over to private operators such traditional loss leaders as Amtrak and the Federal Housing Administration, which insures private mortgages. Other possible initiatives: selling airport landing slots to individual carriers, for example, or letting private companies sort and deliver first-class mail.

Actually, in this country municipal governments have gotten the jump on the feds – contracting out for everything from hospital care to airport management. The town of La Mirada, California, has been one of the leaders, using the private sector for almost all key services – including police and fire protection, social welfare, and public works. Phoenix, Arizona, has saved millions of dollars by having its municipal agencies bid against outside companies for city contracts. A money-losing teaching hospital that the city of Louisville, Kentucky, turned over to a private company in 1983 is not only making money now but also providing better patient care.

Privatization, in short, has meant more efficiency and lower costs – and, usually, better service. And if it involves the sale of an asset, the government gets a whopping one-time capital gain as well. So why has privatization been so long in coming? Fact is, it's been around for some time. Privatization is just a modern-day buzzword for an old, old philosophy. Adam Smith called it the free market. We call it a pretty good deal all around.

Discussion

1. What exactly *is* privatization? Why should a citizen who is not involved in a given industry care whether or not that industry's product is provided to the government by privately owned or publicly owned producers?

2. This article was published as an advertisement paid for by the Mobil Corporation. How could publishing such an ad possibly help to sell gasoline? Does Mobil's decision to publish the ad mean that they are a special interest group? Explain your answers.

3. The advertisement cites a hospital in Louisville, Kentucky. Why do you think that the private hospital was making money while the public hospital was losing money? What sorts of generalizations can you draw from such an example?

5
Government Spending and Taxation

TRUE OR FALSE

T F

☐ ☐   1. As one's marginal tax rate increases, the percentage of each additional dollar earned that the taxpayer is permitted to keep for personal expenditures will decline.

☐ ☐   2. If the supply curve of labor were perfectly vertical, the burden of an earnings (or payroll) tax would fall entirely on the employee in the form of a lower after-tax wage rate.

☐ ☐   3. A tax that takes more dollars from a low-income recipient than it takes from a high-income recipient must be regressive.

☐ ☐   4. A tax that takes more dollars from a high-income recipient than it takes from a low-income recipient must be progressive.

☐ ☐   5. The underground economy's share of GNP can best be measured by calculating the share of income taxes that comes from the underground economy.

☐ ☐   6. Federal expenditures on cash income maintenance constitute a larger share of the federal budget than do expenditures for national defense.

☐ ☐   7. A tax that is equitable is sure to be economically inefficient because the concepts of equity and efficiency are inherently opposed.

☐ ☐   8. If the percentage of income that is taxed away increases as an individual's income increases, the tax must be regressive.

☐ ☐   9. Borrowing and user charges are two alternatives to taxes as sources for government revenue.

☐ ☐ 10. All underground economic activity is illegal economic activity.

☐ ☐ 11. Since the mid-1950s, the purchases of goods and services of the Federal government have declined as a share of GNP.

☐ ☐ 12. Under a proportional income tax, the dollar tax liability of a high-income taxpayer will exceed the dollar tax liability for a low-income taxpayer. (*Hint*: Assume all income is taxable.)

PROBLEMS AND PROJECTS

1. Assume that a massive tax reform bill changes the current federal income tax rate schedule to the following simple tax schedule:

Income (dollars)	Marginal tax rate
Under 20,000	10%
20,000-50,000	20%
Over 50,000	30%

   a. If your income is $30,000, what is your total tax? (*Hint*: it is not $6,000; that would be correct if 20% were the average tax rate.)
   b. If your income is $60,000, what is your total tax?
   c. Is this tax schedule progressive or regressive?
   d. Assume that the tax bill included indexed marginal tax rates and that inflation last year was 10%. Calculate what the new (indexed) tax schedule would be.

2. Exhibit 1 summarizes a portion of the U.S. federal income tax schedule for married couples filing jointly in 1983.

Exhibit 1

Bracket number	Taxable income	Total tax
1	$12,000	$ 1,166
2	24,000	3,518
3	36,000	6,904
4	48,000	11,214
5	60,000	16,014
6	72,000	21,294
7	84,000	26,574

   a. Calculate the average tax rate for brackets 2 and 6. Is your tax rate structure proportional, regressive, or progressive?
   b. Calculate the marginal tax rate for a married couple whose income increases from bracket 1 to bracket 2. From bracket 5 to bracket 6. Are these marginal rates greater or smaller than the corresponding average you calculated in part a?

   c. Suppose that the tax structure in 1982 was the same as that in Exhibit 1. Suppose also that you had the money income of $48,000 in 1982 and that your money income rose to $60,000 in 1983. If the rate of inflation between 1982 and 1983 had been 25 percent, would you have had an increase in your *constant purchasing power* (real) income? Would you have been required to pay a higher percentage of your income in income taxes? What phenomenon does this represent?

3. Exhibit 2 shows average income tax rates and the aggregate amount of taxable income that would be generated by economic activity at each rate.

Exhibit 2

Average tax rate (percent)	Aggregate taxable income (billions)	Tax revenue (billions)
20	$600	$120
30	500	_____
40	450	_____
50	400	_____
60	350	_____
70	300	_____
80	250	_____

   a. Fill in the remaining entries in the tax revenue column.
   b. On a piece of graph paper, plot the relationship between the tax rate (on the vertical axis) and tax revenues (on the horizontal axis). What is this relationship called?

4. Use the diagrams in Exhibit 3 to help you answer the questions below:

Exhibit 3

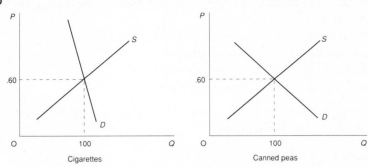

a. Suppose the government imposes a tax of $.40 per unit on cigarettes and on canned peas. Diagram the results. For which good does the incidence of the tax fall more heavily on sellers? On buyers? (*Note*: You do not have to determine actual numerical values.)

b. If the government could only tax one of these products and wanted to generate as much tax revenue as possible, which product should it tax? Why does the product you chose generate more tax revenue?

c. Some have argued that a tax on cigarettes promotes greater efficiency. Why do you think that might be true?

5. Each of the three tax options in Exhibit 4 generates about $40,000 of revenue to finance government spending by taxing three equal-sized families.

Exhibit 4

| | Taxable income | Income taxes | | | | | |
		Option 1	ATR	Option 2	ATR	Option 3	ATR
Family 1	$ 20,000	$13,333	_____	$ 4,444	_____	$ 3,000	_____
Family 2	60,000	13,333	_____	$13,333	_____	$12,000	_____
Family 3	100,000	13,333	_____	$22,222	_____	$25,000	_____

a. Fill in the average tax rate (ATR) for each family under each option.

b. Classify each tax option as either progressive, proportional or regressive.

c. Consider the following statement: "Government programs such as education, fire protection, and defense are equally available to all taxpayers, so it makes economic sense for all taxpayers to contribute an equal amount to finance these programs." Do you agree? If so, explain why. If not, explain why not and then indicate which tax option you prefer and briefly explain why.

LEARNING THE MECHANICS — MULTIPLE CHOICE

1. In the United States, the total tax revenues of the federal, state, and local governments constitute
    a. approximately one-tenth of the gross national product.
    b. approximately one-fifth of the gross national product.
    c. approximately one-third of the gross national product.
    d. approximately one-half of the gross national product.

2. The size of the public sector relative to total output is smaller in one of the following countries than for the United States. Which one?
    a. Japan
    b. France
    c. United Kingdom
    d. Sweden

3. The "incidence" of a tax is the term that indicates
    a. the person who is responsible for paying the tax to the Federal Treasury.
    b. the person why actually bears the burden of the tax.
    c. whether the tax is progressive.
    d. whether the tax results in greater benefits than costs.

4. If we assume that the demand for and supply of Big Jim's Sour Mash Whiskey is described by typically sloped demand and supply curves, which of the following would be the most likely impact of a tax placed on Big Jim's whiskey?
    a. Consumers would pay more, and Big Jim would receive more.
    b. Consumers would pay more, and Big Jim would receive less.
    c. Consumers would pay the same amount, and Big Jim would receive less.
    d. Consumers would pay more, and Big Jim would receive the same amount.

5. A progressive tax
    a. takes a similar percentage from all income brackets.
    b. takes a higher percentage from higher income brackets.
    c. takes a lower percentage from higher income brackets.
    d. is one that does not impede progress.

6. If the tax liability of a couple increases from $1000 to $1200 as their income increases from $10,000 to $11,000, the couple's marginal tax rate is
    a. 10 percent.
    b. 11 percent.
    c. 12 percent.
    d. 20 percent.

7. The underground economy is another name for
    a. unproductive economic activity.
    b. economic activity in underground shopping malls.
    c. unreported production and exchange (usually in cash).
    d. the oil, natural gas, and mineral industries.

8. The largest single source of revenue for local, state, and federal governments (combined) is
    a. the personal income tax.
    b. the sales tax.
    c. the property tax.
    d. the corporate income tax.

9. Which of the following categories represents the largest percentage of total federal expenditures in the late 1980s?
   a. Interest on the national debt
   b. Revenue sharing
   c. National defense expenditures
   d. Cash income maintenance – including such expenditures as social security, Medicare, and veterans' benefits

10. In general, the relative size of the government sector in the United States
    a. is smaller than in countries that are just beginning to develop.
    b. is less than western European nations (such as France, West Germany, and the United Kingdom).
    c. is of no economic significance.
    d. falls primarily on the upper class.

11. Which of the following is clearly an example of a regressive tax?
    a. One that takes more from the rich than the poor
    b. One that is forward looking and leads to future economic growth
    c. One that takes a larger percentage of income as income rises
    d. One that taxes each individual the same number of dollars no matter what his income

12. If families at most income levels consume approximately the same amount of gasoline per year, then gasoline excise taxes are
    a. progressive.
    b. proportional.
    c. regressive.
    d. impossible to classify.

THE ECONOMIC WAY OF THINKING – MULTIPLE CHOICE

1. Assuming that individuals are primarily concerned with their own welfare, which of the following taxes are high-income families *least* likely to prefer?
   a. A progressive tax
   b. A regressive tax
   c. A proportional tax
   d. Any type of sales tax

2. A payroll tax is *not* likely to influence
   a. the quantity of labor supplied.
   b. the quantity of labor demanded.
   c. the price of the final product.
   d. the demand for labor (as a function of *total* labor cost).

3. According to positive economic analysis, the corporate income tax
   a. is bad, compared to other taxes.
   b. is good, compared to other taxes.
   c. is, in the end, paid by individuals, since only individuals can bear the burden of taxes.
   d. is not a burden on consumers.

4. In 1986, Congress approved a new tax bill that decreased marginal tax rates and increased the tax base by eliminating a number of deductions (or tax "loopholes"). Which of the following groups would be most likely to oppose such a tax revision?
   a. Low-income taxpayers with few if any deductions
   b. Middle-income taxpayers with few if any deductions
   c. High-income taxpayers with few if any deductions
   d. Employees of an industry whose product's status as a deduction is in danger of being eliminated

5. A 2-cent-per-gallon increase in the gasoline tax caused the price of gasoline to rise by two cents with no change in quantity. The incidence of the gasoline tax fell on
   a. the producers of gasoline.
   b. gasoline station operators.
   c. gasoline station employees.
   d. the consumers of gasoline.

6. Which of the following is *most* likely to be correct?
   a. An increase in tax rates will lead to a proportional increase in tax revenues.
   b. An increase in tax rates will lead to a more than proportional increase in tax revenues.
   c. An increase in tax rates will lead to a less than proportional increase in tax revenues.
   d. An increase in tax rates will always lead to a decrease in tax revenues.

7. The excess burden of a tax refers to
   a. the loss of private purchasing power due to the revenues transferred to the public sector.
   b. the additional tax that must be levied because some taxpayers engage in tax avoidance activities.
   c. the excess tax levied on high-income taxpayers relative to a taxpayer with an average income.
   d. the additional burden imposed on taxpayers because taxes distort prices and eliminate some mutually advantageous exchanges.

8. Which of the following would occur if a nation's tax structure were fully indexed?
   a. If one's money income rose at the same rate as the nation's inflation rate, one's tax liability would be unchanged.
   b. If one's money income rose more rapidly than the inflation rate, one's average tax rate would be unchanged.
   c. If one's money income rose less rapidly than the inflation rate, one's average tax rate would increase.
   d. If one's money income rose at the same rate as the nation's inflation rate, one's average and marginal tax rates would be unchanged.

9. In order to decide whether it is worthwhile to take a second job, a smart taxpayer would consider the
   a. marginal tax rate.
   b. average tax rate.
   c. before-tax income.
   d. wage rate, independent of taxes.

10. Under which conditions below would the incidence of a tax on a product fall entirely on buyers?
    a. Upward-sloping supply curve and downward-sloping demand curve
    b. Horizontal supply curve and vertical demand curve
    c. Vertical supply curve and horizontal demand curve
    d. The incidence of a tax is always shared between buyers and sellers

11. George Washington is said to have cautioned his colleagues, during the American Revolution, not to increase a particular tax rate too much for fear of raising less, and not more, revenues for the war effort. If this statement is true, which of the following does it imply about the Laffer curve?
    a. George Washington knew about the Laffer curve.
    b. Laffer stole the idea of his curve from Washington.
    c. The principle behind the Laffer curve has been understood, at least at some levels, for many years.
    d. Nothing at all; the Laffer curve has nothing to do with the relationship between tax rates and total tax revenues.

    Questions 12-14 refer to Exhibit 5:

Exhibit 5:

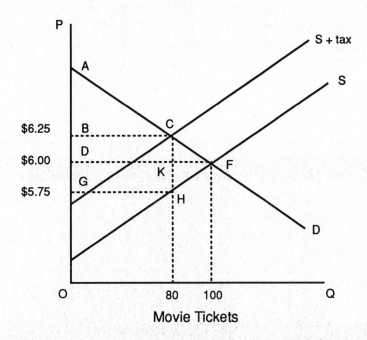

Movie Tickets

12. Suppose the government imposes a tax on movie tickets, causing the supply curve to shift from S to "S + tax." How much was the tax per ticket?
    a. $6.25
    b. $6.00
    c. $0.50
    d. $0.25

13. As a result of the tax, the government collected additional tax revenues of
    a. $50
    b. $40
    c. $25
    d. $20

14. The deadweight loss associated with this tax is best represented by the area
    a. CFK
    b. CFH
    c. BCKD
    d. BCHG

THE ECONOMIC WAY OF THINKING – DISCUSSION QUESTIONS

1. What are the major sources of federal tax revenues? State revenues? Local revenues? Which revenue source do you think is most likely to be progressive? Regressive? Explain your reasoning.

2. By law, Social Security taxes are split 50-50 between employees and employers.
    a. Respond to the following statement: "By the laws of economics, there is no guarantee that the incidence of the Social Security tax is shared evenly by employees and employers."
    b. Evidence suggests that the supply curve for labor is much steeper than the demand curve. Use a labor market supply and demand curve to indicate who absorbs most of the cost of payroll taxes.

3. According to the economic way of thinking, "businesses don't pay taxes, people do." How do you think people end up paying the taxes imposed on business?

4. Consider the following statement: "If we just raised the tax rates of the rich – taxpayers whose incomes are in excess of $50,000 – we could cut the tax rates of the average American." What might be wrong with the logic of this statement?

5. Income taxes are set up in a way that keeps the marginal tax rate higher than the average tax rate for most taxpayers. Social Security taxes are levied at a constant rate until an income ceiling is reached; beyond that income ceiling, no further Social Security taxes are paid. As income rises, what happens to the average income tax rate? The average Social Security tax rate? Support both answers with numerical examples.

6. Suppose that you were running for Congress:
    a. Write a short campaign position paper outlining your platform on government spending and taxation policy. If you advocate any new programs, what would you say about their tax cost?
    b. Do you think your positions will help you raise campaign finances? Will they help you get elected? Why or why not? Address these questions in a letter to your finance chairman.

7. When governments provide electricity and garbage collection services, these services are generally financed with user charges, prices charged to the customers who use the services. Do you think this is a good idea? Why or why not? Would resource use be different if these services were financed by taxation and provided "free" to customers? Explain.

PERSPECTIVES IN ECONOMICS

A Government Health Plan for Free-Marketeers
By Laurence S. Seidman

[From *The Wall Street Journal*, July 23, 1991.
Reprinted with permission from the Wall Street Journal
©Dow Jones & Co., Inc.
All Rights Reserved Worldwide.]

In 1971, Harvard economist Martin Feldstein, chairman of the Council of Economic Advisers in the mid-1980s, set out a simple, elegant plan for the health sector: universal major-risk insurance provided by the federal government. Recently Cornell economist Alfred Kahn, an architect of transportation deregulation in the late 1970s, said he believes major-risk insurance provided by the federal government is the best approach in 1991. What is MRI, and why have these two distinguished economists supported it?

Under MRI, financed by general tax revenue, coverage would be automatic and universal. Every household would have an income-related ceiling on its annual medical financial burden; MRI would thus achieve universal income-related catastrophic protection. At the same time, prior to reaching its out-of-pocket ceiling, every household would pay a share of any medical bill, so each consumer of medical care would have an incentive to be cost-conscious.

For example, a household with $60,000 of income might pay 30% (its "cost-sharing rate") of any medical bill until its annual burden reached 8% of its income, $4,800 (its "out-of-pocket ceiling"). Note that this would occur when its annual medical bill reached $16,000. MRI would then pay 100% of any additional medical bill. The lower a household's income, the lower would be its cost-sharing rate and out-of-pocket ceiling.

Each year, based on its tax return, each household would receive an MRI credit card and be told two numbers: its cost-sharing rate and its out-of-pocket ceiling. For example, the $60,000 household would be told 30% and $4,800. Each household would use its MRI credit card to buy medical care. Households with little or no income would file a short-form tax return in order to obtain an MRI credit card. The government would pay the doctor or hospital and then bill the household for its cost-share (in practice, the government would contract with private insurance companies to process bills). If a household's income dropped sharply, it could file to amend its cost-sharing rate.

MRI is designed to strike a compromise between two conflicting objectives: giving each household an incentive to be cost-conscious, and reducing its financial risk from a medical problem. MRI concentrates on the incentive when the household's financial burden is tolerable but switches to risk reduction when the household's burden threatens to become intolerable.

To protect patient cost-sharing, MRI should not pay any bill for which the household obtains any assistance from a private insurer; nor should employer contributions to health insurance premiums continue to be excluded from employee taxable income. If MRI were enacted with these provisions, many employees would ask their employer to cancel their private insurance and convert the employer's annual premium contribution of several thousand dollars to cash compensation. Employers would welcome an escape from escalating health costs and premiums. Instead of our current mix of myriad private insurance, Medicare, Medicaid, and no insurance, all households (except a minority who bought private insurance) would be covered by MRI.

Why do Messrs. Feldstein and Kahn, economists who generally favor markets over government regulation, support MRI? Because they think it has the best chance to prevent intrusive, inefficient government regulation that tries to micro-manage the practice of medicine. No sector can remain free of government microregulation if its product is "free" to most consumers. When a product is "free' — when there is no consumer cost-sharing — demand escalates, costs escalate, and government must come in to try to get the sector under control. But this inevitably requires detailed micro-management of the behavior of producers and consumers. Such micro-management has already begun for Medicare patients. Like a disease, it will gradually spread to all patients.

While doctors are protesting today, consumers will suffer in the end. Free medical care is not really free, for it requires every consumer to give up some control and power. If patients do not pay for the services they use, then their demands for more services are not credible. "The system" will therefore decide which patients must wait, and which must be denied. By contrast, if the patient pays some of the cost, as he would under MRI, he self-regulates. Government can move away from regulating behavior and fees, letting medical providers respond promptly to self-regulated patient demand.

Will consumer cost-sharing work better than government micro-regulation? True, doctors will continue to make most medical decisions. But with the introduction of MRI, doctors will soon recognize that their patients have a new attitude toward costs. Patients will now want their doctors to weight cost against benefit. So what will happen?

At the time of the decision to enter a hospital, the average patient will probably acquiesce in his doctor's decisions. But a month later, when the recuperating patient receives his bill and estimates his cost-share, he will review his doctor's choices. Was the 10th day really necessary? Was hospital A, the most costly in the area, really best for his problem? Why did he need test Z? Doctors will begin to receive feedback from patients. Knowing this in advance, most doctors will find it in their self-interest to weight cost against benefit in hospital care decisions. The medical market will begin to self-regulate.

What happens if we instead continue down the road of micro-management by regulators? Consider Medicare hospital and physician fee schedules. Hospitals or doctors who provide a particular category of service now must be paid a designated fee regardless of quality. Because a regulator cannot assess quality from a distance, the government fee schedule must ignore it. Hence, hospitals and doctors have little financial incentive to improve the quality of their service. In the long run, the consequences for all patients will be severe.

The only way to cure this worsening regulatory disease is to restore consumer cost-sharing; the only way to make cost-sharing acceptable to the public is to relate it to incomes; and the only way to have income-related cost-sharing is to enact government MRI.

Discussion

1. What exactly *is* MRI? Does its effectiveness depend on the particular cost-sharing rate and out-of-pocket ceiling percentages chosen?

2. What do you see as the major advantages of MRI? What are its major disadvantages? Would you vote to have the federal government provide universal major-risk insurance?

3. Seidman seems to think that Professors Feldstein and Kahn are in favor of MRI because they fear complete government regulation of the health-care industry. What do you think of proposals supported by arguments that, in essence, say "this idea might have flaws, but it sure is a lot better than what everyone else is thinking of."

6
Taking the Nation's Economic Pulse

TRUE OR FALSE

T F

☐ ☐ 1. The gross national product (GNP) is a measure of the market value of all "final product" goods and services that were produced during a period.

☐ ☐ 2. Typically, a gallon of whiskey adds several times more to GNP than does a gallon of water.

☐ ☐ 3. If you paid $800 for a used motorcycle last year, the sale contributed $800 toward last year's GNP.

☐ ☐ 4. GNP minus depreciation is equal to national income.

☐ ☐ 5. Disposable income is that portion of GNP that is left for households to spend or save as they choose.

☐ ☐ 6. In recent years in the United States, disposable income has constituted approximately 70 percent of GNP.

☐ ☐ 7. GNP, net national product (NNP), and national income measure different things; thus, they often move in opposite directions.

☐ ☐ 8. Net national product (NNP) is the GNP minus the negative aspects of production, such as pollution and the depletion of national resources.

☐ ☐ 9. The discovery of a $100 billion Alaskan oil field in 1969 increased GNP by that amount during that year.

☐ ☐ 10. If one wanted to measure the change in the annual output of goods and services between 1981 and 1991, money GNP would be a more reliable indicator than real GNP.

☐ ☐ 11. During a period of deflation, an increase in real GNP would be greater than the increase in money GNP.

☐ ☐ 12. Real per capita GNP in 1990 was approximately twice what it was in 1955. This means that the standard of living in 1990 was two times the 1955 level.

61

PROBLEMS AND PROJECTS

1. Exhibit 1 presents economic data for the United States (in billions of dollars) for 1990.

   ### Exhibit 1

Government purchases	$1098	Indirect business taxes	$ 470
Net exports	-38	Corporate profits	297
Interest income	288	Rents	7
Total personal consumption	3658	Gross private investment	745
Depreciation	576	Compensation of employees	3244
Proprietors' Income	380	Durable goods compensation	482

   a. Calculate GNP and NNP using the expenditure approach.
   b. Calculate GNP and NNP using the resource cost-income approach.

2. Fill in the missing information in Exhibit 2.

   ### Exhibit 2

	GNP (billions)	GNP Deflator (1982 = 100)	Real GNP (1982 dollars)
1970	$1016	42.0	_____
1980	2732	85.7	_____
1990	5463	131.5	_____

3. Given the following information, calculate GNP and NNP.

Employee compensation	10
Rents	20
Government expenditures	30
Depreciation	40
Gross private investment	50
Personal income taxes	60
Net exports	70
Personal consumption	80
Interest income	90

4. In the blank preceding each event described below indicate whether the event would be counted as an increase (+), a decrease (-), or no change (0) in GNP.

_____ a. Ms. A hires a male housekeeper.
_____ b. Ms. A marries her housekeeper.
_____ c. Your family gardener quits (deciding it is more profitable to sell marijuana than to cut grass).
_____ d. Your family adds gardening to your list of chores.
_____ e. A burglar steals your stereo.
_____ f. You buy a new stereo to replace the one that was stolen.
_____ g. The police department hires an extra detective to track down the burglar who stole your stereo.
_____ h. A doctor and lawyer stop billing each other and just trade their services instead.
_____ i. Your parents lose $500 playing blackjack in Las Vegas.
_____ j. You lose $500 playing blackjack in your dorm.
_____ k. Higher world oil prices drive up the price of domestic oil.
_____ l. A self-employed accountant decides to take some time off work "to start enjoying life a little more."
_____ m. You sell an antique writing desk for hard cash.
_____ n. You buy some flour to make a loaf of bread.
_____ o. You burn your bread, throw it away, and buy a loaf of bread from your neighborhood baker.
_____ p. You receive an A grade in this course.

5. Suppose an economy produces and consumes only pizzas and shirts. Consider the following information regarding production, price, and consumption in 1986 and 1989:

	1986				1989		
Total production (millions of units)	Price	Typical consumption (units)		Total production (millions of units)	Price	Typical consumption (units	
300	$ 5	60	Pizzas	360	$ 8	72	
50	10	10	Shirts	180	12	36	

a. Using 1986 as a base year (= 100), what was the value of the CPI for 1989? The GNP deflator for 1989? (*Hint*: Be sure to review the respective definitions.)
b. What was the percentage change in prices from 1986 to 1989 according to the CPI? According to the GNP deflator?

6. Consider the following information for the U.S. economy in 1990 (figures are in billions of dollars):

Gross national product:	$5463
Corporate profits and social insurance taxes:	804
Transfer payments, net interest, and dividends:	1032
Personal taxes:	700
Indirect business taxes:	470
Depreciation:	578

Compute the following values:
a. Net national product
b. National income
c. Personal income
d. Disposable personal income

LEARNING THE MECHANICS – MULTIPLE CHOICE

1. Real GNP, as contrasted with money GNP, refers to
   a. money GNP minus gifts to other countries.
   b. money GNP minus total unemployment compensation.
   c. money GNP adjusted for price changes.
   d. money GNP adjusted for unemployment changes.

2. Assume that between 1980 and 1990 money GNP increased from $1000 billion to $2500 billion, and the index of prices increased from 100 to 200. Which of the following expresses GNP for 1990 in terms of 1980 prices?
   a. $1000 billion
   b. $1250 billion
   c. $2500 billion
   d. $5000 billion

3. From the producer's viewpoint, GNP is best thought of as
   a. an indicator of the good things produced during the period.
   b. an indicator of the total wealth of a nation.
   c. an indicator of the costs that were incurred by the producers of goods during the period.
   d. an indicator of the social welfare of a nation.

4. The GNP deflator is designed to measure the degree to which
   a. incomes are distributed among the poor and rich over time.
   b. the cost of purchasing a bundle of consumer goods has changed with time.
   c. consumption patterns have changed with time because of higher prices.
   d. consumer prices have risen, relative to wages.

5. In terms of 1980 dollars, the 1990 real GNP is the 1990 money GNP (GD stands for GNP deflator.)
   a. multiplied by (GD_{80}/GD_{90}).
   b. multiplied by (GD_{90}/GD_{80}).
   c. divided by the GD in 1980.
   d. divided by the difference between the GD in 1990 and GD in 1980.

6. Which of the following would *not* be counted as part of this year's GNP?
   a. The increase in the value of an antique automobile that was refurbished in the year
   b. The value of a new automobile
   c. The value of a used car at its sale price
   d. The replacement of a worn-out machine used to clean golf balls

7. The largest component of gross national product is
   a. consumption expenditures.
   b. investment expenditures.
   c. government expenditures.
   d. net exports.

8. GNP may be calculated as the sum of
   a. personal consumption expenditures, net private investment expenditures, government purchases, and net exports.
   b. personal consumption expenditures, gross private investment expenditures, and depreciation.
   c. employee compensation, proprietor's income, rents, interest, corporate profits, and net private investment.
   d. net national product and depreciation.

Use the following table to answer questions 9-12.

Personal consumption expenditures	900
Depreciation	130
Indirect business taxes and business transfers	150
Social security contributions	100
Corporate profits	100
Government transfer payments, net interest paid, and business transfer payments	180
Personal taxes	180
Government purchases	300
Dividends	40
Employee compensation	900
Interest income	60
Proprietor's income	100
Rents	40

9. What is net national product?
   a. 1200
   b. 1260
   c. 1350
   d. 1480

10. What is personal income?
    a. 1050
    b. 1110
    c. 1220
    d. 1350

11. What is disposable income?
    a. 1000
    b. 1040
    c. 1110
    d. 1350

12. What is gross national product?
    a. 1200
    b. 1260
    c. 1350
    d. 1480

THE ECONOMIC WAY OF THINKING – MULTIPLE CHOICE

1. The way in which water or air pollution currently affects the measurement of GNP is that the cost of
    a. pollution is completely ignored because it does not affect economic well-being.
    b. any cleaning up of pollution is added to GNP as part of output.
    c. any clean-up campaigns are subtracted from GNP.
    d. pollution damage is subtracted from GNP.

2. Which of the following constitutes a major shortcoming of GNP?
    a. Goods produced but not exchanged during that period are excluded.
    b. It tends to understate the growth of economic welfare.
    c. The value of production that does not involve a monetary exchange is often excluded.
    d. The inclusion of profit is inappropriate, since it does not measure the well-being of the consumers.

3. If you were asked to study the production of the economy during the last three years, you would use the real GNP series rather than the nominal (or money) series because
    a. the nominal series is more complete than the real series, since it includes the production of the government.
    b. the nominal series is less precise, since it does not take into account the externalities from production; the real series does.
    c. the nominal series does not adjust for underemployment of the workers; the real series does.
    d. the nominal series reflects changes in both output and prices; the real series is designed to reflect changes in output only.

4. If the market values of all the goods and services produced during a given year were summed, which of the following would be true with respect to the total for that year?
    a. It would be equal to GNP.
    b. It would be greater than GNP.
    c. It would be less than GNP.
    d. It would ignore the consumer's valuation of the goods and services produced.

5. The GNP deflator
    a. measures the average level of prices now compared with expected prices in the future.
    b. measures the relative dollar value of a given "bundle" of goods and/or services at different points in time.
    c. pertains to all goods and services rather than an array of goods and/or services.
    d. represents a weighted average of price increases adjusted for quality changes.

6. Suppose that the dollar value of GNP increased by approximately 3 percent between January and May of some year, but the real GNP decreased by 2 percent during that period. Which of the following best explains the phenomenon?
    a. Prices rose by approximately 3 percent.
    b. Prices fell by approximately 2 percent.
    c. The real capacity of the economy was increased more quickly than money output.
    d. Prices increased by approximately 5 percent.

7. Some economists prefer the concept of NNP over GNP because
    a. it is more easily calculated.
    b. depreciation is difficult to estimate.
    c. it counts net additions, not gross additions, to the capital stock.
    d. NNP is larger.

8. Real GNP differs from money GNP in that
    a. real GNP measures the value of only tangible products, omitting the value of services.
    b. real GNP is corrected for changes in the price level and is therefore not upwardly biased during inflationary periods.
    c. real GNP corrects for depreciation.
    d. real GNP is more easily calculated than money GNP in that prices need not be known.

9. Real GNP may give a misleading measure of change in national output between two periods because
    a. the price level may change.
    b. the share of production being carried out in the nonmarket sector may change between the two periods.
    c. new goods may be produced in the latter period that cannot be easily compared to earlier goods.
    d. Both b and c are correct.

10. The concept of MEW – measure of economic welfare – modifies traditional GNP data in what way?
    a. The estimated cost of economic "bads" such as pollution are subtracted from GNP, whereas the estimated value of nonmarket goods such as leisure are added to GNP.
    b. The impact of inflation is subtracted from GNP.
    c. Expenditures on necessities such as national defense are added to GNP.
    d. The estimated value of depreciation is subtracted from GNP.

11. Between 1977 and 1987 the federal minimum wage rose from $2.65 per hour to $3.35 per hour, and the CPI rose from 181.5 to 340.4. We can conclude from this that
    a. the minimum wage rose in nominal and in real terms.
    b. the minimum wage fell in nominal terms but rose in real terms.
    c. the minimum wage rose in nominal terms but fell in real terms.
    d. more information is needed to determine what happened to minimum wages over the period.

12. Which of the following is a way to compute GNP?
    a. Wages plus proprietors' income plus interest plus rents plus corporate profits.
    b. National income plus indirect business taxes plus depreciation.
    c. Consumption plus investment plus government purchases.
    d. All of the above equal GNP.

THE ECONOMIC WAY OF THINKING – DISCUSSION QUESTIONS

1. What are the two alternative methods of deriving GNP? Why do both methods yield the same answer?

2. Would you expect real GNP to grow faster or slower over time than nominal (money) GNP? Why? Which do you think better measures changes in the level of economic activity? Why?

3. Why does the government collect data on GNP? The government has elaborate safeguards to keep its information on economic activity secret until the information is publicly announced. Why do you think it is important to avoid leaks of this information?

4. What are some of the deficiencies of GNP as a measure of aggregate output? Consider the following statement: "In terms of measuring *changes* in the level of economic activity, these deficiencies are not important as long as the present method of measuring GNP is applied consistently over time."
    a. Is this statement correct if the structure of our economic activity (the way we operate and the types of things we produce) is fairly stable over time? Why or why not?
    b. Two major changes in recent years include sizeable increases in (i) efforts to control pollution and (ii) the proportion of households with two working parents who pay for services such as child care, housecleaning, and gardening. Is the above quotation correct under these circumstances? Why or why not?

5. If a farmer grows $.30 of wheat, and a miller creates $.35 of value by making flour from the wheat, and a baker creates $.25 of value by baking bread from the flour, and a retailer creates $.10 of value by selling the bread to you, how much GNP results? If intermediate transactions were counted at their market sales prices, how much GNP would be reported? What's wrong with counting the intermediate transactions?

6. How does MEW differ from GNP? What are the advantages of MEW compared to GNP? The disadvantages? Overall, which do you prefer?

7. Can real income increase without an increase in real output? Explain. If there is an increase in real output, what will happen to real income? Why?

PERSPECTIVES IN ECONOMICS

GNP: Pluses and Minuses
Morgan Guaranty Trust Company

[From *Morgan Guaranty Survey*, June 1970, pp. 9-13.
Reprinted with permission of the
Morgan Guaranty Trust Company.]

The gross national product in recent years has basked in the warm glow of nearly universal praise. Economists, quite naturally, have been freest with the encomiums. Where else but the GNP could they get in one tidy number a measure of the growth in the mammoth U.S. economy? Businessmen, though not entirely persuaded of the value of statistics, especially esoteric statistics, nevertheless have been known to quote the GNP – possibly because of its powers to impress audiences with the speaker's grasp of the "big picture." Politicians, too, have been extravagant in their admiration of GNP, most especially when it was rising at a brisk pace. Even the ubiquitous cocktail party has paid homage to the GNP as assorted junior executives,

research assistants, housewives, and dancing instructors have pronounced on the latest GNP numbers with a solemn and knowing air.

Now all that seems to be changing. GNP increasingly is coming under attack. Dr. Arthur F. Burns, Chairman of the Federal Reserve Board, told Congress recently: "The gross national product – which has been deceiving us all along – is a good deal lower than we think it is." Richard A. Falk, a professor of international law at Princeton told a Congressional committee not long ago: If the U.S. were to double its GNP, I would think it would be a much less livable society than it is today." And Representative Henry S. Reuss of Wisconsin warned earlier this year that "as our GNP grows, national pollution also grows every year."

Such comments suggest a need to take a new hard look at GNP, at what it is and – equally significant – what it is not.

Amoral GNP At the outset, it is important to realize that GNP is an estimate of the *market value* of goods and services produced. The unit of account is always dollars. What is equally important to remember is the GNP measures only those goods and services which are exchanged for money in the market place. In other words, what people, or business, or government are willing to *pay for* gets into the national income and product accounts. Few distinctions are made among the types of expenditures. Thus, the dollars spent ind-edicated pursuit of a cancer cure carry the same weight in the GNP as the wages of lackadaisical ecdysiast. Official compilers of the GNP routinely calculate money spent for medical care, new homes, whiskey, tobacco, and plastic objects d'art. To those who object on aes-thetic or even moral grounds, the standard reply is that GNP measures what people actually buy, not what they *ought* to buy. The latter is thought by economists to be more the province of a higher occupational order, such as saints. It should be noted, however, that the accounting rules are not entirely indifferent to moral considerations. Hence, GNP does not include economic activity that stems from illegal operations—such as a bookie parlor, an illicit still, or a doxy's den.

Janus-Faced GNP Thus it is clear that estimating the value of the nation's total spending depends on appli-cation of some fairly rigid—some would say arbi-trary—rules of inclusion and exclusion. Economic schol-ars over the years have discussed ways to improve the GNP. Their suggestions can be conveniently split into two groups, the "pluses" and the "minuses." The for-mer school argues that more items should be added to the accounts when striking a total. This school thinks that the GNP, by excluding nonpaid items such as work done by housewives, significantly *understates* the na-tion's output. Those in the "minuses" group, while not necessarily unreceptive to the other group's pro-posals, nevertheless see a different set of deficiencies. They charge that GNP is *overstating* national income and progress because it does not, for example, take account of the deterioration of the environment.

At present, the "minuses" school seems to be domi-nating the headlines. Dr. Burns, for example, while strongly backing maximum production, is suggesting that the nation develop and stress a more meaningful *net* national product, or NNP. This is GNP after deduct-ing the value of capital goods used up in the production process. Such depreciation or capital consumption cur-rently is running about $80 billion a year. From this NNP (published quarterly along with GNP data), Dr. Burns would additionally deduct some unspecified amount that would represent depreciation in the envi-ronment.

To illustrate the point, assume that a manufacturer flushes waste products into a river. If $1,000 were spent to remove the sludge from the waterway, such spend-ing would increase GNP by a like amount. If no effort is made to deal with the pollution there is no effect on GNP. Economists argue that this is improper since, in fact, the situation is analogous to the depreciation of capital assets. In the waterway case, however, the fixed asset is the environment and its depreciation is called pollution. What is wrong with present accounting pro-cedures, according to these analyses, is that pollution has not been removed from GNP in the calculations of the NNP.

Admittedly, adjusting GNP accounting rules to em-brace allowances for social values presents some ab-struse conceptual problems. Until fairly recently, such social costs were not overwhelmingly important. The elements of the environment were so vast that they

appeared to be inexhaustible. Air, for example, was considered to be a "free good." Although air is neces-sary to life, it was so abundantly available that no one could sell it at a positive price. As a consequence, the destruction of the usefulness of such a prevalent com-modity imposed no costs on society.

Now, of course, things are different. There is much concern about the air these days as more and more people in urban areas have come to realize that they cannot breathe deeply without some risk to lung tissue. Air no longer is "free": there is some "cost" to the user.

But how much do you deduct from GNP for dirty air? Or for streams that no longer support fish or water-fowl? Or for a scenic view bulldozed out of existence? For such as these (the list could easily be expanded), any reasonable person would agree that some deduc-tion should be made. But how much? Calculated in what way?

Goodies and Baddies The only practical method so far discovered is to follow the simple test of marketability —can't be sold for a price? Presumably, if people want breathable air, drinkable water, and the noise levels of a sternly supervised library then they will spend the money needed to pay for it all. Such spending is in-cluded in the GNP. But the offsetting "depreciation" that makes these expenditures necessary is not now deducted from GNP in arriving at NNP. This is not to say, of course, that the market value approach to calcu-lating environmental depreciation would be easy to ap-ply or entirely satisfactory. But inspired intellectual ef-fort surely could produce a method to account for what one observer has called "man-made-bads" to offset the "man-made-goods" that go into the GNP.

It is undoubtedly true, as Dr. Burns states, that a GNP which does not take account of environmental pollution overstates growth and progress of the nation. The affluent society, measured by an expanding GNP, is not so affluent as the official numbers indicate.

Or is it? There are, after all, a number of sizable "pluses" not in the GNP which could be added. If this were done, the "minus" of environmental pollution might very well be more than offset.

The single largest item not counted in GNP is the value of work done in the home by housewives. How-ever much this may appear as an antifeminist manifes-tation, suitable for protestations by women's liberation groups, the plain fact is that placing a value on home-tending presents some very tricky problems in estima-tion. Besides, unpaid productive work done by hus-bands in the home, too, does not get into the GNP. An example of such work would be the turning of a basement into a finished playroom. Only the purchased material would swell GNP; the husband's work would add nothing to GNP even though his house would increase in value as a consequence of the added play-room. However, if the housewife or the husband hired someone to clean the house or finish off the basement, such spending would find its way into GNP.

Other examples of "pluses" that are left out: no allowance is made in GNP for volunteer work, and it is only the out-of-pocket cost, rather than the time spent or the wisdom acquired, that measures the contribution of education. Similarly, no estimates are made of the "income" received by people from services in the public sector—such as use of a park, highway, or library. Peo-ple receive benefits from such facilities year after year, and yet GNP records only the initial cost when the facility is built and its subsequent maintenance. Here again there are immense problems of estimation. Not all people have access to public facilities, the quality of which, in any case, varies widely all across the nation.

Finally, GNP treats the value of spending on consumer durable goods in different ways depending on their ownership. For instance, money spent by an auto rental agency for its fleet of automobiles is included in the GNP. So is the money spent by people and business to rent the autos year after year. On the other hand, money spent by an individual purchasing a car for himself gets into the GNP only once – as a personal consumption expenditure at time of purchase, even though the buyer will get a stream of services, no different from those he would get from a rental auto, for several years. In other words, the "service income" to the owner of any consumer durable good – auto, refrigerator, washing machine, TV – is left out of the GNP.

An exception is made in the case of an owner-occupied house. Since the rent on rented dwellings goes into GNP, the comparable service enjoyed by homeowners from their own dwellings is also included so that the total is not subject to variation resulting merely from changes in the proportion of home ownership. Homeowners simply are regarded as landlords who rent to themselves at going local rates. If all consumer durable goods were to be treated the same way as housing, the result, of course, would be a larger GNP.

Policies that would produce no growth in GNP undoubtedly would hold down pollution. But "costs" to society would be heavy. For one thing, antipollution efforts themselves cost money. Only increased production can provide the resources to tackle pollution – and to reduce poverty, keep up the nation's defenses, meet housing needs, and a thousand other things. Suggestions that consumption of goods be restricted to lessen pollution have a surface kind of logic. But, in practice, what goods would be restricted? From the hands of what groups of people? Would this require the setting up of a new agency: The Department of Consumer Privation? The nation's poor do not have the feeling that they are consuming to an excessive degree. Nor do the millions in the middle class who, after paying taxes and making the mortgage payment, are barely able to keep their heads above water. They would find little comfort if the quagmire that engulfed them when GNP stopped growing were a little purer.

Those who are asking whether the nation can survive with pollution are asking the wrong question. It is unfortunate but true that the nation cannot survive without pollution. The answer is not to jettison growth and push for an anemic GNP, but rather to channel economic growth in new directions. More resources and more talent can be applied to reducing pollution to tolerable levels. In the case of automobiles, for example, increased inputs of capital and labor to produce autos that do not emit noxious fumes would be more sensible than closing down assembly lines to produce fewer automobiles. In short, there need not be a basic contradiction between growth and a livable environment. It is not necessary or even possible to choose one and abandon the other.

Discussion

1. Has the article outlined all the possible errors of commission or omission in the calculation of GNP? If not, what other errors are possible?

2. The authors appear to belittle the concern of many economists that omitting the value of work done in the home causes a sexist bias in GNP calculations. With whom do you agree? Why?

3. If GNP has so many faults as a measure of macroeconomic activity, what value could it possibly have in today's world?

7
Economic Fluctuations, Unemployment, and Inflation

TRUE OR FALSE

T F

☐ ☐ 1. A business cycle is a series of fluctuations in an aggregate measure of current economic production.

☐ ☐ 2. Frictional unemployment implies a lack of jobs available.

☐ ☐ 3. Faster adoption of technological changes would probably increase structural unemployment, since some jobs would disappear more quickly than they would otherwise.

☐ ☐ 4. Unanticipated inflation changes the real prices in long-term contracts.

☐ ☐ 5. If the economy is at its natural rate of unemployment, then employment is well below the full employment level.

☐ ☐ 6. The Consumer Price Index is to nominal consumption as the GNP deflator is to nominal income.

☐ ☐ 7. Insufficient aggregate demand is the root cause of structural, but not frictional, unemployment.

☐ ☐ 8. If a corn blight destroyed half of next year's corn crop and drove corn prices up, the result would properly be called inflation.

☐ ☐ 9. Since the turn of the century, the United States has not experienced deflation.

☐ ☐ 10. The rate of employment plus the rate of unemployment must add up to one because everyone is either employed or unemployed.

PROBLEMS AND PROJECTS

1. Consider each of the following statements about unemployment and inflation. In the space before each statement, mark an "E" if the statement refers *primarily* to a reduction in economic efficiency and an "R" if it refers *primarily* to an income redistribution effect.

    _____ a. Laid-off workers end up collecting unemployment checks paid for by the rest of us.

    _____ b. Unanticipated inflation hurts creditors and helps debtors.

    _____ c. The output lost during periods of cyclical unemployment can never be recovered.

    _____ d. Inflation makes people less willing to enter into long-term contracts.

    _____ e. Inflation hurt Social Security recipients until their benefits were indexed to keep pace with the CPI.

    _____ f. The skills of idle workers erode during periods of prolonged unemployment.

2. Classify the following workers as either (a) frictional, (b) structural, or (c) cyclical.

    _____ (1) Joan Smith, a college student, has spent two weeks trying unsuccessfully to find a summer job so she can return to college in the fall.

    _____ (2) Carol Jones has not been able to find a job after completing high school and initially entering the labor force.

    _____ (3) A sharp cutback in the space program has cost Harold Robinson his $40,000-a-year job as an aerospace engineer. Prospects for employment as an engineer are exceedingly dim. Harold has not been able to find a satisfactory job in other lines of work since his termination six weeks ago.

    _____ (4) Sue Blair is re-entering the labor force after having a baby, but has not yet found work.

    _____ (5) Fred Mack is one of 10,000 auto workers laid off because of a sharp decline in GNP during the last six months.

    _____ (6) Hal Freer, a coal miner, can no longer find work as a miner because automation has reduced the demand for mining labor.

    _____ (7) Sue Colson is one of 70 United Airlines pilots laid off after an economic slowdown caused a sharp reduction in the demand for air transportation.

3. a. Because of the time it takes to publish and distribute a book, the inflation and unemployment figures in the text are recent, but not current. Update your knowledge by investigating (in the library) and discovering the current figures (one source is the *Monthly Labor Review*).

    b. Use the above information to decide exactly where the economy is (boom, recession, etc.) with respect to the business cycle.

4. Exhibit 1 presents information from the *Economic Report of the President* regarding population and employment for selected years. Use the data given to calculate the unemployment and labor force participation rates in the last four columns. (*Hint*: Sufficient data are present to make these calculations.)

Exhibit 1

Year	Civilian non-institutional population	Resident (armed forces) (Millions of persons 16 years and up)	Labor force (including armed forces)	Employment (including armed forces)	Unemployment rate (percent)		Labor force participation rate (percent)	
					Total	Civilian	Total	Civilian
1954	108.3	2.1	65.8	62.3	5.3	5.5	59.6	58.8
1964	124.5	2.0	75.1	71.3	____	____	____	____
1974	150.1	1.7	93.7	88.5	____	____	____	____
1984	176.4	1.7	115.2	106.7	____	____	____	____

5. Official definitions of employment status lead to ambiguities and often strange results. The following list represents a variety of job situations for the individuals involved. In the blank preceding each situation, place *U* to designate when the situation means officially unemployed, *E* to designate officially employed, and *N* to mean not officially in the labor force.

_____ a. Ralph Amey has stopped looking for a job because he believes that employment prospects in his line of work are so poor that it is unlikely he will find work.

_____ b. David Axeen is actively looking for work as a college administrator but meanwhile has worked one hour each weekday as a substitute teacher.

_____ c. Betty Tracy could not find work as a mathematician and decided to re-enroll in school for a refresher course in advanced topology.

_____ d. Rosie Ruiz will start her job at the Jet Propulsion Laboratory in six weeks.

_____ e. Even though he's looking for a job, Scott Richard has decided not to accept a $6.00/hour job offer he received last week because he'd rather go to the beach.

6. Consider the information in Exhibit 2.

Exhibit 2

Year	CPI	Inflation rate	Average hourly earnings	Interest rate*	Hypothetical taxable income, married couple	Actual income taxes
1985	322.2	____	$8.57	11.4%	$20,000	$2,466
1986	328.4	1.9%	8.76	9.0	$20,380	2,438
1987	340.4	3.7	8.98	9.4	21,134	3,049

*Interest on top-rated (Aaa) corporate bonds.

Indicate whether the economic status of each of the following was better (+), or worse (−), or about the same (0) in 1987 compared with 1986:

_____ a. Wage earners.

_____ b. Lenders.

_____ c. Hypothetical married couple, before taxes.

_____ d. Hypothetical married couple, after taxes.

Show a computation to support each decision. (*Hint*: To make the calculations easier, assume that all income is taxable.)

LEARNING THE MECHANICS – MULTIPLE CHOICE

1. Frictional unemployment results from
   a. not enough jobs in the economy.
   b. not enough employers.
   c. not enough employees.
   d. scarce information about job opportunities and the time it takes to acquire that information.

2. The definition of the unemployment rate is
   a. the number of persons in the country who are not employed.
   b. the number of persons in the civilian labor force who are not employed.
   c. the percentage of persons in the country who are not employed.
   d. the percentage of persons in the civilian labor force who are not employed.

3. When an economist states the economy is at "full employment," he/she usually means that
   a. there are no unemployed workers.
   b. all those willing to work have jobs, but those not desiring work are unemployed.
   c. about 95 percent of the labor force is employed.
   d. 100 percent of the people are working or looking for a job.

4. Inflation is *best* described as
   a. high prices.
   b. an increase in the level of prices as indicated by a price index.
   c. an increase in the purchasing power of money.
   d. an increase in the price of a particular good or service that is necessary for all consumers.

5. The natural rate of unemployment equals
   a. the sum of frictional and structural unemployment.
   b. frictional unemployment.
   c. full employment minus all those unemployed.
   d. the sum of frictional and cyclical unemployment.

6. If the Consumer Price Index in 1989 was 150 and the CPI in 1990 was 165, the rate of inflation was
   a. 5 percent.
   b. 10 percent.
   c. 15 percent.
   d. 165 percent.

7. The rate of labor force participation is
   a. the number of persons employed divided by the number of persons unemployed.
   b. the number of persons 16 years of age and older who are either employed or actively seeking work divided by the total noninstitutional population 16 years of age and older.
   c. the number of persons employed divided by the number of persons 16 years of age and older.
   d. the number of persons who are actively seeking work divided by the number of persons who are employed.

8. Debtors gain at the expense of creditors when
   a. prices rise.
   b. prices fall.
   c. prices rise unexpectedly.
   d. prices fall unexpectedly.

9. Which of the following is the best example of inflation?
   a. An increase in the price of food
   b. An increase in the general price level *but not* in every product
   c. An increase in the price of almost every product but (because of some large price decreases) not in the general price level
   d. A decrease in the price of food

10. Structural unemployment means that
    a. employment in the building trades is insufficient.
    b. there are simply not enough jobs to go around.
    c. worker qualifications do not match available jobs.
    d. jobs are plentiful, but workers are scarce.

11. Historical data for the period 1930 to 1990 indicate that
    a. regular business cycles have occurred in the United States approximately every three years.
    b. unemployment has stayed within a rather narrow range, between 1 and 3 percent.
    c. when all the booms and contractions are averaged out, the economy has grown at an average annual rate of approximately 3 to 4 percent.
    d. unemployment has averaged about 6 percent during the 45-year period.

12. Potential GNP
    a. is always less than actual GNP, except during recessions.
    b. minus actual GNP is a measure of production lost due to a business slowdown.
    c. is a measure of the minimum that an economy could be reasonably expected to continue producing at any time.
    d. is 95 to 96 percent of actual GNP, during periods of full employment.

THE ECONOMIC WAY OF THINKING – MULTIPLE CHOICE

1. Even in a truly "efficient" economy, one would expect *some* unemployment because
   a. as an individual, if you wait for a better job offer, you may be better off in the longer run.
   b. wages will increase even when prices are constant.
   c. some persons' expectations are always correct.
   d. unemployment provides the best incentive for stimulating persons to search more diligently for a job.

2. The work force over the last 50 years has changed so that there now is a higher percentage of women in the work force who also have husbands present in the work force. This change quite possibly means that a 10 percent unemployment rate *now* would be
   a. perhaps a bit less catastrophic to families than a 10 percent unemployment rate 50 years ago.
   b. perhaps a bit more catastrophic to families than a 10 percent unemployment rate 50 years ago.
   c. just as catastrophic to families as a 10 percent unemployment rate 50 years ago.
   d. impossible to compare to a 10 percent unemployment rate 50 years ago.

3. Frictional unemployment
   a. would decrease if unemployment compensation payments rose.
   b. would increase if improved methods of disseminating job information among unemployed workers were developed.
   c. would decrease if every individual in the economy had perfect information.
   d. is caused primarily by improper management of government expenditures.

4. As an economy begins to climb out of a long recession, the price index will initially be most likely to
   a. change very little because of an abundance of idle plants, machinery, and manpower.
   b. fall until the deferred consumption demand can be made effective through higher levels of real income.
   c. rise substantially because the expected future increase in prices will stimulate current consumption and investment purchases, thereby giving rise to a situation of excess demand.
   d. rise rapidly because aggregate demand exceeds aggregate supply, thereby forcing inventory levels to fall.

5. In the economy of Myopia, the expected rate of inflation is always zero, and inflation comes as a complete surprise to the Myopians. Their neighbors to the north in Pessimismia, however, always expect 100% inflation and are shocked when the price level rises by less than that (which is always does). Which of the following would you rather be?
   a. A lender in Myopia
   b. A borrower in Pessimismia
   c. A lender in Pessimismia
   d. This question is impossible to answer without knowing more.

6. To most economists, economic growth is
   a. one goal, among others.
   b. not possible without deflation.
   c. clearly undesirable, in view of environmental concerns.
   d. impossible without the decline in demand for labor that generally accompanies high rates of unemployment.

7. The ability to make more accurate forecasts of changes in the aggregate economic conditions would
   a. enable us to adopt policies that would eliminate frictional unemployment.
   b. greatly facilitate our ability to adopt public policy that would reduce cyclical unemployment.
   c. allow us to reduce structural, but not cyclical, unemployment.
   d. make it possible for wise macroeconomic policy to eliminate all unemployment.

8. Unanticipated inflation
   a. will normally hurt creditors, but help borrowers.
   b. has never been a problem for modern economies.
   c. increases the purchasing power of those on fixed incomes.
   d. does not have any noticeable effects.

9. An appropriate description of stagflation is a period when
   a. the male deer gains weight.
   b. an economy is experiencing both substantial inflation and a slow growth in real output.
   c. the rate of employment is rising more slowly than the rate of employment.
   d. an economy is experiencing both inflation and unemployment.

10. Which of the following courses of action does *not* make sense if you anticipate an increase in inflation next year?
    a. Attempt to obtain an increased salary to offset the oncoming inflation.
    b. Lend money at an interest rate that is less than the rate of inflation you expect.
    c. Borrow money at an interest rate that is less than the rate of inflation you expect.
    d. Purchase an asset whose value is likely to increase faster than the expected future rate of inflation.

11. Use I and II to choose the correct answer. **(I)** The natural rate of unemployment is increased by public policy which reduces the worker's opportunity cost of rejecting job offers while he or she continues to search for a more attractive job. **(II)** The natural rate of unemployment rose during the 1970s as the proportion of the labor force made up of youthful workers increased.
    a. I is true, II is false.
    b. I is false, II is true.
    c. Both I and II are true.
    d. Both I and II are false.

12. In a properly operating, dynamic economy
    a. the unemployment rate should remain near zero.
    b. we would expect to have some unemployment, since some labor force participants would temporarily be out of work while changing jobs.
    c. the rate of unemployment will show a slight upward trend as prices rise.
    d. the rate of unemployment will show a slight downward trend as prices fall.

13. Who is least likely to be a loser from unanticipated inflation?
    a. A wage earner working on a union job
    b. A homeowner with a fixed interest rate mortgage
    c. A lender
    d. A retiree on a fixed pension

14. If an unemployed worker becomes too discouraged to keep looking for work,
    a. the unemployment rate will rise and the employment rate will remain the same.
    b. both the unemployment rate and the employment rate will remain the same.
    c. the unemployment rate will fall and the employment rate will remain the same
    d. the unemployment rate will rise and the employment rate will fall.

THE ECONOMIC WAY OF THINKING – DISCUSSION QUESTIONS

1. a. What is inflation? How is it measured? What would a negative inflation rate mean?
    b. Could you predict what would happen to the price of swimsuits compared to sweatshirts during a hot, dry summer, all else equal? Could you predict what would happen to the inflation rate? Explain both answers.

2. Even during periods of high unemployment, newspapers carry listings of numerous available jobs; how can this be? Even during boom periods, some unemployment exists; is this a sign of inefficiency? Explain.

3. "The burden of inflation falls heavily on savers and creditors, for example, upon wealthy bondholders" – Campbell McConnell, *Economics*, 6th ed. (New York: McGraw-Hill, 1975), p. 380. Under what circumstances is this statement likely to be correct? Incorrect?

4. "As long as people are free either to accept or reject a job, some unemployment will be present." Do you agree or disagree? Why?

5. When Ronald Reagan took office the nation's unemployment rate was 7.4 percent. When it reached 9.8 percent two years later, Reagan joked that he would take responsibility for the 2.4 percent increase in the unemployment rate during his term if the Democrats would accept blame for the other 7.4 percent. Should Reagan's joke be taken literally? Explain.

6. Respond to each of the following statements:

    a. "We could eliminate the economic cost of recessions by setting up unemployment compensation so that all unemployed workers receive the same income that they earn when working."

    b. "We could eliminate the economic cost of inflation by indexing all payments, such as wages, interest, retirement benefits, and taxes."

7. Some analysts refer to a misery index, which is the sum of the inflation rate and the unemployment rate. Do you agree with the one-for-one trade-off between inflation and unemployment that is implicit in the misery index? Why or why not?

PERSPECTIVES IN ECONOMICS

Precious Pesos
By Everett G. Martin

[From *The Wall Street Journal*, August 13, 1985. Reprinted with permission from the Wall Street Journal ©Dow Jones & Co., Inc. All Rights Reserved Worldwide. Abridged.]

LA PAZ, Bolivia — When Edgar Miranda gets his monthly teacher's pay of 25 million pesos, he hasn't a moment to lose. Every hour, pesos drop in value. So, while his wife rushes to market to lay in a month's supply of rice and noodles, he is off with the rest of the pesos to change them into black-market dollars.

Mr. Miranda is practicing the First rule of Survival amid the most out-of-control inflation in the world today. Bolivia is a case study of how runaway inflation undermines a society.

Price increases are so huge that the figures build up almost beyond comprehension. In one six-month period, for example, prices soared at an annual rate of 38,000%. By official count, however, last year's inflation reached 2,000%, and this year's is expected to hit 8,000% — though other estimates range many times higher. In any event, Bolivia's rate dwarfs Israel's 370% and Argentina's 1,100% — two other cases of severe inflation.

A Need to Be Quick It is easier to comprehend what happens to the 38-year-old Mr. Miranda's pay if he doesn't quickly change it into dollars. The day he was paid 25 million pesos, a dollar cost 500,000 pesos. So he received $50. Just days later, with the rate at 900,000 pesos, he would have received $27.

"We think only about today and converting every peso into dollars," says Ronald MacLean, the manager of a gold-mining firm. "We have become myopic."

And intent on mere survival, Civil servants won't hand out a form without a bribe. Lawyers, accountants, hairdressers, even prostitutes have almost given up working to become money-changers in the streets. Workers stage repeated strikes and steal from their bosses. The bosses smuggle production abroad, take out phony loans, duck taxes — anything to get dollars for speculation.

Tin production at the state mines, for example, dropped to 12,000 tons last year from 18,000. The miners pad their wages by smuggling out the richest ore in their lunch pails, and the ore goes by a contraband network into neighboring Peru. Without a major tin mine, Peru now exports some 4,000 metric tons of tin a year.

"We don't produce anything. We are all currency speculators," a heavy-equipment dealer in La Paz says. "People don't know what's good and bad anymore. We have become an amoral society."

President Forced Out The blame for the mess is generally laid on the inept administration of Hernan Siles Zuazo, who was recently forced out by an angry Bolivian congress a year before his term ended. Congress has picked as his successor Victor Paz Estenssoro, a 77-year-old, two-time president who was one of the two front-runners in a July 14 presidential election.

He is taking over a nation that functions only because the man in the street bases his finances on the dollar, not the peso. And it is an open secret that practically all the black-market dollars come from the illegal cocaine trade with the U.S. Cocaine traffickers earn an estimated $1 billion a year. Though most of that money goes into overseas bank accounts, U.S. drug-enforcement officials here estimate that between $300 million and $500 million filters back to Bolivia.

Revenues Inadequate The country is suffering from inflation largely because the government's revenues cover a mere 15% of its expenditures and its deficit has widened to nearly 25% of the country's total annual output. The revenues are hurt by a lag in tax payments, and taxes aren't being collected largely because of widespread theft and bribery.

To obtain the extra cash needed to get by, government workers resort to petty corruption. "You have to pay them to hand you any kind of form," says the head of a state agency. meanwhile, immigration officials badger bewildered foreign tourists at the international airport for $20 to stamp their passports so the travelers don't miss their planes.

The agency head says his staffers work about a third of the day and spend the rest of their office time buying, selling or trading among one another things that they have hoarded as an inflation hedge. "It can be cheese, cooking oil, eggs, clothes, anything," he says.

Aided by state railway workers and customs officials, state oil-refinery workers smuggle an estimated 15% of Bolivia's gasoline to Brazil. It is lucrative because the local gasoline price is fixed at the equivalent of 20 cents a gallon, while the Brazilian price is close to $4.

Sen. Gonzalo Sanchez de Losada, a member of President Paz Estenssoro's party, says, "Private indus-try has managed in one way or another to get dollars and stash them abroad, and the miners have at least half their tin ore stockpiled. If we can get the country straightened out, these reserves could start us function-ing again faster than you'd think." But he adds rue-fully:

"We are going to have to go to an Adam Smith economy because no one will ever obey rules again. We've learned you must be an idiot to do things by the rules."

Discussion

1. Why do the Mirandas buy a month's worth of food at once? What is the advantage of changing pesos into dollars as soon as possible? If you moved to Bolivia, what could you do to make inflation's impact on you as small as possible?

2. If you had control over the Bolivian economy, what would you do to halt the inflation? (This question will be significantly easier after you have read the next few chapters, but give it a try now.)

3. Such "hyperinflations" have occurred in countries other than Bolivia. For example, in Brazil, you could buy a television for 13,000 cruzeiros in 1978, but today you can't even buy an ice cream cone for that amount! In Germany in the 1920s, prices went up so fast that the postage stamp on an envelope containing an insurance payment to a beneficiary often cost more than the sum written on the enclosed check. Do you think inflation this bad could happen in the United States? Why or why not?

8
An Introduction to Basic Macroeconomic Markets

TRUE OR FALSE

T F

☐ ☐   1.   Another name for the resource market might be "the market for the exchange of productive inputs."

☐ ☐   2.   The loanable funds market is nothing more than the market for money.

☐ ☐   3.   Aggregate demand for goods and services is composed of consumption, investment, and net exports.

☐ ☐   4.   The aggregate demand curve is negatively sloped, as you'd expect, but the aggregate supply curve is also negatively sloped because of the natural rate of unemployment.

☐ ☐   5.   Saving is disposable income that is not spent on consumption.

☐ ☐   6.   Equilibrium in an aggregate market is slightly different from equilibrium in a microeconomic market, but it still allows for the simultaneous fulfillment of the plans of both buyers and sellers.

☐ ☐   7.   The money (or nominal) interest rate equals the real interest rate plus an inflationary premium.

☐ ☐   8.   The real interest is usually set equal to the expected rate of inflation.

☐ ☐   9.   The real balance effect is the increase in wealth that comes about when aggregate prices fall while the money supply remains constant.

☐ ☐   10.   A bond is nothing more than an IOU; if you own a bond, you owe the issuer of that bond the face amount of the bond plus whatever interest is specified.

☐ ☐   11.   In the loanable funds market, the "price" of money is actually the interest rate, since the money is only loaned, not purchased permanently.

☐ ☐   12.   When an economy is in macroeconomic equilibrium, each of the three basic macro markets (loanable funds, resources, and goods and services) must be equilibrium.

PROBLEMS AND PROJECTS

1. Draw aggregate demand/aggregate supply diagrams below to illustrate the changes in aggregate demand (AD), short-run aggregate supply (SRAS), long-run aggregate supply (LRAS), the price level (P) and real gross national product (RGNP) in response to the events described to the left of the diagrams. First show in the diagrams how AD, SRAS and/or LRAS shift and then fill in the table to the right of the diagrams using + to indicate increase, − to indicate decrease, 0 to indicate no change, and ? to indicate that either a decrease or an increase is possible.

Events	Diagrams	AD	SRAS	LRAS	P	RGNP
a. The government adopts economic policies which lower interest rates.		___	___	___	___	___
b. A technological break-through in robotics significantly raises labor productivity.		___	___	___	___	___
c. Gloomy economic forecasts lead households to save more income for that "rainy day."		___	___	___	___	___
d. An increase in the actual rate of inflation leads to forecasts of higher future inflation.	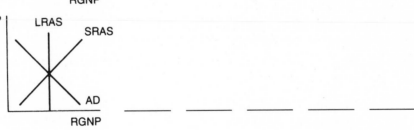	___	___	___	___	___
e. The breakup of the OPEC oil cartel leads to significantly lower oil prices and higher oil supplies. (*Hint*: assume that this country is an oil importer.)	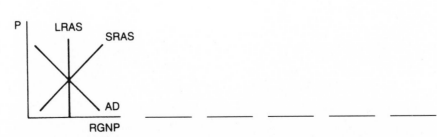	___	___	___	___	___

2. Consider once again the data from Exhibit 1 of Chapter 8 of this *Coursebook*.
   a. If the economy's self-correcting mechanism operates without impediment, explain how the mechanism leads the economy from its short-run equilibrium in 1969 to a long-run equilibrium. Show the adjustments in aggregate supply and/or demand that would occur in the diagram you constructed for that year.
   b. Do the same for the short-run equilibrium of 1933.
   c. The rate of unemployment in 1933 was 24.9%. Six years later, in 1939, the unemployment rate had fallen only to 17.2%, still far above the natural rate. Why might the self-correcting mechanism have worked so slowly?

3. Using an AD/AS model for the U.S. economy, explain what happens to the price level, the output level, and unemployment in each of the following cases. Assume that the economy is initially in long-run equilibrium and the events initially catch people by surprise.

Event	Prices	Output	Unemploy-ment Rate
a. Due to election promises, inflationary expectations fall even though there is no change in actual inflation.	_____	_____	_____
b. The President embargoes wheat and computer sales to the USSR.	_____	_____	_____
c. To pay for lobbying expenses, the Teamsters press for higher wages.	_____	_____	_____
d. A Federal tax revision bill is passed giving additional incentives for saving.	_____	_____	_____
e. The U.S.'s trading partners slip into recession, lowering demand for U.S. exports.	_____	_____	_____

4. Use the diagrams in Exhibit 1 to help you label each of the statements below as true or false:

Exhibit 1

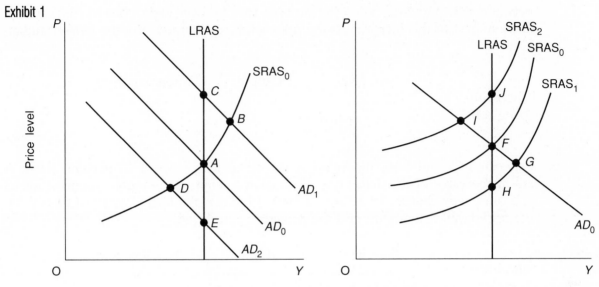

Output of goods and services—Real GNP

_____ a. Profits are higher at B than at D.

_____ b. Profits are higher at G than at I.

_____ c. Inflationary expectations are higher at B than at D.

_____ d. Over time, if the economy were at point B inflationary expectations would tend to fall, while if the economy were at point D inflationary expectations would tend to rise.

_____ e. The self-correcting mechanism tends to work faster from point I than from point G.

_____ f. If the economy were at point D, a fall in interest rates would help restore full employment.

_____ g. If the economy were at point B, an increase in U.S. net exports would help restore full employment.

_____ h. If the economy ended up at point C instead of point E, real profits would be higher.

5. Use AD/AS diagrams to help you fill in the blanks below. Use + to indicate increase, − to indicate decrease, and 0 to indicate no change. In each case assume the economy is initially at full employment.

   a. Between 1980 and 1982, real interest rates rose by over eight percent. Indicate the likely impact of this increase on the price level, real output, and the percent unemployed:

	Price level	Output	Unemployment
Short run	_____	_____	_____
Long run	_____	_____	_____

   b. Between 1985 and 1990, the value of the dollar fell by about 33 percent. (*Hint*: A fall in the value of the dollar typically makes foreign goods more expensive for us and our goods cheaper for foreign citizens.) Indicate the likely impact of this fall on the price level, real output, and the percent unemployed:

	Price level	Output	Unemployment
Short run	_____	_____	_____
Long run	_____	_____	_____

LEARNING THE MECHANICS – MULTIPLE CHOICE

1. All of the following will reduce aggregate demand *except*
   a. a decrease in real wealth.
   b. higher real rates of interest.
   c. increased consumer optimism about the future.
   d. a decline in the expected rate of inflation.

2. An increase in the long-run aggregate supply curve simply means
   a. shifting the curve up.
   b. shifting the curve down.
   c. shifting the curve to the right.
   d. shifting the curve to the left.

3. When there is a reduction in the anticipated rate of inflation, which of the following is most likely?
   a. Short-run aggregate supply will decrease.
   b. Long-run aggregate supply will increase.
   c. Aggregate demand will increase.
   d. Aggregate demand will decrease.

4. With more workers available, we should be able to produce more. This will tend to
   a. shift the SRAS and the LRAS to the right.
   b. shift the SRAS to the right and the LRAS to the left.
   c. shift the SRAS to the left and the LRAS to the right.
   d. shift the SRAS and the LRAS to the left.

5. Other things constant, a decline in the exchange rate value of the dollar will
   a. cause foreign goods to become more expensive for U.S. consumers, stimulating our net exports and aggregate demand.
   b. cause foreign goods to become less expensive for U.S. consumers, stimulating our net exports and aggregate demand.
   c. cause foreign goods to become more expensive for U.S. consumers, slowing the growth of our net exports and aggregate demand.
   d. cause foreign goods to become less expensive for U.S. consumers, slowing the growth of our net exports and aggregate demand.

6. An unanticipated increase in the short-run aggregate supply curve will cause
   a. an increase in the price level.
   b. a decrease in the price level.
   c. a decrease in output.
   d. an increase in the real interest rate.

7. In the short-run, equilibrium output in the goods and services market may be either above or below the output at which the long-run aggregate supply curve intersects the X (goods and services) axis, but in the long run
   a. it must be less than that output.
   b. it must be greater than that output.
   c. it must be equal to that output.
   d. it depends on aggregate demand, not just aggregate supply.

8. If unanticipated, which of the following will decrease short-run equilibrium aggregate output in the goods and services market?
   a. A decrease in the real interest rate
   b. A decrease in the cost of resources
   c. A decrease in the money interest rate
   d. A decrease in the expected rate of inflation

9. Which of the following is most likely to result from an unanticipated increase in aggregate supply due to favorable weather conditions in agricultural areas?
   a. An increase in the inflation rate
   b. An increase in the unemployment rate
   c. A decrease in the price level
   d. A decrease in the natural rate of unemployment

10. Which of the following is most likely to accompany an unanticipated reduction in aggregate demand?
    a. An increase in the price level
    b. An increase in employment
    c. An increase in real GNP
    d. An increase in the unemployment rate

11. Which of the following is most likely to accompany an unanticipated reduction in aggregate supply?
    a. An increase in nominal income
    b. A reduction in the real rate of investment
    c. An increase in the price level
    d. A decrease in the unemployment rate

12. In the aggregate demand/aggregate supply model, an economy operating below its long-run potential capacity will experience
    a. falling real wages and resource prices which will stimulate employment and real output.
    b. rising interest rates which will stimulate employment and real output.
    c. inflation which will stimulate additional spending and thereby restore full employment.
    d. a budget deficit that will cause policy makers to increase taxes, which will help restore full employment.

13. The permanent income hypothesis, developed by Milton Friedman, states that
    a. if incomes rise temporarily, consumption spending will increase by a smaller proportion.
    b. if incomes rise permanently, consumption spending will not change at all.
    c. if incomes rise temporarily, consumption spending will also rise by a proportional amount, but only temporarily.
    d. none of the above.

14. In the aggregate demand/aggregate supply model, what market adjustments cause the economy to return to its long-run capacity when output is temporarily *greater than* the economy's long run potential output?
    a. Lower wage rates and resource prices reduce short-run aggregate supply.
    b. Lower interest rates increase aggregate demand and thereby stimulate output.
    c. Higher wage rates and resource prices reduce short-run aggregate supply.
    d. A decrease in the price level reduces aggregate demand.

THE ECONOMIC WAY OF THINKING — MULTIPLE CHOICE

For questions 1-4, assume that the economy is in long-run equilibrium in the aggregate demand/aggregate supply model and that some sort of event takes place. In each case, mark the most likely impact of the event on the aggregate demand/aggregate supply diagram: Feel free to refer to the diagram in Exhibit 2 before answering.

Exhibit 2

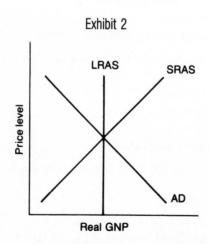

1. Good weather allows crop yields to double in the South.
    a. The aggregate demand curve would shift to the right.
    b. The aggregate demand curve would shift to the left.
    c. The short-run aggregate supply curve would shift to the right.
    d. The short-run aggregate supply curve would shift to the left.

2. The real interest rate suddenly goes up by 2%.
   a. The aggregate demand curve would shift to the right.
   b. The aggregate demand curve would shift to the left.
   c. The short-run aggregate supply curve would shift to the right.
   d. The short-run aggregate supply curve would shift to the left.

3. Consumers and businesses all suddenly decide that the future looks much better than it previously had.
   a. The aggregate demand curve would shift to the right.
   b. The aggregate demand curve would shift to the left.
   c. The short-run aggregate supply curve would shift to the right.
   d. The short-run aggregate supply curve would shift to the left.

4. Legislation is adopted that improves labor productivity.
   a. The aggregate demand curve would shift to the right.
   b. The aggregate demand curve would shift to the left.
   c. The short-run aggregate supply curve would shift to the right.
   d. The short-run aggregate supply curve would shift to the left.

5. What will force an economy that is producing more than its long-run capacity to decrease its output?
   a. Eventually, an adverse supply shock will come along.
   b. Wages and prices will rise until equilibrium is restored at full employment output but a higher price level.
   c. Wages and prices will fall until equilibrium is restored at full employment output and a lower price level.
   d. Nothing; the concept of long-run capacity is only a theoretical one which can be surpassed without difficulty even in the long run.

6. A reduction in aggregate supply that is expected to be temporary will
   a. have no effect on the economy.
   b. cause a higher real interest rate.
   c. eventually cause a lower price level.
   d. cause more spending on capital goods to offset the reduction.

7. An economy operating on its long-run aggregate supply schedule will remain on the schedule if
   a. resource prices rise, while product prices decline.
   b. resource prices are unchanged, while product prices increase.
   c. resource prices rise, while product prices are unchanged.
   d. resource and product prices rise proportionally, leaving the incentive to supply resources unchanged.

8. If an economy is in equilibrium at a given price level and a given output level, the aggregate demand/aggregate supply (AD/AS) model indicates that an unanticipated decrease in aggregate demand will cause
   a. real output to decline.
   b. the price level to fall, while real output remains unchanged.
   c. nominal output to decline, while real output remains unchanged.
   d. real output to decline, while nominal output remains unchanged.

9. During the mid 1980s, the real price of crude oil declined sharply on the world market. Other things constant, how would such a decrease in oil prices have influenced the price level and output of oil-importing nations?
   a. Both real output and the price level would have fallen.
   b. Both real output and the price level would have risen.
   c. Real output would have fallen, and the price level would have risen.
   d. Real output would have risen, and the price level would have fallen.

10. Which of the following is most likely to accompany an unanticipated reduction in aggregate demand?
    a. An increase in the price level
    b. A decrease in the unemployment rate
    c. A decrease in real GNP
    d. A reduction in the real rate of interest

11. When an economy is temporarily operating at less than capacity, then a market economy will tend to be self-correcting (move towards equilibrium at full employment capacity) since
    a. lower resource prices will increase aggregate supply.
    b. lower retail prices will increase aggregate demand.
    c. both a and b.
    d. neither a nor b.

12. Other things constant, what impact did the sharp increase in the price of imported oil during the 1990-91 Gulf War have on aggregate supply, growth of real GNP, and the inflation rate of the U.S.? The oil-price increase caused:
    a. aggregate supply to fall, the growth rate of real GNP to increase, and the inflation rate to decelerate.
    b. aggregate supply to fall, the growth rate of real GNP to decline, and the inflation rate to accelerate.
    c. aggregate supply to rise, the growth rate of real GNP to decline, and the inflation rate to accelerate.
    d. aggregate supply to rise, the growth rate of real GNP to increase, and the inflation rate to accelerate.

13. Suppose an economy is at full employment with stable prices, and workers demand and receive a 10 percent increase in their wages. All else constant, when comparing the short-run and long-run effects,
    a. the price level and unemployment rate will be higher in the short run than in the long run.
    b. the price level will be lower and the unemployment rate higher in the short run than in the long run.
    c. the price level will be higher and the unemployment rate lower in the short run than in the long run.
    d. the price level and unemployment rate will be lower in the short run than in the long run.

THE ECONOMIC WAY OF THINKING – DISCUSSION QUESTIONS

1. Between 1980 and 1985, the value of the dollar rose by about 56 percent, and the U.S. inflation rate dropped from 13.5 percent to 3.6. Does AD/AS analysis suggest that the rise in the value of the dollar could have been a factor in the decrease in inflation? (*Hint*: A rise in the value of the dollar makes foreign currencies cheaper for us and dollars more expensive for foreign citizens.)

2. Recent improvements in the quality of South Korean goods have made Americans more willing to "buy Korean." Use an AD/AS diagram to show the impact of this development on the U.S. economy.

3. Do you really believe that the entire economy can be analyzed in one diagram? In three diagrams? What does the AD/AS model leave out? How do you think you might go about attempting to analyze these left-out topics while still using the AD/AS model when it is appropriate?

4. The topic of tax rate changes won't be dealt with specifically until the following chapters, but you won't be surprised to hear that taxes have a profound effect on the economy. Could you analyze the impact of an income tax reduction on the economy with the AD/AS diagram? How?

5. What if everyone started saving quite a bit? What would happen to the economy? What would happen to aggregate demand, output, prices and interest rates? How does this impact fit in with the concept that our economy would be better off with *more* savings? (*Hint*: Think about the aggregate supply curve as well.)

10
Keynesian Foundations
of Modern Macroeconomics

TRUE OR FALSE

T F

☐ ☐   1. Keynes believed that during a time of depression, people could induce more production by saving more.

☐ ☐   2. The multiplier concept indicates the amplified effect that a change in income will have on investment.

☐ ☐   3. Their views on price and wage flexibility were one important distinction between Keynes and the classicists who came before him.

☐ ☐   4. An increase in disposable income, other things being equal, will cause consumption to increase.

☐ ☐   5. One, divided by one minus the MPC, yields the multiplier.

☐ ☐   6. Investment and saving are quite different; they are done by different people for different reasons.

☐ ☐   7. In the Keynesian model, the responsiveness of aggregate demand to changes in supply will be directly related to the availability of unemployed resources.

☐ ☐   8. The marginal propensity to consume (MPC) is defines as the total amount of consumption in the economy divided by the change in disposable income.

☐ ☐   9. Business pessimism can increase the severity of recessions by reducing investment.

☐ ☐ 10. In general, the rate of government expenditures is determined by market forces.

☐ ☐ 11. Since disposable income can only be consumed or saved, the knowledge of an economy's aggregate consumption function will permit one to calculate the economy's aggregate saving function with respect to disposable income.

☐ ☐ 12. Within the Keynesian model, prices are typically assumed to be constant; if inflation does occur due to an increase in autonomous expenditures, then the multiplier effect of that increase is absent.

☐ ☐ 13. The idea that the Keynesian model implies an aggregate supply curve that is horizontal below potential output and vertical at potential output is probably a simplification; instead, the SRAS turns from horizontal to vertical more gradually.

PROBLEMS AND PROJECTS

1. Calculate the marginal propensity to consume for the following situations:
   a. Consumption increases by $2,000 when disposable income increases by $3,000.
   b. Consumption increases from $6,000 to $7,000 when disposable income increases from $8,000 to $9,500.
   c. Disposable income decreases from $10,000 to $9,000 causing consumption to do the same.
   d. Disposable income increases by $4,000 causing savings to increase by $1,000. (*Hint:* disposable income must be either spent or saved.)

2. Calculate the value of the multiplier for all four cases in question 1 above.

3. In the country of Buyevermore, households have the following consumption schedule:

Disposable income:	10,000	11,000	12,000	13,000	14,000
Consumption:	5,000	6,200	7,400	8,600	9,800

   a. What is the value of the marginal propensity to consume?
   b. According to your computation from part a, how much does consumption change when income rises by 100? Where does the money for the extra consumption come from?
   c. Consider the multiplier process. In the table below, fill in the first three rounds of additional income if investment spending rises by 100:

Expenditure stage	Additional income ($ billion)	Additional consumption ($ billion)
Round 1	100	_____
Round 2	_____	_____
Round 3	_____	_____

   d. Does the Buyevermore economy converge to a new equilibrium? Explain briefly.

4. Suppose that the economy's initial equilibrium is at $4,000 billion and the marginal propensity to consume is 1/2. Autonomous expenditure then rises by $200 billion.
   a. Complete the following table:

Expenditure stage	Additional income ($ billion)	Additional consumption ($ billion)
Round 1	200	100
Round 2	_____	_____
Round 3	_____	_____
Round 4	_____	_____
Round 5	_____	_____
Subtotal:	_____	_____
:	:	:
:	:	:
Grand total:	_____	_____

   b. The diagrams below illustrate the close relationship between the Keynesian aggregate expenditure model of Chapter 10 and the AD/AS model when the economy's SRAS is highly elastic (flat). Each round of additional income in the upper panel pushes out the AD curve in the lower panel. Complete the diagrams (RGNP denotes real GNP).

Fig. 10-1

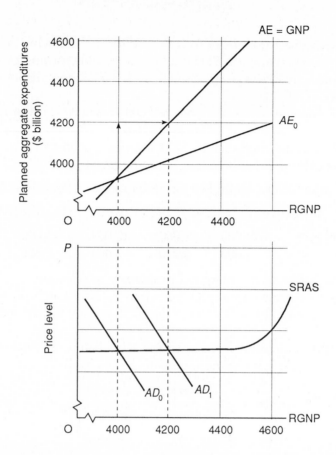

5. Calculate the equilibrium level of output within the framework of the Keynesian model in each of the following cases (assume net exports are zero throughout):

    a. From a starting equilibrium level of output equal to $600 billion, assume an autonomous increase in gross investment of $50 billion in an economy with a fairly stable MPC of 2/3.

    b. From a starting equilibrium level of output equal to $800 billion, assume an autonomous decrease in gross investment of $100 billion in an economy with a fairly stable MPC of 3/4.

    c. Planned government expenditure is $300 billion (as are expected taxes), planned gross investment is $100 billion, and 3/4 of all disposable income is spent on consumption.

    d. Planned gross investment is $150 billion, government expenditures are $600 billion (while taxes are only $500 billion), and the aggregate consumption function is $C = \$200$ billion $+ 4/5$ (disposable income).

6. Imagine two economies, Savit and Spendit, which are identical in all respects except that Savit has a marginal propensity to consume of 1/2 while Spendit has an MPC of 9/10. Exhibit 1 traces the impact of additional investment spending of $25 million in each economy.

Exhibit 1

Expenditure stage	Savit		Spendit	
	Additional income	Additional consumption	Additional income	Additional consumption
Round 1	25.0	12.5	25.0	22.5
Round 2	____	____	____	____
Round 3	____	____	____	____
Round 4	____	____	____	____
Round 5	____	____	____	____
All others	____	____	____	____
Total	____	____	____	____

a. Fill in the missing entries for the expenditure stages in each of the two countries.
b. In which economy does the increased investment spending have the larger impact? Explain briefly.
c. From the "Total" row, calculate the ratio of total additional consumption to total additional income for each country. Are the magnitudes of these ratios surprising? Explain briefly.

7. Suppose that the current equilibrium level of aggregate income is $500 trillion while the *full employment* level of income is $600 trillion. If the marginal propensity to consume is 4/5, how much would investment spending need to increase for the equilibrium level of income to equal the full employment level? Explain briefly. Attempt to show this situation on both AD/AS and aggregate expenditure diagrams.

LEARNING THE MECHANICS – MULTIPLE CHOICE

1. The multiplier is used to calculate
   a. the change in spending caused by a change in income.
   b. the change in income resulting from a change in saving.
   c. the change in income resulting from an independent change in spending.
   d. the change in investment caused by a change in consumption.

2. Which of the following is *not* a major insight of the Keynesian model?
   a. Changes in output, as well as changes in prices, play a role in the macroeconomic adjustment process, particularly in the short run.
   b. A general overproduction of goods relative to total demand is impossible since production stimulates concomitant demand.
   c. The responsiveness of aggregate supply to changes in demand will be directly related to the availability of unemployed resources.
   d. Fluctuations in aggregate demand are an important potential source of business instability.

3. In the Keynesian aggregate expenditure model, which of the following would be the most likely result of an autonomous $5 bill increase in investment?
   a. An increase in the cost of loans for investment
   b. The expectation of a sharp rise in sales during the next six months
   c. An increase of $5 billion in national income
   d. A decrease in government expenditures to offset the increase in investment

4. When planned aggregate demands equals total income, which of the following is true?
   a. Saving must equal investment plus government spending.
   b. The undesired change in inventories is just equal to the difference between full employment and present employment.
   c. Full employment is achieved.
   d. There is no automatic tendency toward a change in income.

5. In equation form, Keynesian macroeconomic equilibrium is attained when
   a. total output = real GNP.
   b. real GNP = planned consumption.
   c. planned aggregate expenditures = total output.
   d. $C + I + G + X$ = planned aggregate expenditures.

6. Say's law of the markets holds that supply creates its own demand because
   a. there is a buyer for each new product produced.
   b. the act of producing creates income equal to the value of the goods produced.
   c. prices are stable in the short run; thus, producers know how much to provide.
   d. supply prices are always equal to demand prices.

7. If the MPC is 3/4, the multiplier is
   a. 4
   b. 1-1/3
   c. 1-3/4
   d. undefined until the marginal propensity to save is known.

8. John Maynard Keynes
   a. was an American economist.
   b. did not believe that "supply created its own demand."
   c. was the "father of microeconomics."
   d. did not believe that changes in private investment were an important source of economic instability.

9. The primary determinant of consumer spending is
   a. the interest rate.
   b. disposable income.
   c. expectations of inflation.
   d. the stage of the business cycle.

10. Which of the following is most likely to increase investment?
    a. An increase in the interest rate
    b. An increase in saving
    c. An increase in the expected quantity of future sales
    d. An increase in unemployment

11. The greater the MPC
    a. the greater the multiplier.
    b. the larger the change in aggregate expenditure for a given change in spending.
    c. Neither a nor b is correct.
    d. Both a and b are correct.

12. Which of the following best describes a consumption function?
    a. A function that relates consumption to savings
    b. A function that relates investment to the interest rate
    c. A function that relates consumption to disposable income
    d. All of the above are correct; the consumption function includes all three relationships.

13. As income increases, aggregate
    a. consumption spending falls.
    b. consumption spending rises.
    c. consumption spending rises only if the interest rate also rises.
    d. inflation causes consumption and saving to move in opposite directions.

THE ECONOMIC WAY OF THINKING – MULTIPLE CHOICE

1. If consumption equals 800 when disposable income is 1000 and then consumption increases to 1000 when disposable income increases to 1300, the marginal propensity to consume is
   a. 8/10.
   b. 10/13.
   c. 2/3.
   d. 3/4.

2. "If there is unemployment, the average wage rate will decline as the unemployed workers choose lower wages rather than going without a job. The demand curve for labor slopes downward and to the right, so that more workers would be hired at the lower wage rate, restoring full employment" According to the Keynesian view, this quote is
   a. incorrect, because widespread unemployment would cause wages to rise, not decline.
   b. incorrect, because the demand for labor, other things constant, will not be negatively related to wages.
   c. incorrect, because wages and prices tend to be highly inflexible downward.
   d. essentially correct.

3. Which of the following is most likely to lead to an increase in current consumption?
   a. An increase in personal income tax rates
   b. An increase in one's expected future income
   c. A decrease in one's marginal propensity to consume
   d. An increase in the interest rate.

4. According to Keynes, Say's Law was incorrect because
   a. the interest rate adjusts so that planned saving and investment are always identical.
   b. saving and investment are done by different individuals and need not be equal.
   c. it assumed that wages are inflexible.
   d. of the permanent income hypothesis.

5. "Independent changes in investment are high-powered because they generate additional income for workers and factory suppliers. In time, this additional income will be spent on consumption, creating an additional stimulus for investment, employment, and income when the economy is at less than full employment." From the Keynesian view, this quote is
   a. incorrect, because changes in investment will have little impact on consumption.
   b. incorrect, because a change in investment cannot lead to an increase in real income.
   c. incorrect, because the higher level of aggregate demand implicit in the statement will merely cause consumption to increase.
   d. essentially correct.

6. The Great Depression provided support for Keynes's declaration that
   a. government action was necessary to ensure that the saving rate remained at the equilibrium level.
   b. falling interest rates would induce consumers to increase their saving.
   c. the average propensity to consume will increase as disposable income rises.
   d. prolonged periods of unemployment were possible.

   The following information is relevant to the next two questions:
   Assume that IBM decides, despite an ongoing recession, to build a new branch for computer analysis in Bozeman, Montana. The plant will employ 1500 workers, who will be guaranteed a full-time (40 hours per week) job at $4 per hour for 50 weeks. That is, each worker will have an annual income of $8000.

7. If the marginal propensity to consume in Bozeman was 3/4, what would be the total change in income that would result from the operation of the plant for one year?
   a. $12 million
   b. $48 million
   c. $9 million
   d. $27 million

8. If Bozeman citizens decided to spend more than 3/4 of the additional income
   a. the MPC would decrease.
   b. the multiplier would decrease.
   c. the expansion in income would be larger.
   d. aggregate expenditures would decline.

9. "Fluctuations in business investment are the major source of economic disturbances. A high level of aggregate demand is essential; otherwise spending may be insufficient to provide the business sector with the incentive to expand, invest, and employ all workers of the economy." According to the Keynesian view, this quote is
   a. incorrect, because investment is not the major source of economic instability.
   b. incorrect, because it ignores the fact that investment is highly responsive to changing interest rates.
   c. incorrect, because a high level of aggregate demand will mean a decline in savings necessary for investment.
   d. essentially correct.

10. If an economy operating in the Keynesian range of its SRAS has a marginal propensity to consume of 4/5, and the government wants to boost real output by 400, then by how much should it increase autonomous expenditure?
    a. 80.
    b. 320.
    c. 400.
    d. 500.

11. Which of the following is a correct implication of the Keynesian model for the shape of the aggregate supply curve in the goods and services market?
    a. The SRAS is horizontal because prices are assumed to be constant.
    b. The SRAS is vertical because it is impossible to increase real GNP past full employment.
    c. The SRAS is horizontal well below full employment and is vertical at full employment.
    d. The SRAS is vertical well below full employment and is horizontal at full employment.

12. If planned total spending (aggregate expenditures) were $900 billion but GNP were currently $800 billion, Keynesian analysis suggests that
    a. output would fall, incomes would fall, and tax revenues would automatically decrease.
    b. production would be stimulated and output would increase, unless output at full capacity were less than $900 billion.
    c. businesses would accumulate inventories, and output would fall.
    d. businesses would accumulate unplanned inventories, causing output to rise.

13. Which of the following is *not* a reason to prefer the three-market AD/AS macromodel to the aggregate expenditure model of this chapter?
    a. Simultaneous unemployment and inflation are easier to visualize within the AD/AS framework.
    b. The AD/AS model makes it easier to distinguish between long-run and short-run conditions than does the aggregate expenditure model.
    c. The AD/AS model has been at the center of macroeconomics for almost four decades.
    d. Changes in prices and expectations are easier to visualize in the AD/AS model.

THE ECONOMIC WAY OF THINKING – DISCUSSION QUESTIONS

1. What is Say's Law? Explain why classical economists thought that a market economy would always return to a full-employment equilibrium. Do Keynesians agree with Say's Law in the short run? The long run? Explain both answers.

2. Twice during the Reagan administration, income tax rates were cut. Indicate the effect you think such tax cuts have on each of the following: consumption; savings; the value of the multiplier; aggregate demand; and long-run aggregate supply.

3. What do you find most convincing about the economic theory of John Maynard Keynes? Least convincing? On the whole, do you think the influence of Keynes has been good or bad?

4. How would each of the following influence the equilibrium level of output and employment? Explain your answer.
    a. An increase in planned saving
    b. The expectation of a recession in the near future
    c. The expectation of accelerating inflation during the next 12 months
    d. An increase in government spending
    e. A decline in the income tax

5. What is investment? Which of the following adds to current investment?
   a. Kinney Shoes purchases a new cutting machine.
   b. Kinney Shoes increases its shoe inventory 10 percent in anticipation of holiday sales.
   c. General Motors sells 1000 shares of stock.
   d. General Motors uses the stock proceeds to expand its plant in Fremont, California.
   e. Honda expands its U.S. production capacity.
   f. Japanese investors acquire Florida real estate.
   g. Texaco acquires Getty Oil.
   h. Voters approve a bond issue for new school construction.

6. "Business cycles are caused mainly by fluctuations in investment. Investment behavior also makes the swings of business cycles larger than they would otherwise be." Criticize or support this view. What evidence do you have to support your decision?

11
Modern Macroeconomics: Fiscal Policy

TRUE OR FALSE

T   F
☐ ☐   1. The crowding-out effect refers to the hypothesis that high marginal tax rates crowd personal consumption out of the market place and therefore reduce the effectiveness of fiscal policy.

☐ ☐   2. Manipulation of government expenditures is one type of fiscal policy.

☐ ☐   3. A change in fiscal policy usually changes the full-employment level of output.

☐ ☐   4. The lowering of income tax rates is a fiscal policy tool.

☐ ☐   5. A balanced budget is essential if *real* income is to be increased by fiscal policy.

☐ ☐   6. A review of the record of fiscal policy in the United States indicates that there is strong evidence for the contention that governmental budget deficits cause inflation.

☐ ☐   7. Unlike increases in investment expenditures, an increase in government spending has no multiplier effect.

☐ ☐   8. Tax policy can be adjusted in order to encourage or discourage investment.

☐ ☐   9. Given an economy's resource base and current level of technology, it will be impossible to sustain a real output rate greater than the vertical portion of the economy's long-run supply curve.

☐ ☐   10. Higher marginal tax rates coupled with an increase in the size of the planned budget deficit (due to a sharp increase in government expenditures) will tend to decrease aggregate supply and increase aggregate demand, causing acceleration in the rate of inflation.

☐ ☐   11. A budget surplus means that tax revenues exceed government expenditures.

☐ ☐   12. Economic theory indicates that an increase in marginal tax rates will encourage individuals to substitute work for leisure.

☐ ☐   13. New classical economists believe that taxes and debt financing as sources of government expenditure are essentially equivalent in their impact on the economy.

☐ ☐   14. Money income increases faster than real income during a period of inflation.

PROBLEMS AND PROJECTS

1. Label each of the following statements as most likely to be made by a Keynesian (K), a Keynesian critic concerned about crowding-out (C), a new classical economist (NC), or a supply-sider (SS):

   _____ a. "The output lost due to resources left idle during a recession can never be recovered."

   _____ b. "The large budget deficits of the 1980s have been accompanied by historically high real interest rates."

   _____ c. "Most research indicates that there is no link between budget deficits and interest rates; higher deficits may simply be matched by higher savings."

   _____ d. "Countercyclical fiscal policy during a recession can actually promote crowding-in of investment by making investors feel more optimistic."

   _____ e. "The large budget deficits of the Reagan administration eroded the international competitiveness of U.S. industries, since foreign savers were attracted by high U.S. interest rates and bid up the value of the dollar."

   _____ f. "Lower marginal tax rates stimulate people to work, save and invest, resulting in more output and a larger tax base."

   _____ g. "Since taxpayers are concerned about the welfare of succeeding generations, they consider debt financing of government spending to be equivalent to tax financing."

   _____ h. "Tax cuts can reduce inflation by increasing aggregate supply."

2. Indicate which of the following changes will cause a shift in aggregate demand, aggregate supply, or both.
   a. An improvement in technology
   b. An increase in the labor force participation rate of older workers
   c. A change in tax rates
   d. A $100 tax credit (or rebate) for each citizen
   e. A large wheat crop due to excellent weather conditions
   f. An increase in the world price of a country's major export product
   g. An increase in government expenditures
   h. An expansion in the size of the underground economy due to higher marginal tax rates

3. Consider the following two statements made by members of the Reagan administration:

   (I)   According to a news report, "An administration economist calculates that the multiplier effect of an increase in government spending, financed by borrowing, is zero. . . . He estimates that each dollar of such spending crowds out 30 to 70 cents worth of investment. Further, consumption will be reduced" (*The Margin*, October 1985).

   (II) According to a different news report, "A senior Reagan administration official" called for action soon "to ensure that the deficit cuts required by the new budget law (Gramm-Rudman) don't harm the economy" (*Wall Street Journal*, January 29, 1986).

   a. With respect to I, explain carefully the manner in which the deficit spending described there could "crowd out" private spending. In your explanation, be sure to use both an AD/AS diagram and a loanable funds diagram.
   b. With reference to II, explain carefully the manner in which a reduction in the deficit could "harm the economy." In your explanation, be sure to use an AD/AS diagram.
   c. Could both these quotes have been made by members of the same administration? If the official in I feels that the deficit is bad for the economy, then why is the official in II worried about the side effects of reducing that deficit?

4. Suppose the marginal propensity to consume (MPC) is 2/3, and the government responds to a recession by raising its purchases by $90 billion. Answer the following questions using the basic Keynesian model as your framework for analysis.
    a. What is the size of the multiplier?
    b. What is the maximum output effect of the spending increase? Why might the output effect actually be less?

    Suppose instead that the government responds to the recession by cutting taxes by $90 billion.
    c. How much of the tax cut will actually be spent by households in the "first round" response to the tax cut? Why?
    d. Use the multiplier to estimate the output increase associated with the tax cut.
    e. Decide whether the following is true or false: "The Keynesian model suggests that government spending has a more direct and stronger impact on aggregate demand than an equivalent change in taxes." Explain your answer.

LEARNING THE MECHANICS – MULTIPLE CHOICE

1. Fiscal policy is defined as
    a. changes in government expenditure to influence equilibrium GNP.
    b. changes in taxation rates to influence equilibrium GNP.
    c. all of the above.
    d. none of the above.

2. Consider an economy whose aggregate demand (AD) is currently $300 billion below the economy's long-run capacity. If the marginal propensity to consume (MPC) is steady at 2/3, by how much would government spending have to rise in order to push AD to capacity?
    a. $100 billion
    b. $200 billion
    c. $300 billion
    d. $900 billion

3. A balanced budget
    a. means that aggregate consumption is in balance with aggregate saving.
    b. means that government spending is constant from year to year.
    c. means that public spending equals private spending.
    d. means that tax revenues during a period are equal to government expenditures.

4. A decline in marginal tax rates will encourage individuals to
    a. substitute leisure for work.
    b. engage in more barter transactions.
    c. purchase more tax-deductible goods.
    d. allocate more funds into profitable investments expected to yield taxable income.

5. In the simple Keynesian model, inflation
    a. is a problem that cannot arise from fiscal policy.
    b. implies that the full-employment level of income is less than the equilibrium level of income.
    c. automatically leads to unemployment.
    d. is not a problem, since it implies a redistribution of income but has no effect on GNP.

6. The crowding-out effect suggest that
    a. expansionary fiscal policy causes inflation.
    b. restrictive fiscal policy is an effective weapon against inflation.
    c. the reduction in private spending resulting from the higher interest rates caused by a budget deficit will largely offset the expansionary impact of a pure fiscal action.
    d. a budget surplus will cause the private demand for loanable funds, the interest rate, and aggregate demand to fall.

7. Which of the following is indicative of a constant (positive) inflation rate?
    a. A constant price level.
    b. A constant rate of increase in the price level.
    c. A price level that increases at first and then eventually stays constant at a new higher level.
    d. A price level that increases at first but then eventually decreases back to its original level.

8. The new classical model implies that debt financing
    a. substitutes higher future taxes for lower current taxes.
    b. substitutes higher current taxes for lower future taxes.
    c. affects the magnitude of taxes but not their timing.
    d. increases both the current *and* future tax liability of taxpayers.

9. Which of the following is *not* an example of an automatic stabilizer?
    a. Unemployment payments that rise when unemployment increases
    b. Farm-aid payments that fall when the economy moves toward full employment
    c. An income tax whose revenues fall when income drops below the full-employment level
    d. Investment expenditures that rise as income and expectations rise

10. The new focus that Keynesian analysis gives to changes in taxes is
    a. to raise revenue for the government.
    b. to smooth out ups and downs of the business cycle.
    c. to redistribute tax money to lower income groups.
    d. to protect governmental budgets from deficits.

11. Crowding out is
    a. the impact of urbanization on economic activity. As population density increases, productivity tends to fall.
    b. the impact of budget deficits on private spending. As deficits rise, that borrowing pushes up interest rates, cutting back on private borrowing.
    c. the impact of the new classical school on fiscal policy effectiveness. As people come to anticipate policy actions, the impact of those actions is reduced or even destroyed.
    d. none of the above.

12. The new classical model hypothesizes that fiscal policy is an ineffective tool with which to alter aggregate demand because
    a. the substitution of debt for tax financing causes people to save more in order to pay higher future taxes.
    b. current macroeconomic policy ignores the supply side and just focuses on the demand side of the economy.
    c. crowding out causes private spending to be reduced by the amount of the spending increase.
    d. the long-run aggregate supply curve is vertical, so in the long run, macroeconomic policy makes no difference.

THE ECONOMIC WAY OF THINKING – MULTIPLE CHOICE

1. Although the economy was entering the depression, the Hoover administration followed a policy leading to a balanced budget (as opposed to a deficit). According to Keynesian theory, balanced-budget fiscal policy (instead of that leading to a deficit) is inappropriate in periods of depression because
   a. it increases economic activity, but not significantly.
   b. it causes further decreases in economic activity, thus further increasing unemployment.
   c. it leads to a significant increase in the national debt, thus increasing the level of unemployment.
   d. it leads to an increase in spending on automatic stabilizers.

2. The modern synthesis view of fiscal policy stresses:
   a. our capability of timing fiscal policy in a manner that would eliminate the business cycle.
   b. the impotency of fiscal policy, even during periods of widespread unemployment.
   c. the difficulties involved in timing fiscal policy changes so they will exert a stabilizing influence on the economy.
   d. the use of expansionary fiscal policy as a tool to reduce the natural rate of unemployment.

3. A $5 billion tax cut was accompanied by an $8 billion increase in consumer spending during a single year. From a Keynesian viewpoint, the most probable reason why consumer spending increased more than taxes decreased is that
   a. additional spending by those with increased disposable incomes led to increased incomes and additional spending by others.
   b. lower taxes led to a reduction in government spending, which induced additional consumer spending.
   c. the tax reduction caused interest rates to decline, inducing additional consumer spending.
   d. the lower taxes increased investment by the same amount.

4. Which of the following would be most likely to cause inflation?
   a. A reduction in investment at a time when businesses are operating at 50 percent of their capacity
   b. An increase in government spending without an increase in taxes during a period of full employment
   c. An increase in government spending and an increase in taxes during a period of slow economic activity
   d. A budget surplus during a period of full employment

5. Suppose that government policy-makers decide that, because of increased investment, the growth rate of GNP will be higher than they had originally planned. What is needed, they feel, is a reallocation of resources away from the production of investment goods and toward the production of consumption goods. Which of the following policy alternatives would be most likely to accomplish this objective?
   a. Adoption of a national sales tax
   b. A higher tax credit allowance for business investment in capital equipment
   c. An increase in the excise tax on gasoline
   d. A reduction in personal income taxes

6. **(I)** prior to Keynes, when economists focused on aggregate markets, most of their analysis was on the supply side of those markets. **(II)** The great Depression and other economic downturns provide strong evidence that aggregate demand is an important determinant of real output.
    a. Both I and II are true.
    b. Both I and II are false.
    c. I is true, II is false.
    d. I is false, II is true.

7. **(I)** An increase in marginal tax rates will encourage individuals to substitute tax-deductible expenditures for non-tax deductible expenditures. **(II)** An increase in marginal tax rates will increase the incentive of investors to undertake investment projects expected to yield taxable income.
    a. I is true, II is false.
    b. I is false, II is true.
    c. Both I and II are true.
    d. Both I and II are false.

8. In the modern Keynesian model, a permanent increase in the budget deficit will cause (other things being equal)
    a. a permanent increase in unemployment.
    b. a permanent increase in the price level.
    c. a permanently increasing rate of employment.
    d. a permanently increasing rate of inflation.

9. In the real world, it appears that a fiscal policy
    a. has never been a stabilizing influence.
    b. has almost always been a stabilizing influence.
    c. has, at times, been destabilizing.
    d. has had no noticeable impact on the economy.

10. Countercyclical budget policy suggests that
    a. the budget always be balanced.
    b. a deficit is needed if an inflationary gap is present.
    c. a surplus is necessary if full-employment income is less than the present equilibrium level of income.
    d. none of the above.

11. "Expansionary fiscal policy in an economy with some excess capacity will tend to increase current real output." Which of the following models would tend to support such a statement?
    a. The Keynesian model and the new classical model, but not the crowding-out model
    b. The Keynesian model and the crowding-out model, but not the new classical model
    c. The Keynesian model, but not the crowding-out and new classical models
    d. All three models

12. Which of the following is *not* a part of the current modern synthesis which most macro-economists would accept:
    a. During a depression or severe recession, expansionary fiscal policy can stimulate real output and stabilize the economy.
    b. During normal times, the ability of fiscal policy to stimulate real output and stabilize the economy is far more limited than the basic Keynesian model implies.
    c. During inflationary times, fiscal policy is once again capable of having an impact on real output and stabilizing the economy.
    d. Given the potential of ill-timed policy changes, fiscal policy should respond only to major economic disturbances.

13. Which of the following items of evidence is most compatible with the new classical theory of budget deficits?
    a. For most of the years since the Second World War there is little evidence of a relationship between budget deficits and real interest rates.
    b. Across countries, there is no evidence that higher budget deficits are associated with a higher rate of savings.
    c. Evidence suggests that most saving appears to be for precautionary and retirement purposes rather than for inheritances.
    d. All of the above support the new classical theory of budget deficits.

14. The idea that proper timing of fiscal policy is both highly difficult and of crucial importance is
    a. agreed to by most macroeconomists.
    b. of no importance to most macroeconomists because the modern consensus is that fiscal policy does not matter.
    c. supported by new classical economists but not by very many other macroeconomists.
    d. only true if we are operating during a depression or a severe recession.

THE ECONOMIC WAY OF THINKING – DISCUSSION QUESTIONS

1. A reduction in tax rates will lead to a decline in tax revenues and an increase in the size of the budget deficit. The deficit spending will be inflationary. Thus, there is little reason to believe that a tax cut will be able to alter the real output rate of an economy." Evaluate each of these three sentences.

2. What are some historical examples of countercyclical fiscal policy? Procyclical fiscal policy? What change in fiscal policy would you recommend now? Why?

3. Despite a large budget deficit in 1981-1982, the Reagan administration moved to reduce tax rates. Could this move have been recommended by a Keynesian? A supply sider? A new classical economist? You? In each case, why or why not?

4. What do you think of the claim that most of the countercyclical fiscal policy of the last twenty years has been due to automatic stabilizers? (What *are* automatic stabilizers?) If this statement is correct, does it logically follow that discretionary fiscal policy is useless?

5. A leading politician once said, "The government budget should always be balanced, so a tax cut does not make sense without a cut in spending." Would you favor a balanced budget amendment? Why or why not?

6. Suppose that you are the president of a country whose economy is experiencing mild inflation. Assume, too, that political campaign promises restrict you to a balanced government budget. Is there any way in which fiscal policy can solve your problem? If so, what?

CURRENT DEBATES IN ECONOMICS

Debate Number Two:

Should We Always Balance the Federal Budget?

Yes, We Should Always Balance the Federal Budget

To Balance . . .
By Herbert Stein

[From *The Wall Street Journal*, May 12, 1979.
Reprinted with permission from The Wall Street Journal
Originally published as the first half of the following article.]

The unpoetic but Hamlet-like title of this essay reflects my true uncertainty. Whether to bear the ills of the deficits we have or fly to the balanced budgets whose consequences we know not – or have forgotten?

The problem is not that there are strong arguments on each side of this question. The problem rather is that the arguments on both sides are so weak.

I will offer, dogmatically, a summary of reasons for not being dogmatic about either side of the argument.

Why Balance The Budget? 1. *The people want the budget balanced*. Polls show that a large majority of the American people "favor" a balanced budget. But this has been continuously true for the part forty-five years. During this period the budget has been balanced only eight times. The people have not elected government officials who would balance the budget, or turned out of office those who ran deficits. If the people "favor" balancing the budget, they apparently don't care very much.

2. *Deficits cause inflation*. But deficits don't cause inflation all the time. We have had deficits almost all the time since 1929, and haven't had inflation all that time. Whether deficits are inflationary or not depends on their size, their timing, their rate of change and how they are financed. The currently fashionable view of the connection between deficits and inflation is that deficits cause monetary expansion which is inflationary. However, it is not clear that deficits have been a major cause of excessive monetary expansion in the past, or that deficits need to have this effect in the future. And if this is the problem, the appropriate remedy may lie in the monetary system rather than in the budgetary system.

3. *Deficits cause, or permit, excessive government spending*. The argument is that government will tend to spend too much if it does not have to count the costs of its expenditures fully, and that it would have to count the costs if it had to raise all of its funds by taxation. There are several problems with this. One is that the "discipline" argument assumes that there is a correspondence between a Congressman's perception of his constituents' aversion to higher taxes and the real costs that government spending imposes on the society. This correspondence is loose, at most.

But even at its best this is not an argument for equality of total spending and total taxes. It is an argument for balancing taxes and expenditures at the margin – where decisions are made. For example, we may take it as given that federal expenditures will never again be under $400 billion. Then the discipline requirement would be met by saying that we should collect one dollar of taxes for every dollar by which expenditures exceed $400 billion.

4. *Deficits absorb private saving and would otherwise flow into investment, and deficits therefore reduce the rate of economic growth*. This argument assumes, in the first place, that private saving is given, or at least that a deficit does not generate an equal amount of private saving. This assumption has been contested by some economists. Moreover, there is no law of nature or economics which tells us that the right amount of private investment is the amount of private saving. In an economy that is rapidly becoming richer for a variety of reasons, one could argue that it is as reasonable for the government to draw funds out of the private saving-investment stream through borrowing as to draw funds out of the private consumption stream through taxing.

Also, it should be noted that if the government makes expenditures which raise the growth rate this argument would not bar financing such expenditures by deficits.

. . . Or Not To Balance
by Herbert Stein

[From *The Wall Street Journal*, May 12, 1979.
Reprinted with permission from The Wall Street Journal
©Dow Jones & Co., Inc. (1979). All rights reserved worldwide.
Originally published as the second half of the previous article.]

Why Not Balance The Budget? While the arguments for balancing the budget leave many uncertainties, this is also true of the arguments against balance.

1. *Full employment cannot be achieved without a deficit.* This persistent notion is without empirical foundation, and once it is accepted that the money supply matters at all it is without theoretical foundation, since there is always some money supply that will generate full employment, even if the budget is in balance or in large surplus.

2. *The ability to run a deficit of the proper size on the proper occasions increases the government's ability to stabilize the economy.* This proposition is being more and more questioned for several reasons. There is doubt whether variations in the size of the deficit or surplus affect aggregate demand, and also whether the effects on aggregate demand influence the real variables, output and employment, or only the rate of inflation. At a more pragmatic level, there is great skepticism about the ability of the government to manage its deficits and surpluses in a way that contributes to stability rather than to instability.

3. *Unavoidable fluctuations in economic activity affect revenues and expenditures in such a way that even if the government plans to balance the budget a deficit may result.* Of course, if the government made its tax and expenditure decisions so that there would be a large surplus under the forecast economic conditions, there would be a cushion to avoid a deficit even if the economy fell moderately below the forecast path. However, there are probably more realistic solutions to this problem.

One would be to state the budget-balancing requirement in terms of the budget plan, rather than in terms of the budget outcome. Also, the problem is less acute if the requirement is not that the budget be balanced each year but that it be balanced over several years.

4. *Balancing the budget will require that we spend less and/or tax more than we would otherwise have done.* This is obvious, but it is an objection only if it is true that a) there are some expenditures worth borrowing for but not worth taxing for, or b) that some taxes are "worse" than deficits. Many people take one or both of these positions. Undoubtedly there is some truth in both of them. The real question is whether the political process can be trusted to live with this proposition and not make it an excuse for irresponsible behavior.

5. *A requirement that the budget be balanced would be easily and widely evaded.* Government receipts and expenditures as those terms are now defined in the budget are only two of the many ways in which the government can influence the allocation of resources in the economy. "Off-budget" transactions are the most obvious among the other ways available. Probably much more important are regulations which require private parties to make expenditures of kinds specified by the government, as for environmental purposes, or requiring employers to provide certain pension or health benefits to workers, and so on. One can argue that limiting the ability of the government to exert its influence overtly through the budget will force the government's influence into less visible and less efficient forms, which would be a loss.

On the other hand, limitation of the government's options would probably reduce the total scale of its activities, and the options outside the budget are probably less inflationary than financing through the conventional deficit.

Holding a Debate

Many students will enjoy participating in a debate on this topic either in class or in an informal study group. After completing both readings and possibly doing some additional research, get three to four volunteers for each side of the debate, choose a moderator if your instructor is not available, and devote about a half an hour to opening statements, rebuttals, and summaries.

Discussion

1. Review Stein's four arguments in favor of balancing the budget and his five arguments against it. Which side do you find most convincing?

2. Senator Proxmire said (about the time this article came out):

    > If a student in Economics 1 were given this scenario in fiscal policy, that is, there is . . . 8 percent inflation and rapidly expanding employment . . . and asked 'should, under those circumstances, the federal government balance its budget?' [as opposed to running a deficit], there is no way he could get a passing grade if he said no.

    Do you agree with Senator Proxmire? Why or why not? Do you expect to pass this course?

3. If the federal budget were *always* balanced, would the problem of economic instability be solved forever? Why or why not?

12
Money and the Banking System

TRUE OR FALSE

T F

☐ ☐   1.   The two major kinds of money in the United States are paper currency and coins.

☐ ☐   2.   Doubling the supply of money would most likely double the value of money to society as a whole.

☐ ☐   3.   Fractional reserve goldsmithing is analogous to our current system of fractional reserve banking in that newly created money (gold) would, after a time, have a multiplied effect on the total money supply.

☐ ☐   4.   A reserve requirement of 25 percent implies a potential deposit expansion multiplier of 25.

☐ ☐   5.   The Federal Reserve System (Fed) has mainly commercial banks and manufacturing corporations as customers.

☐ ☐   6.   The Fed helps commercial banks with check clearing.

☐ ☐   7.   The monetary base accounts for about half of the total money supply.

☐ ☐   8.   Raising the reserve requirement is one way in which the Fed can reduce the money supply.

☐ ☐   9.   Raising the discount rate encourages consumers to deposit more cash in banks and thereby expand the supply of money.

☐ ☐   10.   The U.S. Treasury is the money-creating branch of the Fed.

☐ ☐   11.   The Fed often purchases bonds issued by the U.S. Treasury.

PROBLEMS AND PROJECTS

1. Compute the value of the actual deposit expansion multiplier for each of the following four cases:

	Required reserve ratio	Proportion of deposits retained by banks as idle excess reserves	Currency leakage ratio*
a.	.20	0	0
b.	.15	.05	0
c.	.10	.05	.05
d.	.20	.15	.05

*The proportion of each addition to the money supply that is not redeposited into the banking system.

2. Suppose that the money supply is $600 billion and the reserve requirement is 20 percent. An Arab nation suddenly withdraws $5 billion from its bank account in New York and fails to deposit the money elsewhere. To what level could the money supply change? (Assume that the level of excess reserves is the same both before and after the withdrawal.)

3. In question 2, if the Fed wanted to respond to the drop in the money supply with open market operations, should it purchase or sell bonds? How many dollars worth of bonds should be involved? (*Hint*: Assume that all transactions are with corporations that adjust their demand deposits to compensate for the transactions.)

4. For each of the following, indicate whether the result will create an increase (+), decrease (−), or no change (0) in the money supply and the national debt.

		Money supply	National debt
a.	The Fed sells $100 million of government securities to the public.	_____	_____
b.	Government purchases exceed tax rereceipts, and the Treasury responds by selling $10 billion of T-bills to the public.	_____	_____
c.	The Treasury sells $5 billion of T-bills to the Fed and uses the proceeds to cover $5 billion of deficit spending.	_____	_____
d.	A U.S. citizen exchanges a T-bill with a German citizen for a BMW.	_____	_____

5. Assume that the required reserve ratio for the U.S. banking system is 20 percent, that banks tend to keep excess reserves of 5 percent, and that the public has no tendency to store money outside of bank accounts. Suppose the Fed buys a U.S. government security from the public for $10,000.
   a. Will the action by the Fed raise or lower the money supply?
   b. Complete the following table to track the possible change in the money supply resulting from the Fed's action:

	Change in demand deposits	Required reserves	Excess reserves	Loans
Round 1	_____	_____	_____	_____
Round 2	_____	_____	_____	_____
Round 3	_____	_____	_____	_____
Round 4	_____	_____	_____	_____
Subtotal:	_____	_____	_____	_____
Total:	_____	_____	_____	_____

6. Most of our analysis of deposit expansion has been from the point of view of the banking system, but the consolidated balance sheet in Exhibit 3 of the textbook (on page 283) is actually a summation of the balance sheets of all the banks in the country. To see how deposit expansion works from the point of view of individual banks, let's consider the following two balance sheets, one for the Continental Bank of Atlanta and the other for the Acme Bank of Pasadena:

CONTINENTAL BANK

Assets		Liabilities	
Reserves	$40,000	Demand Deposits	$100,000
Loans	$60,000		

ACME BANK

Assets		Liabilities	
Reserves	$10,000	Demand Deposits	$50,000
Loans	$40,000		

   a. If we assume that each bank has the same required reserve ratio, 20 percent, and if we assume that the banks have no other assets or liabilities, by how much do Continental's reserves exceed its legal reserve requirement? By how much do Acme's?
   b. Assume now that Continental decides to lend out its entire excess reserves by creating a demand deposit for a borrower who wants to buy a car. Fill in the blanks below indicating what Continental's balance sheet would look like after the loan had been approved (and the deposit had been created) but before the borrower actually bought the car:

CONTINENTAL BANK

Assets		Liabilities	
Reserves $ _____		Demand Deposits $ _____	
Loans $ _____			

By how much has the money supply increased because of this transaction?

c.   Now suppose that the borrower buys the car from the car dealer who deposits the check into his bank, the Acme Bank, and that the Fed transfers the appropriate funds from Continental to Acme. Fill in the blanks below indicating what the balance sheets of the two banks would look like:

CONTINENTAL BANK   *Assets*   *Liabilities*

Reserves $ _____   Demand Deposits $ _____
Loans $ _____

ACME BANK   *Assets*   *Liabilities*

Reserves $ _____   Demand Deposits $ _____
Loans $ _____

By how much has the money supply increased because of this transaction?

d.   By how much do Continental's reserves exceed its legal reserve requirement? By how much do Acme's? If Acme now decides to lend its excess reserves to a borrower who wants to buy a boat from a boat dealer who does business at the Continental Bank, follow through all the same steps you did in the case of the car loan and determine the balance sheets of the two banks after the Fed has transferred funds for the boat to Continental:

CONTINENTAL BANK   *Assets*   *Liabilities*

Reserves $ _____   Demand Deposits $ _____
Loans $ _____

ACME BANK   *Assets*   *Liabilities*

Reserves $ _____   Demand Deposits $ _____
Loans $ _____

By how much has the money supply increased because of this transaction?

e.   You have now followed through the first two steps of deposit expansion in a two-bank world. If this process continues until neither bank has any excess reserves, by what total amount will the money supply ultimately increase?

LEARNING THE MECHANICS – MULTIPLE CHOICE

1.   An important aspect of a decrease in the discount rate is that
   a.   it increases the Federal Reserve System's earnings.
   b.   it increases the interest yield of new issues of U.S. securities.
   c.   it automatically results in a decrease in the interest rate that commercial banks charge to customers.
   d.   it increases the willingness of banks to go into debt, acting as a financial intermediary for the sectors of the economy requesting the funds.

2.   During the last decade, developments in financial markets caused economists to rely more on the M2 definition of the money supply and less on the M1 definition. The most important of these developments was
   a.   the Savings and Loan crisis.
   b.   the invention of the M3 definition of the money supply.
   c.   a dramatic increase in the amount of overnight Eurodollar deposits held by U.S. residents.
   d.   a major shift of funds from savings accounts to interest-earning checking accounts.

3. Money is valuable *to society as a whole*
   a. in proportion to the amount of gold backing the dollars in circulation.
   b. in proportion to the amount in circulation.
   c. in a manner that is largely independent of the total amount in circulation, so long as that total is limited.
   d. only if the supply of money is not limited by the central bank.

4. A tool that is *not* used by the Fed to alter the supply of money is
   a. open market operations.
   b. the discount rate.
   c. taxes.
   d. buying and selling of U.S. securities.

   Suppose that the Fed sells $5 million of U.S. securities to the public. Assume a reserve requirement of 10 percent and that all banks initially have zero excess reserves. (Use in answering questions 5 and 6.)

5. The *direct* result of this action on the money supply is
   a. an increase of $4.5 million.
   b. a decrease of $4.5 million.
   c. an increase of $5 million.
   d. a decrease of $5 million.

6. The *total* impact of this action on the money supply (assuming no leakages in the system and no excess reserves) several weeks later is
   a. an increase of $50 million.
   b. a decrease of $50 million.
   c. an increase of $4.5 million
   d. an increase of $5 million.

7. Monetary expansion and contraction
   a. are the major concern of the Federal Reserve System.
   b. are the concern of the president, under expert advisement from the Federal Reserve System.
   c. are the concern of the Treasury.
   d. are the concern of Congress.

8. A reserve requirement of 10 percent
   a. implies a potential money deposit multiplier of 1.
   b. implies that the discount rate must be less than 10 percent.
   c. implies a potential money deposit multiplier of 10.
   d. implies a smaller multiplier than would be present if the reserve requirement were 25 percent.

9. Suppose that a bank with no initial excess reserves received a demand deposit of $5000 that created excess reserves in the amount of $4000. What was the legal reserve requirement?
   a. 20 percent
   b. 10 percent
   c. 15 percent
   d. 25 percent

10. Fiat money is defined as
    a. deposits denominated in U.S. dollars at banks and other financial institutions outside the United States.
    b. money used to buy small Italian sports cars.
    c. money that has little intrinsic value; it is neither backed by nor convertible to a commodity of value.
    d. vault cash plus deposits with Federal Reserve Banks.

11. In a dynamic setting, which of the following is the best indicator of whether monetary policy is expansionary or restrictive?
    a. The discount rate
    b. The prime interest rate
    c. The total supply of money
    d. The rate of change in the supply of money

12. The primary weapon used by the Fed to control the money supply in recent years has been
    a. NOW accounts.
    b. open market operations.
    c. changes in the discount rate.
    d. changes in reserve requirements.

13. The monetary control act of 1980 restructured the banking industry by eliminating most of the distinctions between
    a. commercial banks and savings and loan associations.
    b. M1 and M2.
    c. the theoretical deposit expansion multiplier and the actual deposit expansion multiplier.
    d. open market operations and changes in the discount rate.

14. The monetary base is defined as
    a. currency plus demand deposits.
    b. the amount of gold the government owns.
    c. currency plus bank reserves.
    d. currency, demand deposits, other checkable deposits, plus traveler's checks.

THE ECONOMIC WAY OF THINKING – MULTIPLE CHOICE

1. If the government wanted to follow an antirecessionary *fiscal* policy, it would plan
   a. a decrease in the money supply.
   b. a government budget deficit.
   c. a government budget surplus.
   d. an increase in the money supply.

2. If the Federal Reserve wanted to expand the supply of money as part of an antirecessionary *monetary* policy, it might
   a. decrease the reserve requirements.
   b. urge the Treasury to buy more U.S. securities.
   c. sell U.S. securities in the open market.
   d. increase the discount rate.

3. The Federal Reserve System, the central bank of the United States, regulates the money supply largely by
   a. regulating the volume of Federal Reserve notes issued, since these notes constitute the major part of the U.S. money stock.
   b. regulating the extent to which the Treasury coins money.
   c. affecting the volume of bank reserves, primarily by its open market policy.
   d. using its power to set the reserve requirements, thereby influencing the ability of banks to issue currency.

4. Our current monetary system resembles early goldsmithing in that
   a. our money is backed mainly by the gold in Fort Knox.
   b. neither goldsmiths nor current banks would have enough gold(money) on hand to pay all depositors simultaneously.
   c. in both cases the required reserves were approximately 20 percent.
   d. excess reserves are not allowed by law.

5. Which of the following is correct?
   a. Federal Reserve purchases of securities put upward pressure on the discount rate.
   b. The Federal Reserve notes in your wallet are an asset of the Federal Reserve System.
   c. Federal Reserve sales of securities reduce the reserves of banks.
   d. The Federal Reserve System controls the currency/demand deposit ratio.

6. The larger the reserve requirement
   a. the larger the potential deposit multiplier.
   b. the smaller the potential deposit multiplier.
   c. the more profitable the banks will be.
   d. the larger the proportion of an additional deposit that is available to the bank for the extension of additional loans.

7. As a result of banking deregulation during the early 1980s
   a. banks can no longer pay interest on checking account deposits.
   b. the Fed's ability to buy and sell U.S. securities was limited.
   c. the Secretary of Treasury was removed from the Board of Governors of the Fed.
   d. The Fed now applies similar regulatory requirements to all depository institutions.

8. Which of the following represents a consistent effort by the Fed to reduce the money supply?
   a. Sell government bonds, lower the discount rate, raise the required reserve ratio.
   b. Buy government bonds, raise the discount rate, lower the required reserve ratio.
   c. Buy government bonds, raise the discount rate, raise the required reserve ratio.
   d. Sell government bonds, raise the discount rate, raise the required reserve ratio.

9. The amount of the actual deposit expansion may fall short of the product of the amount of new reserves times the inverse of the required reserve ratio because
   a. banks may choose to hold some excess reserves rather than lending all excess reserves.
   b. some individuals prefer to hold some excess reserves rather than lending all excess reserves.
   c. instead of a monopoly banking system, there are many banks.
   d. the discount rate may be too low.

10. Which of the following is *not* a method used by the Fed to control the money supply?
    a. An increase in the reserve requirement when restrictive monetary policy is desirable
    b. An increase in the discount rate when restrictive monetary policy is desirable
    c. An open market sale when a restrictive monetary policy is desirable
    d. An increase in government expenditures when expansionary monetary policy is desirable

11. Open market policy concerning purchases and sales of government bonds by the Federal Reserve System is set by
    a. the Treasury Department.
    b. the president in consultation with Congress.
    c. the Federal Reserve Open Market Committee.
    d. the individual commercial banks, which vote according to their share of ownership in the Federal Reserve.

12. A recent development in banking, NOW accounts, allows banks, in effect, to pay interest on checking accounts. This should
    a. cause customers to switch funds from savings accounts to checking accounts.
    b. cause customers to switch funds from cash to checking accounts.
    c. cause customers to switch funds from bonds to checking accounts.
    d. All of the above are correct.

13. The nature of the narrowly defined money supply, M1, is different today than it was prior to the financial deregulation of the early 1980s because
    a. money market deposit accounts, which are part of M1, have increased rapidly.
    b. interest-earning other-checkable deposits, which are part of M1, have increased rapidly.
    c. the definition of M1 has been changed to no longer include deposits at savings and loan associations.
    d. the definition of M1 has been changed to now include credit card purchases.

14. If government purchases exceed tax receipts, and the Treasury sells government securities to the public to cover the difference, then:
    a. both the national debt and the money supply will rise.
    b. the national debt will rise, but the money supply will not.
    c. the national debt will not rise, but the money supply will.
    d. neither the national debt nor the money supply will rise.

THE ECONOMIC WAY OF THINKING – DISCUSSION QUESTIONS

1. Would you be better off if:
   a. the amount of food and clothing *you* have suddenly doubles?
   b. the amount of food and clothing *everyone* has suddenly doubles?
   c. the amount of money *you* have suddenly doubles?
   d. the amount of money *everyone* has suddenly doubles?

   Explain the difference in your answers to parts b and d.

2. "Since our currency can no longer be exchanged for gold, it is only a matter of time until people realize that a dollar bill is worthless. Exchanging pieces of paper that are not backed by valuable minerals cannot go on forever." Do you agree or disagree? Explain.

3. Consider the following paradoxes:
    a. Paradox 1: When the Treasury sells government securities to the public, the money supply doesn't change, but when the Fed sells government securities to the public, the money supply falls.
    b. Paradox 2: When the Treasury buys government securities from the public, the national debt falls, but when the Fed buys government securities from the public, the national debt doesn't change.

    Since both the Federal Reserve Board and the Treasury Department are part of the government, how can you explain these paradoxes?

4. Consider the following questions about fractional reserve banking:
    a. Why do banks need to hold only a fraction of the demand deposits of their customers on reserve?
    b. If the Fed stopped setting required reserve ratios, would bank reserves drop to zero? Why or why not?
    c. Why don't banks keep all of their customer deposits on reserve?
    d. If fractional reserve banking were outlawed and banks had to keep all customer deposits on reserve, would depositors pay more or less for the banking services they receive? Explain.

5. What impact will the following actions have on the money supply?
    a. The Fed buys $2 billion of U.S. securities from the public.
    b. The Fed raises the discount rate from 10 percent to 11 percent.
    c. The Treasury increases the national debt by selling $2 billion of U.S. securities to the public.
    d. The Treasury pays for $2 billion of deficit spending by selling securities directly to the Fed.
    e. The Fed reduces the reserve requirements on transaction accounts from 6 percent to 5 percent.

6. Consider M1 and M2.
    a. How does M2 differ from M1? Which is more liquid?
    b. In the 1970s interest rates rose sharply, but federal laws set ceilings on the interest rates banks could pay their depositors. As a result, many depositors shifted their savings to money market funds. What did this shift do to the size of M1? M2? Explain.

PERSPECTIVES IN ECONOMICS

How the Federal Reserve Decides How Much Money To Put Into The Economy
By Edwin L. Dale Jr.
Special to the New York Times

[From *The New York Times*, May 6, 1976.
©by The New York Times Co.
Reprinted by permission.]

WASHINGTON, May 4 – Only one thing is entirely agreed, accepted and understood about the somewhat mysterious and often controversial subject of the Government's monetary policy, which is conducted by the semi-independent Federal Reserve Board.

This is that the Fed, as it is commonly known, can create money out of thin air by writing a check on itself without any deposits to back that check. It can do so in unlimited amounts. And only it can do so – the Treasury cannot.

Yesterday, Arthur F. Burns, chairman of the Federal Reserve Board, disclosed to Congress the Fed's intentions and targets for creation of money in the year ahead. But he gave his targets in the form of range, not a precise number, and he is the first to admit that he and his colleagues are not at all certain what exactly is the "right" amount of money to create for the good of the nation's economy.

The Government's "printing press" is literally in the Bureau of Engraving and Printing, which turns out currency notes in amounts that depend on the public's demand for them. But the true printing press is a little known man named Alan R. Holmes who sits in an office every day, under instructions and guidelines from a powerful body of the Federal Reserve known as the

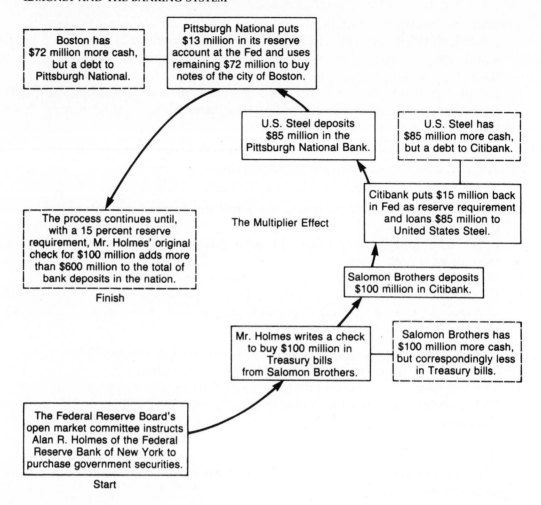

Boston has $72 million more cash, but a debt to Pittsburgh National.

Pittsburgh National puts $13 million in its reserve account at the Fed and uses remaining $72 million to buy notes of the city of Boston.

U.S. Steel deposits $85 million in the Pittsburgh National Bank.

U.S. Steel has $85 million more cash, but a debt to Citibank.

The Multiplier Effect

Citibank puts $15 million back in Fed as reserve requirement and loans $85 million to United States Steel.

The process continues until, with a 15 percent reserve requirement, Mr. Holmes' original check for $100 million adds more than $600 million to the total of bank deposits in the nation.

Finish

Salomon Brothers deposits $100 million in Citibank.

Mr. Holmes writes a check to buy $100 million in Treasury bills from Salomon Brothers.

Salomon Brothers has $100 million more cash, but correspondingly less in Treasury bills.

The Federal Reserve Board's open market committee instructs Alan R. Holmes of the Federal Reserve Bank of New York to purchase government securities.

Start

Open Market Committee, how much money to create.

Orders Securities Mr. Holmes creates money by placing an order in the money market for Treasury bills or other Government securities. He pays for them by writing a check on the Federal Reserve Bank of New York. If the order is for $100 million, an additional $100 million in cash suddenly flows into the economy, possessed originally by the people who sold the Government securities to the Fed.

Mr. Holmes can "extinguish" money, too. If he places a sell order in the market, the Fed sells securities to a money market dealer or bank and gets a check in payment. The amount of money in that check essentially vanishes. The buyer of the securities from the Fed has less cash but the Fed, in effect, tears up the check.

How much money Mr. Holmes creates makes a good deal of difference to the performance of the economy — the rate of inflation, the expansion of production and jobs, interest rates and indeed general well-being — because the amount of money affects how rapidly the wheels of the economy turn.

But what Mr. Holmes does is cause of controversy because the creation of additional money is also linked by economists to inflation. Friedrich Hayek, the Pulitzer Prize-winning Austrian economist, asserts unequivocally that "inflation is an all monetary phenomenon." Mr. Hayek has innumerable followers. While other economists think his view is a little oversimplified, nearly all of them agree that "money matters."

What is more, the check that Mr. Holmes writes is only the beginning of the process of creating money. That initial $100 million starts a process by which the nation's money supply — currency plus deposits in banks — will grow not by $100 million but by some multiple of that amount.

It is at this point that things begin to get a little more complicated. In brief, the "multiplier" effect arises from the way the nation's — any advanced nation's — banking system works. It is called a "fractional reserve" system and it works this way:

Suppose that Salomon Brothers receives Mr. Holmes's check on the Federal Reserve Bank of New York and deposits it in Citibank, where deposits are now higher than $100 million.

Under the Fed's "reserve requirement" regulations, which are crucial to the multiplier process, Citibank must deposit about $15 million of this in its "reserve" account at the Fed. But then it can, and does, lend the remaining $85 million to, say, the United States Steel Corporation, which needs money to pay wages while it waits for its inventories of steel to be bought.

U.S. Steel gets the money from Citibank and deposits it at the Pittsburgh National Bank, and the multiplying process goes on. Pittsburgh National puts about $13 million in its reserve account at the Fed and uses the remaining $72 million to buy notes of the city of Boston, which deposits this income in the First National Bank of Boston.

At this point Mr. Holmes's original $100 million has already become $257 million, as follows:

- Salomon Brothers has $100 million more cash (but correspondingly less in Treasury bills).
- U.S. Steel has $85 million more cash (but a debt to Citibank).
- Boston has $72 million more cash (but a debt to Pittsburgh National).

The process continues until, with a 15 percent reserve requirement, Mr. Homes's original check for $100 million eventually adds more than $600 million to the total of bank deposits in the nation, the nation's money supply. And that money, obviously, can be and is spent. Sometimes more spending is desirable to bring forth production and add to jobs, but by no means always.

The more money there is in circulation, the easier it is for sellers to raise prices, whether to cover higher wages and other costs or to increase profits, because customers around the nation have more to spend. When prices go up all over, this is inflation. But it is impossible to know precisely just how much money is enough or how much is too much at any given time. But there is obviously a point of "too much," as all of history teaches.

For policy makers, there are the two following questions:

- What targets for Mr. Holmes should the Open Market Committee, which consists of seven members of the Federal Reserve Board and the presidents of five of the twelve regional Federal Reserve banks, establish? The relationship of the money supply to the economy at large, including inflation, is by no means clear, even to the experts.
- Because Mr. Holmes's buying and selling affects short-term interest rates as well as the money supply, which should he concentrate on?

At the bottom, the nation's central bank is controversial, and frequently unpopular, because it is a "naysayer." Whenever inflation rears its head, the job of the Fed is to slow the creation of money and, for a while at least, that often means higher interest rates and sometimes a cutback in production and a loss of jobs.

Switching of Funds The right policy will always be a matter of judgement. But at the moment the problem of setting the target for Mr. Holmes is complicated by what Mr. Burns calls the "new financial technology," such as those little electronic "tellers" that many banks now make available to their depositors. Among other services they permit immediate switching of funds from savings to checking accounts by the push of a button and even payment of some bills, such as utilities bills, directly out of savings.

The "money supply" as long defined means currency plus checking accounts (known in the jargon as M1). There were fairly well-established relationships between the growth of M1 and the overall courage of the economy, including the rate of inflation, but now that people, and business, too, have learned to use savings accounts as almost the equivalent of checking accounts, those relationships have gone awry.

"Our equations are all fouled up," a high Federal Reserve official concedes.

The report of the Open Market Committee on its meeting of last January disclosed that the panel, puzzled by a slow growth in money but a rapid growth in the economy, threw up its hands and simply gave Mr. Holmes an unusually wide "target range" for money growth in the period immediately ahead. This meant that he was not to take any special action to create or extinguish money as long as M1 growth stayed within a very wide band.

The Fed also keeps track of and sets targets for M2, which includes savings accounts. But Mr. Holmes cannot tell when he writes one of his checks how much of the ultimate deposits will be in checking or savings accounts. Thus his art will always be imprecise and his results subject to criticism. At present, the Fed does not know whether M1 or M2 is the more important measure, though in the end it controls the growth of both.

The interest rate problem is a different one.

When Mr. Holmes intervenes in the market to buy or sell Government securities, he not only changes the amount of money in the economy but, unavoidably, also affects what are called "money market interest rates" – the rates on very short-term instruments such as Treasury bills.

Rate On Bank Loans The impact of his intervention decisions shows up first in the most sensitive and closely watched of all rates, called the "Federal funds" rate, which is the interest rate charged on loans from one bank to another. In daily operations some banks wind up short of their required reserve deposits with the Federal Reserve and some have an excess, and this gives rise to overnight loans from one bank to another.

Eventually, a rising prime rate brings along with it higher interest rates to ordinary consumers and other borrowers.

Sometimes, as occurred last week, Mr. Holmes is instructed to intervene in such a way as to "nudge up" the Federal funds rate himself, as a signal that the Federal Reserve feels the money supply is growing too rapidly. In either case, whether he "lets" the rate go up or pushes it up himself, the result is higher interest rates. And these days that often means a quick drop in the stock market, as happened in the last few days.

Every time Mr. Holmes writes a check he adds to bank reserves and makes the Federal funds interest rates "easier" – that is, lower or less likely to rise.

Discussion

1. Explain how the Federal Reserve System is actually creating money when Alan Holmes places an order in the money market for Treasury bills or other government securities. How will this money-supply change affect employment and output?

2. The article refers to "the multiplier." Is this the same multiplier that we talked about in Chapter 10? If not, what is it?

3. Who actually decides to expand the money supply — the Treasury, Alan Holmes, the Open Market Committee, or the Board of Governors of the Federal Reserve Board?

PERSPECTIVES IN ECONOMICS

Savings & Loan Regulations Create 'Win-Win' Situation for Risk-Takers
By Jonathan R. Macey

[From the *Los Angeles Times*, February 5, 1989. Reprinted with permission. Abridged.]

In the midst of unprecedented economic growth, it is bewildering that so many U.S. savings-and-loans are in such dire straits. Everyone is pointing fingers at everyone else. Regulators blame bankers, bankers blame Congress and Congress blames the economy.

Recently some of President Bush's advisers seemed to blame innocent depositors. Key officials, such as Treasury Secretary Nicholas F. Brady, advocated a direct charge of 25 cents for each $100 held in federally insured commercial banks, thrifts and credit unions.

There is a clear answer to the question: "Who's to blame for the banking crisis?" Federal regulators — particularly the Federal Savings and Loan Insurance Corp. — are to blame for creating an environment where taking huge risks is the only sensible strategy for the nation's federally insured depository institutions.

S&Ls are failing in record numbers because they operate under a set of regulations that provide huge incentives to take excessive risks. When an entire industry is taking huge risks, many participants are going to come up losers.

The administration of federally insured deposit insurance is the cornerstone of the current regulatory structure. All FSLIC-insured S&Ls pay an annual premium for the privilege of offering deposit insurance. That insurance on deposits is different from all other forms of insurance: The fee bears no relationship to the underlying riskiness of an institution's activities. It is fixed at a flat percentage of deposits.

The insurance-pricing system has lead to a disastrous situation because it creates a "heads I win, tails the government insurers lose" environment. S&L managers can invest federally insured money on high-risk, high-return projects. If these turn out well, the managers reap the reward. If they fail, the FSLIC is left holding the bag. If the federal insurers were acting rationally they would demand compensation for the risks they are bearing — higher insurance premiums for the less prudent S&Ls.

No private auto insurance firm would survive if it charged the same premiums to drunk drivers as safe drivers. Drunk drivers would flock to the company while safe drivers would seek firms offering them the reduced rates they deserve.

Under the current system, S&Ls on the edge of insolvency can attract massive amounts of additional money for a last-ditch gamble because of deposit insurance. Inspection of records of failed institutions shows many did indeed have a last fling with depositors' money in the hopes of hitting the jackpot.

Just as having a single price for car insurance would punish safe drivers, our system of fixed-price deposit insurance punishes safe S&Ls. Not long ago, the FSLIC increased its premiums — an inappropriate gesture, since it signals those trying to operate safely that their prudence offers no advantages.

Logic demands a deposit insurance system where premiums are based on the riskiness of the S&Ls insured. This could be done by requiring federally insured S&Ls to obtain private insurance as well, and then basing government premiums on the rate charged by the private insurer. That way, S&Ls would begin bearing the cost of excessively risky activities.

The most alarming aspect of the current crisis is that it is generally viewed as an isolated event, correctable by a one-time infusion of money from taxpayers or depositors. But the regulatory policies that created this crisis are still in place. Unless the system is reformed, we will suffer future crises that will make this look like small change.

Discussion:

1. Macey says that current S&L deposit insurance premiums encourage risk-takers. Explain how insuring deposits can encourage a failing S&L to make risky loans.

2. Some estimates of the cost of the Savings and Loan "bail-out" run as high as $100 billion, and yet Macey says that "unless the system is reformed . . . future crises will make this look like small change." Why do you think that Congress has refused to make deposit insurance premiums risk-related? If a risky S&L that was barely avoiding bankruptcy was forced to pay higher premiums, what would happen?

3. Why do we have deposit insurance? What would happen if we got rid of mandatory deposit insurance? Would customers have to study the financial stability of their bank or S&L before making a deposit? Would this be good or bad? Why?

13
Modern Macroeconomics: Monetary Policy

TRUE OR FALSE

T	F		
☐	☐	1.	The interest rate is the opportunity cost of *obtaining* money.
☐	☐	2.	If the demand for money does not shift, an increase in the money supply would lower the interest rate in the short run.
☐	☐	3.	If other factors remain unchanged, higher interest rates make fewer investment projects worthwhile.
☐	☐	4.	Purchases of government bonds by the monetary authority tend indirectly to decrease the amount of investment activity.
☐	☐	5.	An unanticipated expansionary monetary policy makes less credit available in the economy, causing interest rates to rise.
☐	☐	6.	The early classical economists did not believe that changes in the supply of money would exert an independent impact on real output and employment.
☐	☐	7.	For monetarists, government itself is often a villain, insofar as monetary instability has led to general economic instability.
☐	☐	8.	Anticipated and unanticipated monetary policies have the same aggregate impact; the main difference between the two is the length of time it takes to achieve that impact.
☐	☐	9.	When aggregate demand expands, the rate of capacity utilization will be approximately equal in all sectors of the economy.
☐	☐	10.	During the Depression, monetary and fiscal authorities undertook policies that made things worse instead of better.
☐	☐	11.	The major consequences of long-run rapid monetary growth are inflation and higher nominal interest rates.
☐	☐	12.	While a modern consensus view of monetary policy is taking shape, some differences between Keynesians and monetarists still remain. Whether or not the velocity of money is stable in the 1990s will help to resolve a remaining difference.

PROBLEMS AND PROJECTS

1. The modern consensus view of monetary policy depends not on whether your views are monetarist or Keynesian but instead on whether the policies are anticipated and on the length of time between the policy and the impact.

Exhibit 1

	Short run	Long run
Unanticipated increase in money supply	Real interest rates fall Aggregate demand increase Aggregate output increases Unemployment falls	
Anticipated increase in money supply		

Attempt to organize each of these views by filling in Exhibit 1, which analyzes the impact of a sudden increase in the money supply caused by open market purchases of bonds by the Federal Reserve System.

2. This question deals with the velocity of money and the quantity theory of money:
   a. Complete the following table of information about the U.S. economy (values for GNP and M1 are in billions of dollars):

Year	P Price Level	Q Real GNP	Nominal GNP	M M1	V Velocity	Interest rate i (nominal)*
1985	110.9	3618.7	_____	620.1	_____	11.4
1986	113.8	3717.9	_____	724.7	_____	9.0
1987	117.4	3845.3	_____	750.4	_____	9.4
1988	121.3	4016.9	_____	787.5	_____	9.7
1989	126.3	4117.7	_____	794.8	_____	9.3
1990	131.5	4155.8	_____	825.5	_____	9.3

   b. Considering the interest rate information in the last column of the table, do the changes in the velocity of money from 1985 through 1990 surprise you? Explain.
   c. Does variability in the velocity of money constitute evidence for or against the quantity theory of money? Explain.
   d. In part a, you calculated velocity using the M1 definition of the money supply. Recall from Chapter 12 that recent developments in financial markets caused M2 to be more stable than M1 was over the last decade. Given that, what impact do you think using M2 to calculate velocity would have on the variability of velocity over the last decade?

3. Exhibit 2 below illustrates the macroeconomy initially in equilibrium at the real GNP level of Y_1 price level of P_1 and nominal and real interest rates of i_1 and r_1 respectively.

Exhibit 2

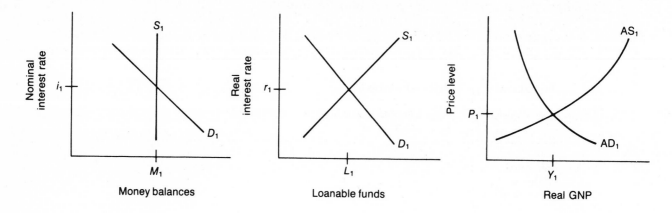

a. Suppose the Fed conducts an open market sale of government securities. Show the short-run impact of this sale in the money balances and loanable funds markets. Briefly explain the changes you make in the diagrams.

b. Now show the short-run impact of these changes in the financial markets on real GNP and the price level. Again, explain briefly the changes you make in the diagram.

4. Exhibit 3 illustrates the macroeconomy in equilibrium initially at real GNP level Y_f (the full-employment level) and price level P_1. There is no long-run growth of real GNP, and initially the money supply is constant. Therefore, prices are stable at P_1. Suppose now that, all else equal, the Fed increases the money supply at some constant percent per period.

Exhibit 3

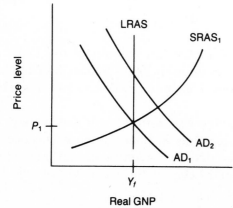

a. If the increase in the money supply raises aggregate demand in the second period to AD_2 what will be the short-run impact on real GNP and the price level? Explain briefly.

b. Will the change in real GNP you described in part a above be sustainable in the long run? Explain, modifying the diagram as necessary.

c. What will happen in the long run if there is no growth in real GNP and the Fed continues to increase the money supply so that aggregate demand continues to increase? Explain briefly and illustrate the process in your diagram.

5. One day you are riding home on the bus and the man sitting on your left is reading a newspaper with the headline, "Fed announces drastic new program of Open Market bond purchases!" In the informal discussion that this headline causes the various bus riders to immediately develop, the woman to your right casually wonders what an aggregate supply/aggregate demand model of the Fed's actions would look like, and everyone (including the bus driver) looks at *you*! What can you do to get the bus going again? You have to show the impact of the purchases (starting from long-run equilibrium shown in Exhibit 4) on the price level, real GNP, and interest rates. (Assume that the change, or at least the size of the change, is unanticipated.)

Exhibit 4

Goods and services—Real GNP

6. This problem concerns the money market effects of spending shocks. The diagrams below depict an initial equilibrium situation:

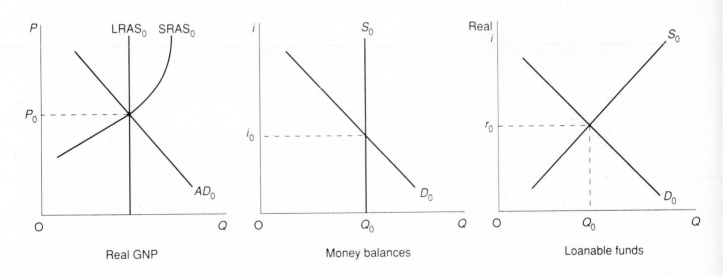

Now suppose that net exports rise as foreigners increase their purchases of domestic output.

   a. Use the AD/AS diagram above to depict the short-run impact of the increased net exports.

   b. Given the economy's new price and output levels, would you expect the demand for money to rise or fall? Which component of money demand (transaction, precautionary, speculative) is affected? Depict the new situation in the money market.

   c. Given the new demand for money, would you expect the supply of loanable funds to rise or fall? Depict this change in the loanable funds market.

   d. What component of domestic spending, if any, might be crowded out by the increased net exports? Explain.

LEARNING THE MECHANICS – MULTIPLE CHOICE

1. Which of the following is *not* a primary determinant of the demand for money balances?
   a. Transactions demand
   b. Nominal demand
   c. Speculative demand
   d. Precautionary demand

2. Which of the following best describes the difference between monetary policy and fiscal policy?
   a. Fiscal policy is used to control the rate of unemployment, whereas monetary policy is used to control the rate of inflation.
   b. Fiscal policy refers to tax changes and monetary policy refers to total payments made by the government.
   c. Fiscal policy determines the volume of government bonds outstanding (national debt), whereas monetary policy determines the interest rate that must be paid on them.
   d. Fiscal policy concerns the tax and expenditure policy of the government, whereas monetary policy concerns interest rate and money supply policy.

3. If the unemployment rate were 8 percent and prices were falling at a rate of 5 percent annually, which of the following would be the most appropriate policy?
   a. An increase in the discount rate
   b. Unanticipated purchases of U.S. securities by the Federal Reserve
   c. An increase in the Fed's reserve requirements
   d. The sale of U.S. securities by the Fed

4. Starting from an initial macroeconomic equilibrium, an increase in the money supply will, in the short run,
   a. lower the demand for money, lower interest rates, and shift the aggregate supply curve to the right.
   b. lower the demand for money, lower interest rates, and shift the aggregate demand curve to the right
   c. leave the demand for money unchanged, lower interest rates, and shift the aggregate supply curve to the right.
   d. leave the demand for money unchanged, lower interest rates, and shift the aggregate demand curve to the right.

5. Suppose the macroeconomy is initially experiencing full employment, stable prices, and zero long-term growth in real GNP. An unanticipated increase in the rate of growth of the money supply will
    a. raise real GNP in the short run, causing temporary inflation in prices and a return to full-employment real GNP.
    b. raise real GNP in the short run, causing permanent inflation at a permanently higher level of real GNP.
    c. raise real GNP in the short run, causing permanent inflation at a level of real GNP close to the full employment level.
    d. leave real GNP unchanged in the short run, causing permanent inflation at the full employment level of real GNP.

6. To the extent that an unanticipated increase in the money supply convinces decision-makers that the Fed will be forced to slow down the rate of growth of the money supply in the future,
    a. monetary policy will become more expansionary.
    b. monetary policy will become less expansionary.
    c. the effectiveness of monetary policy will be unchanged.
    d. decision-makers will be consistently wrong.

7. In the equation of exchange, V stands for
    a. velocity, or the annual rate at which money changes hands in the purchase of final products.
    b. the investment component of aggregate demand.
    c. the amount of money demanded per unit of output.
    d. a constant, 3.1416, discovered by classical economists.

8. The demand curve for money
    a. would shift if the interest rate changed.
    b. shifts with an increase in the reserve requirement.
    c. shows the relationship between the quantity of money demanded and the interest rate.
    d. is a relationship between the quantity of investment demanded and the interest rate.

9. An unanticipated excess supply of money may
    a. cause individuals to increase their demand for a wide range of goods and services as they try to reduce their holdings of money.
    b. cause an increase in real output and/or an increase in the price level.
    c. not have its effect only through a change in the interest rate.
    d. all of the above are correct.

10. Which of the following would be most likely to increase nominal interest rates (according to the consensus view) in the short run?
    a. An unanticipated decrease in the money supply
    b. An unanticipated increase in the money supply
    c. An anticipated decrease in the money supply
    d. An anticipated increase in the money supply

11. According to the consensus view, monetary policy
    a. only works through the interest rate if it is going to be effective.
    b. does not work through the interest rate at all.
    c. can work through the interest rate and also work directly on aggregate demand.
    d. operates by a transmission mechanism involving tax cuts which decrease the interest rate.

12. When we expand the money supply, what actually happens?
    a. The Treasury prints more currency, and then Congress spends it.
    b. The Federal Reserve System prints more currency.
    c. The Treasury prints more money, but it is the Federal Reserve System that actually buys the bonds.
    d. None of the above.

13. Since the introduction of interest-bearing checkable deposits has changed the nature of M1, individuals are less likely to transfer temporarily idle balances from checking accounts to savings deposits. The impact of this tendency will be to
    a. increase M2 and decrease M1.
    b. increase the velocity of money.
    c. both a and b.
    d. neither a nor b.

THE ECONOMIC WAY OF THINKING – MULTIPLE CHOICE

1. In the three-market model, unanticipated expansionary monetary policy
   a. increases aggregate supply in the short run.
   b. increases the supply of loanable funds and aggregate demand in the short run.
   c. decreases aggregate supply but increases aggregate demand in the long run, and also increases the supply of money in the short run.
   d. increases the supply of loanable funds and decreases aggregate demand in the short run, but actually increases aggregate demand in the long run.

2. Professor A. Genius, chief economic adviser to President Ring Leader, informs the president that the present status of the economy is such that the government should adopt a "neutral" macropolicy (that is, a government spending, tax, and monetary policy that is neither significantly expansionary nor restrictive). President Leader has already decided to increase government expenditures on his favorite projects, including an expanded welfare program and the development of a new weapons system. Since President Leader is increasing planned government expenditures, what other actions will Professor Genius most likely suggest?
   a. A tax reduction and/or expansionary monetary policy
   b. A tax increase and/or expansionary monetary policy
   c. A tax reduction and/or restrictive monetary policy
   d. A tax increase and/or restrictive monetary policy

3. Use statements I and II to answer this question. (I) According to the quantity theory of money, the velocity of money and aggregate output are largely determined by factors outside the control of macropolicy-makers. (II) Classical economists, who adhered to the quantity theory of money, believed that an increase in the money supply would cause the general level of prices to increase proportionally.
   a. Both I and II are true.
   b. Both I and II are false.
   c. I is true, II is false.
   d. I is false, II is true.

4. According to the monetarists, a steady (and expected) growth in the money supply would
   a. cause even wider swings in the business cycle.
   b. cause the interest rate to remain unchanged, since inflation would be of less importance.
   c. reduce an important element of uncertainty and make monetary arrangements involving future payments more efficient.
   d. remove any time lag between the point when a policy change is needed and when the impact of fiscal policy is felt.

5. "Inept government monetary policy is the major source of economic instability. Monetary expansion has been the source of every major inflation. Every major recession was perpetuated by monetary contraction. We would have less instability if we simply required the monetary authorities to stabilize the growth rate of the money supply." This quote is indicative of the views of
   a. the classical economists.
   b. both the Keynesians and monetarists.
   c. the monetarists.
   d. the Keynesians.

6. Which of the following may be a reason for opposing the use of restrictive monetary policy as an anti-inflationary tool?
   a. Restrictive monetary policy has no effect, since it may unbalance the budget.
   b. Restrictive monetary policy has uneven effects; the restrictive effects are more severe in interest sensitive sectors.
   c. Restrictive monetary policy cannot have any effect on inflation independent of fiscal policy.
   d. Restrictive monetary policy always causes inflation to accelerate because of its effect on interest rates.

7. All of the following contributed to the severity of the Great Depression except one. Which one was *not* a major cause of the Great Depression?
   a. A sharp reduction in the supply of money in the early 1930s
   b. Tax increases (to balance the budget) in the early 1930s
   c. Tariff increases (to protect domestic industry) in 1930
   d. Farm price supports and increasing farm prices, which made it harder for consumers to be able to afford to eat in the 1930s

8. If the unemployment rate is 8 percent and prices are stable, the *initial* impact of unanticipated expansionary monetary policy would probably be
   a. an increase in prices and a decline in output.
   b. an increase in prices and no change in output.
   c. a small increase in output and a sharp increase in prices.
   d. an increase in output with little change in prices.

9. Which of the following is *least* likely to have an expansionary effect on the economy?
   a. An increase in the demand for money
   b. A decrease in the discount rate
   c. A purchase of government bonds by the Fed
   d. A decrease in reserve requirements of banks

10. The amount of money demanded would probably increase if
    a. the rate of interest rose.
    b. the level of income rose.
    c. individuals began using credit cards for purchases instead of currency or demand deposits.
    d. the Fed sold bonds to commercial banks.

11. Suppose that a federal budget deficit was financed by the sale of U.S. securities to the public. As a result of this action, the money supply will
    a. increase, because the demand deposits of the Treasury will increase.
    b. decrease, because the demand deposits of the public will decrease.
    c. decrease, because the money in the hands of the Fed will increase.
    d. remain unchanged as long as the government spends the proceeds that were borrowed.

12. Starting from a position of macroeconomic equilibrium at the full employment level of real GNP, a one-time increase in the money supply will in the short run
    a. if unanticipated, lower real interest rates, raise the price level, and leave real GNP unchanged.
    b. if anticipated, leave real interest rates unchanged, raise the price level, and leave real GNP unchanged.
    c. if unanticipated, lower nominal interest rates, raise the price level, and leave real GNP unchanged.
    d. if anticipated, leave nominal interest rates unchanged, raise the price level, and leave real GNP unchanged.

13. Suppose we begin from equilibrium in the loanable funds market with the actual and expected rates of inflation equal to zero and the nominal and real rates of interest equal to 4 percent. More rapid monetary expansion leading to an actual and expected inflation rate of 6 percent would
    a. raise both the nominal and real rates of interest to 10 percent.
    b. leave both the real and nominal rates of interest unchanged.
    c. leave the real rate of interest unchanged but raise the nominal rate to 10 percent.
    d. leave the nominal rate of interest unchanged but raise the real rate to 10 percent.

14. Which of the following represents a consistent effort by the government to reduce inflationary pressures?
    a. Sell government bonds, lower the discount rate, raise taxes.
    b. Cut government spending, raise reserve requirements, sell government bonds.
    c. Buy government bonds, raise the discount rate, raise taxes.
    d. Lower reserve requirements, cut government spending, raise the discount rate.

15. The rapid growth of the money supply during the 1982-1986 period may not necessarily indicate that the Fed had shifted to a more expansionary monetary policy because
    a. historically the growth rate of the money supply has not been a good indicator of monetary policy.
    b. while the money supply increased, we don't know what happened to interest rates.
    c. the growth of the money supply during this period was offset by tight fiscal policy.
    d. the nature of money changed during the 1980s with the introduction of interest-earning checking deposits.

THE ECONOMIC WAY OF THINKING – DISCUSSION QUESTIONS

1. "The Great Contraction (1929-1939) is a tragic testimony to the power of money – not as Keynes and so many of his contemporaries believed, evidence of its unimportance" – Milton Friedman.
   a. Explain why you either agree or disagree. Present empirical evidence to support your view.
   b. What other factors contributed to the Great Depression?
   c. Do you think the monetarist or Keynesian view of the business cycle better explains the Great Depression? Why?
   d. What are some of the safeguards we have today against another Great Depression? Do you think there will ever be another Great Depression? Why or why not?

2. Decide whether or not each of the following is true or false, and support your answer:
   a. Sometimes debt financing by the government increases the money supply, and sometimes it doesn't.
   b. Sometimes debt financing by the government puts upward pressure on interest rates, and sometimes it doesn't.
   c. Sometimes a private individual's purchase of government securities from the Fed reduces the money supply, and sometimes it doesn't.

3. "I've read this chapter three times, and I still can't figure out why monetary policy has an effect on output sometimes and not others, and has an effect on prices sometimes and not others. It seems to me that monetary policy *either* should or should not have an effect on output and/or prices. Why doesn't it?"
   a. Consider the contrasting situations of high and low unemployment:
      i. In which situation might monetary policy affect output but not prices?
      ii. In which situation might monetary policy affect prices but not output?
      iii. Draw a SRAS curve that reflects these situations.
   b. Now consider the contrasting time horizons of short run and long run. Over which time horizon is monetary policy likely to affect output? Why? Draw SRAS and LRAS curves which reflect your answer.

4. For most of the postwar years until late 1979, the Fed tried to stabilize interest rates.
   a. With no action by the Fed, what would happen to interest rates as a result of expansionary fiscal policy?
   b. To stabilize interest rates, would the Fed respond by buying or selling government securities?
   c. Would the Fed response make the fiscal policy more expansionary, or less?

5. Refer to "Problems and Projects" exercise #5. Now suppose that someone asks if monetary policy works exactly the same way for decreases in the money supply as it does for increases. Would your answers to the question be identical (except in the reverse direction) for a decrease? Why? If not, how would they differ?

14
Expectations, Inflation, and Unemployment

TRUE OR FALSE

T F

☐ ☐ 1. As it was developed by economist A. W. Phillips, the Phillips curve analysis indicates that inflation causes the rate of unemployment to rise.

☐ ☐ 2. The economic record of the 1970s strengthened the faith of economists in the Phillips curve analysis.

☐ ☐ 3. The adaptive expectations hypothesis suggests that after a few years of inflation, decision-makers begin to anticipate the current rate of inflation. Once the inflation is fully anticipated, the trade-off between inflation and unemployment will tend to disappear.

☐ ☐ 4. Once decision-makers begin to anticipate a 10 percent rate of inflation, a policy of macrodeceleration designed to retard the rate of inflation will result in above-normal rates of unemployment under the adaptive expectations hypothesis.

☐ ☐ 5. Under rational expectations, the anticipated impact of macropolicy change is unpredictable.

☐ ☐ 6. Changes in the composition of the U.S. labor force during the 1970s made it easier for macroplanners to achieve lower rates of unemployment.

☐ ☐ 7. To the extent that decision-makers adjust to demand-stimulus policies, persistent expansionary macropolicy will lead to inflation while permanently reducing the unemployment rate below its normal long-run rate.

☐ ☐ 8. The short-run Phillips curve may be downward sloping, but the long-run Phillips curve is horizontal, or nearly horizontal.

☐ ☐ 9. The exemption of youthful workers from minimum wage regulation would most likely cause an increase in the rate of unemployment of teenagers.

☐ ☐ 10. The rational expectations hypothesis implies that decision-makers are less well informed than proponents of the adaptive expectations hypothesis.

☐ ☐ 11. The unemployment compensation system actually helps lower the unemployment rate in most cases.

☐ ☐ 12. Everything else being equal, the natural unemployment rate in the 1990s will be higher than the natural unemployment rate in the early 1980s because of changes in the composition of the labor force.

☐ ☐ 13. A change in the minimum wage is likely to change the long-run natural rate of unemployment.

PROBLEMS AND PROJECTS

Exhibit 1

1. a. Assume the economy was initially at point A on the Phillips curve P_1 in Exhibit 1. The unemployment rate was 5 percent, and decision-makers expected stable future prices. Political entrepreneurs, planning for the next election, followed an expansionary macropolicy. What would happen to the rates of unemployment and inflation in the short run? In the long run? Explain.
    b. Suppose the economy were at C on the Phillips curve P_2. How could the *short-run* rate of unemployment be reduced to less than 5 percent? What would happen to prices? Could the lower rate be maintained?
    c. When the economy is at point C, what would happen if the macropolicymakers pursued a course that would return the economy to price stability? Would this course be attractive to political entrepreneurs? Explain.
    d. In what ways are your answers affected by the manner in which expectations are developed?

2. Tammy is a great believer in adaptive expectations. Last year, when the inflation rate was 10%, she bought a new car (after borrowing her mom's car for months) that carried a nominal interest rate of 13%. Unfortunately, at least for her, this year's inflation rate is only 4%. For Tammy, calculate the following:
    a. The rate of inflation she expected.
    b. The real interest rate she expected to pay.
    c. The real interest rate she actually paid this year.
    d. Has the fall in the inflation rate made her happy or unhappy (at least with respect to the interest rate she is paying on her car)?

3. Exhibit 2 illustrates the macroeconomy of Lookbak where expectations are of the adaptive variety only. Initially Lookbak is in macroequilibrium at P_{100} and Y_f with unemployment at the long-run natural rate of 6 percent and stable prices. Suppose that the monetary authorities introduce some demand stimulus in an attempt to reach real GNP level Y_2 which represents only 3 percent unemployment.

Exhibit 2

 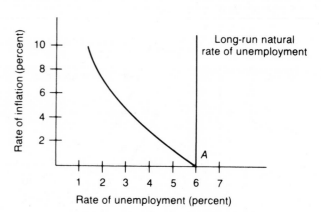

a. If in the short run Lookbak's economy moves to price level P_{105} and real GNP level Y_2, locate the corresponding point in the Phillips curve diagram. (*Hint*: What is the rate of inflation as the price level rises from an index of 100 to 105?) Label this point B. (*Hint*: define the short run as one year.)

b. In the long run (the second year), the SRAS will react to the demand stimulus by shifting to $SRAS_2$ (Be sure you understand why.) Find this point in the Phillips curve diagram and label it C. Illustrate how the Phillips curve will adjust and explain briefly.

c. Now suppose that folks in Lookbak form adaptive expectations regarding the recent inflation they have experienced. Illustrate how the Phillips curve will adjust and explain briefly.

4. Exhibit 3 illustrates the macroeconomy of Lookatall, which is identical to Lookbak except that in Lookatall expectations are of the rational variety. Initially, Lookatall is in macroequilibrium at Y_f and P_{100}, just as for Lookbak in the previous problem, and the monetary authorities raise demand to AD_2

Exhibit 3

 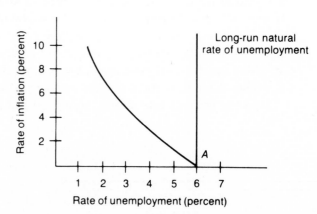

a. Assuming the folks in Lookatall accurately predict the rate of inflation, illustrate how the Phillips curve will adjust and label the new point *B* in the Phillips curve diagram.

b. Under the assumed conditions, will the monetary authorities of Lookatall be able to lower the actual rate of unemployment below the natural rate of unemployment even temporarily? Explain briefly.

5. The following question pertains to the impact of the minimum wage on the natural rate of unemployment.

a. Fill in the last column of the table below and determine whether the real minimum wage rose or fell between 1967 and 1977 and between 1977 and 1987:

Year	Federal Minimum Wage	Consumer Price Index	Real Minimum Wage in 1967 Dollars
1967	$1.00	100.0	$1.00
1977	2.65	181.5	_____
1987	3.35	340.4	_____

b. Indicate whether each of the following increased (+), decreased (−), or remained the same (0), as a result of the change in the real minimum wage from 1977 to 1987. (*Hint*: One way to approach answering the question would be to draw a diagram of the market for unskilled workers and analyze the impact of the change in the real minimum wage, holding all else constant.)

____ Supply of unskilled workers
____ Quantity supplied of unskilled workers
____ Demand for unskilled workers
____ Quantity demanded of unskilled workers
____ Involuntary unemployment of unskilled workers

6. Consider the hypothetical information in Exhibit 4. (For now, ignore the incomplete part of the table and the diagram.)

Exhibit 4

Year	Inflation	Unemployment	Expected Inflation	Actual Minus Expected Inflation
1967	3	5	_____	_____
1968	2	8	_____	_____
1969	4	4	_____	_____
1974	8	5	_____	_____
1975	7	8	_____	_____
1976	9	4	_____	_____

a. In the lefthand panel of Exhibit 4, plot the data for 1967-1969 and draw a Phillips Curve through the plotted points. Do the same for the 1974-1976 data.

b. Now suppose that workers expect current year inflation to equal previous year inflation. Fill in the missing information in the table in Exhibit 4, and diagram the information in the righthand panel in the Exhibit. (*Hint*: Assume that the inflation rate in 1966 was 3 percent and that the inflation rate in 1973 was 8 percent.)

c. Is there a stable trade-off between inflation and unemployment? Between unanticipated inflation and unemployment?

d. What is the economy's natural rate of unemployment?

e. What type of expectations do these workers have?

LEARNING THE MECHANICS – MULTIPLE CHOICE

1. Between 1967 and 1973 the annual rate of inflation exceeded 4 percent. The rate of inflation accelerated during the latter part of this period. Given these conditions, we should expect that, in early 1974
   a. the Phillips curve shifted upward (to the northeast) relative to the position that it would have occupied if prices had been stable during the period from 1967 to 1973.
   b. the money interest rate was low, reflecting the monetary expansion that accompanied the inflation of the period.
   c. the money interest rate was low, reflecting the fact that loans could now be paid back with cheaper dollars.
   d. the Phillips curve was in the same position it would have assumed had prices been stable before 1973.

2. If both monetary and fiscal policy became much more restrictive, Keynesians and monetarists would agree that
   a. the change in fiscal policy would control primarily the rate of unemployment, whereas the change in monetary policy would affect mainly prices.
   b. unemployment would initially rise if the adaptive expectations hypothesis is valid.
   c. real growth would continue as before, but the rate of inflation would decline.
   d. the Phillips curve would remain unchanged with the passage of time.

3. Empirical evidence suggests that, from 1968 to 1980, the Phillips curve in the United States
   a. shifted downward (to the left).
   b. was nearly vertical.
   c. shifted upward (to the right).
   d. was highly consistent with the theory of the Phillips curve developed by economists during the 1960s.

4. During the early 1990s, the proportion of the population in middle-age groupings (ages 35-54) will rise. This demographic change will
   a. decrease the natural rate of unemployment.
   b. decrease the rate of saving from personal income.
   c. reduce the average skill/experience level of the U.S. workforce.
   d. cause the inflation rate to accelerate.

5. The modern view of the Phillips curve indicates that expansionary macroeconomic policy
   a. will reduce the unemployment rate if policymakers are willing to accept the required rate of inflation.
   b. will reduce the unemployment rate only when people underestimate the inflationary effects of the expansionary policy.
   c. will reduce the unemployment rate only when people overestimate the inflationary effects of the expansionary policy.
   d. will reduce the unemployment rate if people accurately anticipate the inflationary effects of the expansionary policy.

6. According to the rational expectations hypothesis
   a. individuals expect the rate of inflation in the past few years to continue into the future.
   b. individuals expect the rate of inflation to be rational and not random.
   c. individuals expect the rate of inflation to be predictable from the direction of current macropolicy.
   d. individuals will continuously underestimate the rate of inflation because they are constantly surprised that monetary acceleration and inflation are linked.

7. If individuals base their expectations on the immediate past, then
   a. the initial effects of macroacceleration will be on prices rather than output.
   b. the initial effects of macroacceleration will be on output rather than prices.
   c. the initial effects of macroacceleration will be unpredictable.
   d. the initial effects of macroacceleration will be the same as the long-run effects.

8. Use statements I and II to answer this question. (**I**) The short-term link between monetary acceleration and inflation is often a loose one. Initially, monetary acceleration often causes real output to increase while the inflation rate increases only slightly, if at all. (**II**) Persistent, prolonged inflation will not occur without an expansion of the money supply relative to the availability of goods and services.
   a. I is true, but II is false.
   b. II is true, but I is false.
   c. Both I and II are true.
   d. Both I and II are false.

9. According to the adaptive expectations hypothesis
   a. people will adapt to whatever income they are earning.
   b. the more people save, the less total savings will be available to the economy.
   c. the anticipated rate of inflation is based on the actual rates of inflation experienced during the recent past.
   d. the expected rate of inflation is adapted to macropolicy changes.

10. Suppose that Congress cuts taxes and that the monetary authorities accelerate the annual growth rate of the money supply from 5 to 10 percent. If decision-makers *underestimate* the impact of these policy changes on the price level
    a. the unemployment rate will rise.
    b. the unemployment rate will fall.
    c. there will be no effect on the unemployment rate.
    d. the unemployment rate will fall if the change in monetary policy dominates but will increase if the change in fiscal policy dominates.

11. Anticipation of an increase in the rate of inflation will
    a. cause the short-run Phillips curve to shift upward (to the right).
    b. cause an increase in the real rate of interest.
    c. reduce the long-run normal rate of unemployment.
    d. cause the rate of inflation to slow, other things constant.

12. One policy implication of an *unexpected* increase in the rate of inflation is
    a. a higher level of unemployment.
    b. the natural rate of unemployment.
    c. a lower level of unemployment.
    d. a new president.

THE ECONOMIC WAY OF THINKING – MULTIPLE CHOICE

Use the Phillips curves diagram in Exhibit 5 to answer questions 1-3.

Exhibit 5

1. Suppose that the economy is initially experiencing stable prices and 6 percent unemployment (point *A*). The incumbent president asks her economic advisers to recommend a policy that will reduce the rate of unemployment in the next 12 months. Which of the following is least likely to be recommended?
   a. A reduction in personal income taxes and monetary expansion
   b. An increase in government spending
   c. An increase in corporate taxes
   d. A decrease in the capital gains tax

2. The president follows the advice of her economic advisers, and unemployment falls to 4 percent. However, prices soon begin to rise at an annual rate of 5 percent. This state of affairs continues for two or three years. Eventually, everyone comes to expect a 5 percent rate of inflation. What will happen to unemployment?
   a. It will remain stable at 4 percent.
   b. It will increase to 9 percent if the macroexpansion continues.
   c. It will increase to 6 percent if the macroexpansion is able to maintain a 5 percent rate of inflation.
   d. It will rise to 6 percent only if the Federal Reserve attempts to counteract the government's policies through a tight money policy.

3. After people come to anticipate correctly the 5 percent inflation, what would happen to the unemployment rate if the administration followed a macropolicy sufficient to stabilize prices completely?
    a. It would initially increase to more than 6 percent.
    b. It would eventually decline to 4 percent after the zero rate of inflation comes to be anticipated by everyone.
    c. It would initially decrease to 4 percent unless the inflation persists.
    d. It would fall in the short run, but later it would return to the 6 percent rate after decision-makers adjust to the lower rate of inflation.

4. Suppose that the rate of unemployment is currently 4.5 percent, and prices are increasing at an annual rate of 6 to 8 percent. If we follow a restrictive macropolicy designed to stabilize prices, what would be the most likely result?
    a. An above-normal rate of unemployment, at least until the expectation of inflation has subsided
    b. Lower interest rates in the short run, reducing unemployment
    c. Unemployment would remain at normal levels, but interest rates would decline
    d. Unemployment would decline, but interest rates would rise.

5. An individual who believed in rational expectations would be most likely to
    a. disregard all current governmental and Fed policies because the impact of macropolicy is unpredictable.
    b. always disagree with the expectations of someone who believed in adaptive expectations.
    c. use all pertinent information when formulating views about the future.
    d. never anticipate stable price, because the monetary authorities continually expand the supply of money rapidly.

6. The program below that might best be expected to reduce the rate of unemployment without causing the rate of inflation to accelerate is
    a. a reduction in government spending on a product for which demand is currently weak.
    b. a reduction in government spending in an industry in which unemployment has increased recently.
    c. an expansion in government spending in states where the unemployment rate is above the national average.
    d. an expansion in government spending in all sectors of the economy.

7. In 1990, the natural rate of unemployment appeared to be lower in the United States than in Europe (11 EEC countries). One reason for this difference is that
    a. unemployment compensation is generally more lucrative in the United States than in Europe.
    b. wages tend to be more flexible in the United States than in Europe.
    c. unionism is more prevalent in the United States than in Europe.
    d. all of the above.

8. Economic analysis suggests that an increase in unemployment benefits (if other factors do not change) increases the average rate of unemployment. This is attributed to the assumption that
    a. higher costs for this program will reduce government expenditures and, thus, aggregate demand.
    b. rational individuals will realize the decreased penalty for failing to accept a job they are not pleased with.
    c. those who are unemployed will discontinue their job search.
    d. unemployed people become lazy when handed money.

9. If policy makers wanted to increase saving they might
   a. make interest (expense) payments a tax credit instead of merely a deduction from taxable income.
   b. make interest income from saving and deduction from taxable income.
   c. decrease government interest payments on government bonds so as to decrease the deficit.
   d. pass laws designed to increase the number of savings and loan institutions in the country.

10. The rapid growth rate in the number of younger people (ages 18-34) and older people (over age 65) during the 1970s probably
    a. reduced the natural rate of unemployment.
    b. reduced the inflation rate.
    c. contributed to the decline in the personal saving rate.
    d. contributed to the increase in the growth rate of real income.

11. Which of the following would be the policy most likely to reduce the rate of unemployment without causing the rate of inflation to accelerate?
    a. An across-the-board increase in government spending
    b. An exemption of youthful workers from minimum wage rates
    c. An increase in unemployment compensation benefits
    d. An increase in the corporate profit tax

12. Which of the following best describes the impact of expectations on the body of economic theory we call macroeconomics?
    a. Expectations help explain stagflation, but they make the task of stabilizing the economy even more difficult.
    b. Expectations make the use of discretionary macropolicy much easier.
    c. Expectations really have no impact on macroeconomics at all; they only allow us to understand the actions of individual consumers better.
    d. Expectations are important, but they do not hinder the ability of policymakers to stabilize the economy.

13. Suppose policymakers think people have adaptive expectations when they in fact have rational expectations. If defense spending rises sharply and the Fed increases it purchases of T-bills, these policies
    a. will have a greater effect on inflation than policymakers expect.
    b. will have a lower effect on inflation than policymakers expect.
    c. will have exactly the effect on inflation that policymakers expect.
    d. will fool everybody because the policies are so irrational.

THE ECONOMIC WAY OF THINKING – DISCUSSION QUESTIONS

1. All else equal, how does each of the following affect the natural rate of unemployment, and why?
   a. An increase in the percentage of workers covered by unemployment compensation.
   b. An increase in the federal minimum wage.
   c. A decrease in workers aged 16 to 24 (as a percentage of the labor force).

2. "It is possible to run a capitalist system at high levels of employment – admittedly, paying the price of a considerable degree of inflation" Robert Heilbroner, *Understanding Macroeconomics*, 4th ed. Englewood Cliffs, NJ: Prentice-Hall, 1972, p. 246.
   a. Do you think Heilbroner would make the same statement in a current edition of his text? Why or why not? What theoretical and historical developments since 1972 influence your answer?
   b. Would you agree with the following revision of Heilbroner's text? "It is possible to run a capitalist system at high levels of employment – admittedly, paying the price of accelerating inflation." Why or why not?

3. Some analysts claim that the economy follows a pattern of "political business cycles" in which incumbent politicians try to get reelected by influencing the timing of booms and busts. If you were trying to document the existence of "political business cycles,"
   a. what macroeconomic policies would you expect to find prior to important elections?
   b. what effects would you expect to find prior to the elections? After the elections?
   c. would you expect to find these cycles if voters have rational expectations? Why or why not?

4. "In the long run, macropolicies can do little to change the average rate of unemployment." Either support or criticize this view.

5. "Increasing unemployment compensation payments reduces the incentive of unemployed workers to take available jobs. High unemployment benefits are a source of high rates of unemployment." Does this view make sense? Explain.

6. "Decision-makers will eventually come to anticipate continued inflation. Once inflation is anticipated, it becomes increasingly difficult to stabilize prices without causing a major recession. Inflation as a means of promoting short-run expansion is like committing suicide with pep pills." Evaluate this view.

7. "There is really nothing we can do to reduce the natural rate of unemployment. Most policies won't work. Even worse, it is impossible to come up with effective policies that are hard-headed but also warm-hearted." Support or criticize this view.

8. In the 1970s, prices in the United States rose by approximately 100 percent. Explain
   a. the major cause of the inflation.
   b. whether public policy could have prevented the inflation.
   c. If so, how? At what cost?

   Use empirical evidence to support the positions that you take.

15
Stabilization Policy, Output, and Employment

TRUE OR FALSE

T F

☐ ☐ 1. At least three kinds of lags seriously undermine the potential of discretionary macropolicy; these lags are the recognition lag, the administrative lag, and the impact lag.

☐ ☐ 2. A major difference between activists and nonactivists is that activists think that the economy is inherently unstable while nonactivists think that the economy is inherently self-correcting.

☐ ☐ 3. Both activists and nonactivists agree that past policy errors have contributed to economic instability.

☐ ☐ 4. The index of leading indicators is more useful to nonactivists than to activists.

☐ ☐ 5. The price level rule is a macropolicy rule proposed by nonactivists as an alternative to the monetary growth rule originally proposed by Milton Friedman.

☐ ☐ 6. Nonactivists admit that recognition lags, administrative lags, and impact lags all make discretionary macroeconomic policy work well, but they still hold to their position that the economy is inherently self-correcting.

☐ ☐ 7. Discretionary macroeconomic policy may be used to pursue political objectives as well as stabilization objectives.

☐ ☐ 8. The theory of rational expectations indicates that predictable changes in macropolicy will help make the economy more stable.

☐ ☐ 9. Monetarists, led by Milton Friedman, favor a policy of constant money supply growth.

☐ ☐ 10. Nonactivists can't agree on a reasonable detailed fiscal policy program.

☐ ☐ 11. Activists, as well as nonactivists, are aware of the difficulties involved in the proper timing of macropolicy.

PROBLEMS AND PROJECTS

1. R. Leader, the head of the House Ways and Means Committee, is convinced that we are heading toward a recession, and he wants to fund a number of public expenditure programs. For each of the possible programs, his staff has estimated (see Exhibit 1) the administrative lag, the impact lag, and the percent of the program expenditures that will go to Congressman Leader's home district.

Exhibit 1

Expenditure program	Administrative lag	Impact lag	District's %
More government buildings	6 months	8 months	25
Big dam	12 months	6 months	0
Lightly used highway	10 months	16 months	100
Acid rain remover	9 months	3 months	10
Trash pickup plan	1 months	4 months	15

   a. Unfortunately, Congressman Leader's staff is uncertain how long or deep the upcoming recession will be. If the public expenditure programs take effect after the economic upturn, then they will be potentially inflationary, since they will come at a time of macroeconomic expansion rather than contraction. If the maximum time before the upturn is a year, which programs should be enacted?

   b. If the maximum time before the upturn is two years, which programs should be enacted?

   c. If R. Leader is especially concerned with next year's Congressional elections, which programs will he support in committee? Why? Does your answer depend on the maximum time before the upturn? Is R. Leader being irrational? Why or why not?

2. Throughout this book, we've given you economic policy changes and asked you how macroeconomic variables would respond to those policy changes (given a particular macroeconomic perspective). In this question, we instead give you the *answer* and ask you to tell us what the question must have been (much like the TV show "Jeopardy"). That is, for each of the sets of short-run movements in macroeconomic variables described in Exhibit 2, label the underlying policy change(s) ("monetary" and/or "fiscal"), and indicate whether the resulting effects are more consistent with an activist or nonactivist macroeconomic perspective. (*Hint*: All spending variables are in real terms.)

Exhibit 2

The Answers:

	C	I	G	Real GNP	Price level	Money supply	Real Interest rate	Unemployment rate
a.	+	−	+	+	+	0	+	−
b.	+	0	+	+	+	+	0	−
c.	−	−	+	0	+	0	+	0
d.	+	+	0	+	+	+	−	−
e.	0	0	0	0	+	+	0	0

The Questions:

a. Policy changes(s):   _____

   Macroeconomic perspective: _____

b. Policy changes(s):   _____

   Macroeconomic perspective: _____

c. Policy changes(s):   _____

   Macroeconomic perspective: _____

d. Policy changes(s):   _____

   Macroeconomic perspective: _____

e. Policy changes(s):   _____

   Macroeconomic perspective: _____

3. Suppose you adopt the monetarist view of the functioning of the macroeconomy. Starting from the initial equilibrium points in the two sets of diagrams below, show both the short-run and long-run impacts on real interest rates (r), the quantity of loanable funds (F), real gross national product (Y), and the price level (P) of a discretionary increase in deficit spending by the government if
   a. the deficit is financed by borrowing from the public, or
   b. the deficit is "monetized" by the Fed.
   c. How would your answers to a and b above be affected by the manner in which expectations are formed?

Loanable funds

The Economy

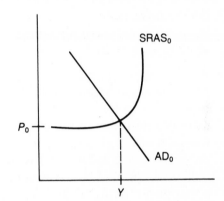

4. Most economists agree that stock market changes anticipate (but do not cause) economic fluctuations. As a result, the behavior of the stock market is a key leading indicator of future economic growth. Decide whether each of the following would tend to make stock prices rise (+), fall (−) or remain the same (0). Unless indicated, assume that each event is unanticipated.

   _____ a. A new survey of corporate executives indicates robust expansion plans for the coming months.

   _____ b. The government reports a sudden decline in the inflation rate, easing pressure on the Fed to enact contractionary monetary policy.

   _____ c. Income tax brackets, now indexed for inflation, automatically rise to offset the inflation rate of the previous year.

   _____ d. The government reports that business inventories have surged over the last three months.

   _____ e. The government releases figures that show the nation's trade deficit fell last month, but by less than previous reports had indicated.

LEARNING THE MECHANICS – MULTIPLE CHOICE

1. The strategy of using discretionary monetary and fiscal policy to moderate economic fluctuations is called
   a. a nonactivist strategy.
   b. a monetarist strategy.
   c. an activist strategy.
   d. a rational expectations strategy.

2. Nonactivists can best be described as wanting to adopt rules and guidelines that will create macroeconomic policies that are
   a. independent of current conditions.
   b. dependent only on inflation but not unemployment.
   c. dependent only on political circumstances.
   d. none of the above; nonactivists do not believe in macroeconomic policies of any sort.

3. A typical activist policy during a recession would be to
   a. increase the rate of growth of the money supply.
   b. decrease tax rates.
   c. increase government spending.
   d. all of the above.

4. A typical nonactivist policy during a recession would be to
   a. increase the rate of growth of the money supply.
   b. decrease tax rates.
   c. increase government spending.
   d. none of the above.

5. The index of leading indicators is
   a. an alphabetical listing of all the most popular indicators in the economy for a given month.
   b. a composite index of indicators that provides information on the future direction of the economy.
   c. an alphabetical listing of the most important indicators of the current economic well-being of the U.S. economy.
   d. a composite index of the most important indicators of the current economic well-being of the U.S. economy.

6. Well-timed discretionary anti-inflationary policy should be undertaken
   a. when the inflation rate is at its highest.
   b. when the inflation rate begins to increase.
   c. before the inflation rate begins to increase.
   d. none of the above; the timing of anti-inflationary policy isn't important as long as it is eventually undertaken.

7. Which of the following is *not* cited by nonactivists in their criticism of discretionary policy's inability to react to economic problems in time?
   a. Recognition lag
   b. Political objectives lag
   c. Administrative lag
   d. Impact lag

8. The policy ineffectiveness theorem offers
   a. the possibility that policy is ineffective because of lags.
   b. the possibility that policy is ineffective because it is anticipated by decision-makers.
   c. the possibility that policy is ineffective because macroeconomic conditions really don't have much of an effect on the lives of individual decision-makers.
   d. the possibility that policy is ineffective because politicians choose policies that are best for their re-election.

9. In the context of macroeconomic policy-makers, knowledge of the current rate of industrial capacity utilization would help an economist
   a. evaluate the current state of the economy.
   b. forecast the future state of the economy by acting as a leading indicator.
   c. decide whether to use nonactivist macroeconomic policies in the current time period.
   d. recommend policies to shorten the administrative and impact lags and therefore to improve the effectiveness of activist macroeconomic policy.

10. Which of the following is a criticism that many activists have of the practical fiscal policy suggestions proposed by the nonactivists?
    a. The monetary targets announced by the Fed cause increased weight to be given to the path of aggregate monetary supply.
    b. Such policy changes cannot be timed properly, and economic instability results.
    c. As policymakers stay on course, the public will develop confidence in the future stability of the policy.
    d. The nonactivists have yet to agree on a detailed, fiscal policy program.

11. Why do nonactivist macroeconomists oppose the use of discretionary monetary and fiscal policies as a stabilization tool?
    a. Nonactivists do not think monetary and fiscal policies affect the economy.
    b. Nonactivists think the use of discretionary policy creates additional uncertainty and thereby exerts a destabilizing rather than stabilizing effect on the economy.
    c. Nonactivists do not think economic instability is a problem.
    d. Nonactivists think that the response of private decision-makers will offset the effects of the policy.

12. Which of the following supports the nonactivist view that the best policy is a steady policy?
    a. Discretionary policy can improve economic stability, but only by a small amount.
    b. Discretionary policy has no effect on the economy.
    c. Discretionary policy can contribute to economic instability.
    d. A market economy is self-correcting.

THE ECONOMIC WAY OF THINKING – MULTIPLE CHOICE

1. Economists with which of the following perspectives would most likely agree that a shift to restrictive monetary policy will reduce output if adopted during a period of full employment?
   a. The Keynesian and monetarist perspectives.
   b. The rational expectations perspective.
   c. The new classical perspective.
   d. The supply side and nonactivist perspectives.

2. The activist view that the best policy is one of discretionary intervention into the macroeconomy is most in keeping with which of the following?
   a. A market economy is inherently self-correcting.
   b. A market economy is inherently unstable because politicians force incorrect policies on the people.
   c. A market economy is inherently unstable because of inevitable economic shocks and investment fluctuations.
   d. A market economy is inherently unstable, but no one really knows why.

prices doubling in about the same time — that served to consolidate stagflation.

The shocks, of course, were not just to the price level, but the economics profession, led by Keynesians. We learned the sad lesson that as to wages and prices, what goes up, propelled by overstimulative monetary-fiscal policy and a series of external shocks, does not necessarily come down when the fiscal-monetary stimulus and supply shocks subside. We have since learned a lot about sticky wages and prices that stay in high orbit even without visible means of fiscal-monetary support. At least, they stayed there until we administered a dose of sadomasochism, better known as the double-dip recession of the eighties, the deepest since the Great Depression.

One should not recite the economic sins of the seventies, without acknowledging one bright fiscal episode, namely, the tax rebate and tax cut enacted in the second quarter of 1975. Granted, it was a bit late to blunt the recession, but it provided a welcome boost to an economy that had fallen into what, until topped by the recession of the early eighties, was the deepest postwar recession. The 1975 tax cut was a winner in both size and timing.

As one surveys the whole postwar period, activist economics and New Deal intrusions into the marketplace can surely take credit not only for building in strong defenses against depression but also for 25 years (1948-73) of high-octane operation of the economy and sharply reduced instability. Within the framework, one can criticize antirecession fiscal policy as often too little and too late, monetary policy as sometimes too easy and other times overstaying tightness. The far-too-late and considerably-too-little tax increase to finance the war in Vietnam, coupled with excessive monetary ease in 1967-68, has to go down in the annals as one of the flat failures of postwar fiscal-monetary policy. And the stagflation experience of the 1970s still hangs like a pall over expansionary policy today.

Still, it is worth reminding ourselves that even in the face of high performance of the economy, inflation in the 1949-72 period rose above 6 percent only once (during the Korean War), and averaged only 2.3 percent. If inflation was the price of activism in public economics, it was a long time in coming.

No, We Should Not Use Activist Macropolicy:

Economic Policy: The Old Tools Won't Work
By Marc Levinson

[Reprinted with permission from *Business Monthly*, January 1987. ©1987 by Goldhirsch Group, Inc. Abridged.]

Since the advent of the New Deal more than half a century ago, the federal government has actively helped shape the course of the economy. Its ability, at least in the short run, to pump up the economy in hard times and slow it down when inflation began to boil up has been unquestioned. As recently as 1981, when a sharp cutback in money supply growth pushed the country into recession, or 1983, when the stimulative effects of a tax cut brought the economy back to health, the old elixirs worked as they had in the past.

But in 1986, things were different. Heady growth in the money supply, repeated cuts in the Federal Reserve Board's discount rate and record federal budget deficits all failed to juice the lackluster economy. The old linkages between the government's actions and the economy's responses have changed in ways economists do not fully understand. As a result, the government's economic tools have been partially blunted. Contends Lawrence Chimerine, chairman of Chase Econometrics, "The ability of policy changes to improve the economy is much smaller than ever."

The reason: the growing internationalization of the U.S. economy. Flexible exchange rates and the resulting mushrooming of international capital markets have made traditional economic policies act in unexpected ways. "No one has a reliable theory of exchange rates," says Paul Krugman, a professor of international economics at the Massachusetts Institute of Technology. "That makes it very difficult to be sure of the effects of macroeconomic policy."

These international connections make it increasingly difficult to aim economic weapons at purely domestic targets. Even thinking of "domestic" in terms of economic problems is misleading. "The problem is global overcapacity and global underconsumption," contends Steve Quick, an economist with the Joint Economic Committee of Congress. "But we have no tools. We have no global fiscal policy. We have no global monetary policy." Adds Harold Rose, chief economist of Britain's Barclays Bank: "It's very hard to see how we can get out of these problems by macroeconomic policy alone."

Certainly, the assumption that the government can "fine tune" the economy has been in disrepute since the early 1970s, when policymakers were helpless as they faced high unemployment and high inflation at the same time. But faith in the government's ability to deal with one of these problems at a time has remained strong. Now, however, the government's very ability to achieve some domestic goals — 3% growth in output, 4% unemployment — appears increasingly limited. The jury is still our on whether these limitations are a temporary phenomenon or a permanent fact of life.

Take monetary policy, the Federal Reserve Board's method of influencing the economy's performance by manipulating the money supply. Financial deregulation, of course, has blurred the meaning of the money supply figures. But international capital flows have also made it much more difficult for the central bank to plot the nation's monetary course.

Suppose, for example, that the Fed wants to boost the economy's growth rate. When international capital flows were small, the central bank could stimulate borrowing by pumping up the money supply or cutting the discount rate. But now, lower real interest rates will spur investors to move their capital out of dollar-denominated investments. Economists can't even begin to estimate the likely extent of those capital flows. If little capital moves abroad, the lower interest rates will powerfully stimulate the U.S. economy. If, on the other hand, lower rates trigger a massive flight from the dollar, higher import prices will inject a strong dose of inflation into the economy, which would discourage the very business spending the Fed wanted to stimulate. Would faster money growth cut the U.S. trade deficit? Nobody knows.

The direction of the overall change remains undisputed: Increasing the rate of money supply growth will stimulate the economy, and reducing it will retard growth. But the magnitude of the change is now almost unpredictable. There is no doubt that a $108 billion budget slash will cut domestic demand. It will also lower deficits and reduce the government's borrowing from abroad, driving down the dollar. But whether a more favorable exchange rate for exports will boost the economy more than lower government spending retards it is an open question. "We don't know the responsiveness of the economy to a changed deficit," contends economist Mickey D. Levy of Philadelphia's Fidelity Bank. "We don't know the lags." Concurs Rudolph Penner, director of the Congressional Budget Office, "If we had been analyzing that big a change twenty years ago, there wouldn't have been much debate that it would cause a recession." The venerable Keynesian multiplier, which links changes in government spending to predictably larger changes in economic output, can, for all practical purposes, be tossed out the window. Using fiscal policy to reach some desired target in terms of, say, unemployment or Gross National Product is thus far more difficult than in the past.

The use of both fiscal and monetary policy has become even more treacherous as government officials have come to realize that they are not operating in an isolated economy. Indeed, the reactions of other governments can blunt or reverse Washington's initiatives, making economic policy a strategic game, according to a brand new line of economic research. The U.S. must figure out how other countries will respond to its moves, and determine the degree to which those responses will counteract the effects that American policymakers seek to achieve. "We can't make policy without taking into account what our competitor overseas is doing," contends University of Illinois economist Stephen J. Turnovsky.

One way to deal with the diminishing effectiveness of monetary and fiscal policies, says the Joint Economic Committee's Quick, is to examine the economic impact of policies long considered unrelated, such as foreign aid of regulation of international lending. Increasing the industrial nations' contributions to the International Monetary Fund, for example, could help stimulate growth in the developing countries, which in turn would step up their purchases of U.S. exports. This viewpoint is catching on in Washington, where Congress has finally come to understand that the debts of developing countries are a major drag on U.S. growth.

Holding a Debate

Many students will enjoy participating in a debate on this topic either in class or in an informal study group. After completing both readings and possibly doing some additional research, get three to four volunteers for each side of the debate, choose a moderator if your instructor is not available, and devote about a half an hour to opening statements, rebuttals, and summaries.

Discussion

1. If you read both articles, it's time to make a judgement. Do the difficulties of accurate policymaking make it better to do nothing? Are there times when even Levinson would agree to activist policy? Explain your answers.

2. If you read the Heller article, it's important to note that Prof. Heller was the chairman of the Council of Economic Advisers under Presidents Kennedy and Johnson and played a major role in shaping the fairly activist macropolicy of that era. Do you think his participation in the policymaking made him a better or worse judge of the effectiveness of activist policy? Why?

3. If you read the Levinson article into what economic "camp" would you group him? Re-read the article for evidence that he is a monetarist or a supply-sider or a new classicist. Why is it unlikely that he is Keynesian?

16
Budget Deficits and the National Debt

TRUE OR FALSE

T F

☐ ☐   1. When the federal government uses debt to finance its expenditures, bonds are sold by the Federal Reserve Bank.

☐ ☐   2. If the budget deficit as a percent of GNP is less than the growth rate of GNP, the national debt as a share of GNP will fall.

☐ ☐   3. The national debt as a share of GNP is higher today than at any time since the end of the Second World War.

☐ ☐   4. Among the Group of Seven industrial countries discussed in the text, the United States ranks in the middle in terms of net public debt as a percent of GNP.

☐ ☐   5. Technically, the nation is bankrupt when the size of the national debt exceeds the size of GNP.

☐ ☐   6. Deficit spending during a recession can improve the welfare of future generations by enlarging the stock of available capital.

☐ ☐   7. To understand how government debt influences future generations, its impact on capital formation must be determined.

☐ ☐   8. According to the new classical view of government deficits, deficit and tax financing of government expenditures have equivalent macroeconomic effects.

☐ ☐   9. The behavior of real investment during the period of expansionary fiscal policy under the Reagan administration provides a clear example of the crowding out phenomenon.

☐ ☐   10. Like the federal government, state and local governments in recent years have tended to run budget deficits.

☐ ☐   11. Including Social Security receipts and expenditures in the budget increases the size of the reported budget deficit.

PROBLEMS AND PROJECTS

1. You've been hired by the government of Letspendit to determine whether the Federal budget deficit rose or fell between 1989 and 1990. Using the data in Exhibit 1, calculate each of the various definitions of the Federal budget deficit listed in Exhibit 1. (All figures are in millions except the CPI.) Now, what's your professional opinion? Did the budget deficit rise or fall? What do you think the popular press will report?

Exhibit 1

	1989	1990
Federal Government Spending	3,000	3,500
Federal Tax Receipts	2,500	2,900
GNP	15,000	20,000
Population	3.0	3.1
CPI	100	120
Federal Budget Deficit	_____	_____
Deficit as a percent of GNP	_____	_____
Per capita deficit	_____	_____
Real deficit	_____	_____
Real per capita deficit	_____	_____

2. Consider the following hypothetical information (figures are in billions of dollars):

Budget receipts in 1990:   1,050
Budget expenditures in 1990:   1,200
Annual growth rate of GNP: 7 percent

a. Complete the following table (some information has already been provided):

	Budget deficit	National debt	GNP	Budget deficit as share of GNP	National debt as share of GNP
1989	$145	$2,700	$4,800	_____	_____
1990	_____	_____	_____	_____	_____

b. Why did the national debt fall as a share of GNP even though the budget deficit rose?

3. In order to illustrate the relationship between inflation, nominal deficits and real deficits, complete the table in Exhibit 2: (*Hint*: Assume the inflation rate is correctly anticipated.)

Exhibit 2

	Case I	Case II
Nominal and real GNP, 1989	2,000	2,000
Nominal and real debt, 1989	1,000	1,000
1990:		
Real growth rate:	5%	5%
Inflation rate:	0%	10%
Real interest rate:	3%	3%
Nominal interest rate:	_____	_____
Tax revenues:	30	30
Interest paid:	30	30
Other budget items:	0	0
Budget expenditures:		
Nominal interest due:	_____	_____
Budget receipts:	_____	_____
Nominal deficit:	_____	_____
Nominal debt:	_____	_____
Inflation-related loss in value of		
outstanding bonds:	_____	_____
Real debt:	_____	_____
Change in real debt:	_____	_____
Real GNP:	_____	_____
Nominal GNP:	_____	_____
Nominal deficit/nominal GNP:	_____	_____
Nominal debt/nominal GNP:	_____	_____

4. Review your answers to question 3 above. Does this economy appear to be better off in Case II or in Case I, with respect to nominal deficits as a share of nominal GNP? What about with respect to the nominal debt as a share of nominal GNP? Which measure gives a more accurate measure of the debt situation of this economy? Why?

LEARNING THE MECHANICS – MULTIPLE CHOICE

1. Which of the following is a true statement about the federal deficit and the national debt?
   a. Both are "flow" concepts.
   b. The deficit is a "flow" concept and the debt is a "stock" concept.
   c. The deficit is a "stock" concept and the debt is a "flow" concept.
   d. Both are "stock" concepts.

2. The external debt is the portion of the national debt
   a. owned by foreigners.
   b. owned by the public instead of the Fed.
   c. owned by any party other than the Treasury Department.
   d. attributable to off-budget federal programs.

3. The correct ranking of ownership of the national debt, from largest to smallest share is
    a. U.S. Government agencies, Federal Reserve Banks, domestic investors, foreign investors.
    b. foreign investors, Federal Reserve Banks, domestic investors, U.S. Government agencies.
    c. domestic investors, foreign investors, Federal Reserve Banks, U.S. Government agencies.
    d. domestic investors, U.S. Government agencies, foreign investors, Federal Reserve Banks.

4. Net federal debt is
    a. total federal debt minus federal debt held by Federal Reserve Banks and U.S. Government agencies.
    b. federal debt held by foreigners, domestic citizens and U.S. Government agencies.
    c. federal receipts minus expenditures.
    d. U.S. government deficits minus state and local surpluses.

5. In contrast to the debt crisis countries (for example Argentina and Mexico), the foreign debt situation of the U.S. is not as difficult because
    a. much of the "debt" is in the form of investments that do not have a contractual obligation of repay.
    b. most of the interest-bearing debt is at fixed interest rates instead of variable interest rates.
    c. the debt is payable in dollars rather than in other currencies.
    d. of all of the above characteristics of U.S. debt.

6. Between 1950 and 1990, U.S. net public debt as a share of GNP
    a. fell consistently.
    b. fell until the mid-1970s and then rose.
    c. rose until the mid-1970s and then fell.
    d. rose consistently throughout the period.

7. Persistent inflation
    a. increases nominal interest rates and the real value of the national debt.
    b. decreases nominal interest rates and the real value of the national debt.
    c. decreases nominal interest rates and increases the real value of the national debt.
    d. increases nominal interest rates and decreases the real value of the national debt.

8. Which of the following statements about the national debt is false?
    a. The greatest percentage of the national debt is held by domestic investors.
    b. The fraction of the debt held by foreign investors is about 13 percent.
    c. In recent years, public debt has increased more rapidly than private debt.
    d. Interest payments on the debt have increased faster than GNP during the 1970s.

9. The national debt does not have to be repaid (reduced to zero) at some date in the future because
    a. the debt can be refinanced indefinitely.
    b. it is owed to domestic citizens who do not have a legal right to sue if the federal government defaults.
    c. repudiation of the debt would exert little impact on the economy.
    d. the debt is insured by the Federal Deposit Insurance Corporation which would pay bondholders if the U.S. Treasury does not.

10. Which of the following is a possible impact of deficits on capital formation?
    a. If deficits hide the true cost of government, then voter-consumers may not support enough government expenditure.
    b. As government's interest obligations increase relative to its potential, the risk of lending to the government increases and lenders may charge a higher interest rate to all borrowers.
    c. Deficit financing imposes severe supply-side disincentives for capital formation.
    d. Deficit financing has *no* effect on capital formation.

THE ECONOMIC WAY OF THINKING – MULTIPLE CHOICE

1. Domestically financed deficit spending shifts the cost of government spending to future generations by
    a. causing a higher future nominal tax liability.
    b. shifting the opportunity cost of the resources used by government onto future generations.
    c. creating deadweight losses and tax-related disincentives.
    d. all of the above.

2. According to the traditional view of deficit financing, an increase in debt-financed government expenditure
    a. causes government spending and consumption to rise, and investment and net exports to fall.
    b. causes government spending to rise, and consumption investment and net exports to fall.
    c. causes government spending and consumption to rise, investment to fall, and net exports to remain unchanged.
    d. causes government spending, consumption and investment to rise, and net exports to fall.

3. Which of the following would *not* be a surprising configuration of events?
    a. a smaller budget deficit, lower interest rates, a depreciation of the dollar, and a smaller trade deficit.
    b. a smaller budget deficit, lower interest rates, a depreciation of the dollar, and a larger trade deficit.
    c. a smaller budget deficit, higher interest rates, an appreciation of the dollar, and a smaller trade deficit.
    d. a larger budget deficit, lower interest rates, a depreciation of the dollar, and a larger trade deficit.

4. Both the U.S. and the debt crisis countries
    a. would owe more on most of their current debt if interest rates increase worldwide.
    b. would find debt repayment easier if the dollar depreciates.
    c. would experience higher interest rates without the foreign loans.
    d. are similar in all of the above respects.

5. An advantage to foreign investors of acquiring U.S. real estate instead of government bonds is that
    a. government bonds are risky compared to real estate.
    b. adjusted for risk, real estate is generally a more profitable investment than are government bonds.
    c. real estate transactions are probably easier to carry out than transactions in government bonds.
    d. real estate is better than government bonds as a hedge against U.S. inflation.

6. The U.S. federal budget includes expenditures for capital investments, while the budgets of many industrial countries include depreciation on their capital assets instead. This difference in *accounting* (holding all else constant) tends to
    a. overstate the size of the U.S. budget deficit compared with other industrial countries.
    b. understate the size of the U.S. budget deficit compared with other industrial countries.
    c. make no difference in comparing budget deficits across countries.
    d. have an indeterminate impact on comparisons of budget deficits across countries.

7. Suppose the United States spends $1 billion in 1991 on a long-lasting waterway project, financed by government bonds paying 8 percent interest. Beginning in 1991, the government collects $100 million per year in user fees from the project. All else equal, the ranking of reported budget deficits from largest to smallest is
    a. highest: 1991, second: 1992, lowest: 1990.
    b. highest: 1991, second: 1990, lowest: 1992.
    c. highest: 1991, second: 1992 and 1990 (tied).
    d. 1991 and 1992 (tied), lowest: 1990.

8. According to public choice economists,
    a. it is surprising that deficit spending persists over time.
    b. it is surprising that deficit spending is such a recent phenomenon.
    c. voters will favor tax increases over budget deficits.
    d. it will be surprising if legislators choose to significantly reduce the budget deficit in the near future.

9. If the proposal by economists Lee and McKenzie that Congressional salaries be inversely linked to the size of the deficit were adopted, then
    a. Congressional support for countercyclical fiscal policies would be reduced.
    b. Congressional support for procyclical fiscal policies would be reduced.
    c. because of automatic stabilizers, Congressional salaries would be inversely related to the level of economic output.
    d. the effectiveness of stabilization policy would be increased.

10. Increased government spending is most likely to help future generations when
    a. it is feasible to finance the spending through taxes.
    b. it is financed by foreigners rather than by domestic citizens.
    c. it occurs during a period of idle capacity.
    d. it is financed by selling government bonds to a government agency rather than to the public.

11. Suppose that the Treasury sells $5 billion of treasury bills to the Fed and uses the proceeds to increase federal government spending by $5 billion. This combination of actions will
    a. cause the money supply to increase but the national debt to decrease.
    b. cause the money supply to decrease but the national debt to increase.
    c. leave the money supply unaffected but cause the national debt to increase.
    d. increase both the money supply and the national debt.

THE ECONOMIC WAY OF THINKING – DISCUSSION QUESTIONS

1. Do you favor or oppose each of the following proposals for reducing the budget deficit? Why?
   a. a balanced-budget amendment
   b. a presidential line-item veto
   c. an aggregate spending constraint adopted prior to the start of each fiscal year
   d. inversely linking Congressional salaries to the size of the deficit.

2. Which popular "costs" of budget deficits are not in fact true costs? What are the real costs of budget deficits?

3. a. How is a budget deficit financed by selling bonds to the Fed different from selling the bonds to another government agency?
   b. How is a budget deficit financed by selling bonds to the Fed or another government agency different from selling the bonds to the public?
   c. How is a budget deficit financed by selling bonds to a domestic resident different from selling bonds to a resident of a foreign country?

4. Respond to the following quote: "Most of the increase in government purchases during the Reagan years was due to increased defense spending. The main beneficiaries of long-term defense projects are U.S. allies and future generations. So it makes perfect sense for foreign citizens and future taxpayers to finance these expenditures."

5. Do you think the budget deficit "problem" is overstated? Why or why not?

6. Do you prefer the traditional view of budget deficits or the new classical view? If you prefer the traditional view, how can you account for the new classical claim that there is no empirical relationship between budget deficits and interest rates? If you prefer the new classical view, how can you explain the simultaneous emergence of large budget and trade deficits in the United States in the 1980s?

7. "Our biggest problem is the national debt. Given the size of the national debt and the number of people in the country, it is clear that every man, woman, and child in the United States is roughly $10,000 in debt!"
   a. What's wrong with the economic thinking reflected in the quotation?
   b. What are some of the true costs of the national debt?

MACROCROSS
By Cindy Kelly and Debbie Shay

[Reprinted with permission from *The Margin*, Fall 1991, p. 83.
If you like this puzzle, please also see MicroCross, by the same authors, on p. 284.]

Across

1. Index of prices of goods and services commonly purchased by families in urban areas.
4. Cash in the vault is one form of this.
7. Ratio of change in income to change in investment.
9. Figures adjusted for inflation.
10. Measure of aggregate output.
11. An important characteristic of 17 across.
13. C/Y_d.
14. The unemployment rate that occurs at potential real GNP.
15. Where an item is bought and sold.
17. Accepted as payment for goods and services.
18. Monetary figures not adjusted for inflation.
19. Federal agency that insures bank deposits.
20. Rate that shows the number of people looking for work as a percentage of the labor force.
22. Schedule that relates quantity of a good consumers wish to buy to the good's price.
23. Model of economic activity showing flow of spending between households and firms.

Down

2. Surplus at price OP in Figure 1.
3. Price floor for labor market
5. The number of times the money stock changes hands during a period.
6. A motive for holding 17 across.
8. A rise in the general price level for a prolonged period.
12. Typically represented on the horizontal axis in demand and supply analysis.
16. Type of promissory note.
19. Monetary authority.
21. $\Delta C/\Delta Y_d$.

Figure 1

17
Demand and Consumer Choice

TRUE OR FALSE

T   F

☐ ☐   1. The consumer's desire for goods usually exceeds what his income can buy; thus choice is essential.

☐ ☐   2. The price of diamonds exceeds that of water; therefore, consumers derive more total utility from diamonds than water, according to the law of diminishing marginal utility.

☐ ☐   3. The law of diminishing marginal utility suggests that you would value the third milk shake on a given day higher than the fourth.

☐ ☐   4. The market demand curve is a reflection of the law of diminishing marginal utility – thus, one would expect price to be negatively related to amount purchased.

☐ ☐   5. When supply is more elastic, suppliers will bear a greater part of the burden of a tax.

☐ ☐   6. A decline in the price of automobiles would almost certainly cause the demand for cars to increase.

☐ ☐   7. An increase in the price of wheat would probably cause a decline in the demand for corn, a substitute product.

☐ ☐   8. An increase in consumer income would cause the demand for most commodities to increase.

☐ ☐   9. If people expected the price of General Electric stock to rise in the near future, the current demand for shares of GE would increase.

☐ ☐ 10. If consumers expected the price of automobiles to increase by 20 percent next week, the current demand for automobiles would fall.

☐ ☐ 11. Economists assume that price or money cost is the only factor that influences consumer decisions.

☐ ☐ 12. The opportunity cost of a bus trip from New York to Los Angeles includes both the money and time cost to the consumer.

☐ ☐ 13. When demand is elastic, an increase in the price of a good causes total revenue to rise.

☐ ☐ 14. The demand for hamburger is more elastic than the demand for beef.

☐ ☐ 15. The short-run demand for gasoline is less elastic than the long-run demand.

172

PROBLEMS AND PROJECTS

Exhibit 1

| | Consumption level | | |
Price of gasoline (per gallon)	Auto tires (millions)	Yellowstone tourists (millions)	Air travel passenger miles (millions)
$0.30	40	3.5	7.500
0.50	38	3.2	8.000
0.75	36	3.0	9.000
1.00	34	2.6	12.000

1. Exhibit 1 presents data on the effect of a change in the price of gasoline on the amount demanded of automobile tires, tourism in Yellowstone National Park, and air travel. Which of the following goods are substitutes: gas and tires? gas and Yellowstone tourism? gas and air travel? Which are complementary? Explain how you could tell from the data.

Exhibit 2

Price	Quantity (million bushels)	Total revenue	Elasticity of demand
$1	1500	_____	_____
2	700	_____	_____
3	550	_____	_____

2. Exhibit 2 indicates the estimated demand schedule for wheat in the United States.
   a. Fill in the total revenue schedule. Is the demand schedule elastic or inelastic between $1 and $2. Between $2 and $3? How can you tell?
   b. Calculate the price elasticity coefficient over the $1 to $2 range; the $2 to $3 range. Use arc elasticity. (*Hint*: The formula for arc elasticity is on page 425 of your textbook.)

Exhibit 3 Demand and Marginal Utility

	Food			Clothing			Housing	
Quantity	Total utility	Marginal utility	Quantity	Total utility	Marginal utility	Quantity	Total utility	Marginal utility
1	30	_____	1	10	_____	1	35	_____
2	55	_____	2	17	_____	2	65	_____
3	75	_____	3	22	_____	3	85	_____
4	90	_____	4	26	_____	4	100	_____
5	100	_____	5	28	_____	5	110	_____
6	105	_____	6	29	_____	6	118	_____

3. Exhibit 3 provides Sam Smith's hypothetical total utility schedule for three goods – food, clothing, and housing.
    a. Fill in the marginal utility schedule for each of the goods.
    b. Assume that the price of food was $20, clothing $10, and housing $30. What is the marginal utility *per dollar* derived from consumption of the first unit of each of the three commodities? If Smith had only $20 to spend, which good(s) would he buy?
    c. Assume that Smith's income is $130 per week. If he purchased only the three commodities and faced the price structure indicated in b, how many units of each good would he demand per week?
    d. Assume that Smith's weekly income, the price of clothing, and the price of housing remain constant, but the price of food increases from $20 to $30. How much would he buy? How much food would Smith demand at $15 per unit? Indicate these points on Smith's demand schedule for food, assuming that his weekly income is $130 and the prices of clothing and housing are $10 and $30, respectively.
    e. What would happen to Smith's demand curve for food if his income rose from $130 to $250 per week? (Assume prices indicated in b.)

4. Suppose that in reviewing the material of this chapter you were sitting in your college cafeteria sipping coffee for two or three hours. Exhibit 4 below shows some information about your preferences regarding coffee. The column "Marginal valuation" refers to the maximum amount you would be willing to pay for the particular unit of goods in the first column (e.g., you would be willing to pay a maximum of $0.10 for the 5th cup).

Exhibit 4

Quantity of cups	Marginal utility	Marginal valuation
1	200	$2.00
2	100	1.00
3	50	.50
4	25	.25
5	10	.10
6	5	.05
7	0	.00

    a. If you behave according to the theory of consumer choice developed in this chapter, how many cups of coffee will you purchase if the price of coffee is $0.25 per cup?
    b. Calculate the value of your consumer surplus at a price of $0.25 per cup.
    c. Suppose (again at a price of $0.25) you bought seven cups of coffee. Calculate the value of your consumer surplus in this case. How does it compare to the value for consumer surplus in part b above?
    d. How would your answers to this questions change if the price of a cup of coffee were $.10?

5. Fill in the missing entries in Exhibit 5.

Exhibit 5

Price elasticity	Change in price	Change in total revenue
0.2	down	_____
3.5	_____	down
1.0	up	_____
0.9	_____	up
_____	down	none
6.3	down	_____

6. For each of the following events, fill in the table in Exhibit 6 to indicate which curve shifts – demand (D) or supply (S) – and whether price, quantity, and total expenditure rise (+), fall (−), stay the same (0), or change in an unpredictable direction (?).
    a. Personal income in the United States rises this year.
    b. The government imposes an excise tax on all cars.
    c. New environmental standards require that all new cars be equipped with more expensive pollution control devices.
    d. The federal government passes a law requiring that all imported cars contain at least 90 percent U.S.-made parts.

Exhibit 6

		a	Event b	c	d
New U.S. cars (price elasticity less than 1)	Shift P Q TE	D + + +			
New foreign cars (price elasticity less than 1)	Shift P Q TE				
Used cars, an inferior good (price elasticity equal to 1)	Shift P Q TE				
Auto repairs, a complement of used cars (price elasticity greater than 1)	Shift P Q TE				

D = demand; S = supply; P = price; Q = quantity; TE = total expenditure

7. Suppose that the demand and supply curves for denim jeans are given by the following equations:

$$\text{Demand:} \quad Q_d = 81 - 3P$$
$$\text{Supply:} \quad Q_s = -27 + 6P$$

where P is the price in dollars, and the Q's represent the quantities of denim jeans (in thousands of pairs).

a. Complete the table in Exhibit 7:

Exhibit 7

P	Q_d	Total expenditure	Value of price elasticity of demand
18	_____	_____	
15	_____	_____	_____
12	_____	_____	_____
9	_____	_____	_____

b. Based on your computations, does price elasticity of demand rise, fall, or remain the same as we move down a linear demand curve?

c. Choose the term "elastic," "unit elastic," or "inelastic" to fill in the blanks below:

(1) Price and total expenditure move in the same directions when demand is

_____

(2) Price and total expenditure move in opposite directions when demand is

_____

(3) Total expenditure remains constant when price changes if demand is

_____

d. What are the equilibrium values for the price and quantity of denim jeans?

LEARNING THE MECHANICS – MULTIPLE CHOICE

1. A rise of 15 percent in the price of beef reduces the consumption of beef by 30 percent. As the result of the price increase, households
   a. spend more money on beef.
   b. spend less money on beef.
   c. spend the same amount on beef as before.
   d. spend more on goods that are complimentary with beef.

2. Which of the following would *not* cause a shift in the demand curve for green peas?
   a. An increase in the income of consumers
   b. A decrease in the price of potatoes (a complement)
   c. A decrease in the price of green peas
   d. A decrease in the price of beans (a substitute)

3. Which of the following statements most accurately reflects the basic postulate of demand theory?
   a. Individuals act purely out of selfish motives, but they will be less likely to pursue selfish ends as these actions become more costly.
   b. Individuals act primarily out of humanitarian motives; this explains why less of a product is bought at a higher price.
   c. Individuals respond from a variety of motives, including both selfish and humanitarian impulses; however, they are less likely to follow a course of action (for example, purchase a commodity) as the cost of the action increases.
   d. Individuals' behavior has many causes, but their actions are affected by changes in the cost of activities only when they are motivated by self-interest, narrowly defined.

4. Consumer surplus is
   a. the surplus of goods owned by consumers that has not been consumed.
   b. the difference between the amount that consumers would be willing to pay and the amount they actually pay for an item.
   c. the surplus of goods produced for consumption that have not been purchased.
   d. the difference between the amount that consumers would be willing to pay and the producer's cost of an item.

5. An inferior good is distinguished by
   a. a negative price elasticity of demand.
   b. a positive price elasticity of demand.
   c. a positive income elasticity of demand.
   d. a negative income elasticity of demand.

6. If the price of grapefruit rose, the market demand curve for the substitute good (oranges) would
   a. shift to the right.
   b. shift to the left.
   c. remain stationary.
   d. become horizontal.

7. When an economist says that the demand for a product has increased, she means that
   a. the demand curve has shifted to the left.
   b. product price has fallen and, as a result, consumers are buying more of the product.
   c. the product has become particularly scarce for some reason.
   d. consumers are now willing to purchase more of this product at any given price.

8. If the money income of consumers decreased and, as a result, the demand for product A increased, it could be concluded that product A is
   a. an inferior good.
   b. a substitute good.
   c. a complementary good.
   d. a normal good.

9. An increase in the demand for milk can be explained most reasonably by which of the following?
   a. The supply of milk has increased because costs of production have declined.
   b. The price of milk has declined and, as a result, consumers want to purchase more of it.
   c. Consumers preferences have changed in favor of milk so that they now want to buy a larger quantity at the current market price.
   d. The price of milk has increased and, as a result, consumers want to purchase less of it.

10. "After listening to nothing but rock music on my vacation, I was anxious to return home and play something different." This statement most clearly reflects the law of
    a. the budget constraint.
    b. consumer irrationality.
    c. greater demand elasticity with time.
    d. diminishing marginal utility.

11. Which of the following would be most likely to cause the demand for beef to increase?
    a. A decrease in the price of pork
    b. An increase in the price of catsup, a complementary good
    c. An increase in consumer income
    d. A decrease in the price of bean curd, a substitute good

12. Demand theory implies that, for pork chops, price is negatively related to quantity demanded, all other things constant. The "all other things" include each of the following *except*
    a. the price of pork chops.
    b. consumer preferences.
    c. the price of hamburger.
    d. consumer income.

13. If a 50 percent increase in the price of hula hoops led to a 10 percent reduction in the quantity of hula hoops purchased, this would suggest that
    a. an additional 20 percent increase in price would surely cause a sharp reduction in sales.
    b. the demand for hula hoops was elastic over this range.
    c. the income elasticity for hula hoops was low.
    d. households increased their spending on hula hoops.

THE ECONOMIC WAY OF THINKING – MULTIPLE CHOICE

1. "The year 1963 was a year tobacco makers are unlikely to forget. It was a year that regular-size cigarettes received their worst publicity ever. The discussion of a possible link between cigarette smoking and cancer reached alarmist proportions. Increasingly, people were buying aids designed to reduce the smoking habit." This statement indicates that
   a. the supply of cigarettes was reduced because of the possible adverse effects of cigarette smoking.
   b. as income increases, the demand for cigarettes declines because their income elasticity is negative.
   c. the price of cigarettes had finally reached the point at which people began to turn to substitute products.
   d. the demand for cigarettes decreased because of a change in the preferences of consumers.

2. "Because of the unseasonably cold weather, Florida orange growers expect (a) fewer bushels of oranges to be harvested and (b) larger total revenues from this year's crop." Assuming that the demand for Florida oranges is constant, the statement would most likely be correct if
   a. the demand for Florida oranges were elastic.
   b. the supply of Florida oranges were highly inelastic.
   c. the demand for Florida oranges were inelastic.
   d. the supply of Florida oranges were elastic.

Exhibit 8

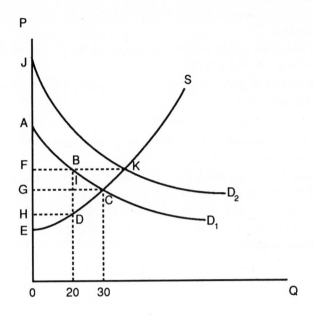

Questions 3 and 4 refer to the market for ballpoint pens depicted in Exhibit 8:

3. Consider demand curve D1. The buyer of the twentieth good on that curve receives a consumer surplus from that purchase of
   a. ACG.
   b. ABIG.
   c. (B − I).
   d. (B − D).

4. Assume that demand shifts to D2. As a result of this increase in demand, the total consumer surplus in the market should
   a. increase because ACG will be greater than TKF.
   b. decrease because ABF will be smaller than ACE.
   c. increase or decrease, depending on whether JKBA is greater than or less than FBCG.
   d. increase or decrease, depending on whether JKCG is greater than or less than FKE.

5. Which of the following will most likely cause a decrease in the *current* demand for fuel oil?
   a. An increase in income
   b. The expectation that the future price of fuel oil will increase
   c. A decline in the price of fuel oil
   d. A decline in the price of electricity, a substitute good

6. As the price of precious gems (diamonds, pearls, etc.) increases, other things constant, the quantity demanded may also increase. Which of the following offers the best explanation of this phenomenon?
   a. The demand for precious gems is like the demand for other goods.
   b. Precious gems are an inferior good.
   c. The demand for precious gems is subject to a "snob" effect, in which higher prices increase their marginal utility.
   d. The demand for precious gems is inelastic.

7. "A number of mass transit systems have been experiencing declining revenues despite fare increases." This statement suggests
   a. that the automobile is a poor substitute for mass transit in urban areas.
   b. that the demand for the mass transit service was inelastic.
   c. that the demand for the mass transit service was elastic.
   d. that a profit-maximizing firm would have raised the price charged for mass transit service by a larger amount.

8. Operators of the midway at the Seattle Center reduced the price of admission to their carnival rides after Labor Day even though "for all practical purposes, once our weekly schedule is announced, all our costs are fixed costs," as one manager explained. The change in prices would increase the firm's profits if
   a. marginal costs were now zero.
   b. the elasticity of demand were unitary.
   c. the demand for rides at the Seattle Center were elastic.
   d. the income elasticity for carnival rides were negative.

9. The Radio Corporation of America (RCA) is considering a 10 percent price reduction on its black-and-white television sets, whereas the firm's price for color television sets (a substitute) is held constant. With this information, what can we say about how the price reduction will affect the firm's total revenue?
   a. Revenues from black-and-white sets will fall, whereas revenues derived from color sets may either increase or decrease.
   b. Revenues from black-and-white sets will increase, whereas revenues derived from color sets will fall.
   c. Revenues from color sets will fall, whereas revenues from black-and-white sets could either increase or decrease.
   d. Revenues from color sets will increase, whereas revenues derived from black-and-white sets will fall.

10. (I) The number of fly rods owned by a fishing enthusiast will probably be limited because income necessitates choice. (II) The number of fly rods owned by an angler will probably be limited because of the law of diminishing marginal utility.
    a. Both I and II are true.
    b. Both I and II are false.
    c. I is true, but II is false.
    d. II is true, but I is false.

11. Use the diagram below to answer this question.

For this demand curve, the price elasticity of demand is
a. more elastic at $3 than at $2.
b. more elastic at $2 than at $3.
c. identical at $2 to that at $3.
d. equal to 1.0 over the range from $3 to $2.

12. If the owners of Pac-Kong, a video arcade game, increased the price they charged for one play of the game from 25 cents to 50 cents, what can be said about their perception of the elasticity of demand with respect to the price of a game of Pac-Kong?
a. It is impossible to say anything about the owners' perceptions without interviewing them.
b. The owners expect that the price elasticity of demand for Pac-Kong is elastic.
c. The owners expect that the price elasticity of demand for Pac-Kong is unitary (equal to one).
d. The owners expect that the price elasticity of demand for Pac-Kong is inelastic.

13. All else equal, if bus fares rise by 20 percent and bus fare receipts rise by only 10 percent, then
a. the demand for bus rides must be elastic.
b. the demand for bus rides must be inelastic.
c. the demand for bus rides must be unit elastic.
d. we can't be sure about elasticity, but we do know that the demand for bus rides will fall.

14. For a consumer who initially buys 8 ice cream cones per month, if the price of an ice cream cone suddenly falls by $.25,
a. consumer surplus will rise by $2.00, and total expenditure will fall by $2.00.
b. consumer surplus will rise by at least $2.00, and total expenditure will fall.
c. consumer surplus will rise by at least $2.00, and total expenditure will change in an uncertain direction.
d. consumer surplus will rise by $2.00, and total expenditure will change in an uncertain direction.

THE ECONOMIC WAY OF THINKING – DISCUSSION QUESTIONS

1. a. What causes a change in quantity demanded? In demand?
    b. Decide whether the following is true or false: "A change in demand causes a change in quantity supplied, and vice versa."
    c. What factors should you hold constant when constructing a demand curve? A supply curve?

2. Will each of the following cause a shift of or movement along the demand curve for electricity? Will equilibrium quantity rise or fall in each case?
    a. An increase in consumer income
    b. An increase in price of natural gas, an alternative source of energy
    c. Higher electricity prices, due to increased fuel costs
    d. The expectation that electricity prices will rise sharply in the future
    e. Lower prices for electrical appliances

3. For each of the following pairs of products, indicate which you think will have the lower price elasticity of demand. Explain your reasoning.
    a. Salt or green peas
    b. Volkswagens or all automobiles
    c. Electricity (short run) or electricity (long run)
    d. Tires (short run) or tires (long run)
    e. Physician services or bus transportation

4. "Affluent customers spend much of their income on useless items. If consumers limited their purchases to those items they needed, our economic problems would be reduced to manageable proportions."
    a. What items do people spend their money on that are not necessary? Do you buy things you do not need? If so, why?
    b. "If people spent less time working to purchase more things that they do not need, they would have more leisure time." Is leisure a "useless" item that people do not need? Explain.
    c. How can you determine if an item is useful or needed? Are demand and usefulness the same thing?

5. List three goods you buy that you think of as necessities and three goods you buy that you think of as luxuries.
    a. Are the necessities you listed always used for essential purposes? Why or why not?
    b. Are the luxuries you listed entirely wasteful? Why or why not?
    c. Is leisure time a necessity or a luxury? Why would a person who is already wealthy choose work over leisure?

6. Explain in your own words why diamonds, which appear to be useless, are more expensive than water, which is life supporting? Which law of economics helps to explain why diamonds are more expensive than water?

7. What's wrong with this way of thinking? "Although economists argue that the amount demanded is negatively related to price, the evidence doesn't always support this view. For example, in 1970 the average price for the installation of a 20 x 40 home swimming pool was $4000. By 1980 the price had soared to more than $8000. Yet Americans bought 50 percent more swimming pools in 1980 than 1970. The higher price did not discourage sales."

8. Suppose that the "Helpful Navy," a local charity, takes in donations of clothes and food in order to assist the needy. The Navy sells the better donated clothes at their second-hand shop, which last month had total sales of $1400, while the cost of rent, utilities, and shopkeeper salaries was $1350.
   a. Did the store earn an economic profit? Why or why not?
   b. According to economic theory, is more consumer surplus created by selling the clothes or by giving the same clothes away? Explain.

PERSPECTIVES IN ECONOMICS

Moonshiners in South Find Sales Are Down as Their Costs Go Up
by Jonathan Kwitney

Habersham County, Ga.

"There probably isn't a family around here that hasn't had at least one member involved with a still," observes Clyde Dixon, executive vice president of the Peoples Bank in Cleveland, Ga. "It hasn't been so long around here since moonshine was the only way to make money. My father made moonshine," Mr. Dixon says.

But two years ago the price of sugar — an essential ingredient in moonshine — tripled, and life in the laurel thickets changed rapidly. It takes at least 10 pounds of sugar to make a gallon of barnyard whiskey. With other inflationary factors added, moonshine that sold a few years ago for $6 a gallon at the still began pushing $15 a gallon.

At that price the moonshine market contracted severely, because for $15 plus retail markup, a customer can buy government whiskey. ("Government whiskey" is the hill country term for legal booze — stuff on which the tax has been paid. Unlike hastily made moonshine, its manufacture relies on slowly drawing natural sugars form the grain being distilled, and therefore its price is unaffected by the sugar market.)

Revenuers Look Elsewhere The price squeeze on moonshine has forced new occupations on a lot of people who were engaged, one way or another, in what may have been, even as late as the 1950s, the largest industry in such counties as Habersham, Dawson and Gilmer. Not all of those people whose employment depended on illegal booze were moonshiners themselves, however.

Billy Corbin is a revenue agent with the Treasury Department's Bureau of Alcohol, Tobacco and Firearms (ATF). He chased moonshiners in North Georgia for 10 years and says his team of five agents used to bust up an average of 10 stills a month. Then, in December, he was transferred to a new office with emphasis on non whiskey violations. "When I left (the moonshine post) it was down to no more than one still a month," Mr. Corbin says.

Mr. Corbin's boss, Bill Barbary, agent in charge of ATF's Gainsville, Ga., office, says the 108 revenue agents in Georgia used to spend 75% of their time on liquor offenses, the rest on other crimes, mostly the unlicensed sale of firearms. Now, he says, agents spend only about 25% of their time on moonshine patrol. To help fill the slack, the Treasury Department this year reassigned its gambling tax enforcement to ATF from the Internal Revenue Service.

So, for the government, one beneficial by-product of the sugar inflation and moonshine depression is an increase in arrests for firearms violations and illegal wagering. Some 15 or 20 revenue agents from the countryside were reassigned to Atlanta this spring and broke up a big numbers ring there, federal officials say; they promise to follow up with the indictment of 30 or 40 gambling operators.

The Pot Shuttle On the other hand, with the whiskey business in turmoil, many former moonshine overlords — Mr. Barbary says most of them — have simply reapplied their resourcefulness to trafficking in other illicit goods that are still profitable. They are suspected of being responsible for the recent big increase in the airlifting of drugs, particularly marijuana, from South America to small airstrips in Georgia and neighboring moonshine states.

For example, two long-reputed North Georgia moonshine czars, Garland "Bud" Cochran and Ben Kade "Junior" Tatum, were indicted in federal court in South Carolina last summer for allegedly masterminding a DC-4 pot shuttle from Colombia. Mr. Tatum was convicted and is appealing. Mr. Cochran — who the ATF says was shipping 7,000 gallons of moonshine a month into Atlanta in trailer trucks during the 1960s — has been a fugitive since the smuggling indictment came down. Officials believe he is in South America directing more smuggling operations.

Radical as the change in North Georgia life has been since the price of sugar rose, it actually is the culmination of an evolutionary change that began in the early 1940s.

Revenue agents agree that the old-time, 100% corn liquor made in pure copper stills — the fabled "white lightning" — was as good as or better than bonded whiskey. But when copper became scarce at the start of World War II, moonshiners turned to sheet metal vats, and in more recent times began cooling the liquor in automobile radiators instead of copper coils. The result often is a fatal dose of lead poisoning. In probably the most famous case of this, the late Fats Hardy, a Gainesville moonshine king, was sentenced to life in prison in the late 1950s after many persons died from drinking the moonshine he shipped to Atlanta.

The people who do drink it, authorities say are almost exclusively poor, urban blacks. The biggest retail distribution centers are so-called "shot-houses," operated in private homes or stores in black neighborhoods of Atlanta, Macon and other cities throughout the Southeast. Because the price of a shot has soared to 75 cents, almost the price of safer, stronger legal bar whiskey, the ATF estimates that there are only a few hundred shot-houses in Atlanta now, down from a few thousand before the crunch.

Assistant U.S. Attorney Owen Forrester in Atlanta – who says his grandmother had a still on her land, though she didn't drink – says he doubts that even a new rise in sugar prices could wipe out moonshine entirely. "The revenue agents who work the shot-houses here tell me that there are still a lot of old-timers who like the taste of it," Mr. Forrester says. "There's a certain zang, or sizzle, going down."

How To Make It Hill folks and revenue agents have described the methods moonshiners use to get that "zang" and "sizzle" in there.

First, there's a widespread belief, often put into practice, that horse manure added to the corn mash speeds its fermentation. In addition, sanitary conditions aren't always up to FDA standards. Mr. Dixon, the country banker, says, "I've seen a hog get in (the vat) to drink some of that slop and drown. They just take the hog out and go ahead. They can't afford to lose all that money (by throwing out the contaminated mash). I'll tell you, Jack Daniel's does it a lot cleaner." Mr. Forrester, the prosecutor, recalls a moonshiner who "put in dead possums at the end to flavor it."

Later, still other foreign matter is added. Moonshine usually is 110 proof when it's sold at the still to a "tripper," who usually is either an independent truck driver or an employee of an urban distributor. To stretch the product, the distributors usually water it down as much as 50%. Then, to make it look its original strength, they add beading oil, which stimulates the swirls that alcohol makes in liquor.

"It's damn hard work to make whiskey," Mr. Dixon says. "They have to hide the stills in laurel thickets on a mountain. You have your barrels and boxes of malt – it's corn meal mostly, some barley malt. They'll carry 200 or 300 pounds of sugar up that mountain at a time on their backs. All the time (the mash) is working it has to be stirred. That corn meal has a tendency to lump up. I've seen them get stark naked and get in there and mash it. If you don't think it's hard work, try it."

Much of the hard work, high price and poor quality is caused by the revenue agents, whose presence puts constant pressure on moonshiners to finish their work fast and get out. Moonshiners need costly sugar because they must dash off each batch of their product in about 72 hours. Bonded distillers have controlled conditions and plenty of time, so they can apply even heat as required and wait out the two weeks or so it takes to get sugar out of the natural grains.

Byron Davis of Gainesville, who retired in 1968 after 31 years as a revenue agent because "it's a young man's job," says he remembers capturing a lot of moonshiners by cruising the hills looking for smoke. In fact, he attributes the switch in still materials from copper to other metals at least in part to a switch in cooking fuels from wood to butane gas. The butane largely eliminated the telltale smoke trail, he says, but didn't work well with copper equipment.

Keeping tabs on sugar sales also has helped agents to corral a few moonshiners. "One of these little country stores starts selling 500 pounds of sugar a week, you smell a rat," Mr. Corbin says.

Nowadays, however, agents say they make most of their arrests through tips from informants. Moonshiners love to tell on each other, Mr. Corbin says. Certainly the ATF needed information 18 months ago in order to discover a fabulous 2,000-gallon-a-week underground still, which was entered by opening the trunk of an old Ford sitting in a Habersham Country junkyard, and climbing down a ladder. Agents believe that the operator obtained electric power for his still by tapping into nearby underground Tennessee Valley Authority lines.

On the whole, authorities say their problem is less in catching moonshiners than in obtaining justice afterwards.

Judges and juries just "didn't consider whiskey to be a crime," Mr. Forrester recalls of his moonshine trial days. The operator of the underground still beneath the old Ford, for example, pleaded guilty and received a suspended sentence, Mr. Forrester says.

Professional So relaxed is the atmosphere at moonshine trials that one notorious moonshiner from Adairsville, Ga., used to feel comfortable attending them. Mr. Forrester recalls, "Every term he'd come to court with mash all over his pants and listen to testimony in other cases to learn new techniques."

A typical still operation is financed and overseen by a man with substantial income from legitimate business, such as a farm or store. He hires three to six still hands and one or two women who live with them while the still is in operation, to keep house and to make the group appear to be a normal family. While the still hands sometimes wind up serving a year or two in federal prison, the boss, if convicted, usually gets probation, often impressing the judge and jury with letters of commendation from leaders in the community.

Discussion

1. Did the increase in the price of sugar affect the supply of or the demand for moonshine? Use the principles of supply and demand to analyze the moonshine market.

2. Use supply and demand diagrams to analyze the market for federally regulated whiskey and for federal regulatory agents. Would owners of regulated whiskey distilleries be helped or hurt by the sugar price increase? Explain your answer.

3. The title of the article says that sales went down as costs went up. If by sales the author meant total revenue, and if by costs the author meant price, what can we determine about the elasticity of demand for moonshine? Explain your answer.

18
Costs and the Supply of Goods

TRUE OR FALSE

T F

☐ ☐   1. Implicit costs involve the foregoing of opportunities, even though monetary costs are not incurred.

☐ ☐   2. Rental income foregone because the Widget Manufacturing Company uses its business-owned 200,000-square-foot structure to produce widgets is an example of an implicit cost.

☐ ☐   3. The economists's concept of costs imputes an implicit market rate of return to capital assets that are owned by a business firm.

☐ ☐   4. Average fixed costs (AFC) will always decline as output is expanded in the short run.

☐ ☐   5. Average per unit cost is defined as total cost divided by the number of units produced.

☐ ☐   6. The law of diminishing returns alone implies that the long-run average total cost (ATC) curve will be U-shaped.

☐ ☐   7. When a firm's output level is small (relative to plant size), ATC is high because of the high AFC.

☐ ☐   8. Marginal cost (MC) represents the opportunity cost of producing an additional unit.

☐ ☐   9. MC is equal to ATC at the point where ATC is a minimum.

☐ ☐ 10. ATC will always decline when MC is less than ATC.

☐ ☐ 11. A profit-maximizing business entrepreneur never sells a good for less than his ATC.

☐ ☐ 12. The owner of a drugstore may fail to make an economic profit even though her total revenues exceed her costs on labor, wholesale products, and equipment.

☐ ☐ 13. A firm can reduce its total fixed cost by reducing output.

☐ ☐ 14. A firm can avoid the opportunity cost of interest by using its own monetary resources in the business.

PROBLEMS AND PROJECTS

Exhibit 1   Income Statement

Revenues		Costs	
Sales	$55,000	Wholesale clothing	$30,000
Inventory adjustment	2,000	Equipment	2,000
		Labor	15,000
		Utilities and insurance	1,000
Total revenues	$57,000	Total costs	$48,000

1. Exhibit 1 represents the annual income statement of Joe's Clothing Store for 1991. Joe worked full time in the store and invested $30,000 to buy the store and stock it with merchandise. He recently turned down an offer of a salaried position paying $10,000 per year to manage another clothing store. He did not pay himself a salary during the year. According to Exhibit 1:
   a. what were Joe's accounting profits?
   b. what major items did he exclude from his costs?
   c. assuming that the market rate of interest was 10 percent recalculate Joe's total costs.
   d. what was the economic profit or loss of Joe's Clothing Store in 1991?

Exhibit 2   Costs and Output

Output (per week)	Total cost	Total fixed cost	Total variable cost	Average total cost	Average variable cost	Marginal cost
1	$100	$50				
2	140					
3	177					
4	216					
5	265					
6	324					
7	399					
8	496					

2. Jaynie owns a small shop and produces dining room sets. Exhibit 2 presents data on her expected total cost per set at various output levels.
   a. Complete Exhibit 2.
   b. At what output level is Jaynie's average total cost at a minimum?
   c. At what output level are diminishing marginal returns (given the current plant size) confronted?
   d. Graph the firm's average total cost, average variable cost, and marginal cost curves.

3. The data necessary to evaluate the cost of owning and operating two alternative automobiles are in Exhibit 3.

Exhibit 3

	Auto A	Auto B
Purchase price	$5000	$4000
Annual fee for insurance and license	200	100
Operating cost per mile including gas, oil, and maintenance	0.15	0.14
Resale value one year from now	4000	2800

a. Assuming that the market rate of interest is 10 percent, calculate the average cost per mile of owning the automobile one year and driving it 10,000 miles for both auto A and auto B. Which is cheaper?

b. If the automobiles were driven 20,000 miles during the year, their respective resale values would be $3700 for A and $2200 for B. Which would be cheaper to purchase, own, and drive 20,000 miles during the year? Explain.

c. What happens to the average total cost per mile as the miles driven per year increase? Explain.

4. Carl Bergstrom is harvesting some wheat that he planted in the spring. Bergstrom uses a variety of fixed inputs (land, machines, and so on), the fixed costs of which are $100 per day. The only variable input is labor. Exhibit 4 shows the relationship between the quantity of labor Bergstrom can hire at $50 per day and the total output.

Exhibit 4

Daily labor inputs	Total product (bushels/day)	Marginal product (bushels/day)	Marginal cost (dollars/ bushel)	Total cost (dollars/day)
1	20			150
		30	1.67	
2	50			200
		___		___
3	70			___
		___		___
4	85			___
		___		___
5	95			___
		___		___
6	100			___
		1	50.00	___
7	101			

a. Fill in the missing information in the table.

b. On a piece of graph paper plot the marginal product curve and the marginal cost curve. Does marginal cost rise when marginal product falls? Explain your answer.

5. Complete the table in Exhibit 5 based on the information from the diagram in that exhibit.

Exhibit 5

Q	TC	TVC	TFC	MC
3	___	___	___	___
6	___	___	___	___

6. Suppose that you want to start a cable TV channel. You learn that the local cable company charges a flat fee of $1,000,000 per year to lease a channel. You figure production and broadcast costs for each 30 minutes of programming will equal $20,000. In other words, the cost equation for your operations is:

$$TC = 1,000,000 + 20,000 \cdot Q$$

where Q is the number of programs you produce and broadcast.

a. Indicate whether each of the following rises (+), falls (−), or remains constant (0) as your output rises:
   ___ i. marginal cost
   ___ ii. average variable cost
   ___ iii. average total cost

b. Is your overall production characterized by economies of scale, diseconomies of scale, or constant returns of scale? Why?

c. How large will your average total cost be if you decide to produce 20 shows? If an advertiser offers to sponsor a twenty-first show for $50,000, would you accept her offer? Why or why not?

LEARNING THE MECHANICS – MULTIPLE CHOICE

1. Economists argue that the short-run average total cost curve is U-shaped because
   a. initially the law of diminishing marginal returns is operating, but later the law of increasing returns takes effect.
   b. factor prices will be higher for both small and large firms.
   c. the average fixed costs are high when output is low, and marginal costs are high when a plant is used too intensively.
   d. large plants are usually more efficient that small ones, but eventually bureaucratic inefficiency causes costs to rise.

2. The law of diminishing marginal returns indicates why
   a. beyond some point, the extra utility derived from additional units of a product will yield the consumer larger and larger additional amounts of satisfaction.
   b. the demand curve for goods produced by purely competitive industries is downward sloping.
   c. a firm's long-run average total cost curve is U-shaped.
   d. a firm's marginal costs will eventually increase as the firm expands output in the short run.

3. Which of the following is most likely to be an implicit cost?
   a. Rental income foregone on assets owned by the firm
   b. Salaries paid to the firm's board of directors
   c. Transportation cost on raw materials
   d. Interest payments on an outstanding loan of the firm

4. Use statements I and II to answer this question. (**I**) The demand for a product represents the voice of consumers instructing firms to produce the good. (**II**) Costs of production represent the desire of consumers for other items that could be produced with the resources.
   a. I is true, II is false.
   b. I is false, II is true.
   c. Both I and II are true.
   d. Both I and II are false.

5. The short run is a time period of insufficient length for the firm to change its
   a. output.
   b. amount of labor utilized.
   c. plant size and heavy equipment.
   d. price.

6. Sunk or "historical" costs are
   a. costs associated with current operational decisions.
   b. costs that have already been incurred as the result of past decisions.
   c. costs that add to the firm's marginal costs.
   d. costs that form the major component of the firm's variable costs.

7. The corporation enables a single business firm to raise large amounts of capital because
   a. stockholders like to participate in the operation of large firms.
   b. the limited liability concept protects the stockholder from potential debts incurred by the corporation.
   c. stockholders usually participated in the daily operations of the firms in which they own shares.
   d. large firms are operated more efficiently than small firms.

8. The average variable cost curve and average total cost curve tend to converge as output rises because
   a. the marginal cost curve intersects the average total cost curve at its minimum.
   b. average fixed costs are constant as output rises.
   c. the difference between them (average fixed cost) declines.
   d. output is rising more rapidly than inputs are being increased.

9. Which of the following factors is *not* likely to have shifted the cost curve for Slaughter's Demon Rum upward?
   a. The demand for rum has increased, pushing up its price.
   b. The price of glass for bottling the rum has increased.
   c. The excise tax on alcoholic beverages has increased.
   d. A new law requiring the purchase of an extra rum filtration machine was enacted by the Federal Demon Rum Administration.

10. The firm's average total costs will be a minimum at the output level where
    a. the firm just begins to confront diminishing returns to the variable factors.
    b. the marginal costs are a minimum.
    c. the firm's profits would always be a maximum.
    d. the marginal cost curve crosses the firm's average total cost curve.

11. Economic profit is frequently
    a. greater than total revenue.
    b. defined as total revenue minus total fixed cost.
    c. irrelevant to the owner of a firm who is concerned instead with accounting profit.
    d. less than accounting profit.

12. The law of diminishing returns states that
    a. as we continually add variable factors to a fixed amount of other resources, output eventually increases at a decreasing rate.
    b. as we increase plant size, costs must diminish.
    c. old industrialists never die, they just get smaller returns on their investments.
    d. as fixed costs increase, profits diminish.

Questions 13-15 refer to the following cost curves for one very small firm in a large market:

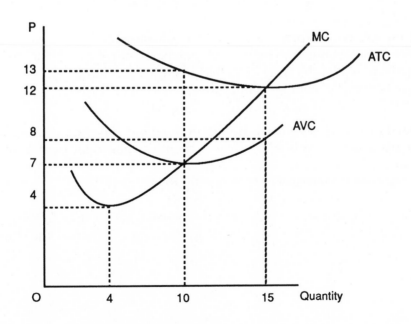

13. If the firm produces at Q = 15, the average fixed cost is:
    a. 4.
    b. 5.
    c. 6.
    d. 60.

14. Total fixed costs for the firm
    a. fall until Q = 15 and then increase.
    b. fall until Q = 10 and then increase.
    c. fall until Q = 15 and then remain constant.
    d. none of the above.

15. Diminishing marginal returns to the variable factor of production for this firm set in at
    a. Q = 6.
    b. Q = 10.
    c. Q = 15.
    d. Q > 15.

THE ECONOMIC WAY OF THINKING – MULTIPLE CHOICE

1. "During the past five years, the prices of raw materials in our industry have increased, and the costs of both labor and machinery are up. Yet we have held our product price constant, and our profits have actually increased." Which of the following statements offers the best explanation for this phenomenon?
    a. Technology and/or economic efficiency has improved in the industry, making it possible to produce at low per unit cost, in spite of the increase in input prices.
    b. Economically speaking, the statement is a logical impossibility.
    c. The number of firms in this competitive industry has decreased so that the law of diminishing marginal returns decreased fixed costs.
    d. The demand for the product has increased enough to offset the higher per unit costs of output.

2. Which of the following represents a long-run adjustment?
    a. A steel manufacturer cuts back on its purchases of coke and iron ore.
    b. A farmer uses an extra dose of herbicide on his zucchini crop.
    c. The owner of a hamburger stand hires an additional carhop.
    d. A publisher builds a new plant to produce paperback books.

3. The fact that the physical constraints (size of buildings, number of operational machines, etc.) of a plant are more binding over a month's time than over a six-month period explains why
    a. it is less costly to increase output rapidly than slowly.
    b. the long-run average cost curve is U-shaped.
    c. it is less costly to product output in the present, rather than in the future.
    d. the quantity supplied is more flexible in the long run than in the short run.

4. "Actually, big businesses are generally no more and no less efficient than medium-sized businesses even when the gains wrung by monopoly power are included in efficiency. This is the one general finding in comparative cost studies and comparative profitability studies." This quotation from Professor George Stigler would most accurately reflect that
   a. the minimum long-run per unit costs of medium-size firms are similar.
   b. the short-run average costs fail to increase as medium-size and large-size firms are similar.
   c. the long-run average total cost curve is U-shaped.
   d. the law of diminishing marginal returns is the major explanation of why long-run marginal cost increases.

Exhibit 6

Purchase price	$2000
Gas and oil (10¢ per mile – 5000 miles)	500
Depreciation	600
Insurance	800
Maintenance	400
License tag	100
Total	$3400

5. A political science major has calculated the cost of *owning and operating* a used car for one year. He included the items in Exhibit 6. Which of the following constitutes the best appraisal of his calculations?
   a. They are correct.
   b. There is only one error – depreciation should not be included.
   c. They contain only one error – omission of the interest earnings.
   d. There are two errors – the purchase price should not be included, but the interest earnings foregone because of buying the car should be.

6. A homeowner will be away from her house for six months. The monthly mortgage payment on the house is $300. The local services, *to be paid by the owner*, cost $100 per month if the house is occupied; otherwise zero. If the owner wishes to minimize her losses from the house, she should rent the house for as much as the market will bear, as long as monthly rent is greater than which of the following? (Assume wear and tear to be zero regardless of whether the house is occupied.) *Hint*: Remember the concept of opportunity cost.
   a. $0
   b. $100
   c. $200
   d. $400

7. The best way to think about marginal product is as
   a. the profit margin due to production.
   b. total product divided by average product.
   c. the change in total output associated with each additional unit of an input (like labor).
   d. total output divided by the total number of units of an input (like labor).

8. Craig inherited a pizza store and enough money to pay the inheritance tax. The store did not cost him a cent. If Craig operated it, paying himself the full opportunity cost of his time, plus interest on the money he used to buy supplies and the like, his accounting profits would apparently be
   a. equal to his economic profit.
   b. less than his economic profit by the amount of salary he could earn elsewhere.
   c. greater than his economic profit by the value of the store's rental value.
   d. greater than his economic profit by the amount of salary he could earn elsewhere.

9. Which of the following constitutes a good reason for selling a product for less than it cost to produce?
   a. The product is about to spoil and will become worthless.
   b. Market conditions have changed, and the equilibrium price is now well below what it was expected to be.
   c. Both of the above.
   d. Neither of the above; it never pays to sell a product for less than its production costs!

10. Mark owns a firm that makes waterbeds. Last year his average total cost per bed was $210 while his selling price was $195. He tells his banker that if the bank would lend him more money, he could keep his price the same, and make a profit by selling more beds. The banker knows that rent, labor, materials, and other resource costs will not decline. Mark says he is losing money on each unit, but plans to make it up by selling more and more units. Mark is
    a. clearly a con artist – he is not telling the truth.
    b. correct, if fixed costs were a small enough part of last year's costs.
    c. correct, if fixed costs were a large enough part of total costs.
    d. correct, if the law of diminishing marginal returns had already begun to affect his firm.

11. If consumers suddenly increased their demand for oranges, the average total cost curve would probably shift upward for growers of
    a. bananas, if bananas were frequently consumed with oranges.
    b. apples, which consumers often substitute for oranges.
    c. exotic hogs, which often eat discarded orange peels.
    d. grapefruit, since grapefruit growers use the same land and labor pool as orange growers.

12. Which of the following factors is most likely to shift the cost curves of an Iowa corn farmer downward?
    a. An increase in the price of fertilizer
    b. An increase in the tax on diesel fuel, which is used by the farmer
    c. The development of a new, more efficient corn harvester
    d. An increase in the demand by soybean farmers for land such as his

13. From an economics perspective, accounting methods tend to
    a. overstate profits and losses.
    b. overstate profits and understate losses.
    c. understate profits and overstate losses.
    d. understate profits and losses.

14. The shaded area in the diagram in Exhibit 7
    a. should be larger than area 0abc.
    b. should be smaller than area 0abc.
    c. should be the same size as area 0abc.
    d. could be larger, smaller or the same size as area 0abc.

Exhibit 7

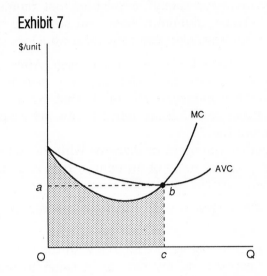

THE ECONOMIC WAY OF THINKING – DISCUSSION QUESTIONS

1. a. What are the reasons that economic profit differs from accounting profit?
    b. In the real world, which reason do you think is the most significant?
    c. Could it make economic sense for a firm to leave an industry when the firm's accounting profits are positive? When its economic profits are positive? Explain both answers.

2. a. Suppose you compute the average weight of the students present at the start of class. Then a student weighing 175 pounds shows up late and your computed average rises. If another student weighing only 145 pounds shows up, could your computed average rise again, even though the second late student weighs less than the first?
    b. Suppose you are part way through a course, and then your course grade falls because you do poorly on an assignment. Will your course grade necessarily rise back up again if you do better on the next assignment than you did on the last one?
    c. Decide whether the following is true or false, and explain: If average cost is falling (rising), then we can conclude that marginal cost is also falling (rising).

3. What are the main reasons that per unit production costs are often lower for large firms than for small firms in the same industry? Why don't the small firms go bankrupt because of their higher production costs?

4. How would each of the following influence the cost of producing new housing?
   a. An increase in the price of lumber
   b. The development of a new lighter brick that reduced labor requirements without increasing the costs of material
   c. A reduction in the price of cement
   d. A new "occupational safety" regulation that required all construction workers to wear safety glasses, aluminum hats, and steel-toed shoes.
   e. Passage of state legislation requiring all contractors to pay a $10,000 licensing fee.

5. a. Suppose some friends of yours buy a trailer. After some time, you ask them if they are glad they bought the trailer and they respond, "No, we wouldn't buy one again, but we spent so much on it that we do travel more now." Does their reasoning make sense? If so, why? If not, why not, and why do you think they do travel more now?
   b. Decide whether you agree or disagree with the following, and explain: "In deciding whether to produce more of an item, a firm should consider total cost in the long run, but only variable cost in the short run."

6. What are the advantages of corporations compared to proprietorships? The disadvantages?

7. Indicate why you either agree or disagree with the following statements:
   a. "I have to keep driving my old car in order to make up for the loss that I took when the transmission went out." (*Hint*: Remember the relevance of sunk costs.)
   b. "It does not make sense to keep operating an old machine when new machines can produce more efficiently."
   c. "Accounting costs yield valuable information, but they are not the relevant cost consideration when making business decisions."
   d. It does not make sense for a profit-maximizing firm to sell a product for less than it costs to produce.

8. In 1911, Thomas Edison wrote in the *Wall Street Journal*:

   Thirty years ago my balance sheet showed me that I was not making much money. My manufacturing plant was not running to its full capacity. I couldn't find a market for my products. Then I suggested that we undertake to run our plant on full capacity and sell the surplus products in foreign markets at less than the cost of production. Every one of my associates opposed me. I had my experts figure out how much it would add to the cost of operating the plant if we increased this production 25 percent. The figures showed that we could increase the production 25 percent at an increased cost of only about 2 percent. On this basis I sent a man to Europe who sold lamps there at a price less than the cost of production in Europe.

   a. When Edison suggested that he would sell in foreign markets "at less than the cost of production," of what cost was he speaking?
   b. What was happening to Edison's marginal cost as he expanded output by 25 percent?
   c. Edison's pricing idea was opposed by his associates. Assuming that he was motivated by profit, who was right — Edison or his associates? Explain.

9. What is the nature of the principle agent problem? How does the principle agent problem affect the cost-efficiency of large corporations in the market sector? Can you think of factors that limit the ability of corporate managers to follow policies that are inconsistent with economic efficiency (cost-effectiveness)?

PERSPECTIVES IN ECONOMICS

Marginal-Cost Policy Making and the Guy Next Door
by Thomas L. Wyrick

[From *The Wall Street Journal*, April 12, 1984, abridged. Reprinted with permission of Thomas L. Wyrick, Southwest Missouri State University]

Imagine yourself in a supermarket when the manager announces that for the next five minutes bottles of your favorite soft drink will be sold two for $1 rather than the regular price of $1 each. "Buy one, get one free."

Back at home a half-hour later, a neighbor with unexpected company calls to ask if you would sell him a bottle of the same soda. You agree, but before he gets there you must decide how much to charge him. Three possibilities come to mind — $1, 50 cents or nothing — but there doesn't seem to be any way of knowing which is appropriate.

It doesn't take long to narrow your choices to two. Only the most altruistic would figure that the neighbor was getting the free bottle anyway, and shouldn't have to pay for it.

If you concentrate on the average price per bottle, then 50 cents will seem correct. After all, it is impossible to say which bottle was purchased and which one was "free," so it may appear reasonable to split the difference and charge your neighbor 50 cents.

But before the neighbor arrives, you have two bottles of soda. Once he leaves you will have one bottle and 50 cents, if you charge according to average cost. Since the two-for-one sale was a one-time thing only, it will be necessary to spend an additional 50 cents of your own money to replace the bottle once it is gone.

So averaging costs to set a price reduces your wealth by the difference between replacement cost for the soda and its average cost to you.

Now, you may charge the neighbor 50 cents just to prevent hard feelings in case he later learns about the two-for-one special. But that is the consequence of placing friendship above economic considerations. If the deal is purely an economic one, then it is proper to charge the neighbor $1. This represents the soda's replacement cost, or the marginal cost incurred by you when selling the soda.

Sound simple? That's because it is. Unfortunately, however, government officials often have difficulty translating such ideas into policy.

Our nation's energy policies have usually been based on the naive view that firms set prices according to their average costs of doing business. Instead, profit-seeking firms use marginal-cost pricing. Thus policies can (and often do) have consequences opposite to those intended.

Recall the experience with oil price controls in the 1970s. The price of domestic crude oil was held down to artificially low levels to try to lower the costs of producing gasoline. As everyone knows, though, gasoline prices have declined (rather than increased) since President Reagan abolished controls in early 1981. This is contrary to what price controllers had expected, so they generally explain the (three-year) decline as temporary.

But a different explanation emerges from the marginal-cost pricing perspective. Oil refiners produce gasoline (and other products) from crude oil purchased from both domestic and foreign sources. Controls held the price of U.S. oil to $2 or $3 a barrel while foreign suppliers charged $36 or more in 1979. Refiners rationally bought all of the U.S. crude available, and turned to OPEC members only as a last resort.

Like a person selling soda to his neighbor, however, refiners charge customers a price based on their marginal costs of selling oil. That is, because Exxon or Texaco had only a limited amount of $2 oil available, a sale of that oil meant they had to rely on OPEC sources to replenish their inventories. Since that meant an additional (marginal) outlay of $36 a barrel, then the price of gasoline had to be high enough to reflect this cost rather than the lower controlled price.

So price controls on oil allowed refiners to pay less than a market price on some of their inputs, while they charged a market price on all of their output. Thanks to Congress, refiners' profits were at an all-time high during the price-control years. Of course, U.S. landowners and others who sold crude to refiners were harmed in proportion to the latter's gain.

The 1981 removal of price controls gave domestic owners of oil reserves more incentive to find and sell crude, and they responded in kind. As new domestic supplies came into competition with foreign oil, OPEC and others were forced to lower their prices to the current range of $28 to $29. This lowered refiners' marginal costs of doing business, and allowed them to lower the price of gasoline.

Meanwhile, because of the average cost-marginal cost confusion, Congress remains unwilling to remove price controls from certain categories of natural gas. Doing so, it is thought, would result in price increases for consumers perhaps by 50% or more within a few months.

In reality, however, controls cause owners of artificially low-priced gas to hold down production, so pipeline companies must turn to more expensive (uncontrolled) sources to satisfy customer demands. That drives up the latter's price, increases marginal costs for pipelines and utility companies, and pushes up prices to consumers.

Decontrol would allow all natural gas to sell for the same price. the owners of decontrolled gas would increase production to profit from higher prices, and the now familiar dynamic would be seen again. Lessened demand for higher-priced gas on the margin would bring down the market price of gas. And lower marginal costs for pipelines would ultimately help reduce the heating bills of consumers.

The lesson to be learned is that market participants respond to marginal costs, not average costs. If a firm's costs rise by X dollars when it produces and sells one more unit of output, then price will tend toward X dollars regardless of the firm's costs averaged over all units of output.

Policy makers intent on helping consumers, borrowers and others would do well to stop trying to control the various components of production costs. Such efforts usually end up reducing the total supply of the good or service in question, and customers pay higher retail prices as a result. Public officials should spend more effort understanding how the private economy works; then they wouldn't waste so much energy trying to fix it.

PROBLEMS AND PROJECTS

Exhibit 1

Monthly output	Total cost	Average total cost	Average fixed cost	Average variable cost	Marginal cost
1	$ 25	_____	0	_____	_____
2	50	_____	_____	_____	_____
3	69	_____	_____	_____	_____
4	84	_____	_____	_____	_____
5	100	_____	_____	_____	_____
6	119	_____	_____	_____	_____
7	140	_____	_____	_____	_____
8	168	_____	_____	_____	_____

1. The student government of a major university arranges a monthly campuswide "flea market" sale where talented students can sell products they produce in their leisure time. Mary brings her handmade wallets to sell at the flea market. Since there are several other suppliers, Mary has no control over the market price. Mary's estimated cost and output data are presented in Exhibit 1.
   a. Fill in the missing cost information.
   b. If Mary was a profit maximizer, how many wallets would she produce monthly if the market price was $20? Indicate her economic profit (or loss).
   c. Indicate what Mary's monthly output and maximum profit would be if the price rose to $25.

Exhibit 2

Housing units per month	Total cost per month	Fixed cost (FC)	Variable cost (VC)	Average total cost (ATC)	Average fixed cost (AFC)	Average variable cost (AVC)	Marginal cost (MC)
0	$ 40,000	_____	_____	_____	_____	_____	_____
1	60,000	_____	_____	_____	_____	_____	_____
2	80,000	_____	_____	_____	_____	_____	_____
3	100,000	_____	_____	_____	_____	_____	_____
4	120,000	_____	_____	_____	_____	_____	_____
5	142,000	_____	_____	_____	_____	_____	_____
6	168,000	_____	_____	_____	_____	_____	_____
7	198,000	_____	_____	_____	_____	_____	_____
8	232,000	_____	_____	_____	_____	_____	_____
9	270,000	_____	_____	_____	_____	_____	_____
10	315,000	_____	_____	_____	_____	_____	_____

2. Joe Green operates a construction firm, Joe's Construction Company, Inc., that specializes in the production of small frame houses. Joe's expected cost schedule is presented in Exhibit 2.
   a. Complete the chart indicating Joe's FC, VC, ATC, AFC, AVC, and MC.
   b. The current market price for houses of the quality produced by Joe's Construction is $29,500. Assume Joe wants to maximize profits. How many houses should he produce per month? What is his profit (or loss)?
   c. Suppose that there is population growth in the area, causing the demand for housing to expand. The market price of houses increases to $32,000. Indicate Joe's new profit-maximizing monthly output and profit (or loss).
   d. Indicate Joe's output and maximum profit (or minimum loss) if the market price were to fall to $25,000; to $21,000. Should Joe continue in business at the latter price? Explain.

Exhibit 3

Price	Quantity demanded (new housing)	Quantity supplied (new housing)
$21,000	850	400
25,000	700	500
29,000	600	600
31,000	500	700
35,000	450	900

3. Market conditions stabilize in the market area served by Joe's construction firm. The market demand schedule for housing of the quality produced by Joe is presented in Exhibit 3.
   a. Suppose that there are 100 competitive firms – including Joe's Construction – that supply the market area. Each firm has the cost conditions indicated in Exhibit 2. What is the market supply schedule?
   b. What is the short-run market-clearing price?
   c. What is the profit or loss of the firms? Is there any incentive for new firms to enter the market?
   d. Given competitive conditions, what will happen to the market price with time? Explain.

4. Exhibit 4 presents selected monthly information relating to a single firm in a purely competitive market.

Exhibit 4

Price.	$ 8
Total Revenue.	8000
Total Variable Cost	7000
Output.	————
Average Total Cost	8
Total Cost.	————
Marginal Revenue	————
Marginal Cost	8
Total Profit	————

   a. Fill in the missing information in the exhibit.
   b. Is this firm in *long-run* equilibrium?

Suppose the government decides that firms in this market must be licensed to operate and establishes a licensing fee of $6000 payable by each firm yearly regardless of the economic circumstances of the firm.
   c. In the *short-run*, how will the firm adjust its output in response to the licensing fee?
   d. If the firm expects market conditions to remain the same in the long run, how will it adjust its output?

5. Exhibit 5 shows a situation of long-run equilibrium for both the market and a typical firm in the cheese industry. Suppose that government decides (perhaps to raise incomes for dairy "farmers") to place a price support on dairy products at the level P_s and enforces this price by agreeing to purchase any quantity of dairy products produced but not sold to the private sector.

Exhibit 5

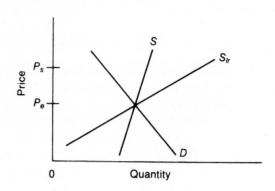

a. For the short run, indicate in the diagrams how the market and the typical firm will adjust to this price support policy. (Indicate the new quantity demanded in the market and the new quantity supplied both in the market and by the typical firm.) How much cheese will the government need to buy in the short run in order to maintain the price, P_s?

b. Now indicate how the market and the typical firm will adjust to the price support policy in the long run. (Remember that an upward-sloping long-run supply curve indicates that the industry is an increasing-cost industry.) Will the government be required to purchase more cheese per period in the long run than in the short run?

c. Is this policy consistent with the achievement of *productive efficiency* in the dairy products industry? Is it consistent with the achievement of *allocative efficiency*? Explain. (*Hint*: Be sure to decide how long the "long" run is.)

6.   Use the diagram in Exhibit 6 to answer the questions below:

Exhibit 6

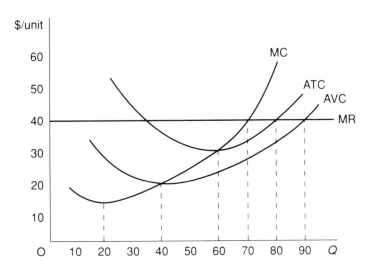

Suppose the price of output is $40 per unit. What output level is implied by each of the following statements?

_____   a.   Ms. A: "I work for the sales department of my employer. My annual bonus is tied to the company's sales revenue, so I push the firm to sell as much as possible – without causing overall losses, of course."

_____   b.   Mr. B: "My specialty is cost control. My plan for moving up in my department is maximizing the spread between price and marginal cost. Avoid diminishing returns, I always say."

_____   c.   Mr. C: "I am a middle level manager, and I have a strategy for reaching the top: maximizing profits as a share of sales." [*Hint*: profits as a share of sales = (TR – TC)/TR, where TR = P • Q and TC = ATC • Q.]

_____   d.   Ms. D: "I own this company, and I would like all of you to maximize the return on my capital investment, in short, my profits."

7. Suppose you own a hotel at a ski resort. The left-hand panel of Exhibit 7 depicts the market supply of rooms and the demand for rooms in the winter (W), spring (Sp), summer (Su) and fall (F). The right-hand panel depicts your unit costs per room rented; these costs are the same for each season.

Exhibit 7

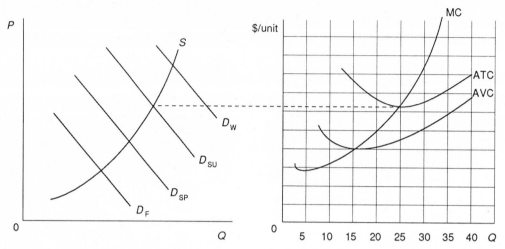

a. Use the diagrams in Exhibit 7 to help you complete the table below. For the profits column, indicate whether your profits for the season are positive (+), negative (−), or zero (0).

Season	Number of rooms rented	Profits
Winter	_____	_____
Spring	_____	_____
Summer	_____	_____
Fall	_____	_____

b. Given the fluctuations in demand and profits, how would you decide whether or not to remain in this industry?

LEARNING THE MECHANICS – MULTIPLE CHOICE

1. The reason we do not refer to long-run variable cost as distinguished from long-run cost is that
   a. all costs are fixed in the long run.
   b. all costs are constant in the long run.
   c. all costs are variable in the long run.
   d. all costs decline in the long run.

2. A decrease in demand that results in economic losses in industry A will
   a. induce new, more efficient firms to enter the industry.
   b. cause the existing firms in industry A to expand the scale of their operation.
   c. induce both new and existing firms in industry A to bid more resources away from other industries.
   d. encourage owners of resources to move their resources from industry A to other industries.

3. If the firms in a competitive industry were incurring costs that were less than the prices they were charging, the firms
    a. would enjoy short-run economic profits that would be offset by long-run economic losses.
    b. would face new competition, which would drive price down to the cost of production in the long run.
    c. would enjoy long-run economic profit.
    d. must be colluding or otherwise "rigging the market."

4. Which of the following statements is correct?
    a. In order to maximize profits in the short run, a purely competitive firm should produce at the output level where marginal cost is equal to price.
    b. In long-run equilibrium, a purely competitive firm will produce at the level of minimum average variable cost.
    c. A purely competitive firm will produce in the short run, so long as total receipts are sufficient to cover total fixed costs.
    d. A purely competitive firm will always close down in the short run, whenever price is less than average total cost.

5. Which of the following would be most likely to lead to a reduction in the price of a competitively produced product X?
    a. An increase in the price of Y, a substitute
    b. A decrease in the price of Z, a complementary product
    c. A decrease in the price of K, a factor of production that is utilized to produce X
    d. A decrease in the price of L, a factor of production utilized to produce Z, the complementary product

6. In an industry with low barriers to entry, when positive economic profits are present and expected
    a. firms will exit from the industry.
    b. the marginal cost curve will shift down.
    c. the average fixed cost curve will shift up.
    d. firms will enter the industry, forcing the price down such that only zero economic profits will be possible.

7. The long-run supply curve is more elastic than the short-run supply curve because, given sufficient time
    a. production techniques become more expensive.
    b. new firms can enter the industry and old firms can increase their plant size.
    c. producers become less competitive.
    d. consumers become more demanding.

8. In the short run, the basic relationship between an individual firm's supply curve under perfect competition and the market supply curve under perfect competition is
    a. the individual firm's supply curve is horizontal, but the market supply curve is upward sloping.
    b. the individual firm's supply curve is vertical, but the market supply curve is upward sloping.
    c. the market supply curve is the summation of all the individual firms' supply curves.
    d. the market supply curve is equal to the average of all the individual firms' supply curves.

9. The actions of a firm in a purely competitive industry have no effect on market price; therefore, the demand curve faced by the firm is
   a. unknown.
   b. a downward-sloping curve.
   c. a horizontal line at the level of market price.
   d. the firm's total revenue curve.

10. A study of the dairy industry indicates that the long-run elasticity of supply of milk with respect to its price is
   a. much more elastic than would have been expected.
   b. much more inelastic than would have been expected.
   c. dependent on the demand for milk.
   d. none of the above.

11. The difference between the short-run and the long-run supply curves for a product is that the short-run supply curve is usually
   a. horizontal.
   b. more inelastic than the long-run curve.
   c. more elastic than the long-run curve.
   d. of unitary elasticity.

12. Laboratory experiments in economics:
   a. are part of a field called experimental economics.
   b. tend to support the concept of the competitive model.
   c. have been undertaken mainly since the 1950s.
   d. all of the above are correct.

Questions 13 and 14 refer to the following cost curves for a firm in a competitive market:

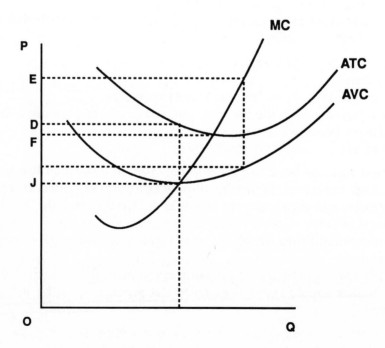

13. In order for the above firm to be BOTH allocatively and productively efficient, the market price P must equal
    a. OE.
    b. OD.
    c. OF.
    d. OJ.

14. For the firm to be in long-run equilibrium (given the cost curves above and a price equal to OE):
    a. other firms must leave the industry.
    b. demand for the industry's good must increase.
    c. the firm must invest in cost-cutting equipment.
    d. the market supply curve must shift out (increase supply).

THE ECONOMIC WAY OF THINKING – MULTIPLE CHOICE

1. If firms in a competitive industry were forced to install antipollution devices that increased their production costs, we should expect
    a. the demand for their product to decline.
    b. the market price of their product to increase in the short run, but not in the long run.
    c. that the firms in the industry would be saddled with long-run economic losses.
    d. that the firms in the industry would make normal economic profits in the long run, as the higher production costs were passed along to consumers.

   Use the following table in answering the next two questions:

	Price, July 1972 (bushel)	Price, August 1973 (bushel)
Wheat	$1.70	$ 4.90
Oats	0.80	2.06
Rye	1.01	3.86
Soybeans	3.50	12.00

2. In July 1972, the Nixon administration announced it had concluded the largest agricultural commodity sale in history – selling 25 percent of the American wheat crop to the Soviet Union. Which of the following best explains the impact of this transaction?
    a. The demand for American wheat increased sharply, the short-run supply was highly inelastic, and price rose sharply.
    b. The domestic production of wheat declined, and price rose sharply in spite of the highly elastic demand.
    c. The demand for American wheat increased, but the price change suggests that the short-run supply was highly elastic.
    d. The supply of American wheat fell sharply, but the price change suggests that the current demand was elastic.

3. Which of the following would *not* result from the Russian wheat deal?
    a. The income and profits of American farmers would increase.
    b. The price of agricultural land – particularly land suitable for growing grain products – would rise.
    c. The price of wheat would rise more in the short run than over a longer period of time that would allow for a supply response.
    d. The price of breakfast foods, bread, and beef to the American consumer would be unaffected by the wheat deal.

4. The agricultural sector is often said to approximate closely the competitive market structure because of the large number of firms and the low barriers to entry. Assume that the government fixes the price of wheat above the market equilibrium price and pledges to purchase quantities of wheat that cannot be sold to private purchasers. Wheat farmers will
   a. expand the output of wheat and bid up the prices of factors used in the production of wheat.
   b. expand the output of wheat and continue to make long-run economic profits.
   c. increase their sales of wheat to private consumers because of the higher price.
   d. produce less wheat because of higher factor prices and therefore increased cost.

5. If the demand for food increased drastically over the next ten years in the United States, and farmers became much more productive during the same period, then
   a. the price of food would definitely fall over the next ten years.
   b. the price of food would definitely rise over the next ten years.
   c. it is possible that the price of food would not increase over the next ten years, relative to its current level.
   d. the supply curve for food would shift to the left because of increased farm productivity and the increased demand for food.

6. The competitive market tends toward a state of long-run normal rate of return (zero economic profits) because
   a. firms will moderate their price demands under fear of government legislation.
   b. with firms able to enter and leave the industry freely, competition between rivals will drive prices down to the level of production costs.
   c. cutthroat competition will cause some firms to incur losses, but barriers to entry will result in profits for others.
   d. barriers to entry will prevent firms from earning excess profits.

7. Suppose that there is a sharp increase in the demand for small cars as drivers seek to conserve fuel during the energy crisis. The most likely long-run market adjustment would be
   a. lower short-run small car prices because of greater sales volume, but higher prices as the long-run stock of small cars is depleted.
   b. higher short-run prices, leading to an increase in long-run quantity supplied which would moderate the long-run price increase.
   c. moderate increases in short-run prices, followed by larger long-run price increases as the stock of small cars is depleted.
   d. higher short-run prices because of greater sales volume and still higher prices later, as plant sizes are adjusted.

8. During peak periods, like the middle of the day during a summer hot spell, power companies often experience brownouts because the quantity of electricity demanded exceeds the capacity of the power company. These brownouts are costly, since they reduce available electricity without regard to the need for that electricity, and they may damage sensitive machinery. These costs could be reduced if
   a. the barriers to entry in the utility industry were reduced.
   b. the long-run demand for electricity was perfectly elastic.
   c. the long-run supply of electricity was perfectly elastic.
   d. the power company had the right to charge a higher price for electricity consumed during peak periods.

9. Which portion of the marginal cost curve is used to create a firm's short-run supply curve?
   a. the entire marginal cost curve
   b. the marginal cost curve above its intersection with the average variable cost curve
   c. the marginal cost curve above its intersection with the marginal revenue (demand) curve
   d. the marginal cost curve above its intersection with the average total cost curve

10. "My fixed costs are killing me. I am only covering my variable costs plus a third of those fixed costs. I see no change coming in either my costs of production or in product prices." Economic analysis indicates that this producer will minimize her losses by
    a. shutting down and selling out immediately.
    b. shutting down only when variable costs cannot be covered.
    c. continuing to produce, recognizing that true economic profits do not include fixed costs.
    d. continuing to produce as long as marginal costs are covered.

11. "I have been making furniture for 27 years. I have never heard of either marginal costs or Adam Smith. Fancy economic theories mean nothing to me. I just know how to do well in this business. Common sense and watching the market are good enough for me." For producers like this, the competitive model
    a. will not usually predict their behavior accurately.
    b. indicates nothing about the behavior of such producers.
    c. will probably predict their actions fairly accurately.
    d. does not apply, because the producers do not understand the terminology.

12. "Our marginal cost exceeds our marginal revenue at current factor prices." In plain English, this means that
    a. profit would increase if one more unit were produced.
    b. producing one more unit right now would either reduce the profit or enlarge the loss of the firm.
    c. management must be operating correctly right now.
    d. the firm should shut down and cease production even in the short run.

13. Use the diagram in the left-hand panel in Exhibit 8 to answer this question. From the information in the diagram we can conclude that:
    a. Q_0 is more profitable (has smaller losses) than Q_1.
    b. Q_1 is more profitable (has smaller losses) than Q_0.
    c. Q_0 and Q_1 are equally profitable.
    d. we don't have enough information to determine which output level is more profitable.

Exhibit 8

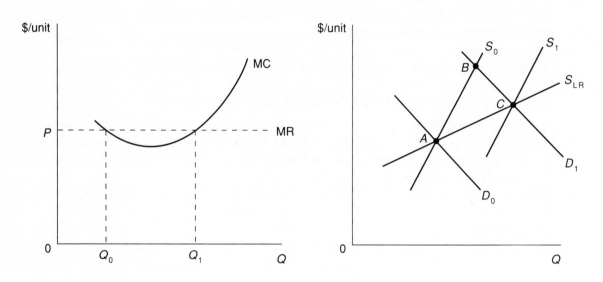

14. Use the diagram in the right-hand panel in Exhibit 8 to answer this question. Which of the following is correct ranking of profits for the firms in this industry?
    a. A is more profitable than B which is more profitable than C.
    b. B is more profitable than A which is more profitable than C.
    c. B is more profitable than C which is more profitable than A.
    d. B is more profitable than A which is just as profitable as C.

15. Suppose that the demand curve for playing cards is downward sloping and that the cards are produced in a constant cost competitive industry. If a 50 cent per deck tax is levied on playing cards, by how much will the price of a deck of cards increase in the short run and in the long run?

	short run	*long run*
a.	50 cents	more than 50 cents
b.	less than 50 cents	50 cents
c.	less than 50 cents	more than 50 cents
d.	50 cents	less than 50 cents

THE ECONOMIC WAY OF THINKING – DISCUSSION QUESTIONS

1. When price is above minimum average variable cost, why is the firm's marginal cost curve its supply curve in the short run? Why isn't the same thing true when price is below minimum average variable cost?

2. Use the competitive model to indicate how each of the following would affect the market price of green vegetables:
   a. Higher fertilizer prices
   b. Development of a hybrid bean seed that triples output per acre
   c. An increase in meat prices
   d. Increased demand for potatoes, which can be grown instead on the land used for green vegetables.
   e. Passage of a general sales tax on agricultural products including vegetables

3.
   a. Clearly distinguish between competition in the rivalry sense and pure competition.
   b. What type of competition applies to wheat farmer Smith and wheat farmer Smythe? To Boeing and Lockheed?
   c. From an economic perspective, how would Smith fare if misfortune befell Smythe? How would Boeing fare if misfortune befell Lockheed?

4. A winter freeze destroys 50 percent of the orange trees in Florida. What impact would the freeze have on
   a. the current supply of oranges?
   b. the price of grapefruit?
   c. the incomes of California orange growers?
   d. the incomes of Florida orange growers?

5. Use the competitive model to explain fully how a reduction in demand for shrimp would affect (a) the economic profit or loss of shrimp producers and (b) the market price and output in both the short and long run. Use diagrams relating the adjustments of the producers (firms) to the market in explaining your answer.

6. Consider the following statement: "Profits and losses are merely signals providing producers with the incentive to produce what consumers want." Do you think this is true when industries are competitively structured? When they are not competitively structured? Explain both answers.

7. Our economy is in a continuous process of change: new firms start up and many existing firms go bankrupt.
   a. Do bankruptcies increase or decrease efficiency?
   b. Who loses when a firm goes bankrupt? Who gains?
   c. If a firm is producing a good or service at a loss, how is it affecting national wealth? Explain.
   d. The government occasionally rescues bankrupt firms, such as Chrysler and many savings and loan associations. Do you approve of these bailouts? Why or why not?

8. Do you think economics ever can become a true laboratory science like chemistry or biology? Why or why not?

PERSPECTIVES IN ECONOMICS

The Economic Organization of a Prison Camp
by Richard A. Radford

[Abridged from "The Economic Organization
of a Prison Camp," *Economica*,
November 1945, pp. 189-201.
Reprinted with permission.]

After allowance has been made for abnormal circumstances, the social institutions, ideas and habits of groups in the outside world are to be found reflected in a Prisoner of War Camp. One aspect of social organization is to be found in economic activity, and this is to be found in any P.O.W. camp. True, a prisoner is not dependent on his exertions for the provision of the necessaries, or even the luxuries of life, but through his economic activity, the exchange of goods and services, his standard of material comfort is considerably enhanced.

Everyone receives a roughly equal share of essentials: it is by trade that individual preferences are given expression and comfort increased. All at some time, and most people regularly, make exchanges of one sort of another. Our essential interest lies in the universality and the spontaneity of this economic life: it came into existence not only by conscious imitation but as a response to the immediate needs and circumstances. Any similarity between prison organization and outside organization arises form similar stimuli evoking similar responses.

The Development And Organization Of The Market We reached a transit camp in Italy and received one-quarter of a Red Cross food parcel each a week later. At once exchanges, already established, multiplied in volume. Starting with simple direct barter, such as a non-smoker giving a smoker friend a cigarette issue in exchange for a chocolate ration, more complex exchanges soon became an accepted custom. Stories circulated of a padre who started off round the camp with a tin of cheese and five cigarettes and returned to his bed with a complete parcel in addition to his original cheese and cigarettes: the market was not yet perfect. Within a week or two, as the volume of trade grew, rough scales of exchange values came into existence. Sikhs, who had at first exchanged tinned beef for practically any other foodstuff, began to insist on jam and margarine. It was realized that a tin of jam was worth one-half pound of margarine plus something else; that a cigarette issue was worth several chocolate issues, and a tin of diced carrots was worth practically nothing.

By the end of the month, when we reached our permanent camp, there was a lively trade in all commodities and their relative values were well known, and expressed not in terms of one another, but in terms of cigarettes. The cigarette became the standard of value. In the permanent camp people started by wandering through the bungalows calling their offers — "cheese for seven" (cigarettes) — and the hours after parcel issue were bedlam. The inconvenience of this system soon led to its replacement by an Exchange and Mart notice board in every bungalow, where sales and wants were advertised. When a deal went through, it was crossed off the board. The public and semi-permanent records of transactions led to cigarette prices being well known and thus tending to equality throughout the camp, although there was always opportunities for an astute trader to make a profit from arbitrage. With this development everyone, including non-smokers, was willing to sell for cigarettes, using them to buy at another time and place. Cigarettes became the normal currency, though, of course, barter was never extinguished.

The unity of the market and the prevalence of a single price varied directly with the general level of organization and comfort in the camp. A transit camp was always chaotic. Organization was too slender to include an Exchange and Mart board, and private advertisements were the most that appeared. Consequently a transit camp was not one market but many. The price of a tin of salmon is known to have varied by two cigarettes in 20 between one end of a hut and the other. Despite a high level of organization in Italy, the market was morcellated in this manner at the first transit we reached after our removal to Germany. In this camp there were up to 50,000 prisoners of all nationalities. French, Russian, Italian and Jugo-Slavs were free to move about within the camp: British and Americans were confined to their compounds, although a few cigarettes given to a sentry would always procure permission for one or two men to visit other compounds. The people who first visited the highly organized French trading center, with its stalls and known prices, found coffee extract — relatively cheap among the tea-drinking English — commanding a fancy price in biscuits or cigarettes, and some enterprising people made small fortunes that way.

The permanent camps in Germany saw the highest level of commercial organizations. In addition to the Exchange and Mart notice boards, a shop was organized as a public utility, controlled by representatives of the Senior British Officer, on a no-profit basis. People left their surplus clothing, toilet requirements and food there until they were sold at a fixed price in cigarettes. Only sales in cigarettes were accepted and there was no haggling. The capital was provided by a loan from the bulk store of Red Cross cigarettes and repaid by a small commission taken on the first transaction. Thus the cigarette attained its fullest currency status, and the market was almost completely united.

There was an embryo labor market. Even when cigarettes were not scarce, there was usually some unlucky person willing to perform services for them. Laundry advertised at two cigarettes a garment. A good pastel portrait cost thirty. Odd tailoring and other jobs similarly had their prices.

There were also entrepreneurial services. There was a coffee stall owner who sold tea, coffee or cocoa at two cigarettes a cup, buying his raw materials at market prices and hiring labor to gather fuel and to stoke: he actually enjoyed the services of a chartered accountant at one stage. After a period of great prosperity he overreached himself and failed disastrously for several hundred cigarettes. Such large-scale private enterprise was rare but several middlemen or professional traders existed. One man capitalized his knowledge of Urdu by buying meat from the Sikhs and selling butter and jam in return: as his operations became better known more and more people entered this trade, prices in the Indian Wing approximated more nearly to those elsewhere, though to the end a "contact" among the Indians was valuable, as linguistic difficulties prevented the trade from being quite free. Some were specialists in the Indian trade, the food, or even the watch trade. Middlemen traded on their own account or on commission. Price rings and agreements were suspected and the traders certainly cooperated. Nor did they welcome newcomers. Unfortunately the writer knows little of the workings of these people: public opinion was hostile and the professionals were usually of a retiring disposition.

One trader in food and cigarettes, operating in a period of dearth, enjoyed a high reputation. His capital was originally about 50 cigarettes, with which he bought rations on issue days and held them until the price rose just before the next issue. He also picked up a little by arbitrage; several times a day he visited every Exchange or Mart notice board and took advantage of every discrepancy between prices of goods offered and wanted. His knowledge of prices, markets and names of those who had received cigarette parcels was phenomenal. By these means he kept himself smoking steadily – his profits – while his capital remained intact.

Credit entered into many transactions. Naturally prices varied according to the terms of sale. A treacle ration might be advertised for four cigarettes now or five next week. And in the future market "bread now" was a vastly different thing from "bread Thursday." Bread was issued on Thursday and Monday, and by Wednesday and Sunday night it had risen at least one cigarette per ration. One man always saved a ration to sell then at the peak price: his offer of "bread now" stood out on the board among a number of "bread Monday's" fetching one or two less, or not selling at all – and he always smoked on Sunday night.

The Cigarette Currency Although cigarettes as currency had certain peculiarities, they performed all the functions of a metallic currency as a unit of account, as a measure of value and as a store of value, and shared most of its characteristics.

Cigarettes were also subject to the working of Gresham's Law. Certain brands were more popular than others as smokes, but for currency purposes a cigarette was a cigarette. Consequently buyers used the poorer qualities and the Shop rarely saw the more popular brands: cigarettes such as Churchman's No. 1 were rarely used for trading. At one time cigarettes hand-rolled from pipe tobacco began to circulate. Pipe tobacco was issued in lieu of cigarettes by the Red Cross at a rate of 25 cigarettes to the ounce and this rate was standard in exchanges, but an ounce would produce 30 home-made cigarettes. Naturally people with machine-made cigarettes broke them down and re-rolled the tobacco, and the real cigarette virtually disappeared from the market. For a time we suffered all the inconveniences of debased currency.

While the Red Cross issue of 50 or 25 cigarettes per man per week came in regularly, and while there were fair stocks held, the cigarette currency suited its purpose admirably. But when the issue was interrupted, stocks soon ran out, prices fell, trading declined in volume and became increasingly a matter of barter. This deflationary tendency was periodically offset by the sudden injection of new currency. Private cigarette parcels arrived in a trickle throughout the year, but the big numbers came in quarterly when the Red Cross received its allocation of transport. Several hundred thousand cigarettes might arrive in the space of a fortnight. Prices soared, and then began to fall, slowly at first but with increasing rapidity as stocks ran out, until the

next big delivery. Most of our economic troubles could be attributed to this fundamental instability.

Price Movements The general price level was affected by other factors. An influx of new prisoners, proverbially hungry, raised it. Heavy air raids in the vicinity of the camp probably increased the non-monetary demand for cigarettes and accentuated deflation. Good and bad war news certainly had its effect, and the general waves of optimism and pessimism which swept the camp were reflected in prices. Before breakfast one morning a rumor of the arrival of parcels and cigarettes was circulated. Within ten minutes I sold a treacle ration for four cigarettes (hitherto offered in vain for three). By 10 o'clock the rumor was denied, and the treacle that day found no more buyers even at two cigarettes.

Changes in the supply of a commodity, in the ration scale or in the make-up of Red Cross parcels, would raise the price of one commodity relative to others. Tins of oatmeal, once a rare and much sought after luxury in the parcels, became a commonplace in 1943, and the price fell. In hot weather the demand for cocoa fell, and that for soap rose. A new recipe would be reflected in the price level: the discovery that raisins and sugar could be turned into an alcohol liquor of remarkable potency reacted permanently on the dried fruit market. The invention of electric immersion heaters run off the power points made tea, a drug on the market in Italy, a certain seller in Germany. Any change in conditions affected both the general price level and the price structure.

Public Opinion Public opinion on the subject of trading was vocal if confused and changeable. Certain forms of trading were more generally condemned; trade with the Germans was criticized by many. At one time, when there had been several cases of malnutrition reported among the more devoted smokers, no trade in German rations was permitted, as the victims became an additional burden on the depleted foot reserves of the Hospital. But while certain activities were condemned as antisocial, trade itself was practiced, and its utility appreciated, by almost everyone in the camp.

Taken as a whole, opinion was hostile to the middleman. His function, and his hard work in bringing buyer and seller together, were ignored; profits were not regarded as a reward for labour, but as a result of sharp practice. Despite the fact that his very existence was proof to the contrary, the middleman was held to be redundant in view of the existence of an Official Shop and the Exchange and Mart. Appreciation only came his way when he was willing to advance the price of a sugar ration, or to buy goods spot and carry them against a future sale. In these cases the element of risk was obvious to all, and the convenience of the service was felt to merit some reward. Particularly unpopular was the middleman with an element of monopoly, the man who contacted the ration wagon driver, or the man who utilized his knowledge of Urdu.

There was a strong feeling that everything had its "just price" in cigarettes. While the assessment of the just price, which incidentally varied between camps, was impossible of explanation, this price was nevertheless pretty closely known. It can best be defined as the price usually fetched by an article in good times when cigarettes were plentiful. The "just price" changed slowly; it was unaffected by short-term variations in supply , and while opinion might be resigned to departures from the "just price," a strong feeling of resentment persisted.

Conclusion The economic organization described was both elaborate and smooth-working in the summer of 1944. Then came the August cuts and deflation. Prices fell, rallied with deliveries of cigarette parcels in September and December, and fell again. In January 1945, supplies of Red Cross cigarettes ran out; and prices slumped still further; in February the supplies of food parcels were exhausted and the depression became a blizzard. Food, itself scarce, was almost given away in order to meet the non-monetary demand for cigarettes. Laundries ceased to operate, or worked for £'s or Reichmarks: food and cigarettes sold for fancy prices in £'s, hitherto unheard of. The Shop was empty and the Exchange Mart notices were full of unaccepted offers for cigarettes. Barter increased in volume, becoming a large portion of a smaller value of trade.

By April, 1945, chaos had replaced order in the economic sphere: sales were difficult, prices lacked stability. Economics has been defined as the science of distributing limited means among unlimited and competing ends. On 12 April with the arrival of elements of the 30th U.S. Infantry Division, the ushering in of an age of plenty demonstrated the hypothesis that with infinite means economic organization and activity would be redundant, as every want could be satisfied without effort.

Discussion

1. The prisoners used cigarettes as their medium of exchange. Was this a good choice? What else could they have used?

2. Were the prisoners' exchanges *really* similar to what would take place under perfect competition? Could you diagram these exchanges on supply and demand graphs? Try it!

3. How moral is it to use the price mechanism to allocate food when life and death may be at stake? Can you think of a better method than the one that was used?

20
Monopoly and High Barriers to Entry

TRUE OR FALSE

T F

☐ ☐ 1. It is not easy to regulate a monopoly well. The cost – plus orientation toward which pricing methods gravitate tends to weaken incentives for efficiency.

☐ ☐ 2. In some industries (for example, telephone), per unit costs may decline with size of firm, generating a tendency for the industry to be monopolized.

☐ ☐ 3. Like pure competition, the barriers to entry of a monopoly are fairly low.

☐ ☐ 4. A profit-maximizing monopolist would expand output, as long as price exceeds her marginal cost.

☐ ☐ 5. The marginal revenue curve of the monopolist will lie below the firm's demand curve.

☐ ☐ 6. Since an unregulated monopolist is assured of economic profit, there is little incentive for such a firm to produce efficiently.

☐ ☐ 7. Within the framework of the hypothetical model of monopoly, high barriers to entry prevent competitive pressures from driving the market price down to the level of production cost.

☐ ☐ 8. In the long run, the profits of a monopolist will be eliminated.

☐ ☐ 9. The price of goods produced by a monopolist may substantially exceed their opportunity cost of production.

☐ ☐ 10. Economists usually argue that the output of a monopolized industry is less than the socially ideal level of output.

☐ ☐ 11. Ideal price regulation could improve resource allocation by forcing a monopolist to charge a price equal to her average (or marginal) cost of production.

☐ ☐ 12. Practically speaking, the advantages of government regulation are greatly limited because of imperfect information about cost and demand conditions.

☐ ☐ 13. Monopolists have little incentive to influence regulatory agencies, whereas the typical consumer has a great incentive to be concerned with regulatory activities.

☐ ☐ 14. Historically, regulatory agencies have sometimes been used as vehicles to maintain high prices and limit competition.

PROBLEMS AND PROJECTS

Exhibit 1

Price	Quantity demanded (per week)	Marginal cost	Total revenue	Marginal revenue	Fixed cost	Total cost
$60	1	$50	_____	_____	$40	_____
55	2	20	_____	_____		_____
50	3	26	_____	_____		_____
45	4	30	_____	_____		_____
40	5	40	_____	_____		_____
35	6	50	_____	_____		_____

1. Suppose that you produce and sell dining tables in a localized market. Past experience permits you to estimate your demand and marginal cost schedules. This information is presented in Exhibit 1.
   a. Fill in the missing revenue and cost schedules.
   b. If you were currently charging $55 per dining table set, what should you do if you wanted to maximize profits?
   c. Given your demand and cost estimates, what would be the maximum weekly profit you could earn?

2. Exhibit 2 indicates the demand and long-run cost conditions in an industry.
   a. Explain why the industry is likely to be monopolized.
   b. Indicate the price that a profit-maximizing monopolist would charge and label it P.
   c. Indicate the monopolist's output level and label it Q.
   d. Indicate the maximum profits of the monopolist.
   e. Will the profits attract competitors to the industry? Why or why not? Explain.

Exhibit 2

3. The food service at many university campuses is operated by a single firm. Suppose that Exhibit 3 indicates the monthly demand for meals and total operating cost for the food service firm on your campus.

Exhibit 3

Sales (in 1000s)	Price (per meal)	TR	MR (per 1000)	Total cost	MC (per 1000)
4	$1.60	————	————	$ 6000	————
5	1.40	————	————	6400	————
6	1.30	————	————	6800	————
7	1.20	————	————	7300	————
8	1.10	————	————	8000	————
9	1.00	————	————	9000	————
10	0.90	————	————	10200	————

a. Fill in the firm's TR, MR, and MC schedules.
b. What price (of those shown) would a profit-maximizing monopolist choose?
c. Is the monopolist making economic profits? If so, how large per month?
d. Students often complain about the price and quality of food. Suppose that a group of economics majors was asked to regulate the monopolists by setting a price for meals that would maximize consumer welfare. What price would they choose? (Total costs must be covered or service will cease.)
e. In the absence of student regulation, suppose that the university competitively auctioned the food service rights to the highest bidder. How much would a firm pay for this property right for one year? Who would reap the monopoly profits under this arrangement?

4. Exhibit 4 indicates the demand, marginal revenue, marginal cost, and average cost curves for a monopolist.
   a. What price would an unregulated private monopolist set? Indicate with a colored pen or pencil the border of the area on the graph that represents the monopolist's profit or loss.
   b. Suppose that a regulatory agency wanted to force a normal rate of return (zero economic profit) on the monopolist. What price would the regulatory agency set? Would this price necessarily force a zero economic profit on the monopoly? Why or why not?
   c. What price would be most efficient from the viewpoint of allocative efficiency? (Assume any profit or loss would be absorbed by the government and that all else remains constant.) Indicate with another colored pen or pencil the border of the area on the graph that represents the monopolists's profit or loss. Does this area represent a profit or a loss?

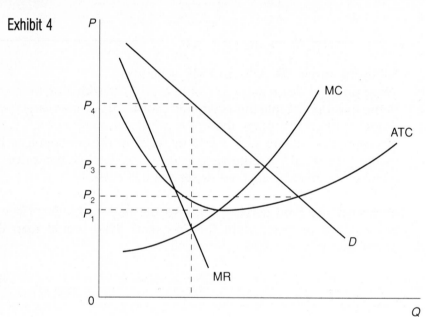

Exhibit 4

5. When a seller can effectively separate his or her total market into two segments, the theory of price discrimination indicates that a higher product price will be charged in the market segment with the lower elasticity of demand. For each of the markets below, indicate in the blank which segment, (1) or (2), you think will be charged the higher price and be ready to explain why you think that segment has a lower elasticity of demand.
   ____ a. Sales of movie tickets to (1) adults (2) children
   ____ b. Sales of airline tickets to (1) business travelers (2) spouses traveling with them
   ____ c. Sales of new cars to (1) those who presently own a car (2) those who do not
   ____ d. Sales of cosmetic surgery to (1) the poor (2) the rich

6. Suppose the diagram in Exhibit 5 depicts the situation facing the seller of a special prerecorded cassette tape. The quantity is in millions of units.

Exhibit 5

Consider each of the following alternative output strategies for the cassette seller, and complete the table below:
a. The firm produces the efficient level of output.
b. The firm produces the profit-maximizing level of output.
c. The firm produces the total revenue-maximizing level of output.

	Q	P	Total revenue	Total cost	Firm profits	Consumer surplus	Efficiency loss
a.	___	___	___	___	___	___	___
b.	___	___	___	___	___	___	___
c.	___	___	___	___	___	___	___

7. Suppose you are a Buster's ice cream fanatic. Your demand for scoops of Buster's ice cream is given in the first two columns of Exhibit 6 (ignore the remaining columns for now):

Exhibit 6

Price	Scoops per day	For questions a and b:		For questions c and d:	
		Total revenue	Marginal revenue	Total revenue	Marginal revenue
$1.20	0	0	xxxx	0	xxxx
1.10	1	_____	_____	_____	_____
1.00	2	_____	_____	_____	_____
.90	3	_____	_____	_____	_____
.80	4	_____	_____	_____	_____
.70	5	_____	_____	_____	_____
.60	6	_____	_____	_____	_____
.50	7	_____	_____	_____	_____
.40	8	_____	_____	_____	_____

a. Complete the middle two columns of Exhibit 6.
b. Suppose Buster's average and marginal cost of ice cream is $.50 per scoop. If Buster's wants to maximize the profits it earns from sales to you, what price should it charge you? How many scoops will you buy? How large will Buster's profits be?

Now suppose you go into Buster's one day and see the following new pricing schedule for ice cream:

1 scoop	$1.00
2 scoops	1.90
3 scoops	2.70
4 scoops	3.40
5 scoops	4.00
Additional scoops $.50 each	

c. Complete the last two columns of Exhibit 6. (*Hint*: Recall that the price you are willing to pay for a scoop reflects the marginal value you place on that scoop.)
d. How many scoops will you buy? How large will Buster's profits be?
e. Is Buster's new pricing system a smart strategy? Why or why not?

LEARNING THE MECHANICS – MULTIPLE CHOICE

1. Which of the following best defines a monopoly?
   a. A firm that is the sole producer of a product for which there are no good substitutes
   b. A firm that produces a differentiated product
   c. A firm that is licensed by the government
   d. A firm that has made profits over a long-run time period

2. Which of the following is a major economic criticism of monopoly as a source of economic inefficiency?
   a. Monopolists fail to expand output to the level where the consumer's valuation of the additional until is just equal to its opportunity cost.
   b. Monopolists have no incentive to produce efficiently, because even the inefficient monopolists can be assured of high economic profits.
   c. Monopolists will always make profits, and profits are an indication that prices are too high.
   d. Monopolists have an unfair advantage since they can purchase inputs, including labor, at a lower price than competitive firms in other industries.

3. If economies of scale could not be realized in an industry, imposition of the monopoly industrial structure on an otherwise purely competitive industry would result in
   a. higher prices and a smaller industry output.
   b. higher prices and a larger industry output.
   c. lower prices and a larger industry output.
   d. lower prices and a smaller industry output.

4. Use statements I and II to answer this question. (I) If a monopolist's marginal revenue exceeded marginal cost at the current price and output level, the monopolist should reduce price and expand output in order to maximize its profits. (II) A monopolist will maximize its profits by charging a price that maximizes the difference between its sale price and its average total cost.
   a. I is true, II is false.
   b. I is false, II is true.
   c. Both I and I are true.
   d. Both I and I are false.

5. When economies of scale are important, and therefore when an industry tends toward natural monopoly, breaking the industries into several firms of small size would
   a. lead to lower short-run prices.
   b. lead to higher prices or at least to a higher per unit cost for the smaller firms.
   c. cause prices to rise if demand were inelastic, but fall if it were elastic.
   d. cause prices to fall because of the decline in producer profits.

6. Which of the following best describes the supply policy of a monopolist? The monopolist will expand supply until
   a. total revenues equal total cost.
   b. per unit profits are at a maximum.
   c. average total costs are at a minimum.
   d. marginal costs equal marginal revenues.

7. All of the following except one are sometimes a source of monopoly. Which one is not a source of monopoly?
   a. Substantial economies of scale
   b. Government licensing of producers
   c. Control over an essential resource
   d. Inefficiency because of bureaucratic decision-making procedures

Use the following quotation in answering questions 8 and 9.

"It is commonly argued that, for criteria of ideal economic efficiency to be met, production of a good should be expanded as long as consumers are willing to pay a price that is greater than the cost of producing one more unit."

8. How will the actions of an unregulated, profit-maximizing, *competitive* firm compare with this standard of efficiency?
   a. Output will be too small, and price will be too low.
   b. Output will be too small, and price will be too high.
   c. Output will be too large, and price will be too high.
   d. Output and price will be consistent with the ideal standard.

9. How will the actions of an unregulated, profit-maximizing *monopolist* compare with this standard?
   a. Output will be too small, and price will be too low.
   b. Output will be too small, and price will be too high.
   c. Output will be too large, and price will be too high.
   d. Output and price will be consistent with the ideal standard.

10. Which of the following factors limits the monopoly power of a firm?
    a. Competition from producers of substitute products
    b. Potential competition from entrepreneurs who may develop substitute products
    c. Competition from all other producers seeking the dollar votes of consumers
    d. All of the above

11. The oldest and most effective way to protect a business from competition is through
    a. legal barriers.
    b. economies of scale.
    c. natural monopoly.
    d. understocking the market.

12. Use statements I and II to answer this question. **(I)** Since patent rights give firms a monopoly on the production and marketing of a product, the patent system is a potential source of static economic inefficiency. **(II)** Since a patent system enables owners to enforce their property rights over a new product and technique, it encourages the development of new lower-cost products, essential to dynamic economic efficiency.
    a. I is true, II is false.
    b. I is false, II is true.
    c. Both I and II are true.
    d. Both I and II are false.

THE ECONOMIC WAY OF THINKING – MULTIPLE CHOICE

1. A major problem with regulatory agencies is that they
   a. have no real legal power over the industries they are supposed to regulate.
   b. tend to be too tough on the firms they are regulating.
   c. often underestimate the firm's cost of production, and consequently force regulated firms into a loss position.
   d. often become a vehicle to be used by the existing producers to limit the competition of potential rivals.

2. If a monopolist selling in the inelastic region of its demand curve raises its price, then
   a. profits will rise.
   b. profits will fall.
   c. profits will remain the same.
   d. we can't predict what will happen to profits without production cost information.

3. Suppose that all wholesale liquor distributorships in your state were brought under the control of a single firm and that government licensing was used to eliminate the potential competition of rivals. Relative to a competitive situation, economic theory suggests that the monopoly firm would
   a. charge higher prices and restrict output.
   b. charge lower prices and restrict output.
   c. charge higher prices and expand output.
   d. charge lower prices and expand output.

4. "A firm with a secure monopoly in its market and with no fear of regulation or new entrants will never want to operate at a price at which its demand curve is inelastic." Economic theory suggests that this statement is
   a. correct.
   b. correct only if the firm's costs are constant.
   c. correct only if the firm's costs are rising.
   d. correct only if the firm's costs are decreasing.

5. For which of the following reasons do regulatory agencies sometimes fail to bring the price and output of a natural monopoly to the ideal level?
   a. The regulatory agency does not have all the information concerning opportunity costs.
   b. Monopolists may conceal profits by inflating the costs of items that are in accord with their personal objectives.
   c. Regulatory agencies often come to reflect the views of the industries they are supposed to regulate.
   d. All of the above.

6. Economic theory suggests that government-operated monopolies will
   a. be highly efficient and follow policies that are in the consumers' interest.
   b. be dominated by persons who, while seeking to serve the public interest, are not hard nosed enough to run a business efficiently.
   c. be inefficient, because no small group of persons is in a position to capture the benefits from operational efficiency.
   d. favor the consumer at the expense of special interest groups in and out of government.

7. Which of the following firms best fits the description of a monopolist?
   a. General Motors
   b. Columbia Broadcasting System
   c. Your local power company
   d. Exxon Corporation

8. Suppose you invent a new product and sell your patent to a firm in exchange for a percentage of the firm's total sales receipts from making and selling your product. If both you and the firm want to make as much income as possible, then
   a. you and the firm will agree about how much output should be produced.
   b. the firm is likely to produce more than you would like.
   c. the firm is likely to produce less than you would like.
   d. the firm will go bankrupt if it produces the amount you would like.

9. In a famous antitrust case, the government charged the DuPont Company with attempting to monopolize the cellophane industry. The company argued that, while it was the major producer of cellophane, it was competing in the broader market of "flexible packaging," a very competitive industry. Waxed paper, glassine, and aluminum foil all had sizable shares of the flexible packaging market. To determine whether DuPont was, in fact, competing in the flexible wrap industry, one would be interested in determining
   a. evidence of collusion between flexible wrap producers.
   b. the per unit cost as a function of output for cellophane.
   c. the income elasticity of demand for cellophane, relative to the other flexible wraps.
   d. whether other potential flexible wraps were actually good substitutes for cellophane.

Questions 10-14 refer to Exhibit 7:

Exhibit 7:

10. The maximum profits this monopolist can earn are
    a. less than $240
    b. $240
    c. between $240 and $528
    d. $528

11. If total fixed costs increased by $48, the monopolist will
    a. increase price by $1, and profit will be unchanged.
    b. increase price by $1, and profit will fall by $48.
    c. leave price unchanged, and profit will be unchanged.
    d. leave price unchanged, and profit will fall by $48.

12. Return to Exhibit 6 (without the increase in fixed costs mentioned in question #11). Now suppose that the government imposes a tax of $2.00 per unit, payable by the monopolist. What will be the profit maximizing marginal revenue per unit?
    a. $6.00
    b. between $6.00 and $8.00
    c. $8.00
    d. more than $8.00

13. Suppose that instead of imposing the tax mentioned in question #12 above, the government were to announce a price ceiling of $8.00. The monopolist would choose to produce
    a. 40 units.
    b. 52 units.
    c. between 52 and 60 units.
    d. 60 units.

14. In order to induce the monopolist to supply the allocatively (socially) efficient amount of output, the price ceiling in question #13 above would have to be set at
    a. $P = \$6.00$
    b. $P = \$8.00$
    c. $P = \$9.00$
    d. $P = \$11.00$

THE ECONOMIC WAY OF THINKING – DISCUSSION QUESTIONS

1. Economists have historically had a very negative view of monopoly. What are the major criticisms of monopoly? Which, if any, of the criticisms might be a distributional issue rather than an efficiency issue? Why might it be an efficiency issue after all?

2. a. List some real-world examples of price discrimination.
   b. Why do you think price discrimination is more common in the sale of services than in the sale of physical goods?
   c. Phone prices are generally lower on weekends than on weekdays. Do you think this is price discrimination? Explain.

3. "In some industries, pure competition would result in higher prices and a greater waste of resources than monopoly." Do you agree? Can you think of any such industries? Discuss.

4. What are the advantages of regulating the activities of a monopolist? The major problems? Why does regulation, over time, tend to become a source of economic inefficiency?

5. What are the major sources of monopoly? Can a monopolized industry sometimes be transformed into a competitive industry? Why may it sometimes be costly to break up a monopoly into several smaller independent firms? Explain.

6. Use economic analysis to evaluate the government-operated firm as an alternative to monopoly. What factors will influence the price, output, and operational efficiency of the public sector firm? Explain.

7. Under Former Chairman Dennis Patrick, the Federal Communications Commission (FCC) recently replaced profit regulation with price regulation. Which do you think is easier administratively, profit regulation or price regulation? Explain. Which seems more economically efficient? Why?

PERSPECTIVES IN ECONOMICS

The Parable of the Parking Lots
by Henry G. Manne

[From *Public Interest*, No. 23 (Spring 1971), pp. 10-15,
Copyright ©by National Affairs Inc. 1971.
Reprinted by permission.]

In a city not far away there was a large football stadium. It was used from time to time for various events, but the principal use was for football games played Saturday afternoons by the local college team. The games were tremendously popular and people drove hundreds of miles to watch them. Parking was done in the usual way. People who arrived early were able to park free on the streets, and late comers had to pay to park in regular improvised lots.

There were, at distances ranging from 5 to 12 blocks from the stadium, approximately 25 commercial parking lots all of which received some business from Saturday afternoon football games. The lots closer to the stadium naturally received more football business than those further away, and some of the very close lots actually raised their price on Saturday afternoons. But they did not raise the price much, and most did not change prices at all. The reason was not hard to find.

For something else happened on football afternoons. A lot of people who during the week were students, lawyers, school teachers, plumbers, factory workers, and even stock brokers went into the parking lot business. It was not a difficult thing to do. Typically a young boy would put up a crude, homemade sign saying "Parking $3." He would direct a couple of cars into his parent's driveway, tell the driver to take the key, and collect the three dollars. If the driveway was larger or there was yard space to park in, an older brother, an uncle, or the head of the household would direct the operation, sometimes asking drivers to leave their keys so that shifts could be made if necessary.

Some part-time parking lot operators who lived very close to the stadium charged as much as $5.00 to park in their driveways. But as the residences-turned-parking-lots were located further from the stadium (and incidentally closer to the commercial parking lots), the price charged at game time declined. In fact houses at some distance from the stadium charged less than the adjacent commercial lots. The whole system seemed to work fairly smoothly, and though traffic just after a big game was terrible, there were no significant delays parking cars or retrieving parked cars.

But one day the owner of a chain of parking lots called a meeting of all the commercial parking lot owners in the general vicinity of the stadium. They formed an organization known as the Association of Professional Parking Lot Employers, or APPLE. And they were very concerned about the Saturday parking business. One man who owned four parking lots pointed out that honest parking lot owners had heavy capital investments in their businesses, that they paid taxes, and that they employed individuals who supported families. There was no reason, he alleged, why these lots should not handle all the cars coming into the area for special events like football games. "It is unethical," he said, "to engage in cutthroat competition with irresponsible fender benders. After all, parking cars is a profession, not a business." This last remark drew loud applause.

Thus emboldened he continued, stating that commercial parking lot owners recognize their responsibility to serve the public's needs. Ethical car parkers, he said, understand their obligations not to dent fenders, to employ only trustworthy car parkers, to pay decent wages, and generally to care for the customers' automobiles as they would the corpus of a trust. His statement was hailed by others attending the meeting as being very statesmanlike.

Others at the meeting related various tales of horror about nonprofessional car parkers. One homeowner, it was said, actually allowed his fifteen-year-old son to move other peoples' cars around. Another said that he had seen an $8,000 Cadillac parked on a dirt lawn where it would have become mired in mud had it rained that day. Still another pointed out that a great deal of the problem came on the side of the stadium with the lower-priced houses, where there were more driveways per block than on the wealthier side of the stadium. He pointed out that these poor people would rarely be able to afford to pay for damage to other peoples' automobiles or to pay insurance premiums to cover such losses. He felt that a professional group such as APPLE had a duty to protect the public from their folly in using those parking spaces.

Finally another speaker reminded the audience that these "marginal, fly-by-night" parking lot operators generally parked a string of cars in the driveways so that a driver had to wait until all cars behind his had been removed before he could get out. This he pointed out, was quite unlike the situation in commercial lots where, during a normal business day, people had to be assured of ready access to their automobiles at any time. The commercial parking lots either had to hire more attendants to shift cars around, or they had to park them so that any car was always accessible, even though this meant that fewer cars could park than the total space would actually hold. "Clearly," he said, "driveway parking constitutes unfair competition."

Emotions ran high at this meeting, and every member of APPLE pledged $1 per parking space for something mysteriously called a "slush fund." It was never made clear exactly whose slush would be bought with these funds, but several months later a resolution was adopted by the city council requiring licensing for anyone in the parking lot business.

The preamble to the new ordinance read like the speeches at the earlier meeting. It said that this measure was designed to protect the public against unscrupulous, unprofessional and undercapitalized parking lot operators. It required, *inter alia*, that anyone parking cars for a fee must have a minimum capital devoted to the parking lot business of $25,000, liability insurance in an amount not less than $500,000, bonding for each car parker, and a special driving test for these parkers (which incidentally would be designed and administered by APPLE). The ordinance also required, again in the public's interest, that every lot charge a single posted price for parking and that any change in the posted price be approved in advance by the city council. Incidentally, most members were able to raise their fees by about 20 percent before the first posting.

Then a funny thing happened to drivers on their way to the stadium for the next big game. They discovered city police in unusually large numbers informing them that it was illegal to pay a non-licensed parking lot operator for the right to park a car. These policemen also reminded parents that if their children were found in violation of this ordinance it could result in a misdemeanor charge being brought against the parents and possible juvenile court proceedings for the children. There were no driveway parking lots that day.

Back at the commercial parking lots, another funny thing occurred. Proceeding from the entrance of each of these parking lots within twelve blocks of the stadium were long lines of cars waiting to park. The line got larger as the lot was closer to the stadium. Many drivers had to wait so long or walk so far that they missed the entire first quarter of the big game.

At the end of the game it was even worse. The confusion was massive. The lot attendants could not cope with the jam up, and some cars were actually not retrieved until the next day. It was even rumored about town that some automobiles had been lost forever and that considerable liabilities might result for some operators. Industry spokesmen denied this, however.

Naturally there was a lot of grumbling, but there was no argument on what had caused the difficulty. At first everyone said there were merely some "bugs" in the new system that would have to be ironed out. But the only "bug" ironed out was a Volkswagen which was flattened by a careless lot attendant in a Cadillac Eldorado.

The situation did not improve at subsequent games. The members of APPLE did not hire additional employees to park cars, and operators near the stadium were not careful to follow their previous practice of parking cars in such a way as to have them immediately accessible. Employees seemed to become more surly, and a number of dented-fender claims mounted rapidly.

Little by little, too, cars began appearing in residential driveways again. For instance, one enterprising youth regularly went into the car wash business on football afternoons, promising that his wash job would take at least two hours. He charged five dollars, and got it — even on rainy days — in fact, especially on rainy days. Another homeowner offered to take cars on consignment for three hours to sell them at prices fixed by the owner. He charged $4.00 for this "service," but his subterfuge was quickly squelched by the authorities. The parking situation remained "critical."

Political pressures on the city council began to mount to "do something" about the inordinate delays in parking and retrieving cars on football afternoons. The city council sent a stern note of warning to APPLE, and the local university's computer science department to look into the matter. This group reported that the managerial and administrative machinery in the parking lot business was archaic. What was needed, the study group said, was less goose quills and stand-up desks and more computers and conveyor belts. It was also suggested that all members of APPLE be hooked into one computer so that cars could be really shifted to the most accessible spaces.

Spokesmen for the industry took up the cry of administrative modernization. Subtle warnings appeared in the local papers suggesting that if the industry did not get its own house in order, heavy-handed regulation could be anticipated. The city council asked for reports on failures to deliver cars and decreed that this would include any failure to put a driver in his car within five minutes of demand without a new dent.

Some of the professional operators actually installed computer equipment to handle their ticketing and parking logistics problems. And some added second stories to their parking lots. Others bought up additional space, thereby raising the value of vacant lots in the area. but many simply added a few additional car parkers and hoped that the problem would go away without a substantial investment of capital.

The commercial operators also began arguing that they needed higher parking fees because of their higher operating costs. Everyone agreed that costs for operating a parking lot were certainly higher than before the licensing ordinance. So the city council granted a request for an across-the-board ten percent hike in fees. The local newspaper editorially hoped that this would ease the problem without still higher fees being necessary. In a way, it did. A lot of people stopped driving. They began using city buses, or they chartered private buses for the game. Some stayed home and watched the game on TV. A new study group on fees was appointed.

Just about then several other blows fell on the parking lot business. Bus transportation to the area near the stadium was improved with a federal subsidy to the municipal bus company. And several new suburban shopping centers caused a loss of automobile traffic in the older area of town. But most dramatic of all, the local university, under severe pressure from its students and faculty, dropped intercollegiate football altogether and converted the stadium into a park for underprivileged children.

The impact of these evens on the commercial parking lots was swift. Income declined drastically. The companies that had borrowed money to finance the expansion everyone wanted earlier were hardest hit. Two declared bankruptcy, and many had to be absorbed by financially stronger companies. Layoffs among car parkers were enormous, and APPLE actually petitioned the city council to guarantee the premiums on their liability insurance policies so that people would not be afraid to park commercially. This idea was suggested to APPLE by recent congressional legislation creating an insurance program for stock brokers.

A spokesman for APPLE made the following public statement: New organizations or arrangements may be necessary to straighten out this problem. There has been a failure in both the structure of the industry and the regulatory scheme. New and better regulation is clearly demanded. A sound parking lot business is necessary for a healthy urban economy." The statement was hailed by the industry as being very statesmanlike, though everyone speculated about what he really meant.

Others in the industry demanded that the city bus service be curtailed during the emergency. The city council granted every rate increase the lots requested. There were no requests for rate decreases, but the weaker lots began offering prizes and other subtle or covert rebates to private bus companies who would park with them. In fact, this problem became so serious and uncontrollable that one owner of a large chain proclaimed that old-fashioned price competition for this business would be desirable. This again was hailed as statesmanlike, but everyone assumed that he really meant something else. No one proposed repeal of the licensing ordinance.

One other thing happened. Under pressure from APPLE, the city council decreed that henceforth no parking would be allowed on any streets in the downtown area of town. The local merchants were extremely unhappy about this, however, and the council rescinded the ordinance at the next meeting, citing a computer error as the basis for the earlier restriction.

The ultimate resolution of the "new" parking problem is not in sight. The parking lot industry in this town not very far from here is now said to be a depressed business, even a sick one. Everyone looks to the city council for a solution, but things will probably limp along as they are for quite a while, picking up with an occasional professional football game and dropping low with bad weather.

MORAL. If you risk your lot under an apple tree, you may get hit in the head.

Discussion

1. In this fable, who was protected by the regulations? From what? At what cost?

2. Do you see similar situations in regulated businesses in your own area? In state or federally regulated industries? How are they similar? How do they differ? Who gains, and at what cost?

3. In this article, businesses that lobbied to protect themselves form competition ended up hurting themselves in the long run. Do you think that this is a typical result, or did author Manne stretch things a bit to make it come out this way? Explain your answer.

21
Between Competition and Monopoly: Models of Rivalry and Strategy

TRUE OR FALSE

T F

☐ ☐   1.   Oligopolistic industries will be dominated by a small number of firms.

☐ ☐   2.   Economies of scale are an important reason for oligopoly in the automobile, typewriter, and steel industries.

☐ ☐   3.   There are no local restraints on collusive behavior by oligopolistic firms.

☐ ☐   4.   Firms in oligopolistic industries make profits because they are free from competitive pressures.

☐ ☐   5.   Collusion would be easier (less costly) if the barriers to entry were higher and the number of producers in the industry were smaller.

☐ ☐   6.   Inability to police the nonprice characteristics of a product offered by a competitive firm reduces the likelihood of successful collusion among oligopolists.

☐ ☐   7.   The monopolistic competitor who is better able to correctly anticipate changes in consumer demand and adjust to those changes is, *ceteris parabus*, more likely to make economic profits.

☐ ☐   8.   A monopolistically competitive firm maximizes profits by producing at a level of output at which price is equal to short-run marginal cost.

☐ ☐   9.   In recent years, concentration has increased in almost all manufacturing industries.

☐ ☐ 10.   Monopolistically competitive firms often emphasize quality, location, and advertising as competitive weapons (in addition to price competition).

☐ ☐ 11.   The smart investor will purchase the stock of firms in oligopolistic industries since the high average rate of profit in these industries will mean a greater return on the investor's dollar.

☐ ☐ 12.   The larger the number of competitors and the more similar the products offered by the firms of a monopolistically competitive industry, the greater will be the elasticity of the individual seller's demand curve.

PROBLEMS AND PROJECTS

Exhibit 1

Output (market)	Price	Total revenue (market)	Total revenue (each firm)	Average total cost (firm)
1,000	$750	_____	_____	$200
2,000	500	_____	_____	170
3,000	450	_____	_____	150
4,000	400	_____	_____	150
8,000	300	_____	_____	150
12,000	250	_____	_____	150
16,000	200	_____	_____	150
20,000	175	_____	_____	150
24,000	150	_____	_____	150
28,000	125	_____	_____	150
32,000	100	_____	_____	150

1. Currently there are four rival firms in the typewriter industry. Assume that the four firms are of identical size, produce similar products (consumers think they are homogeneous), and have identical cost schedules. The cost schedule for a *firm* along with the market demand schedule is presented in Exhibit 1.
   a. Fill in the missing information.
   b. What price would prevail if there were no collusion and each firm sought to offer the consumer a better deal than that available from rivals (as long as the firm's opportunity cost of production was covered)? How many units would be sold in the market? How many would each firm sell?
   c. If each firm produced one-fourth of the total market, what market price would prevail when *each firm* supplied 1000 units? 2000 units? 3000 units?
   d. Which of the listed prices would prevail if the firms acted cooperatively (so as to maximize their joint profit)?
   e. Given the demand and cost conditions in this oligopolistic industry, what outcome would be most likely to prevail in the real world? Explain.

2. Johnson Tricycle Manufacturers currently sells 20,000 tricycles per month at a price of $10 each. The firm's fixed costs are currently 60 percent of sales revenues. At the current level of production, the firm's average variable cost per tricycle is $4. The firm is just covering its total cost. The sales manager argues that a reduction in the price of tricycles to $9 would enable the firm to earn a monthly profit of $5000 as the results of increased sales. Since the firm has ample capacity, the necessary expansion in output could be accomplished without any increase in the average variable cost of tricycles.
   a. Does the sales manager's argument make sense? Explain.
   b. How much would sales have to increase in order for the firm to earn a monthly profit of $5000? (*Hint*: Remember that fixed costs will not vary with output.)
   c. What price elasticity of demand is necessary for the sales manager's prediction to be realized?

3. Sociable Corporation (SC) produces and sells gizmos in an oligopolistic market comprised of only a very few firms. Exhibit 2 presents two different demand schedules for SC. The first one shows how SC's quantity demanded varies when the industry price varies, and the second one shows how SC's quantity demanded varies when only SC's price varies. Assume throughout that SC's marginal cost is constant at $10 per gizmo and that fixed costs are zero.

Exhibit 2

| | Demand when industry price varies | | | | Demand when only SC's price varies | | |
Quantity	Price	Total revenue	Marginal revenue	Quantity	Price	Total revenue	Marginal revenue
1	$130	$130	$130	1	$100	$100	$100
2	110	220	90	2	90	180	80
3	90	___	___	3	80	___	___
4	70	___	___	4	70	___	___
5	50	___	___	5	60	___	___
6	30	___	___	6	50	___	___
7	10	___	___	7	40	___	___
8	0	___	___	8	30	___	___
9	0	___	___	9	20	___	___
10	0	0	0	10	10	___	___

a. Fill in the missing information (*Hint*: Remember that marginal revenue can be negative as well as positive.)

b. Suppose the industry could engage in successful collusion. What price would SC want the industry to set? Calculate SC's profits at this price. Explain your answer.

c. Suppose the industry has established the collusively determined price of part b above and that SC believes it could "cheat" on the agreement and not be detected. Assuming that sales of gizmos must be in whole units, what quantity would SC decide to sell? What price would it charge? Compare SC's new profit level to the level it achieved in part b.

d. If each firm in the industry believes what SC believes, could each firm increase its profits the way SC believes it can? Explain.

4. International Oil, Incorporated (IOI), has come under public criticism for earning excessive profits. In its defense, IOI releases information indicating that profit constitutes only $0.01 of the firm's price of $1.00 per gallon of gasoline. Is this information useful in resolving the issue? If no, what type of profit information would you want in order to attempt a resolution?

5. Consider the following production information about the U.S. steel industry (units are in millions of tons):

Firm	Production	Firm	Production
Armco Steel	8.1	National Steel	9.4
Bethlehem Steel	16.6	Republic Steel	9.2
Inland Steel	7.8	United States Steel	28.8
Jones and Laughlin	7.0	Remaining (small) producers	33.3
Lykes Corporation	4.5		

  a. Construct a four firm concentration ratio (CR4) for the U.S. steel industry.

  b. A loose rule of thumb suggests the following tentative classification of industry structure:

  CR4 of 70 or more: tight oligopoly;
  CR4 between 50 and 70: loose oligopoly;
  CR4 below 50: competitive.

  What category describes the steel industry? What is the minimum average market share of the top four firms in a loose oligopoly?

6. Suppose the cardboard box industry is suspected of collusion (the industry has, in fact, been accused of collusion in the past). Classify each of the following items as likely evidence in support (+) or against (−) successful collusion.

  _____ a. The four firm concentration ratio of cardboard box manufacturers is 19.

  _____ b. Members of an industry trade association exchange invoice information about the prices charged to specified customers.

  _____ c. The members of the trade association account for 90 percent of the cardboard box output.

  _____ d. Cardboard boxes are standardized (homogeneous) products and prices are pretty uniform throughout the industry.

  _____ e. At the current price level, demand is inelastic.

  _____ f. Throughout the period of trade association activity, cardboard box prices have been falling and entry has been occurring.

LEARNING THE MECHANICS – MULTIPLE CHOICE

1. Long-run economic profit requires
  a. barriers to market entry that limit potential competitors.
  b. an inelastic market demand for the product.
  c. free entry, but a small number of competitors.
  d. a differentiated product.

2. Which of the following factors will weaken the ability of an oligopolist to charge a price in excess of production cost?
  a. The existence of a small number of competitors
  b. An inelastic demand for one's product
  c. Quality competition from one's rivals
  d. Licensing procedures and other factors that limit entry into the industry

3. For the monopolistic competitor
    a. price will exceed the firm's short-run marginal cost at the profit-maximizing output level; in the long run, however, economic profit will be eliminated.
    b. price will equal marginal cost at the profit-maximizing output level; long-run profits will be positive.
    c. price will always equal average total cost in the short run; in the long run either profits or losses may result.
    d. marginal revenue will equal average total cost in the short run; long-run economic profits will be zero.

4. Which of the following factors will make it more difficult for oligopolistic firms to collude on prices?
    a. A reduction in the number of firms
    b. A homogeneous product
    c. High barriers to entry
    d. Instability and uncertainty concerning the demand and cost conditions in the industry

5. Economic theory suggests that prices in oligopolistic industries will
    a. be above the cost of production, but less than what a monopolist would charge.
    b. be below the firms' marginal costs, but higher than their average total costs.
    c. be equal to the firms' per unit costs.
    d. rise as the number of rival firms in the industry increases.

6. Suppose you were asked to determine whether a firm was perfectly competitive or monopolistically competitive by looking at a graph of the firm's cost and revenue curves. The key is that for the monopolistically competitive firm,
    a. the firm's marginal revenue curve lies to the left and below the demand curve, not above and to the right.
    b. there are only total costs, not variable costs, on the graph.
    c. the firm's demand curve is downward sloping.
    d. all of the above.

7. Using industrial concentration ratios as the measure of competitiveness, one finds that during the last three decades, the U.S. economy has
    a. become more competitive.
    b. become less competitive.
    c. on balance, changed little in competitiveness.
    d. become fully dominated by highly concentrated, oligopolistic industries.

8. Amy is widely known among restauranteurs in Seattle as the best fast-food restaurant manager in town. Since the restaurant business is monopolistically competitive, Amy
    a. would make more money if she could establish her own restaurant.
    b. would make just as much money working for one of the many firms bidding for her services as she would with her own firm.
    c. can never be paid what she is really worth in such an industry.
    d. could make long-run economic profit if she established her own restaurant.

9. It would be difficult for a group of oligopolists to follow a price and output policy similar to that of a monopolist if
    a. there were many producers.
    b. firms could not compete on the basis of quality (of the product).
    c. supply of substitute products were highly inelastic.
    d. prices charged in some states were higher because of higher sales taxes.

10. The concentration ratio of an industry provides
    a. an excellent measure of competitiveness in the industry.
    b. an indication, albeit an imperfect one, of competitiveness in the industry.
    c. a measure of the availability for the products of the industry.
    d. no indication at all of competitiveness in the industry.

11. Which of the following is the most accurate description of the conditions that exist under the monopolistically competitive market structure?
    a. Barriers to entry are low; firms will consistently incur economic losses in the short run.
    b. Barriers to entry are low; firms will realize normal profits in the short run, but losses in the long run.
    c. Barriers to entry are low; firms may realize either profits or losses in the short run, but they will tend to realize a normal profit in the long run.
    d. Barriers to entry are high; firms will consistently realize economic profits in the short run.

12. If economic profits were present in a monopolistically competitive industry
    a. production inefficiency would develop, causing costs to increase until the profits had been eliminated.
    b. firms would operate in the short run, but they would be forced out of business in the long run as competition eliminated the economic profit.
    c. competition from new entrants would expand supply and depress prices until the economic profits had been eliminated.
    d. the firms would lower their prices, since profits would attract government regulation.

13. Comparative profitability studies between oligopolistic and competitive industries suggest that
    a. dynamic competitive forces are one important determinant of profitability in oligopolistic as well as competitive industries.
    b. collusion and monopoly profit are prevalent in almost all oligopolistic sectors.
    c. competition has little effect on the profitability of firms.
    d. large firms almost always earn a higher rate of return than their smaller counterparts.

14. If one firm produced 60 percent of an industry's output, the industry's four-firm concentration ratio would be
    a. about 15 percent.
    b. about 30 percent.
    c. between 60 and 100 percent.
    d. about 240 percent.

THE ECONOMIC WAY OF THINKING – MULTIPLE CHOICE

1. If large automobile manufacturers were to collude secretly on prices, as has often been charged, what short-run factor might tend to undermine the effectiveness of their agreements?
    a. The economies of scale in the industry
    b. The size of the firms in the industry
    c. The ease with which a new competitor could enter the industry if profitability increased
    d. The difficulty of policing style and quality competition among firms.

2. Which of the following would be the most likely to happen if the firms in a monopolistically competitive industry were suffering economic losses?
    a. The firms would eliminate production inefficiencies, which must be the source of the losses.
    b. Some firms would leave the industry, and the market price would rise.
    c. Some firms would operate in the short run, but all firms would go out of business in the long run.
    d. All firms in the industry would continue producing at their current output levels, but they would charge a higher price.

3. If you were going to invest in the stock market, you would be
    a. wise to purchase the stock of an oligopolist so that you could share in the oligopoly profits.
    b. unwise to purchase only the stock of an oligopolist, because the inefficiency of oligopoly often leads to losses.
    c. wise to purchase the stock of an oligopolist if the firm had made economic profit in the long run.
    d. unwise to purchase only the stock of an oligopolist, because the expectation of future profits has already increased the current market value of the stock.

4. Neither pure nor monopolistic competitors will be able to earn long-run economic profit because
    a. with free entry and exit, competition between rivals will drive prices down to the level of production costs.
    b. high barriers to entry will prevent the firms from earning excess profits.
    c. government legislation will cause firms to moderate their price demands.
    d. cutthroat competition will cause some firms to incur losses, but barriers to entry will result in profits for others.

5. A profit-maximizing oligopolist who has invested heavily in brand-name advertising does not want adverse publicity. The owner of such a firm would pay more to avoid shoddy output and to keep its good (brand) name if
    a. it were part of an oligopolistic group of firms that looked forward to high economic profits.
    b. government price regulation were about to be imposed, ensuring low future profits.
    c. it were part of an oligopolistic group of firms in which secret competition was hindering collusion.
    d. it dealt with buyers who shopped only for the lowest available price.

6. The local plumbing contractors have called a meeting to discuss ways to improve their long-run profitability. Of the four plans being discussed seriously, which would most likely increase their long-run profits?
    a. An "off-the-record" agreement that each plumbing contractor would increase his or her prices by an average of 7 percent.
    b. Passage of legislation requiring the local government to share the cost of installing all private sewage systems
    c. Passage of legislation requiring *new* contractors to pass a stiff licensing exam and to pay a $5000 fee to obtain a contractor's license
    d. Repeal of the current tax on installations of plumbing units

7. "If a few firms colluded successfully and looked forward to long-run economic profits, they would lose all monetary incentive to innovate. Successful collusion eliminates any contribution to profit that innovation would otherwise make." This statement is
   a. essentially correct.
   b. correct, if quality competition had been eliminated.
   c. correct, if there were few substitutes for the product produced by the colluding firms.
   d. incorrect, because lower costs for producing the same good *or* a better product for the same cost would benefit even a group of colluding oligopolists.

8. Suppose that recent fuel shortages and rising fuel prices have raised the delivery costs for diaper services in Los Angeles. If that industry were characterized by monopolistic competition, we could expect that
   a. competition would keep the price of diaper service the same as before, until eventually some firms were forced out of business by rising costs.
   b. diaper service prices would rise quickly (by the full amount of the cost increase multiplied by the market rate of interest.)
   c. diaper service prices would rise, and in the long run the full amount of increase in cost would be passed along to consumers.
   d. if the diaper service industry were in long-run equilibrium before the cost increase, its economic profits would absorb the cost increase; there would be no change in price.

9. Introducing a new process that produces widgets at half the current cost with identical product quality would be most valuable in the long run to a firm in
   a. a purely competitive industry.
   b. a monopolistically competitive industry.
   c. an oligopolistic industry with little hope of successful collusion.
   d. an oligopolistic industry with successful collusion and little fear of new entrants in the future.

10. An oligopolist's incentive to "cheat" on a secret collusive agreement increases when
    a. quality competition is more easily detected.
    b. the demand for his product at the current price is shrinking.
    c. the demand for his product at the current price is expanding.
    d. his marginal cost is closer to the oligopoly price.

The following information applies to the next two questions: The taxicab industry is basically competitive. However, taxicab operators must generally obtain licenses, and regulators in many large cities use these licenses to artificially restrict entry into the profession. (In Boston, for example, the number of licenses has not risen since 1930.) New cab drivers must then purchase a license from existing drivers.

11. A taxicab license costs $35,000 in Boston and $65,000 in New York.
    a. It is probably more profitable to become a taxicab driver in Boston than in New York.
    b. It is probably more profitable to become a taxicab driver in New York than in Boston.
    c. It is probably equally profitable to become a taxicab driver in New York and in Boston.
    d. Taxicab drivers probably lose money in both cities.

12. Suppose you decide to become a taxicab driver in New York and pay $65,000 to buy a license. Right after you start operating, the taxi industry is deregulated, and your license becomes worthless.
    a. You entered the industry just in the nick of time.
    b. You should now exit the industry.
    c. You should sell your license in Boston.
    d. You may as well stay in the industry.

13. One large motel chain uses the slogan "the best surprise is no surprise" to advertise that its motels are always about the same. Critics charge that this approach fails to take advantage of local architecture, local customs, and – in general – is just too "drab" and "plastic." The motel's profits have been high enough to attract many competitors. Since the motel industry is monopolistically competitive, our economic model
    a. is contradicted, since this firm does *not* offer much variety.
    b. is contradicted, since *economic* profits do not fit into the model.
    c. is contradicted by the fact that the firm advertises.
    d. indicates that some travelers appreciate predictability at the expense of other values.

THE ECONOMIC WAY OF THINKING – DISCUSSION QUESTIONS

1. Do firms in oligopolistic industries have an incentive to collude? What factors will reduce the likelihood of successful collusion (from the viewpoint of the firms)? Will the threat of potential new rivals in an oligopolistic industry influence the price and output policies of the existing firms in the industry? Explain.

2. Suppose the only information you have about an industry is that it is highly concentrated. Will the firms in the industry make high profits? What factors may limit their ability to do so?

3. Consider the alternatives of pure competition, monopolistic competition, oligopoly, and contestable markets.
    a. How is the structure of monopolistic competition different from pure competition? How is it similar?
    b. How is the structure of oligopoly different from pure competition? How is it similar?
    c. How is the structure of contestable markets different from oligopoly? How is it similar?
    d. Compared to pure competition, what tends to be true about the levels of price and profitability under monopolistic competition? Oligopoly? Contestable markets?

4. Does the town where you live have too many gas stations or quick-stop mini food stores? Is this duplication and competitiveness wasteful? Does it result in higher prices than those that would prevail under alternative arrangements? Explain why you think that monopolistic competition is either
    a. wasteful and inefficient, or
    b. consistent with efficiency and a consumer-directed economy.

5. Explain why economic theory predicts that collusion to rig the market against consumers will be far more prevalent under oligopoly than under monopolistic competition.

6. Do you think that the long-run profits that an oligopolist may be able to earn will make the oligopolist less concerned about holding down production costs? Why or why not?

7. Assume that the Barbers Association for Short Hair (BASH) successfully convinced the state of Florida to pass legislation increasing the price of haircuts to $15. Suppose that there are no barriers to entry into the barbering profession, but that everyone who charges a price for cutting hair must comply with this legislation (i.e., charge $15). What would you expect to happen to the
   a. sales revenues of Florida barbers?
   b. profits of Florida barbers in the short run? Long run?
   c. waiting time to get a haircut?
   d. quality of a haircut and the auxiliary services provided with it?
   e. number of black market haircuts?

8. What is meant by competition? How does the element of monopoly in monopolistic competition affect the process of competition? Why is competition important if markets are to work efficiently? Can competition protect the consumer from the market power of sellers? Is competition sometimes destructive or counterproductive? Defend or criticize competition as a method of allocating goods and resources. Be specific. Feel free to suggest and defend alternatives that you think are superior to the competitive market process.

22
Business Structure, Regulation, and Deregulation

TRUE OR FALSE

T F
□ □   1. Bigness and lack of competition are not always synonymous.

□ □   2. Predatory pricing is another term for high, monopolistic pricing.

□ □   3. An exclusive contract is commonly involved in dealerships.

□ □   4. One of the shortcomings of regulatory agencies is that with the passage of time they tend to represent broad groups such as consumers at the expense of labor and business interests.

□ □   5. The effectiveness of the Sherman Act encourages Congress to pass the Clayton Act.

□ □   6. Most economists believe that antitrust policy has had a dramatic impact on market structure.

□ □   7. While there are a number of difficulties involved in applying anti-trust policy in the United States, distinguishing between competitive and anti-competitive behavior is not one of those difficulties.

□ □   8. Social regulation seeks to provide a cleaner, safer, healthier environment for workers and consumers.

□ □   9. The antitrust position of the Reagan administration might best be characterized as "bigness necessarily means badness."

□ □ 10. American cars are approximately 500 pounds heavier than they would have been without the CAFE standards.

□ □ 11. The merger wave of the 1980s relied on a new method of financing, called leveraged buyouts, in which the acquiring firm borrowed large amounts of money to purchase another firm.

PROBLEMS AND PROJECTS

1. Consider the problem of regulating your local water company. Originally, huge amounts of money had to be spent to install pipe, build water treatment plants, and construct aqueducts between your town and the local sources of water. The costs of building these facilities were met with a bond issue, the annual payments on which are fixed. Given the existence of these facilities, however, the marginal cost of an extra gallon of water is quite low (consisting mainly of the marginal cost of treating the water plus mainte-nance and billing activities). Suppose that the following chart describes the cost structure of your local water company:

Exhibit 1

Quantity supplied (millions of gallons)	Total fixed cost (millions of dollars)	Average fixed cost (cents per gallon)	Marginal cost (cents per gallon)	Average total cost (cents per gallon)
40	$10	.25	.06	.31
50	10	.20	.06	_____
60	10	_____	.06	_____
70	10	_____	.06	_____

a. Fill in the missing information in Exhibit 1 above.
b. Suppose regulators set price equal to marginal cost (which will make consumers happy and increase the quantity demanded.) What is the water company's profit/loss situation at each output level?
c. Suppose regulators set price equal to average total cost (which will make consumers unhappy and decrease the quantity demanded). What is the water company's profit/ loss situation at each output level?
d. Is either pricing mechanism a good option in this case? How do you balance the goal of economic efficiency with that of fairness to the owners of the water company? What would you do if you were on the town's water regulation board?

2. For each of the following historical cases, indicate which antitrust law applies and which side you think won the case. (Some research may be necessary to fully answer this question.)

   a. Plaintiff: United States
      Defendant: Standard Oil

   Standard Oil aggressively protected its 90 percent share of the petroleum market with practices that included receiving a rebate from railroads of the price charged for shipping oil (both its own oil and the oil shipped by competitors).

   Antitrust law: _____

   Winning side: _____

   b. Plaintiff: United States
      Defendant: Vons Grocery Store

   Vons, the Los Angeles area's third largest grocery store chain, merged with Shopping Bag, the sixth largest, resulting in the second largest chain with a market share of 7.5 percent.

   Antitrust law: _____

   Winning side: _____

   c. Plaintiff: Curt Flood
      Defendant: Major League Baseball

   Curt Flood accused baseball owners of a collective boycott of his services because of a player contract clause that prevented Flood from becoming a free agent and offering his services to the highest bidding team.

   Antitrust law: _____

   Winning side: _____

   d. Plaintiff: United States
      Defendant: Alcoa

   Alcoa maintained its monopoly position beyond the expiration date of its legal patents, mainly by constantly adding capacity in anticipation of future aluminum demand.

   Antitrust law: _____

   Winning side: _____

   e. Plaintiff: United States
      Defendant: International Salt

   International Salt required that firms using its patented machines for injecting salt into canned foods also purchase their salt from International Salt.

   Antitrust law: _____

   Winning side: _____

3. The insurance industry, whose activities are generally exempt from U.S. antitrust laws, is often suspected of collusion. California voters recently passed a law ("Proposition 103") requiring a twenty percent rollback in auto insurance rates. The diagrams in Exhibit 2 contrast two alternative initial situations in the California auto insurance industry, pure competition and perfect collusion:

Exhibit 2

Pure competition

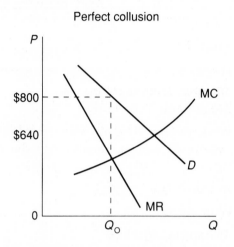

Perfect collusion

a. For the two alternative initial situations, indicate below whether quantity demanded and quantity supplied will rise (+), fall (−), remain the same (0), or change in an uncertain direction, as a result of California's price ceiling on insurance rates:

	Pure competition	*Perfect collusion*
Quantity demanded:	_____	_____
Quantity supplied:	_____	_____

b. Will the insurance rate rollback necessarily result in a shortage if the industry is perfectly competitive? If it is perfectly collusive?

Research and write a short paper on one of the following topics:

4. The size, power, and role of big business in the U.S. economy. [Selected references that might be helpful: Walter Adams, *The Structure of American Industry*, 4th ed. (New York: Macmillan, 1971); William N. Leonard, *Business Size, Market Power, and Public Policy* (New York: Crowell, 1969); M. A. Adelman, "Two Faces of Economic Concentration," *Public Interest*, Fall 1970; Joe Bain, *Barriers to New Competition* (Cambridge, MA: Harvard University Press, 1956); John S. McGee, *In Defense of Industrial Competition* (New York: Praeger, 1971); Yale Brozen, *The Competitive Economy: Selected Readings* (Morristown, NJ: General Learning Press, 1975); and William Shepherd, *The Economics of Industrial Organization* (Englewood Cliffs, NJ: Prentice-Hall, 1979).]

LEARNING THE MECHANICS – MULTIPLE CHOICE

1. Predatory pricing would involve charging some customers a price that is
   a. lower than the price of a competitor.
   b. lower than average total cost.
   c. lower than marginal cost.
   d. any of the above.

2. The concept of economic regulation typically involves
   a. the regulation of product price and production processes in various industries.
   b. the regulation of product price but not production processes or industrial structure in various industries.
   c. the regulation of product price and industrial structure but not production processes in various industries.
   d. the regulation of industrial structure in various industries.

3. Economists who defend the merger and acquisition wave of the 1980s point to several ways in which the recent corporate reorganizations have enhanced economic productivity. Which of the following is *not* one of their points?
   a. The new larger firm may be a more efficient size than either of the smaller ones were.
   b. The merged firms may have complementary strengths.
   c. The new managers of the firm may be more capable of making needed management/ production changes than were the old ones.
   d. There are often tremendous tax benefits to merging a high-profit firm with one with substantial losses.

4. Data on national income by sector suggest that the private economy in the United States is
   a. dominated by small firms that produce in industries approximating the conditions of pure competition.
   b. dominated by large firms that produce in industries approaching monopoly conditions.
   c. increasingly dominated by an effectively competitive sector.
   d. increasingly coming to be dominated by manufacturing – a sector whose revenues are increasing more rapidly than our national income.

5. All but one of the following are clearly illegal under current antitrust laws. Which is usually *not* legal?
   a. collusion and conspiracies to restrain trade
   b. horizontal mergers that tend to lessen competition
   c. serving on the board of directors of a competing firm with assets of more than $1 million.
   d. conglomerate mergers

6. An example of a government action designed to promote competition among producers is
   a. the institution of higher tariffs (import taxes) on Volkswagens.
   b. an extension of occupational licensing procedures to many additional occupations.
   c. imposition of additional regulations on small businesses.
   d. legislation prohibiting interlocking corporate directorates.

7. Use statements I and II to answer this question. (**I**) Regulation of business firms and labor interests tends to be inflexible. It often fails to adjust very rapidly to dynamic changes that affect a competitive market. (**II**) The demand for regulation often stems from organized groups seeking to profit from the regulation, rather than from forces seeking an economically efficient solution.
   a. I is true, II is false.
   b. I is false, II is true.
   c. Both I and II are true.
   d. Both I and II are false.

8. Since 1950, which of the following sectors has grown most rapidly in the United States?
   a. Agriculture
   b. Manufacturing
   c. Service and government
   d. Construction

9. Which of the following is not prohibited by current antitrust legislation?
   a. Tying contracts that substantially lessen competition
   b. Collusion to fix prices of products in competitive markets
   c. Quantity discounts that reflect cost savings stemming from a large purchase
   d. Horizontal mergers that serve to lessen competition

10. The Herfindahl index is a fairly sophisticated tool for measuring the level of
   a. market concentration in an industry.
   b. merger and acquisition activity in a given year.
   c. vigor with which a given administration is enforcing antitrust policies.
   d. deregulation in an industry.

11. Buick and Oldsmobile are divisions of General Motors. If we were to consider the incentives facing the officers of each division, we would expect
   a. complete cooperation and no rivalry between them.
   b. a good deal of rivalry, as well as cooperation, between them.
   c. no cooperation, but simply an intense rivalry between the two.
   d. no interest in what the other is doing.

12. Use statements I and II to answer this question. (**I**) The new social legislation seeks to improve the health, safety, and quality of the environment. (**II**) Whereas the older economic regulation generally increased costs of production, social regulation usually reduces the cost of production and, in turn, the price of products to the consumer.
   a. Both I and II are true.
   b. Both I and II are false.
   c. I is true, II is false.
   d. I is false, II is true.

THE ECONOMIC WAY OF THINKING – MULTIPLE CHOICE

1. When state governments use business licensing to limit the entry of potential competitors into an industry and create a situation whereby the licensed firms can earn *long-run* economic profit, profit-seeking business entrepreneurs
   a. have an incentive to use both economic and political means in attempting to obtain the valuable licenses.
   b. have little incentive to enter the licensed industry.
   c. would enter the industry only if the licenses were free.
   d. would use economic methods, but not political ones, in attempting to obtain the valuable licenses.

2. Which of the following best explains why competitive private firms seek to produce efficiently?
   a. The pressures of competition demand efficient production, which, other things constant, is rewarded with larger profits or smaller losses.
   b. Efficient production results because private decision-making is invariably less bureaucratic.
   c. Employees in the private sector know that they must produce, whereas waste and inefficiency characterize public sector production.
   d. Analysis of incentives does *not* suggest that competitive firms will produce efficiently.

Use the following quotation to answer the next question.

The world's first plant for the manufacture of gasoline from natural gas will be shut down as uneconomical, it was announced today by the Amoco Chemicals Corporation. J. H. Forrester, president of Amoco, a subsidiary of Standard Oil Company (Indiana), said, "We have determined that the plant cannot make gasoline and chemicals from natural gas at present market prices as cheaply as they can be made by other processes." [*New York Times*, September 14, 1957.]

3. If the facts in this quotation are correct, a decision by the firm to close down the plant
   a. results in economic inefficiency, because of the abandonment of a technically sound project.
   b. is consistent with economic efficiency, because lower-cost alternative production methods were available.
   c. will increase the demand for gasoline because its lower cost.
   d. is sound from the firm's point of view, but not from the point of view of society.

4. Suppose that the Barbers' Association of Florida (BAF) was designing legislation to increase the average earnings of its members. Which of the following proposals would be most likely to lead to large and permanent net income gains for those already in the barbering profession in Florida?
   a. Legislation fixing the minimum price of haircuts at $6, and instituting the free licensing of any graduate of a U.S. barber college
   b. Establishment of strict licensing requirements that would prevent any new entrants into the barbering business without the approval of BAF
   c. Legislation requiring that all employees in the barbering profession be paid double time for any hours worked beyond the normal 40-hour week
   d. Establishment of a $6-per-hour minimum wage for barbers who are paid hourly wages

5. Which of the following is most descriptive of public policy toward competitive markets?
   a. Public policy has consistently promoted competitive markets.
   b. Public policy has tolerated big business while following a regulatory and taxation policy that favors smaller businesses.
   c. Public policy has sometimes promoted competition, but it also has used regulatory, tariff, and subsidization powers to stifle and weaken competitive markets.
   d. Public policy has attempted to promote competition, although the effort has been negated by the rapid growth of the manufacturing sector, which has been spurred on by modern technology.

6. The experience of very large firms over the last several decades indicates that bigness
   a. is a virtual guarantee of success in the corporate world.
   b. is a guarantee of success, at least in manufacturing.
   c. is a guarantee of success, except in manufacturing.
   d. is no guarantee of success over time, since so many firms come and go from the "top 50" or "top 100" firms over a 20- or 30-year period.

7. "Big firms in the United States are growing primarily because the manufacturing sector, which is dominated by big firms, is growing in importance." This statement is
   a. essentially correct.
   b. incorrect, because bigness is declining among U.S. firms.
   c. incorrect, because manufacturing has produced 75-80 percent of the output in the United States for many years.
   d. incorrect, because since 1950 manufacturing has constituted a shrinking percentage of our output.

8. Which of the following would increase an economist's expectations that competitive pressures were present in an industry?
   a. A high concentration ratio
   b. An increase in the availability of close substitutes made by another industry
   c. Few entrants into the industry
   d. A decrease in the availability of foreign products similar to those produced in the industry

9. Regulation that requires the producers of a product to adopt more costly production techniques will
   a. increase supply and lead to a lower market price of the product.
   b. decrease supply and lead to a higher market price of the product.
   c. increase demand and lead to a higher market price of the product.
   d. leave the market price unchanged, since producers are forced to bear the burden of regulatory costs.

Questions 10-13 refer to the following description of the market for the services of midwives (non-doctors who deliver children) in Pasadena, California. Assume that midwives are in a perfectly competitive industry with an equilibrium quantity of 100 children delivered per year at a price of $400 each.

Now suppose that local doctors convince the city council to pass a law requiring that an MD must be "on-call" for all midwife-handled births even if the midwife does all the work. The doctors establish a fixed fee of $100 (to be paid by the midwives) for being on call. After the enactment of the new law, the midwife industry experiences a decrease in the equilibrium number of children delivered per year to 80 and the price rises to $450.

10. By how much did the total annual income (after paying doctors' fees) of all the midwives in Pasadena fall due to the new law?
    a. $28,000.
    b. $12,000.
    c. $8,000.
    d. $4,000.

11. By how much did the total annual income of doctors in Pasadena rise due to the 80 midwife births covered by the new law?
    a. $28,000.
    b. $12,000.
    c. $8,000.
    d. $4,000.

12. What is the deadweight loss caused by the new law? (*Hint*: Assume that the only deadweight losses caused by the new law are in the midwife industry and that the supply and demand functions in the relevant range are straight lines.)
    a. $4,500.
    b. $1,000.
    c. $500.
    d. zero.

13. If the Pasadena City Council is responsive to lobbying, which of the following describes the likelihood of the new law being repealed during the next few years?
    a. Very likely, because the midwives will point out the large deadweight loss due to the new law.
    b. Very likely, since the midwives lost more money than the doctors gained, and they'll spend it on lobbying.
    c. Very unlikely, because the doctors will point out the zero deadweight loss due to the new law.
    d. Very unlikely, because the doctors gained not only the fees from the 80 midwife-handled births but also from the 20 births no longer handled by the midwives. Thus, they'll have more to spend on lobbying than the midwives.

THE ECONOMIC WAY OF THINKING – DISCUSSION QUESTIONS

1. Some economists have proposed that the United States repeal its antitrust laws except for Section 1 of the Sherman Act. Do you agree or not? Explain.

2. How much of the U.S. economy is competitive today? Is the economy less competitive today than three or four decades ago? What are some of the major changes in the economy in recent years that have affected its competitiveness?

3. In recent years there has been considerable dissatisfaction with regulatory policies in the airline and trucking industries. This has led to significant movements toward deregulation in these industries. How successful has deregulation been? Do you think deregulating these industries is a good idea? Why or why not?

4. How does social regulation differ from economic regulation? Why is social regulation more difficult to administer than economic regulation? Do the higher costs of social regulation make it less desirable than economic regulation? Explain.

5. Suppose that the government uses licensing to limit the number of firms in the retail liquor industry. Thus, ignoring the cost of a license, firms in the industry make substantial economic profit.
    a. Analyze the price, costs, and profits of firms when the limited number of licenses (good for five years) are auctioned off to the highest bidders. Assume that ownership of the licenses is widespread, so there is no problem in collusion.
    b. Analyze the price, costs, and profits of firms when the limited number of licenses are granted "free" to persons approved by a committee appointed by the legislature (or governor).
    c. When choosing between these two, state legislatures have almost exclusively chosen alternative b. Can you explain why?

6. Do you think General Motors is too big? Would you vote to have it broken up into several smaller firms? What are the major factors that influence your views on this question? Assume that the head of the Pontiac division of General Motors earns his bonuses and promotions on the basis of how Pontiac division (not GM as a whole) performs. The same applies to the heads of Chevrolet, Buick, and other GM divisions. Can you explain why rivalry and competition among divisions should be expected? Will there also be cooperation? What kinds? Will testing laboratories be shared? Will consumers gain? What might consumers lose if GM is *not* broken up? Write a short essay either defending GM or arguing for its breakup. Address the questions raised here.

7. Present your case for or against each of the following:
    a. Laws to make mergers and takeovers more difficult.
    b. A "no-fault" monopoly law that breaks up large, dominant firms unless the firms can prove that major inefficiencies will result.

PERSPECTIVES IN ECONOMICS

Single-Digit Oil and Auto Mileage Standards Don't Mix
by Robert W. Crandall

[From *The Wall Street Journal*, April 3, 1986, p. 26. Reprinted with permission of the Wall Street Journal; ©Dow Jones & Co., Inc. (1986). All rights reserved.]

As we watch the demise of the world petroleum cartel, debate continues whether fuel-economy standards for automobiles prescribed by Congress during the heyday of OPEC should be adjusted slightly. We are even treated to the unsightly spectacle of the Big Three auto company – Chrysler – arguing for the retention of the Corporate Average Fuel Economy program just to hobble the other two companies. Surprisingly, almost no one has suggested the abolition of the entire fuel-economy program – the only sensible decision.

To understand why we have government-mandated fuel-economy standards for cars, one has to return to the 1970s and the unstable oil market of that time. In 1975, most people believed that the real price of fossil fuels would rise ad infinitum. In this environment, Congress enacted the CAFE program for all manufacturers selling new passenger cars in the U.S., requiring that their fleet averages rise from 18 to 27.5 miles per gallon between 1978 and 1985 with subsequent years' standards to be set by the secretary of transportation.

At the time, this policy seemed a not too irrational antidote to a truly irrational policy of regulating crude-oil and gasoline prices. If Congress was not going to allow gasoline prices to rise to world market clearing levels, thereby encouraging conservation, it would have to mandate conservation more directly by requiring that automobiles be produced to deliver more fuel economy than consumers would desire at artificially low prices.

Of course, we finally came to our senses and abandoned oil-price controls. After the Iranian debacle, oil prices made one last surge. By early 1981, crude-oil prices had risen to the range of $35 a barrel and gasoline prices had climbed to about $1.40 a gallon. Since that time, as we all know, oil and gasoline prices have declined dramatically. In fact, gasoline prices in Februpary were less than 70% of their 1981 level in real terms despite an increase in the federal gasoline tax, and they will continue to drop. The cost of the crude oil in a gallon of gasoline has fallen from about 65 cents to 30 cents in the past three months. With real gasoline prices falling so rapidly, why do we want to require auto makers to direct their scarce capital and trained manpower to increasing fuel economy far beyond the level that consumers would willingly pay for? Obviously, if the price of gasoline is falling, you and I are likely to be less willing to pay more for each additional mile per gallon promised by Detroit's newest models.

Visionaries say we need CAFE to protect us against another round of OPEC price increases somewhere in the distant future. But are they better equipped to predict these price increases than today's market participants? And if they are, why do they focus only on the gasoline consumed by new cars, which are only about 8% of all cars on the road and account for less than 3% of oil consumption? Why don't they argue for conservation standards on industrial boilers, home furnaces, locomotives and plastics producers?

If the conservationists were truly interested in reducing oil consumption, they would advocate a tax on all petroleum products. If they were concerned about OPEC-led embargoes or other supply disruptions, they would press for more rapid accumulation of oil in the Strategic Petroleum Reserve, which Congress has chosen to ignore just when the reserve could be filled at low prices.

In the past year, the debate over CAFE standards has taken a number of twists that suggest fuel economy is not really the issue. The United Auto Workers union has become an ardent supporter of CAFE even though the program raises Detroit's costs and thereby leads to fewer new-car sales. The reason for this anomalous behavior is to be found in the law's curious distinction between imported and domestic cars. Manufacturers must tote up their CAFE numbers for cars they produce in the U.S. separately from those they import. Given General Motors' and Ford's success with large cars, they have fallen short of the CAFE standard the past three years. As a result, they will have to increase their production of small cars in the U.S. or make heroic progress on their larger cars if they are to comply.

Recent studies suggest that the U.S. companies are not competitive with Japan or Korea in producing small cars. Therefore, without CAFE, it would make sense for Ford and General Motors to import their small cars. Unfortunately, CAFE makes this difficult because these companies are required to pay $50 a car for every mile per gallon they fall short of CAFE. In short, CAFE serves as a nontariff trade barrier for small-car imports.

Even more curious are the strategic battles among the domestic Big Three companies. Chrysler insists that the CAFE program not be weakened because the company has complied easily while Ford and GM will owe potentially hundreds of millions of dollars of fines a year for not meeting the standard. Last year, Chrysler argued strenuously but unsuccessfully against the secretary of transportation's decision to lower the standard to 26 mpg for the current (1986) model year, saying that since Chrysler had spent the capital resources to meet the standard, GM and Ford should be forced to do so as well. In fact, Chrysler has the worst fuel economy of the Big Three for given weight of car and engine power. It has succeeded in meeting CAFE because it was forced to end its production of large cars during its brush with bankruptcy in the late 1970s. Now it wants to penalize Ford and GM for having the foresight and financial wherewithal to keep their full line of cars.

Even Ford and General Motors are not arguing for an abolition of this misguided program. They simply want the 26-mile-per-gallon standard to be extended to the 1987 and 1988 model years. Why? Could the answer be that a 26 mpg standard severely constrains the major large-car competitors in the world – Mercedes, Volvo, BMW, Peugeot, and Saab-from exporting freely to the U.S.? These European companies are forced to offer diesels or simply lower-performing cars in order to comply with the standards. Incidentally, the first company to pay CAFE penalties was not an American company, but Jaguar.

The CAFE program has become an anomaly or even an absurdity in an era of declining oil prices. If the visionaries in congress wish to protect us from unforeseen disasters, they should look to improving our ability to survive a shock, perhaps by enlarging the Strategic Petroleum Reserve. CAFE standards simply penalize U.S consumers by offering them cars with too much fuel economy and too little performance, and a reduced choice between imported and domestically produced smaller models. Or Congress could enact an oil-consumption tax. Who knows, such a tax might even help to solve certain other pressing problems of the day.

Discussion

1. Is Crandall saying that auto mileage standards are *always* a bad idea or just a bad idea when gasoline prices are low? Explain your answer.

2. If the free-market system worked, wouldn't high gasoline prices lower the demand for gas guzzlers (and increase the demand for fuel-efficient cars) and make auto mileage standards redundant? Did this happen?

3. Crandall seems to find it "curious" that at least one of the same automobile makers who opposed the mileage standards when they were introduced is now arguing to have them retained. Would the special interest effect make this more understandable? How?

23
The Supply of and Demand for Productive Resources

TRUE OR FALSE

T F

☐ ☐   1. An increase in demand for wheat would cause the price of wheat-producing land to rise.

☐ ☐   2. Under pure competition, the marginal revenue product of a resource would be equal to the resource price.

☐ ☐   3. A profit-maximizing firm will continue to employ a resource as long as its marginal revenue product exceeds its marginal cost to the firm.

☐ ☐   4. The availability of good substitutes for a resource will tend to make the demand for it less elastic.

☐ ☐   5. In the short run, the supply of doctors is quite inelastic.

☐ ☐   6. In the short run, the supply of filling station attendants is quite inelastic.

☐ ☐   7. Physical capital and human capital cannot be substituted for each other.

☐ ☐   8. The marginal products – and therefore wage rates – of employees will be positively influenced by the amount of physical capital per worker in a firm.

☐ ☐   9. An increase in the price of a resource increases the incentive of producers to find a substitute for it.

☐ ☐ 10. The demand for a resource will be negatively related to its price partly because producers will substitute other factors of production for the resource as it increases in price.

☐ ☐ 11. A firm that purchases resources competitively must buy at the price that is determined in the market.

☐ ☐ 12. An employer will hire workers as long as their marginal revenue product is positive.

☐ ☐ 13. Because of the law of diminishing marginal returns, the value of a worker's marginal product eventually declines as more workers are hired in a given plant.

☐ ☐ 14. The demand for a resource is strongly dependent upon its contribution to the production of a good demanded by consumers.

☐ ☐ 15. A unique resource will command a high price, regardless of demand conditions.

PROBLEMS AND PROJECTS

Exhibit 1

Units of labor	Total output (per week)	Marginal physical product (per week)	Product price	Total revenue	Marginal revenue product (per week)
1	5	_____	100	_____	_____
2	9	_____	100	_____	_____
3	12	_____	100	_____	_____
4	14	_____	100	_____	_____
5	15	_____	100	_____	_____

1. Nichole sells building materials in a competitive industry. Her firm receives $100 for each unit of material. Given the firm's current fixed capital, Exhibit 1 shows how total output changes as additional units of labor are hired. Assume that Nichole hires labor from a competitive market in which the market-determined wage is $200 per week.

   a. Fill in the marginal physical product, total revenue, and marginal revenue product columns.

   b. How many employees should Nichole hire if she wants to maximize profits? (*Hint*: If two different labor levels maximize profits, assume Nichole will produce at the higher of the two levels.)

   c. How many units of labor should Nichole hire if the wage rate goes up to $300?

Exhibit 2

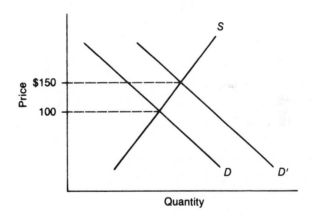

d. The supply-and-demand conditions in the building market are represented in Exhibit 2. Suppose that the demand for building materials increases as indicated by D'. Given the new wage rate in part c, indicate the firm's new employment level, total revenue, and profits (refer to Exhibit 3).

Exhibit 3

Units of labor	Units of output	Product price	Total revenue	Variable cost	Profit
0	0	$150	_____	_____	_____
1	5	150	_____	_____	_____
2	9	150	_____	_____	_____
3	12	150	_____	_____	_____
4	14	150	_____	_____	_____
5	15	150	_____	_____	_____

e. Nichole has a weekly fixed charge of $800 in addition to her variable cost for labor. Given her *fixed costs*, would Nichole stay in business if she operated at the level of output you determined in part d?

2. Magic Carpet, Inc., produces and sells handmade oriental rugs in a competitive industry. The firm receives $100 per square meter for each rug produced. Given the firm's current fixed capital, Exhibit 4 shows how total output (in square meters) changes as additional units of skilled labor are hired.

Exhibit 4

Units of skilled labor	Total output (square meters per week)	MPP	Price per square meter	TR	MRP
0	0	_____	$100	_____	_____
1	5	_____	100	_____	_____
2	12	_____	100	_____	_____
3	18	_____	100	_____	_____
4	21.5	_____	100	_____	_____
5	24	_____	100	_____	_____
6	25	_____	100	_____	_____

a. Complete the table.
b. What is the firm's demand schedule for labor?
c. Given the equilibrium wage rate as $200 per week, indicate how many workers the firm would hire if it wanted to maximize profits.
d. How many workers would Magic Carpet hire if the market wage increased to $300 per week?

3. Use the diagrams below to indicate the changes in demand (D), supply (S), equilibrium price (P) and equilibrium quantity (Q) in response to the events in the resource markets. First show in the diagrams how the described event or events affect demand and/or supply of the resource, and then fill in the table to the right of the diagrams using + to indicate increase, − to indicate decrease, 0 to indicate no effect, and ? to indicate uncertain (*Hint*: The diagrams are of the resource markets themselves; for example, the diagram in part a. is of the market for high-school math teachers.)

	Resource market	Events	Diagrams	D	S	P	Q
a.	High school math teachers	Wages for mathematicians employed in industry rise.					
b.	Computers	Technological change raises the speed of computer calculations.					
c.	Computer technicians	The cost of obtaining computer training falls.					
d.	Welders	Technological change lowers the cost of robots used to weld auto parts on auto assembly lines.					
e.	Agricultural land in Southern California	Population migration raises homesite values; a vitamin C fad raises the price of oranges.					

4. In the growing of corn a farmer uses two fertilizers, Vitacorn and Cornpower. The farmer has estimated that at the current rate of usage of the two fertilizers, the marginal (physical) product of one ton of Vitacorn is 200 bushels per acre and the marginal product of one ton of Cornpower is 400 bushels per acre. The best price quotations the farmer has been able to get are $800/ton for Vitacorn and $1200/ton for Cornpower.
   a. From the above information, does the farmer's current usage of the two fertilizers meet the "condition for cost minimization when multiple resources are employed"?
   b. Suppose the farmer used one more ton of Cornpower and two fewer tons of Vitacorn. How would total output change? How would total cost change? Would this substitution be consistent with the goal of profit maximization?
   c. If the farmer continued to substitute Cornpower for Vitacorn, assume that the marginal product of Cornpower would fall. Would these changes lead toward fulfillment of the condition for cost minimization you discussed in part a? How?

5. Suppose that the world's long-run and short-run demands for crude petroleum can be represented by the diagram in Exhibit 5.

Exhibit 5

Billions of barrels

a. From the information in the diagram, calculate the arc-price elasticity of demand (between $15 and $20) for crude petroleum in the short run and in the long run.
b. Of the many possible reasons behind the demand for petroleum being more elastic in the long run than in the short run, which do you think is most important? Which is second most important? Explain your reasoning.

6. Thin Air is a monopolistic seller of breathing devices. Labor is the firm's only variable input.
   a. Complete the following table:

Units of labor	Units of output	Price of output	Total revenue	Marginal revenue product
1	10	50	_____	_____
2	19	48	_____	_____
3	27	46	_____	_____
4	34	44	_____	_____
5	40	42	_____	_____
6	45	40	_____	_____
7	49	39	_____	_____
8	52	38	_____	_____
9	54	37	_____	_____
10	55	36	_____	_____

   b. If fixed costs are $100 and labor costs $100 per unit, what are the profit-maximizing values of units of labor hired, output, profits, and average cost?
   c. What is the value of the marginal product of the last worker hired? Is the worker paid the full value of his or her marginal product?

LEARNING THE MECHANICS – MULTIPLE CHOICE

1. The short-run supply of a human resource will be more elastic the
   a. more elastic the demand for the product to be produced.
   b. more inelastic the demand for the product to be produced.
   c. lower the skill level necessary to perform the job.
   d. harder it is to acquire the skill and knowledge necessary to provide the resource.

2. A decrease in the demand for a product will cause
   a. the price of resources to decrease and, therefore, output to increase.
   b. output to decrease, and demand for (and prices of) resources used to produce the product to decrease also.
   c. output to decrease, but the demand for resources to remain constant.
   d. output to decrease and resource prices to fall if, and only if, their supply is elastic.

3. Empirical evidence indicates a close relationship between quantity of schooling and income. A cost-minimizing firm would be willing to pay a highly educated person higher wages than those with less education if
   a. the marginal revenue product of the highly educated person were greater.
   b. the demand for the highly educated group was inelastic.
   c. the supply of the highly educated group was smaller.
   d. the total cost of schooling was greater for the highly educated employee.

4. The more elastic the demand for a product
   a. the more inelastic the demand for the productive resources used.
   b. the less elastic the supply of factors used in producing the product.
   c. the more elastic the demand for the productive resources used.
   d. the longer the time period before the product will be sold.

5. Which of the following expresses the correct decision-making rule for a profit-maximizing firm hiring units of labor?
   a. If the MRP were rising, less labor would be employed as time passed.
   b. The firm should continue to hire workers as long as their MRP is greater than the wage rate.
   c. The firm should continue to hire workers until the total costs of all workers equals the total revenue from the output of the workers.
   d. The firm should continue to hire workers until the wage rate equals the price of the product.

6. The demand for a productive resource
   a. is a derived demand.
   b. is independent of the selling price of the product.
   c. is dependent on the supply side of the resource at the time.
   d. shifts when the price of the resource changes.

7. Increasing the price of a natural resource will
   a. cause consumers to choose substitute goods that do not use the natural resource intensively.
   b. decrease the demand for the natural resource.
   c. increase the demand for the natural resource.
   d. increase the quantity of the resource demanded.

8. Compared to the short-run demand, the long-run demand for carpenters is
   a. less elastic.
   b. more elastic.
   c. equally elastic.
   d. either more or less elastic; we cannot predict which.

9. In a purely competitive industry, the marginal revenue derived from the sale of an additional unit of the product is equal to the market price of the product. In these circumstances, the additional revenue derived from the employment of an additional unit of a resource is referred to as the resource's
   a. marginal cost.
   b. value of marginal product.
   c. marginal physical product.
   d. marginal productivity.

10. If the cost of using skilled labor was twice the cost of using unskilled labor, and both were used by a profit-maximizing firm, the firm would adjust the quantity of each type of labor until
    a. the marginal physical product of each was the same.
    b. twice as much unskilled labor was used.
    c. half as much unskilled labor was used.
    d. the marginal physical product of unskilled labor was half that of skilled labor.

11. If a firm used only two factors of production, labor (L) and capital (K), which of the following conditions would be present if the firm were minimizing its costs of production?
    a. The $MPP_L/P_L = MPP_K/P_K$.
    b. MPP_L times the price of labor $= MPP_K$ times the price of capital.
    c. $MRP_L = MRP_K$.
    d. $MPP_L = MPP_K$.

12. A shift in the demand for a particular resource can be caused by all the following *except*
    a. a change in the demand for the product that uses the resource as a factor of production.
    b. a change in the productivity of the resource.
    c. a change in the price of *other* resources that could be used as substitutes for the resource in question.
    d. a change in price of the resource.

Questions 13 and 14 refer to the market for midwestern law clerks. Law clerks produce materials that law firms need to provide law services to their clients. Assume that the law clerks currently work in a perfectly competitive market.

13. Suppose a major toxic waste disaster causes damages throughout the midwest, and everyone expects an increased demand for legal services to result. (All else constant.) Law clerks should expect
    a. an increase in wages as their marginal products increase.
    b. an increase in wages as their marginal revenue products increase.
    c. a decrease in wages as their clients no longer afford high bills.
    d. a decrease in wages as the firm hires more clerks.

14. Suppose that all the midwestern law firms consolidate, becoming a monopoly in the area. We'd expect the wages of midwestern law clerks to
    a. fall, but more clerks would be hired.
    b. fall, and fewer clerks would be hired.
    c. rise, but fewer clerks would be hired.
    d. rise, and more clerks would be hired.

15. A firm in Clinton, N.Y., currently employs 80 units of labor and 50 units of capital equipment to produce 300 hamster cages. Given the current input levels utilized, the marginal product of labor is 4 and the marginal product of capital is 10. If we assume that labor costs $20 per unit and capital costs $10 per unit, then
    a. if the firm wants to expand output, when doing so, it should use the same proportions of labor and capital it now does.
    b. the firm could increase its output with no extra costs by using more capital and less labor.
    c. the firm could lower its production costs by using more labor and less capital.
    d. the firm is maximizing profits.

THE ECONOMIC WAY OF THINKING – MULTIPLE CHOICE

1. Which of the following resources will have the most inelastic supply in the short run?
    a. Land in downtown Chicago
    b. Trucks used to transport a variety of products
    c. Elevator operators
    d. Secretaries in Eagle Rock, California

2. Suppose that the number of economists engaged in teaching positions in 1985 decreased 10 percent from the 1975 level, while the number of economists in all positions declined 5 percent. Furthermore, suppose the median salary of those teaching declined relative to the average for economists as a group. The apparent paradox of a relative decrease in economists in teaching positions concurrent with their lower salaries relative to all economists can be explained by which of the following?
    a. The demand for teachers in economics is positively sloped, as evidenced by the smaller quantity employed at the lower salary rate.
    b. The demand elasticity for teachers in economics was smaller than that of the demand for all economists.
    c. The demand for economists decreased, and the demand for teachers in economics decreased relative to the demand for all economists.
    d. The larger decrease in the demand for research economists increased the relative median salaries of all economists.

3. Given the education required to become an engineer, which of the following best describes the expected market reaction to an increase in demand for the services of engineers?
    a. A large decrease in the wages of engineers in the short run, but a small increase in wages over time
    b. A substantial increase in the wages of engineers, followed (later) by an increase in the number of engineers, moderating the initial wage increase
    c. A substantial increase in the number of engineers and no increase in the wage level
    d. A substantial increase in the wages of engineers in the short run, and no change in the number of persons choosing to become engineers

4. In which of the following resource markets do you think supply would be most elastic in the short run?
   a. Pharmacists
   b. Physicians
   c. Unskilled labor
   d. Airplane pilots

5. During his administration, President Carter advocated a $1.46 billion aid program for college students from low- and middle-income families. The program was designed to halt the decline in college enrollments. If the program had been implemented, which of the following would have been the most likely outcome?
   a. Starting salaries for new college graduates would have risen because of an increase in the number of high-quality graduates.
   b. Starting salaries for college graduates would have been unaffected.
   c. Inflation would have decreased as more young people chose to be students instead of workers.
   d. Starting salaries of new college graduates would have fallen as the supply of graduates increased.

6. Suppose that a school board adopted a policy whereby all teachers were paid at the same wage rate. Furthermore, suppose that there was a vacancy in economics for which there were no applicants, and there was no vacancy in political science but there were 50 inquiries regarding any possible vacancy. Economic analysis implies that
   a. the nation needs to train more economists.
   b. the wage rate paid the teachers is below the market wage for economists.
   c. economists have fewer alternatives to teaching than do political scientists.
   d. the wage rate offered is below the market wage for political scientists.

7. Suppose that the United Auto Workers Union is successful in obtaining a 15 percent increase in the wages of auto workers and that the large wage increase necessitates an increase in automobile prices. Employment in the automobile manufacturing industry would be *least* likely to fall if
   a. the demand for American automobiles was relatively constant, but highly elastic.
   b. the supply of foreign-produced automobiles was highly elastic.
   c. American consumers felt that foreign automobiles were a good substitute for American automobiles.
   d. the demand for American automobiles was increasing and highly elastic.

8. Human capital differs from physical capital in that
   a. only physical capital depreciates.
   b. the use of physical capital is affected by working conditions and monetary return; human capital is predominantly affected by monetary return.
   c. physical capital may be purchased and sold; human capital may not be sold in a non-slave society (only the services of human capital may be purchased and sold).
   d. only human capital depreciates.

9. According to marginal productivity theory, a law forcing firms to pay higher wages to HHLs (heads of households with large families) would tend to
   a. decrease the employment and marginal productivity of HHLs.
   b. decrease the employment of HHLs, but lead to a higher marginal productivity for those HHLs hired.
   c. reduce the wages of workers without families.
   d. have no impact on HHLs.

10. The cost of electricity is a large component of the cost of making aluminum. In the Pacific Northwest, federal agencies sell electricity to aluminum manufacturers at roughly one-fourth its market value. Among those eager to eliminate this implicit subsidy would be
    a. firms that make wooden bats and wooden canoes.
    b. firms that supply aluminum ore to aluminum makers, since ore would then be a smaller part of the total cost of producing aluminum.
    c. buyers of aluminum products (who gain when aluminum profits decline).
    d. employees of the aluminum makers (who would then be justified in asking for higher wages when aluminum prices go up).

11. Where human capital is concerned, nonpecuniary considerations are likely to be
    a. irrelevant, since owners' decisions are based on money prices.
    b. unimportant, since people are very mobile.
    c. important, since workers have objectives other than money.
    d. important, since human capital is not transferable.

12. If the demand for chemical engineers suddenly increased, salaries for them would be higher one year later if
    a. several other kinds of engineers became chemical engineers by enrolling in a special one-semester training course.
    b. the price of goods produced by the chemical engineers was highly sensitive to changes in price.
    c. chemical engineering was so specialized that few persons in other areas could become chemical engineers without taking at least three additional years of training.
    d. there were many unemployed chemical engineers before the increase in demand.

13. If a college education did not increase worker productivity,
    a. no one would go to college.
    b. wages would tend to be the same for workers with and without a college education.
    c. wages would still be higher for workers with college degrees because of the cost of going to college.
    d. the total lifetime earnings of workers who go to college and those who don't would tend to be the same.

THE ECONOMIC WAY OF THINKING – DISCUSSION QUESTIONS

1. In recent years, the computer industry has grown quite rapidly as a result of technological advances. Suppose that the application of computers in the workplace continues at an accelerated rate.
   a. What would happen to the supply of computer technicians in the short run? In the long run?
   b. What would happen to the earnings of computer technicians in the short run? In the long run?
   c. What would happen in the long run to the supply and earnings of workers in industries that compete for the type of workers who become computer technicians?
   d. What would happen to the demand for inputs (for example, bookkeepers and clerks) for which computers are substitutes?

2. Is human labor really a "thing" that can be bought and sold like any other productive resource? What about the feelings of the human beings involved? While we can buy a person's time, we can't buy his or her enthusiasm or loyalty so easily. What sort of advantages and disadvantages does the "human element" in purchasing labor inputs have?

3. a. Why is the amount demanded of a productive resource negatively related to the price of the resource? Why is the demand likely to be more elastic when buyers have more time to respond?

   b. If the price of unskilled labor rises, what will tend to happen to the demand for substitute resources? For complementary resources?

   c. Will the demand for unskilled labor be more or less elastic as a result of the demand change described in part b for substitute resources? For complementary resources?

4. Do individuals seek to maximize their income from supplying resources? How does the rate of return to resource suppliers influence their investment decisions? Do investors necessarily seek the highest possible rate of return on their resources? Why or why not?

5. Suppose that the question in part e of Problem and Project #1 had specified the weekly fixed cost at $1,000 instead of $800. How would this have changed your answer to the question?

6. What impact would each of the following have on the demand for economists?

   a. An increase in government research funds for the study of wage-price controls

   b. A reduction in government-financed scholarships and loans for students

   c. The establishment of a planning agency that must analyze and decide whether labor-management contracts are inflationary

   d. Reduced emphasis on government planning and an increased reliance on the market mechanism

PERSPECTIVES IN ECONOMICS

Baseball's $5 Million Man: Is He Worth It?
by Timothy Tregarthen

[Reprinted with permission from *The Margin*, Fall 1991, pp. 34-36, abridged.]

Boston Red Sox pitcher Roger Clemens became baseball's first $5 million man when he signed a $21.5 million, four-year contract early this year.

"We are all delighted to get this contract finished," said Red Sox general manager Lou Gorman after the signing. "He is not only one of the best pitchers in history, but the premier pitcher in baseball today."

Not everyone was as delighted as Mr. Gorman — or, presumably, Mr. Clemens. "It's another classic example of how ownership is tearing the heart out of baseball for no good reason," snapped Pittsburgh Pirates President Carl Berger.

Mr. Clemens is undoubtedly a great pitcher. He has twice won baseball's Cy Young award. Prior to the 1991 season he had won 69.5 percent of the games in which he pitched, while the Red Sox had won just 50.1 percent of the games in which Mr. Clemens had not pitched since he joined the club. But is he worth more than $5 million per season?

In one sense, the answer is obviously "yes." The Red Sox franchise chose to pay Mr. Clemens his huge wage; they must have thought he was worth $5 million.

"Clubs will typically do a calculation of what kind of additional revenue a player will generate," says Lou Guth, an economist and senior vice president of National Economic Research Associates, a consulting firm in White Plains, New York. "It may well be that the greater attendance and better TV and radio contracts that having Roger Clemens on the roster could bring will prove to be worth it."

Apparently, many teams have high estimates of their players' ability to generate big revenues. Thirty-five players now earn $3 million or more. Mr. Clemens was joined in the $5 million club last spring by New York Mets pitcher Dwight Gooden, who signed a three-year pact for $15.45 million. The contract could be worth as much as $16.2 million, depending on Mr. Gooden's performance.

Economic theory suggests that firms will be willing to pay for a factor of production, whether it is an ace hurler or a ton of fertilizer, a price equal to its marginal revenue product — the additional revenue attributable to an additional unit of the factor.

Presumably, the Red Sox calculated Mr. Clemens' likely impact on team revenues. As long as his efforts bring fans to the stadium, viewers to the TV set and listeners to radio who will generate at least $5 million in revenue each year, Mr. Clemens will pay his way. It is the fans a player attracts that ultimately determine his worth.

In the words of Yankee owner George Steinbrenner, "You measure the value of a ballplayer by the number of fannies he puts in the seats."

The notion that Mr. Clemens might account for $5 million in additional revenues is not implausible. The Red Sox drew 2,528,986 fans last year to Fenway Park and are thought to have grossed $40 million. "If you think about what might happen to their (the Red Sox) revenues if Mr. Clemens switched to another team, it's easy to see him being worth $5 million a year," Mr. Guth says.

Wins and Losses

Economists generally measure the marginal revenue product of a player using a method developed by

Gerald W. Scully, an economist at the University of Texas at Dallas. Writing in the December 1974 issue of the *American Economic Review*, Mr. Scully proposed a two-step process to gauge a player's contribution to team revenues. First, Mr. Scully figured out what determines team revenue. Several factors are involved, including the population of the city in which the team plays, its average income level and whether there are other professional sports teams in the city. A crucial factor is the team's win-loss record. Winners draw more fans than losers, all other things equal.

The second step was to identify the factors that determine how many games a team will win. Mr. Scully found that win-loss records are determined almost entirely by hitting and pitching ability.

Once these relationships were estimated, Mr. Scully could calculate the impact of a player with a given hitting or pitching record on his team's record and then compute the effect that would have on that team's revenues. Mr. Scully then subtracted costs associated with having a player on the roster, such as for training and transportation, to estimate the player's net marginal revenue product. Finally, he compared these figures to actual player salaries.

Startling Results

Mr. Scully's results were startling. He found that hitters and pitchers with average records earned salaries equal to only about 20 percent of their estimated net marginal revenue products. "Star" quality players earned just 15 percent of net marginal revenue products. Mr. Scully based his estimates on data for the 1968-69 season and compared salaries and net marginal revenue products over the likely course of a player's entire career.

The sharp disparity, Mr. Scully argued, resulted from a key provision then in effect under the Uniform Player's Contract. The provision, called the reserve clause, stipulated that players belonged to the teams that hired them. A team could sell or trade players to another team, but at no time could a player offer his services to other teams. If a player wanted a career in baseball, he had to agree to a system in which he would always be limited to negotiations with the team that owned his contract. Teams thus had monopsony power over their players' services.

A monopsony team faced an upward-sloping supply curve for players of a particular quality; getting more players of the same skill level requires paying higher salaries. Hiring another player that good is likely to require a higher salary not only for that player but for the other players of that quality on the team's roster. The additional, or marginal, cost of the player will thus exceed his salary.

The accompanying graph illustrates the argument in the case of star pitchers. The net marginal revenue product curve (MRP) measures the contribution of additional star pitchers to a team's revenues, less their associated training, transportation and other costs. The supply curve (S) shows the number of players of that quality available at each wage. Because a team must offer a higher wage to obtain more star pitchers, its marginal factor cost curve (MFC) lies above this supply curve.

Theoretically, a profit-maximizing team will hire additional star pitchers up to the point at which the marginal factor cost equals net marginal revenue product. The wage – the player's salary – will then be determined by the supply curve. The monopsony model

Monopsony Exploitation of Star Pitchers

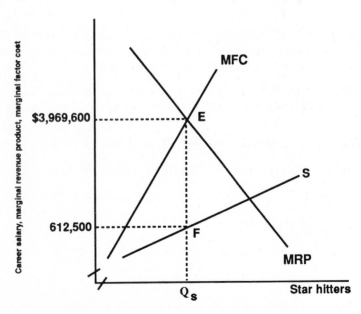

A monopsony firm hires addtional units of an input up to the point that margninal factor cost and marginal revenue product are equal. It pays a wage determined by the supply curve. That results in a wage ($612,500) considerably below marginal revenue product ($3,969,600).

Fig. 23-5

thus predicts that wages will fall short of net marginal revenue product, just as Mr. Scully observed.

An even sharper test of the theory was provided in the mid-1970s. Two players challenged the reserve clause, arguing it was an illegal restriction of their rights. An arbitrator agreed and ordered that baseball players be given status as "free agents" – able to seek offers from other teams – after six years of professional play.

At the close of the 1976 season, 25 players became free agents under the new stipulation. Paul M. Sommers, an economist at Middlebury College, and a student, Noel Quinton, analyzed the salaries won by the top 14 free agents.

Economic theory predicts that the shift to more competitive bidding should have moved player salaries closer to marginal revenue product. Using an approach similar to Mr. Scully's, the two researchers estimated each player's marginal revenue product in the 1977 season and compared that to the salary the player received that year.

Their results, reported in the Summer 1982 issue of the *Journal of Human Resources*, were consistent with the theory. The salaries of the hitters in the group rose to about half of marginal revenue product. The salaries of the pitchers were roughly equal to their marginal revenue product. The economists could not explain why pitcher salaries came so much closer to estimated marginal revenue product than hitter salaries.

Villanova University economist John Leonard reported in 1985 on a study of hitter salaries for the 1982 season. He found that they had risen to 75 percent of estimated marginal revenue product.

And today? "I think that salaries are, on average, about equal to the marginal revenue products of players," Mr. Leonard says. "Of course, it's difficult to predict just how well a player might perform, so some salaries end up being too high and some end up being too low. But on average, they're about right."

Mr. Guth notes that another factor that contributes to high player salaries is arbitration. Beginning in a player's third year, he can demand that his salary be set by an arbitrator. The arbitrator, whose rulings are binding, then determines a salary that he or she thinks is justified, based on what other players of similar quality receive. Thus, according to Mr. Guth, the market affects a player's salary even before he can become a free agent.

The models economists use to analyze the player market assume that teams act as profit-maximizing entities. Is that a reasonable assumption?

"You hear a lot about owners being in it for the 'love of the sport' and things like that," Mr. Guth says. "And that might well be true. But profit considerations surely affect their choices. Every academic study I've seen suggests that the owners make choices that are consistent with the assumption of profit-maximizing behavior."

Certainly the business has been profitable. Professional baseball reported a profit of $214 million in 1989, the most recent year for which figures have been released. Another gauge of expected profitability is the price new teams are willing to pay for the right to a franchise. Six ownership groups were vying last spring for two new major league expansion franchises. The teams chosen will have to pay a franchise fee of $95 million for the right to operate a major league team.

Discussion

1. The results cited in this article seem to be at odds with the general view that "professional athletes are overpaid, spoiled brats." What reasons can you think of that would explain this difference of opinion?

2. As Tregarthen admits, one of the weaknesses of this analysis is the manner in which marginal revenue product was measured. How would *you* go about measuring the marginal revenue product of an employee?

3. What about players who are hurt or who are in the minor leagues still improving their skills (human capital). If owners have to pay players whose marginal revenue products are zero, then shouldn't they be allowed to pay the other players less than their MRPs to even things out? Why or why not?

24
Earnings, Productivity, and the Job Market

TRUE OR FALSE

T F

☐ ☐ 1. Immobility of labor is a major source of wage differentials.

☐ ☐ 2. Higher productivity generally leads to higher wages.

☐ ☐ 3. Firms seeking to maximize monetary profit will tend to hire very few minority workers.

☐ ☐ 4. Owners of physical capital in the United States receive about 40 percent of national income.

☐ ☐ 5. Automation always reduces production costs and employment within a firm.

☐ ☐ 6. Automation almost always reduces the demand for labor in the economy.

☐ ☐ 7. An expansion in production per worker is the primary source of high living standards.

☐ ☐ 8. Minimum wage legislation helps low-wage workers, particularly teenagers, whereas the burden of the legislation is imposed almost exclusively on high-wage workers.

☐ ☐ 9. The average wage rate in the United States in high in comparison with that of other countries largely because of the large amount of physical and human capital with which the average American works.

☐ ☐ 10. Other things constant, the more dangerous a job, the higher the wage rate it will command.

☐ ☐ 11. The wages of workers on jobs that require special skills or technical know-how will necessarily be high.

☐ ☐ 12. The job opportunities of a minority group would be reduced if consumers discriminated against firms that hired minorities.

☐ ☐ 13. The almost total exclusion of women from many high-paying professional occupations is consistent with the employment discrimination explanation of earnings differences according to gender.

PROBLEMS AND PROJECTS

Exhibit 1

Quantity demanded per month	Price	Quantity supplied per month
0	$600	6000
1000	500	5000
2000	400	4000
3000	300	3000
4000	200	2000
5000	100	1000
6000	0	0

1. Exhibit 1 is a hypothetical, demand-and-supply schedule for sophisticated pocket calculators in a competitive industry.
   a. What will be the equilibrium quantity and price in this market?
   b. Suppose that a new labor-saving technology is developed, resulting in an increase of 2000 in quantity supplied at every price. What will happen to the equilibrium quantity and price?
   c. The new technology reduces the quantity of labor used *per calculator* by 20 percent. What will happen to total employment in the industry? (Original employment was 120 workers.)
   d. Owing to the new technology, the computer industry substituted more machines for labor. Using the elasticity-of-demand argument, refute or support the following statement: "If we continue to allow machines to replace workers, we will run out of jobs. Automation is the major cause of unemployment."

2. The diagram in Exhibit 2 depicts the situation in the unskilled labor market with a minimum wage of $4.55 per hour:

Exhibit 2

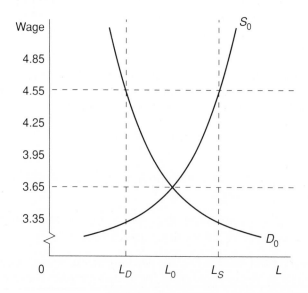

Suppose a proposal is made to replace the current minimum wage law with a wage subsidy. With the subsidy, employed unskilled workers would receive a $.90 per hour subsidy in addition to their regular wage.

a. How many workers would be hired with the subsidy, L_O, L_S, L_D, or some different amount?

b. What is the total cost to the government of providing the subsidy?

c. Indicate whether the wage subsidy (compared to the $4.55 minimum wage) would raise (+), lower (−), leave unchanged (0), or change in an uncertain direction (?) the well-being of each of the following:

_____ i. Consumers of products that use unskilled labor
_____ ii. Currently employed unskilled workers
_____ iii. Currently unemployed unskilled workers
_____ iv. Skilled workers
_____ v. Taxpayers

d. How would you expect employers to adjust their cost minimizing combination of machinery and unskilled workers? Explain.

3. The text describes the following determinants of earnings differentials:

a. Nonhomogeneous labor
   A1: Worker productivity and specialized skills
   A2: Workers preferences
   A3: Race and gender

b. Nonhomogeneous jobs
   B1: Location of jobs
   B2: Nonpecuniary job characteristics

c. Immobility of labor
   C1: Temporary disequilibrium
   C2: Institutional restrictions

Indicate the main reason from the list above for each of the following wage differentials:

_____ a. Urban wages are higher than rural wages.
_____ b. Police officers in metropolitan areas with high violent crime rates earn higher wages than police officers elsewhere.
_____ c. White basketball players receive about 20 percent higher salaries than equally talented black basketball players.
_____ d. Primary care parents tend to choose jobs with flexible working conditions.
_____ e. Taxicab drivers charge higher-than-average fares in cities with marketable taxi licenses.
_____ f. Computer programmers earn higher salaries than computer operators.

4. Consider the following hypothetical information about productivity in Canada and Brazil:

Labor output per week

	Tons of steel	Bushels of wheat	Autos
Canada	10	5000	1
Brazil	5	500	1/5

a. If wages depend on productivity, how high would Canadian wages be compared to Brazilian wages if both countries produced
    i. only steel? _____
    ii. only wheat? _____
    iii. only autos? _____

b. Suppose that the actual wage rate per week is $200 in Canada and $40 in Brazil. Assuming that other input costs are the same in both countries for each of these goods, indicate below which country is the low-cost producer of
    i. steel _____
    ii. wheat _____
    iii. autos _____

c. Based on your answers to parts a and b, decide whether the following is true or false: "High-paid Canadian workers can't compete with cheap foreign labor." Explain.

LEARNING THE MECHANICS – MULTIPLE CHOICE

1. In 1989, the female-male earnings ratio indicated that the earnings of single women relative to the earnings of single men were
    a. much higher than the relative earnings of women in other marital status groupings.
    b. about the same as the relative earnings of women in other marital status groupings.
    c. much less than the relative earnings of women in other marital status groupings.
    d. not directly comparable to the relative earnings of women in other marital status groupings.

2. Real wages would be most likely to decrease over a period of time if
    a. the rate of inflation was higher than 3 percent.
    b. the demand for consumer goods decreased relative to the demand for capital goods.
    c. automation increased.
    d. output or productivity per labor-hour decreased.

3. If all persons were identical regarding preferences and productivity factors (ability, skill level, education, experience, etc.), the highest-paying jobs would be the most
    a. prestigious.
    b. convenient.
    c. pleasant.
    d. disagreeable.

4. If a minimum wage law was enacted and the demand for workers was inelastic
    a. employers would substitute machines for most of the present workers in the short run.
    b. the total income for workers would fall.
    c. the reduction in employment would be small.
    d. employers would hire more low-skill workers to keep the wage rate from rising even further.

5. Evidence suggests that education raises the earnings of the work force mainly by
   a. increasing the marginal productivity of labor.
   b. keeping young people out of the labor force, thereby reducing the supply of labor.
   c. teaching workers how to demand more pay.
   d. teaching people to read and write, although education beyond the point does not seem to increase worker productivity.

6. Increasing the minimum wage will probably result in
   a. lower profits and the same level of product prices.
   b. greater employment, since more people want to work at the new wage than at the previous equilibrium wage.
   c. reduced employment of the unskilled, as firms produce less output and substitute away from the more expensive unskilled labor.
   d. a decrease in the demand for workers in previously unionized high-wage firms.

7. Within an occupation, when a given job provides steadier work (fewer layoffs), the hourly wage tends to be
   a. lower than wage rates in jobs that are otherwise similar.
   b. higher than wage rates in jobs that are otherwise similar.
   c. no different from wage rates in jobs that are otherwise similar.
   d. determined by factors other than supply and demand.

8. Employment discrimination against members of a minority group invariably exists when the minority group members
   a. are paid less than other workers.
   b. are hired less frequently than other workers.
   c. are treated differently than other workers.
   d. are treated differently than other workers who are similarly qualified.

9. Indicate which of the following most accurately represents the capital formation rate of the United States relative to other countries.
   a. The United States invests a larger share of its GNP than most other industrial countries.
   b. The United States invests a smaller share of its GNP than most other industrial countries.
   c. The United States invests about the same share of its GNP as Japan and Germany.
   d. The United States invests about the same share of its GNP as most other industrial countries.

10. Automated production methods are attractive to a producer when
    a. they reduce cost.
    b. they replace workers.
    c. output is increased.
    d. wages are low.

Questions 11-14 refer to the following information:

Suppose that the labor force of an imaginary country is equally divided between men and women, who are equally skilled and productive, with similar preferences with respect to laboring. However, due to recent social upheavals, the labor market is rigidly segmented: the majority of occupations are reserved for men, the remainder for women. Important figures are given below.

Labor Market as a Whole			Segmented Markets			
quantity supplied total	quantity demanded total	wage	quantity supplied female	quantity demanded female	quantity supplied male	quantity demanded male
60	140	$60	30	35	30	105
66	132	70	33	33	33	99
80	120	80	40	30	40	90
100	100	100	50	25	50	75
120	80	120	60	20	60	60
140	60	140	70	15	70	45

11. The best description of the current rigidly segmented labor market situation is that
    a. more men than women are hired, with men earning a higher wage.
    b. equal numbers of men and women are hired, with men earning a higher wage.
    c. equal numbers of men and women are hired, with women earning a higher wage.
    d. equal numbers of men and women are hired, with equal wages for both genders.

12. The impact of the market segmentation on employers is
    a. zero, since men and women are equally skilled.
    b. minor, since employers are paying only $10 more for men to do something that women could do equally well.
    c. major, since employers are paying more than 50% more for men to do something that women could do equally well.
    d. impossible to determine from the information given.

13. Suppose that the government decides to ensure that men and women earn the same wage. As a result, a law is passed mandating that the female wage be comparable in worth to the male wage that previously existed in the segmented male market. The market remains segmented. As a result,
    a. the total number of men working and their wages is unchanged.
    b. the total number of women working falls, but their wages rise.
    c. 40 women are unemployed (willing to work at the existing wage), but no men are unemployed.
    d. all of the above.

14. The Opposition floats a different proposal, which would outlaw segmentation. Gender differences would no longer be allowed to affect hiring. (Remember, the two groups are otherwise identical.) If this proposal could be perfectly enforced, the best description of the labor market would be that:
    a. more men than women would be hired, with men earning a higher wage.
    b. equal numbers of men and women would be hired, with men earning a higher wage.
    c. equal numbers of men and women would be hired, with equal wages of $100 for both genders.
    d. equal numbers of men and women would be hired, with equal wages of $120 for both genders.

THE ECONOMIC WAY OF THINKING – MULTIPLE CHOICE

1. Use statements I and II to answer this question (**I**) Differences in worker productivity are one major reason why individual earnings differ. (**II**) Even if all workers were identical, differences in the desirability of jobs would still cause earnings differentials.
    a. Both I and II are true.
    b. I is true, II is false.
    c. I is false, II is true.
    d. Both I and II are false.

2. When wage rates for a group of workers (teenagers, for example) are far above the equilibrium level, discrimination by employers on noneconomic grounds becomes
    a. more costly.
    b. more costly, but necessary.
    c. necessary and less costly.
    d. more costly and unnecessary.

3. One potential problem with Congress mandating that employers supply their employees with free child care services is that
    a. if employers can change wages, the wages of employees will be likely to eventually absorb the cost of the child care.
    b. if employers cannot change wages, the increased total compensation package will make employers likely to attempt to hire fewer employees, causing increased unemployment.
    c. total compensation will be greater for workers with children that can use child care than it will be for other workers.
    d. all of the above are potential problems.

4. Suppose that the government passed a law that required that all government employees be paid the average wage rate in the private sector. Which of the following would be true?
    a. Output would be maximized.
    b. Costs would be maximized.
    c. Those individuals with higher skills (and thus more options) could be expected to leave government employment for higher-paying alternatives.
    d. There would be no change in the allocation of resources.

5. Which one of the following would be *least* likely to occur if Congress passed legislation exempting teenagers from the minimum wage?
    a. The training opportunities available to teenagers would improve.
    b. The white-black unemployment differential would increase.
    c. The rate of unemployment for teenagers would decline.
    d. The rate of labor force participation for black teenagers would increase.

6. After correcting for differences in age, education, marital status, language, and regional characteristics, the earnings of women are not as great as those of men. This differential is due in part to
    a. discrimination against women in employment.
    b. work specialization within the family following traditional male-female patterns.
    c. both and b.
    d. neither a nor b.

7. Which of the following most correctly states the relationship between machinery and the earnings of labor?
   a. Machines tend to reduce the demand for labor, thereby reducing the earnings rate of labor.
   b. Production of machinery creates jobs, thereby increasing the demand for (and wages of) labor.
   c. High productivity per worker-hour is a necessary ingredient for the attainment of high real earnings, and adoption of labor-saving machinery enhances the ability of labor to attain such high productivity.
   d. Output and real earnings can always be increased whenever a machine can be substituted for a function previously performed by labor.

8. A marketing representative for a firm selling equipment to automate car washes would probably be happy to see the minimum wage law
   a. abolished.
   b. changed to exempt teenagers from the law.
   c. extended to cover all car-wash establishments (including weekend operations run by service clubs).
   d. changed so that car-wash establishments would not be covered by the law (but other businesses would be).

9. Economic theory suggests that the standard of living for American workers would rise if
   a. the minimum wage was doubled.
   b. automation was outlawed.
   c. a new law required all wage rates to double.
   d. technological progress continued.

10. If large numbers of young American men thought the life of a cowboy was great (despite the hardships), we would expect
    a. an increase in the wages of cowboys, to fit the image.
    b. a decrease in the wages of cowboys, since supply would be enlarged.
    c. no impact on wages, which are determined by supply and demand, not romantic notions.
    d. a decrease in the wages of cowboys, since demand would be reduced.

11. "One way to get higher labor productivity is to set higher wages. If bricklayers had to be paid $30 per hours next year, we could trust that virtually every bricklayer *working at that time* would be worth (have a marginal revenue product of) at least $30 per hour." This statement is
    a. true, and everyone would gain because of the higher productivity.
    b. true, although many of the current bricklayers would be unable find employment at the $30 wage rate.
    c. false, since the marginal productivity of bricklayers could not rise so fast in one year.
    d. false, unless very rapid technological change occurred.

12. The effects of job discrimination in a given time period are
    a. not likely to carry over into the future.
    b. likely to carry over into the future, since human capital formation is often influenced.
    c. measured without consideration of past experience or discrimination.
    d. strictly dependent on employer actions at the time, not on what came earlier in the worker's career.

13. If customers are racist but employers are not, then employment discrimination will be
    a. less profitable than nondiscrimination.
    b. more profitable than nondiscrimination.
    c. equally profitable as nondiscrimination.
    d. easier to eliminate than if employers were racist but customers were not.

THE ECONOMIC WAY OF THINKING – DISCUSSION QUESTIONS

1. Suppose that a new invention halves the cost of making automobiles.
   a. What will happen to output in the auto industry?
   b. What will happen to auto industry employment if demand for automobiles is elastic? Inelastic?
   c. What will happen to output and employment elsewhere in the economy if the auto demand is elastic? Inelastic?
   d. Is it more likely for the new invention to make auto industry employment rise in the short run and fall in the long run or fall in the short run and rise in the long run? Explain.

2. What are the major determinants of the elasticity of demand for a specific category (for example, physicists, craftsmen) of labor? Explain. Be specific. How does time affect the elasticity of demand for labor?

3. Substantial differences, sometimes up to 150 percent, in wage rates for essentially the same kind of labor (for example, semiskilled labor) prevail between different industries even in the same locality.
   a. What are some of the causes of interindustry wage differentials? List an industry that illustrates each cause.
   b. Which kinds of industries are likely to be at the top of the wage scale? At the bottom?

4. Two components of U.S. antidiscrimination laws are (1) "equal pay for equal work" and (2) "equal opportunity."
   a. Which type of discrimination (wage rate or employment restriction) is addressed by each component? Explain.
   b. If employers practice racial discrimination, do you think "equal pay for equal work" alone would promote or discourage "equal opportunity" for employment?
   c. What are the pros and cons of actual hiring quotas as a method for eliminating employment discrimination?

5. If you owned a firm, how would you expect the wages and racial composition of your employees to compare with your competitors' employees if
   a. firms in general practice employment discrimination, but you don't.
   b. firms in general do not practice employment discrimination, but you do.

   Explain both answers.

6. A recent issue of importance has been that of illegal immigration from one country to another. Analyze the impact of such illegal immigration on (a) the immigrants, (b) the new employers of the immigrants, (c) workers who remained in the home country of the immigrants, and (d) workers in the country to which the immigrants came. Given this analysis, attempt to develop a solution for the problem of illegal immigration.

7. The following statement was made by John Kendrick of George Washington University:

> I might point out that investment is a smaller portion of gross national product in the United States than in most other industrialized countries. And I believe this is one reason that we have a slower rate of advance in productivity than most other advanced nations.

Assuming that Kendrick's data are correct, do you agree with his conclusion? Why or why not?

CURRENT DEBATES IN ECONOMICS

Debate Number Four: Should We Adopt a Comparable Worth Program?
Yes, We Should Adopt a Comparable Worth Program:

Fair Pay
By Jodie T. Allen

[Reprinted with permission from *The Washington Post*, February 13, 1985.]

Quiz: Who wrote the following? "Comparable worth is an extension of women's demand for equal pay for equal work, an idea that is both reasonable and fair as a way of correcting the undeniable, historic wage discrimination against women."

Answer: the editors of Business Week magazine.

That's right. The quotation comes not from the annual report of the Radical Feminist League to Disrupt the American Economy, but from an editorial in a recent issue of a distinguished business journal. They recognize that "comparable worth" – the misnomer that generally refers to the idea that employers should not pay low wages for certain jobs just because they are typically held by women – is an idea that should not be dismissed by ridicule or misrepresentation.

Economists predict that, as skills of working women increase, the pay gap between men and women will narrow to "only" 25 percent by the end of the century. Part of the larger discrepancy is accounted for by differences in training, work experience, responsibility and, perhaps, such intangibles as "drive" and the distractions of family responsibilities. But there is no serious dispute that many employers pay less for jobs in which women are concentrated than those in which men predominate.

Women for centuries were crowded into a few occupations. It would have been remarkable if employers had *not* taken advantage of that fact by paying them less than their skills and responsibilities would have commanded in an open marketplace. Vestiges of this discrimination still exist. How else to explain the fact that New York City pays its police dispatchers (mostly black women) several thousand dollars less than it pays its predominantly white male fire dispatchers – to cite one current but far from isolated example?

Using similar examples, women have been pressing employers in wage negotiations (such as those recently concluded at Yale University) and in court suits alleging illegal discrimination (such as the successful suit brought against the State of Washington). The comparable pay practices being sought would not, as administration spokesmen and other pooh-poohers of the idea claim, require that ballet dancers be paid as much as football players, or nurses as much as lab technicians. Nor would the changes being asked of individual employers require the creation of another ghastly federal bureaucracy charged with assigning worth and wages to every worker.

In fact, as a recent report sponsored by 23 House Republicans pointed out, Title VII of the Civil Rights Act, as interpreted by the Supreme Court in the state of Washington case, already prohibits employers from adopting pay-setting schemes that discriminate between men and women in similar though not identical jobs. These Republican legislators did not find that the drive for comparable pay presaged the decline and fall of the free-enterprise system. Instead, they called on employers to eliminate bias from their pay practices and on federal agencies to speed up investigation of discriminatory practices.

Ending sex discrimination in wage-setting would not prohibit employers from setting pay scales that were different from those of other employers or from responding to skill shortages in male-dominated jobs. But fair pay would require that individual employers review their formal or informal job classification practices and ask themselves, for example, whether the differences in what they pay secretaries (who are in short supply) and truckdrivers (who are currently in great surplus) are really the result of impartial market forces.

In fact, most wages are not determined by the free interplay of supply and demand in a fluid market. Convention, monopoly power, unionization and employer preferences have had far more to do with the wags paid in many occupations. The relatively high pay for surgeons compared with other doctors for example, has been traced to the surgeons' dominance in fee setting arrangements when Blue Shield insurance was invented in the 1930s. The relatively low pay for nurses and secretaries has been charged to collusive practices among employers in some areas.

Like earlier legally enforced changes in the labor market – minimum wage, child-labor, health and safety, fair labor standards and equal-pay laws – reviewing comparable pay would be inconvenient and, in some cases, costly to employers. But forward-looking private and public employers – such as the editors of business Week and the 23 House Republicans – are recognizing that inexplicable differences in pay for jobs requiring comparable skills are not only hard to justify but very likely to result in costly litigation.

By moving voluntarily to straighten out its pay practices, the state of Minnesota, for example, avoided both prolonged litigation and a costly settlement. By willfully ignoring repeated findings by independent job reviewers, the state of Washington ended up owing – deservedly – a costly back-pay award. Moreover, contrary to predictions of opponents, Minnesota's new pay practices seem to have encouraged women to move into traditionally male jobs – a trend that will ultimately help in narrowing the gap between male and female earnings.

The importance of pay equity is easy to exaggerate on both sides. While egregious pay discrimination because of gender surely exists, the evidence is that it does not account for a substantial portion of the total wage bill. That means that eliminating it neither would be very costly to the average employer nor would do much for the average female worker. But comparable worth – or pay equity or sex discrimination or whatever you want to call it – is important as part of the continuing drive to make the job market a fairer and more open place.

No, We Should Not Adopt a Comparable Worth Program:

Against 'Comparable Worth'
By Morris B. Abram

[Reprinted from *The New York Times*, November 4, 1985.
©1985 by The New York Times Company. Reprinted by permission.]

Both houses of Congress and a number of courts are grappling with the question of whether wages should be fixed on the basis of equal pay for work of comparable value to the employer – a proposed remedy for lower pay received by women. One can already see developing many complications and dangers built into the concept of "comparable worth."

These proposals would tie us up in a tangle of definitions that would reduce options for women and ultimately be a detriment to all of society. Comparable worth proposals do not attempt to equalize the wages of men and women doing the same job but to arbitrarily equate jobs that have entirely different market values.

What is the actual situation with regard to women's wages in this country? During the last Presidential campaign, Geraldine A. Ferraro frequently repeated that women are "paid 59 cents on the dollar for the same work as a man," implying a wage gap of 41 percent. This misleading statistic has been the basis for much well-meaning support of the proposals now before us.

But the 59 percent wage scale, with a 41 percent gap, comes from statistics for 1977; by 1983, that 41 percent gap had narrowed to 36 percent. This figure declines to 28 percent when the number of hours worked by women and men is taken into account, and then to 14 percent when other factors, including schooling and work experience, are considered.

The 14 percent gap, the real starting point for discussions of comparable worth, has not been adequately explained. Of course, part of it may be attributable to discrimination, but the Equal Pay Act of 1963 and the Civil Rights Act of 1964 already prohibit such practices. An alternative explanation could be that women may be willing to accept lower paying jobs that permit them to spend more time with their families.

More meaningful insights can be drawn from statistics of particular groups of employees. Among men and women between the ages of 20 and 24, for instance, the wage gap is only 10 percent. And for single men and women who have never been married, the gap is almost nonexistent – 2.4 percent to 4 percent.

One of the dangers of comparable worth is that it would create a new claim by certain advocacy groups on the right to legislate economic equality. These groups would have us adopt a system of permanent wage and salary controls, first in Federal employment and inevitably in private business. Under their plan, wages and salaries would be decreed by "experts" and bureaucrats, and deviations from their edicts would generate lawsuits in which the employer would bear the burden of proof that discrimination did not exist.

What's more, gender-based legislation is only the start. A bill introduced last July in the House brought race and ethnic qualifications into the wage formula as well. The latest proposals are likely to become a mechanism to give leverage to any subgroup of employees seeking a raise.

How would women fare in the proposed brave new world of comparable worth? Women would suffer a decline in the standard of living as does everyone in society when wages are inflated artificially. To maintain their previous standard, more women than at present would find work a necessity rather than an option. Even women in occupations targeted for wage raises would not benefit. For example, if secretarial wages were mandated to rise to a certain level, one could expect more businesses to opt for automation. The result would be fewer jobs for women and further narrowing of their options.

The attempt to write comparable worth into Federal laws marks a reversal of the civil rights revolution. Comparable worth moves from the assertion of civil and political equality, which we all support, to economic and social equality, which many of us do not support.

Guaranteed economic and social equality have never been part of the heritage of a free country because they ultimately impinge on freedom, by making government the arbiter of the rewards of human effort. This raises the old question of whether government should be dependent on the people or people on government.

Holding a Debate

Many students will enjoy participating in a debate on this topic either in class or in an informal study group. After completing both readings and possibly doing some additional research (for example, see pages 612-615 of the text), get three to four volunteers for each side of the debate, choose a moderator if your instructor is not available, and devote about a half an hour to opening statements, rebuttals, and summaries.

Discussion

1. What exactly *is* comparable worth? Pick two occupations you know fairly well and describe how a comparable worth program would work in those occupations. Is it possible to be in favor of equal pay for equal work and still be against a comparable worth program? How?

2. If you read the Allen article, note that one of the hardest problems to solve when implementing a comparable worth program is choosing the jobs which have equivalent "worth." In particular, some jobs which are similar in terms of skills required have differences in terms of working conditions (such as more flexible hours). Are such jobs comparable or not? Explain.

3. If you read the Abram article, note that there is an unexplained gap of at least 14 percent between the earnings of male and female workers. How then could he be against legislation that would get rid of this discriminatory difference?

25
Capital, Interest, and Profit

TRUE OR FALSE

T F

☐ ☐ 1. We must divert resources from the production of current consumption in order to expand the availability of capital goods.

☐ ☐ 2. The net present value of a payment to be received one year from now can be expressed as the ratio of the amount of money to be received divided by the interest rate.

☐ ☐ 3. Suppose that an investor hears that the supply of loanable funds has just increased but that inflation (and expected inflation) has not. This news might encourage her to borrow to buy a machine that she previously had thought was too expensive.

☐ ☐ 4. Agricultural price support programs don't always work perfectly, but they are unquestionably effective at increasing farmers' incomes.

☐ ☐ 5. The net present value of a payment to be received a year in the future can be expressed as the receipts one year from now divided by one plus the interest rate.

☐ ☐ 6. A higher rate of time preference implies a higher interest rate.

☐ ☐ 7. If a governmental price control and acreage allotment program increases the price of raw tobacco above the market equilibrium level, the price of land with an acreage allotment to grow tobacco will rise.

☐ ☐ 8. The real rate of interest rises when the rate of inflation accelerates.

☐ ☐ 9. Risk usually influences the interest rate agreed to by business decision-makers.

☐ ☐ 10. The interest rate charged by a lender has three components: the inflationary premium, the risk premium, and the pure nominal interest rate component.

☐ ☐ 11. Changes in a corporation's stock price happen too slowly to give corporate officers much feedback on how market investors evaluate their investment decisions.

☐ ☐ 12. Entrepreneurial decision-making usually involves choosing under conditions of uncertainty.

PROBLEMS AND PROJECTS

You will need to use the net present values in Exhibit 3 on page 638 of the text to work various problems in this chapter.

1. Suppose that you have $1000. Broker A offers an opportunity that should pay $2000 after six years. After considering the expected rate of inflation and the risk involved, you determine that a 12 percent discount rate is appropriate. Broker B offers a different opportunity that will pay $1000 in five years and another $1000 in ten years. Since it is safer, an 8 percent discount rate is appropriate.
   a. What is the value to you, today, of broker A's option? Broker B's option?
   b. Suppose you learn that broker B's option is a bit more risky, and it, too should be evaluated with a 12 percent discount rate. Now what is it worth today?
   c. Having evaluated both options at 12 percent, you are advised that an extra 2 percent should be allowed as an annual inflation factor. If 12 percent was the initial appropriate rate (and the money payoff and timing remain the same), what interest rate is appropriate now that the expected rate of inflation has risen by 2 percent?

2. The owner of a small forest in Florida is raising trees as a cash crop. A forester friend mentions that certain silvicultural practices, costing $334 now, will yield an extra 10,000 board feet of timber when the forest is harvested in 30 years. Harvesting and other costs will not change significantly. What price of timber per board foot would be required for the silvicultural practices to be worthwhile if the appropriate discount rate is 12 percent?

3. Reconstruct Exhibit 4 on page 640 of the text by using $14,000 per year as the expected income, and 12 percent as the discount rate. What is the net present value? (*Hint*: Be sure to round the discounted value to three digits, as the text does, for your answers to check exactly.)

4. It was noted in the text that the present value of an equal payment received or paid each year forever is:

   Present value = payment / interest rate.

In fact, this formula can be used to approximate present value whenever the payments last for a fairly long time. Try the following examples to see how well this simple formula works as an approximation.
   a. Recently, Life Cereal held a "Life Cereal Lifetime Allowance Sweepstakes." Each grand prize winner was promised $1,000 per year for life. At an interest rate of 8 percent, what would be the approximate present value of the grand prize? (If you expect to live for another 50 years, the true present value is $12,234.)
   b. A few years ago households across the country received a letter from Ed McMahon (of the Johnny Carson show) urging them to enter the American Family Publishers sweepstakes which offered America's "first TEN MILLION DOLLAR prize!" The winner of the prize was promised $333,333 per year for 30 years. At 7 percent interest, what is the approximate present value of this stream of receipts? (The true present value is $4,136,329.)
   c. Suppose you or your parents borrow $150,000 to buy a new home. If the interest rate is 10 percent, what is the approximate size of the mortgage payments each year? (*Hint*: rearrange the terms of the formula. Assuming annual payments, the actual payment size for a 30-year mortgage would be $15,912 per year.)

5. You have an opportunity to attend a six-month course in computer programming. The course meets every afternoon and would require that you work at your present job only half-time, in the mornings. Your employer has agreed to your half-time absence, but you must accept only half-time pay for the duration of the course, which would reduce your take-home pay by $1,250 per month. You have personal savings which would comfortably cover the $6,000 cost of the course itself. In discussions with your present employer, you have decided that if you acquire the skills offered by the course it will raise your take-home pay by $2,000 per year for the next ten years until you retire. If the appropriate discount rate is 8 percent, should you make this investment in your "human capital"?

6. The table in Exhibit 1 is available to help you answer the questions below. The middle column is similar to Exhibit 3 from Chapter 25 of the text. The right-hand column gives the total present value of $100 received each year rather than at one time.

Exhibit 1

Interest rate: 10 percent

	Present value of $100 received	
Year (t)	at the end of year t	each year for t year(s)
1	$90.91	$ 90.91
2	82.64	173.55
3	75.13	248.68
4	68.30	316.98
5	62.09	379.08
6	56.45	435.53
7	51.32	486.84
8	46.65	533.49
9	42.41	575.90
10	38.55	614.46

    a. According to the figures in the middle column, what is the total present value of $100 received at the end of one year, another $100 received after two years, and a final $100 received after three years? How does this compare to the value listed in the right-hand column for $t = 3$?

    b. Suppose you decide to rent an apartment for 7 years. Further suppose that the owner offers to let you use an old refrigerator for free and promises to keep the refrigerator repaired for all 7 years. You also have the option of buying a new energy efficient refrigerator (with a 7-year free maintenance agreement) for $700. The new refrigerator will reduce your electric bill by $150 per year and will have a market value of $100 after 7 years. With an interest rate of 10 percent, which option should you chose?

LEARNING THE MECHANICS – MULTIPLE CHOICE

1. The development and construction of machines that enhance our ability to produce goods and services in the future require
    a. the owners of these capital assets to borrow.
    b. the owners of these capital assets to reduce the growth rate of their consumption.
    c. that current consumption be sacrificed.
    d. that future consumption be sacrificed.

2. If the rate of time preference increased, we would expect
   a. the interest rate to fall.
   b. more capital investment.
   c. less capital investment.
   d. more *future* consumption.

3. A higher rate of inflation mainly tends to
   a. raise the real rate of interest.
   b. reduce the real rate of interest.
   c. raise the money rate of interest.
   d. lower the money rate of interest.

4. The net present value of $100, delivered one year from now, would
   a. rise, if inflation rose.
   b. fall, if the money rate of interest fell.
   c. rise, if the money rate of interest rose.
   d. fall, if the money rate of interest rose.

5. If the interest rate were 6 percent, the net present value of $100 to be received one year from now would be
   a. $94.34.
   b. $93.04.
   c. $100.00.
   d. $106.00

6. The pure interest yield, a component of the cost of an investment project
   a. is positively related to the risk of undertaking the project.
   b. is negatively related to the risk of undertaking the project.
   c. is unaffected by the riskiness of the project.
   d. is irrelevant to whether the project will be undertaken.

7. The net present value of $100 received one year from now will
   a. increase with the interest rate.
   b. be greater than $100 as long as the interest rate is positive.
   c. be greater than the net present value of $100 to be received two years from now.
   d. be unaffected by the money rate of interest.

8. Use statements I and II to answer this question. (**I**) Discounting procedures apply to decisions to invest in physical capital, but are not relevant to human capital investment decisions. (**II**) Nonmonetary considerations are usually more important in human capital investment decisions than in nonhuman capital investment decisions.
   a. I is true, II is false.
   b. I is false, II is true.
   c. Both I and II are true.
   d. Both I and II are false.

9. Monopoly profit that stems from a patent
   a. will quickly be eliminated by competitive imitators.
   b. can never be reduced by close (but slightly different) imitations.
   c. becomes capitalized into the value of the patent, which could then be sold.
   d. has no impact on resource allocation, but only makes the present owner wealthy, in a dynamic economy.

10. Pure interest is the payment to
    a. an investor bearing little or no risk.
    b. business entrepreneurs.
    c. owners of capital items.
    d. people who clip coupons, but contribute nothing to production.

11. According to Joseph Schumpeter, what is the major source of economic growth within the framework of a capitalist economy?
    a. Pure competition
    b. Innovative behavior by entrepreneurs
    c. Financial capital provided by bond holders
    d. Consumer expenditure

Questions 12-14 refer to the following information:

You manage a local widget factory and have to decide whether or not to buy a new improved widget machine. The machine will last for one year and then turn to dust. The machine will produce 100 widgets. The factory currently earns economic profit at a rate of 12%, the real interest rate is 4%, the inflation rate (and expected inflation rate) is 3% and the riskiness of the investment is evaluated at 2%. Your expectation is that each widget produced will sell for $100.00. (For simplicity, assume you sell all of them at the end of the year.)

12. The nominal rate of interest on a totally secure loan would be
    a. 9%.
    b. 7%.
    c. 6%.
    d. 4%.

13. The most you would be willing to pay for the machine is
    a. $9,345.
    b. $9,174.
    c. $8,928.
    d. $5,263.

14. Now assume that the nominal rate of interest is 10% and that the price of the machine is $9,000. In order for you to invest in the machine you would have to expect that the price of widgets would be at least
    a. $100.80.
    b. $100.00.
    c. $99.00.
    d. $97.20.

THE ECONOMIC WAY OF THINKING – MULTIPLE CHOICE

1. If an era of new inventions began next year, with many and new promising investment opportunities suddenly appearing, we would expect
    a. a lower interest rate as many people saved more.
    b. a higher interest rate as the demand for loanable funds increased, along with investment.
    c. more investment, but no change in the interest rate.
    d. a higher interest rate with no change in investment.

2. In an economy without money, an interest rate
   a. would be meaningless.
   b. could not exist.
   c. would simply be the price of earlier availability.
   d. would always be zero.

3. For an individual, the rate of time preference
   a. indicates irrational decisions.
   b. is greater whenever inflation is greater.
   c. is a subjective valuation.
   d. could never be negative, whatever the circumstances.

4. Economic analysis indicates that if usury laws held the interest rate below the equilibrium level
   a. saving would increase.
   b. borrowers would demand less from the loanable funds market.
   c. anyone who wanted to borrow would be happy with the lower interest rate.
   d. funds must be rationed to borrowers by some means other than price (the interest rate).

5. If inflation increased during a year, the dollar price of existing corporate bonds would
   a. rise because during times of inflation it takes more dollars to buy an asset.
   b. rise because the bond is really a loan, and loans rise in value with inflation.
   c. fall because each bond promises a fixed return, which falls in value as the price level rises.
   d. fall because the risk element (the likelihood of not receiving payment) is roughly proportional to inflation.

6. In the West, many people dream of being cattle ranchers, even if it means a low income. On the other hand, few if any people seem to dream of raising hogs or sheep. Thus, if we examined the financial records of ranchers raising cattle, we would expect to find that (relative to hog and sheep ranches)
   a. cattle ranches would show a higher rate of return.
   b. cattle ranches would show a lower rate of return.
   c. there would be no difference in the rates of return.
   d. the preference for cattle ranching would have no effect on the financial rate of return.

7. We would expect most risky investment ventures to be financed by owners rather than by bankers lending money because
   a. bankers are always cautious.
   b. bankers want interest payments, not profits.
   c. with a bank loan, the bank might lose all it puts in, but can never get more than the agreed-upon principal and interest.
   d. most entrepreneurs think bank interest rates are too high.

8. Theresa spends $1000 on General Motors stock and $1000 on General Motors bonds. However, inflation develops unexpectedly, and prices rise steadily at a rate 5 percent faster than what was previously anticipated. GM product prices rise with inflation, and its sales are unaffected. Theresa will probably find that the
   a. real value of her bonds rises, whereas the real value of her stocks falls.
   b. real values of her bonds and stocks fall equally.
   c. real values of her bonds and stocks rise equally.
   d. real value of her bonds falls *relative* to the real value of her stocks.

9. A company that mines coal on federally owned land is about to be told by the federal government that, beginning in five years, it must abandon the mine it expected to operate for another 20 years. This will mean a reduction in accounting profits beginning in five years. If the announcement of this ruling was made tomorrow, the price of the firm's stock would
   a. fall in about five years, just before the reduction in accounting profits was to begin.
   b. fall gradually, as the reduction in the firm's accounting profit drew near.
   c. fall immediately by the full amount of the discounted value of the decrease in future profit.
   d. fall immediately, since some investors would panic irrationally, whereas smart investors would put the same value on the stock as before, up to the time of the decline in accounting profit.

10. Use statements I and II when answering this question. (**I**) When the government restricts the number of acres that farmers can utilize to raise a crop such as wheat, the supply of the product will decline, making it possible for farmers to receive a higher price for the product. (**II**) If a price support and acre restriction program increases the price of a farm product, persons purchasing farm land with an acreage allotment for that product will be able to make a higher rate of return on their investment than would be true in the absence of the government program.
    a. I is true, II is false.
    b. I is false, II is true.
    c. Both I and II are true.
    d. Both I and II are false.

11. Which of these are the major sources of economic profit?
    a. Uncertainty, entrepreneurial alertness, and barriers to entry
    b. Competition, perfect information, and elasticity of market demand
    c. Size of firm, economies of scale, and freedom from unionism
    d. Externalities, inflation, and size of firm

12. The value of farmland is approximately equal to the present value of the expected future receipts from farming the land, net of other expenses. Which of the following would most likely raise the price of farmland?
    a. Higher interest rates
    b. Higher government price supports for farm products
    c. Higher fertilizer prices
    d. Higher value of the dollar in foreign exchange markets

13. Which of the following would reduce the net present value of your college education?
    a. Higher interest rates
    b. Earlier retirement age
    c. Higher wages for high school graduates
    d. All of the above

THE ECONOMIC WAY OF THINKING – DISCUSSION QUESTIONS

1. Assume that Congress is debating two plans to increase the profitability of wildcat oil-drilling firms. Those in Congress agree that more profits in drilling would lead to more drilling. Plan A would give a tax break on current drilling activities, so that profits on current drilling operations would rise by $10 billion – providing that much extra capital for future investment. Plan B would give tax breaks on *future* discoveries. The tax breaks derived from plan B would be worth $3.4 billion per year for the next three years to the same wildcat drillers. Which plan is likely to generate more oil production? (*Hint*: Remember the effects of marginal price changes *and* the discount rate.)

2. U.S. government bonds are considered risk-free in the sense that there is a negligible chance of default.
   a. What uncertainty is still involved in purchasing government bonds?
   b. How can you earn a profit from the purchase and resale of government bonds? How can you suffer a loss?

3. a. What are the components of the money interest rate? The real interest rate?
   b. Are risk premiums efficient since the result is that different borrowers pay different interest rates? Explain.
   c. From the self-interested viewpoint of a future generation responsible for interest payments, it is beneficial to use a positive, market-clearing interest rate for rationing loanable funds among competing investment opportunities? Why or why not?

4. If you were going to lend someone money, would the following events cause you to increase, decrease, or leave unchanged the nominal interest rate you were thinking of asking for?
   a. You hear a news report that causes you to increase the inflation rate you expect to exist over the life of the loan.
   b. You discover documents that cause you to think that there is a reasonable chance that the loan might not be completely repaid. (Assume that you still want to loan the money.)
   c. You read in the newspaper that most major banks have lowered the interest rate they charge their prime customers.

5. "When a firm's total costs are less than its sales, the firm has increased the value of the resources it has used. Such firms will be rewarded with profits. In contrast, losses indicate that the resources used to produce a good were more valuable than the good that was produced. Profits are evidence of the wise utilization of resources, whereas losses are indicative of waste and inefficiency." Is this statement always true, never true, or sometimes true? Explain your answer.

PERSPECTIVES IN ECONOMICS

State's Lottery 'Millionaires' Will be Somewhat Less Than
By Lee Dembart

[From the *Los Angeles Times*, August 16, 1985. Reprinted with permission.]

When the California lottery gets into full swing this fall, it will offer jackpots of $1 million, $2 million and $3 million. The lucky winners, therefore, will be "millionaires," according to common parlance.

Not so fast. There's a rub. "All million-dollar prizes will be awarded as annuities over a 20-year period," said an article in The Times. In other words, if you win, say, a million dollars, the Lottery Commission won't hand you a check for a million. It will pay you $50,000 now and promise to pay another $50,000 a year for 19 more years, for a total of $1 million.

Now, $50,000 a year for 20 years is not worth a million dollars by a long shot. In fact, according to Bill Seaton, spokesman for the Lottery Commission, if you win "a million dollars" in the lottery, what they actually will give you is not a million dollars but an annuity worth $400,000 today.

A $400,000 annuity winds up being worth $1 million over 20 years because of the miracle of compound interest. Think about it. Money that is put aside today earns interest and is worth more in the future. The longer the future is, the more it grows.

So if the state promises to pay you $50,000 19 years from now – the time of the last payment – how much does it have to put aside in order to have the $50,000 then? It depends, obviously, on the interest rate. The higher the interest rate, the less that has to be set aside initially. If it earns 8%, $11,585.60 will yield $50,000 in 19 years. At a 10% rate, $8,175.40 will grow to $50,000 in 19 years. And at 12%, it would take just $5,805.34 today to produce $50,000 in 2004.

This is a well-known bit of straight-forward mathematics, which is called the present-value or present-worth calculation. It involves running the formula for compound interest backward, and it answers the question, "What is the present value of a future sum of money?" Everybody understands that if a person invested $1,000 today at 10% interest it would earn $100 in a year and then be worth $1,100. The question can be asked the other way: If you wind up with $1,100 in a year at 10% interest, how much did you start with? The answer is $1,000, and that is called the present value of $1,100 in a year at 10% interest.

Occasionally, when athletes sign multiyear, multi-million-dollar contracts, someone points out an owner who promises to pay $2 million 30 years from now can do it with much less than $2 million today.

How does the lottery figure the present value of $1 million doled out in 20-year installments of $50,000 a year? The same calculation is done for year 19 – the last year – can also be done for years 18, 17, 16 and so on to determine the amount of money that must be set aside today to pay the $50,000 in each of the subsequent years. Then those present values can be added to yield the total present value of the state's "million-dollar lottery." The following is a table showing the present values of 20 once-a-year payments of $50,000 each, assuming earnings of 12.8%:

Year	Payment	Present value
0	$50,000	$50,000.00
1	50,000	44,326.24
2	50,000	39,296.31
3	50,000	34,837.16
4	50,000	30,884.00
5	50,000	27,379.44
6	50,000	24,272.55
7	50,000	21,518.22
8	50,000	19,076.43
9	50,000	16,911.73
10	50,000	14,992.67
11	50,000	13,291.38
12	50,000	11,783.13
13	50,000	10,446.04
14	50,000	9,260.67
15	50,000	8,209.82
16	50,000	7,278.21
17	50,000	6,452.31
18	50,000	5,720.13
19	50,000	5,071.04

The total present value of $1 million handed out in $50,000 chunks over 20 years is $401, 007.48.

So it is at least misleading to call $50,000 a year for 20 years "a million dollars." (This analysis ignores income tax, inflation, life expectancy and all other factors related to the question of which is the better deal, $400,000 today or $50,000 a year for 20 years.)

The Lottery Commission says further that, based on the same calculation, a winner of a $2-million jack-pot will receive an $800,000 annuity. In addition, the commission says, the odds against wining a $2-million pot are 25 million to 1.

So a person who buys a $1 ticket will have a 25 million-to-1 shot at winning a "$2-million" prize. That sounds like bad odds to begin with. The odds are made worse by the fact that the $2-million prize is really only $800,000.

Discussion

1. After reading the article, a friend says, "it seems to me that a million dollars is a million dollars. As long as you get the money eventually, it's still worth the same amount!" How would you convince your friend that it matters quite a bit when you get the money? Be specific.

2. The present values in the article were calculated assuming earnings of 12.8%, but this might seem a bit high. Use the exhibit on page 638 of the text to calculate the present value of $50,000 a year for twenty years if the interest rate (earnings) were only 6 percent a year. Does the total go up or down? Why?

3. How ethical is it of the State of California to advertise a $2 million dollar prize when it knows the actual value is less than half of that? What could be done to change the lottery (or at least its advertising) to make the truth obvious? Is making such changes worth the trouble? (After all, gambling is illegal in California anyway!)

MICROCROSS
By Cindy Kelly and Debbie Shay

[Reprinted with permission from *The Margin*, Fall 1991, p. 82.
If you like this puzzle, please also see MacroCross, by the same authors, on p. 171.]

Across

1. Tax imposed on importation of a good.
6. A good for which demand increases if income increases, other things constant.
7. Results when quantity supplied is greater than quantity demanded.
8. Costs that do not vary with output.
9. The additional cost of one more unit of output.
12. The exchange value of a commodity.
13. Ratio of the change in total revenue to the change in quantity.
14. Monopoly profit per unit in Figure 1.
16. Type of good for which consumption is nonrival and exclusion prohibitively difficult.
19. Market with only two sellers.
20. One sector in the circular flow.
21. What 20 across seeks to maximize.
22. Workers organization.
23. What chicken is to beef.

Down

2. Return to a good or service with a vertical supply curve.
3. Machines, tools and factories are examples of this.
4. What one more worker contributes to a firm's total revenue.
5. Schedule that relates quantity of a good producers are willing to provide to the price of the good.
7. The fundamental problem in economics.
10. What tires are to cars.
11. If price falls below P in Fig. 2 the firm will ___ .
15. What economists assume decision-makers do.
17. Goods and services purchased from foreign countries.
18. Competition with many sellers and buyers, homogeneous product, full information and no barriers to entry and exit.

Figure 1

Figure 25-2

Figure 25-3

26
Labor Unions and Collective Bargaining

TRUE OR FALSE

T F

☐ ☐ 1. Union membership as a percentage of the labor force has steadily increased since 1960.

☐ ☐ 2. Approximately one-half of all workers in the United States belong to a labor union.

☐ ☐ 3. A union shop labor contract requires all workers to join a union after a specified length of employment.

☐ ☐ 4. Right-to-work laws require all union-management contracts to contain a union shop provision.

☐ ☐ 5. Unions have played a central role in the development of contractual or formal rules and procedures that govern promotions, raises, layoffs, terminations, and other aspects of the relationship between employers and employees.

☐ ☐ 6. Each year, approximately 4 percent of the total work time in the United States is lost because of strikes.

☐ ☐ 7. The amount of work time lost because of strikes has steadily increased since World War II.

☐ ☐ 8. Strikes involving public employees and community services often result in inconvenience and reductions in output in other sectors of the economy.

☐ ☐ 9. The greater the ability of management to substitute machines and nonunion labor for union labor, the weaker the bargaining power of a union.

☐ ☐ 10. A monopsony is to a monopoly as a seller is to a buyer.

☐ ☐ 11. The evidence from other countries indicates that unions raise the wages of workers, including nonunion workers.

☐ ☐ 12. Failure to organize all of the firms in an industry does not greatly limit the ability of a union to attain large wage gains from the individual firms of the industry that are unionized.

☐ ☐ 13. Most unions have been able to increase the wages of their members by at least 40 percent.

☐ ☐ 14. The share of national income going to labor has increased steadily as more and more workers have joined unions.

PROBLEMS AND PROJECTS

Exhibit 1

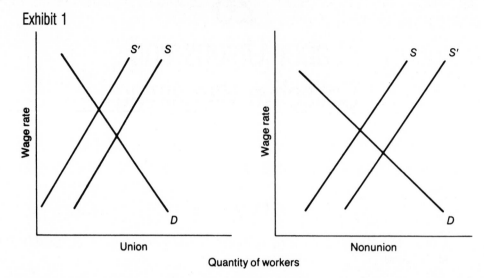

Quantity of workers

1. "The problem with unions is that they bring higher wage rates for workers and thus force all employers to raise wages in order to compete in the labor market." Refute this statement by explaining the phenomenon described by the supply-and-demand conditions in Exhibit 1.

Exhibit 2

Quantity of labor demanded	Wage rate	Quantity of labor supplied
100	$10	1000
300	9	900
500	8	800
700	7	700
900	6	600

2. Exhibit 2 is a demand-and-supply schedule for the competitive engineering labor market. Suppose that you are the president of the American Machines Corporation, and you must hire a group of engineers for your firm.
   a. What wage rate will you offer the hired engineers?
   b. Assume the UEU, the United Engineers Union, is formed, reducing the quantity supplied of engineers at every wage rate by 300 because of increased qualifications in this discipline. What will be the new wage rate?
   c. What effect will the union have on employment and total incomes of the unionized engineers?
   d. Calculate the elasticity of demand for engineers between these two equilibrium points.

3. International Manufacturing, Incorporated (IMI) is a monopsonistic employer of labor. Exhibit 3 shows the quantity of labor IMI demands at each wage and the supply curve that IMI faces in its hiring of labor.

Exhibit 3

Labor demanded (hundreds of hours)	Hourly wage (dollars)	Labor supplied (hundreds of hours)	Total labor cost (dollars)	Marginal labor cost (dollars)
450	$16	100	$1600	
				$20
400	18	200	3600	
350	20	300	_____	_____
300	22	400	_____	_____
250	24	500	_____	_____
200	26	600	_____	_____

a. Fill in the missing information in the table.
b. On a piece of graph paper plot IMI's labor demand curve, labor supply curve and marginal labor cost curve. (Be sure to plot values for marginal labor cost at the appropriate *midpoints* of the quantities.)
c. What quantity of labor will IMI hire? What wage will it pay?
d. Suppose that IMI workers form a union and establish a wage floor of $22 per hour. Will this new (and higher) wage result in more or less employment at IMI? Exactly how many hours of labor will IMI employ at this minimum wage?

4. It is difficult to know exactly what income goal unions try to achieve. Suppose a hotel clerks' union faces the following demand and supply situation in Exhibit 4:

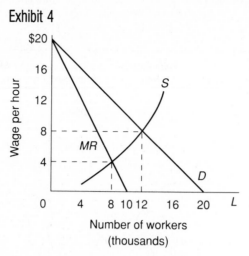

Exhibit 4

The market is initially in a competitive equilibrium.

For each of the following union goals, determine the wage level the union will bargain for and the resulting number of workers hired. Record your answers in the table that follows the list of goals:

Goals
a. Maximize employment.
b. Get the highest wage that at least half of the membership will approve. (Workers with the greatest seniority will retain their jobs.)
c. Maximize the total wage bill paid by hotel owners.
d. Maximize union members' "profits" (the excess of total wages over worker opportunity cost).

Goal	Wage	Number of workers hired (thousands)
a.	___	_____
b.	___	_____
c.	___	_____
d.	___	_____

5. According to the text, unions can raise wages three ways:
(1) supply restrictions
(2) bargaining power (resulting in a wage floor above the equilibrium level)
(3) increase in the demand for union workers

For each of the following union strategies, list the number given above for the type of effect the strategy illustrates, and indicate whether employment in the unionized industry rises (+) or falls (−) as a result. The first case is completed as an example:

Type of effect 3	Change in employment +	Union strategy
_____	_____	a. In a practice called featherbedding, railroad unions require that all trains carry firemen, even though modern locomotives pose little fire danger.
_____	_____	b. The American Medical Association restricts accreditation of medical schools.
_____	_____	c. Garment workers run an ad campaign with the jingle, "Look for the union label."
_____	_____	d. Unions commonly bargain for wage increases indexed to inflation plus a negotiated premium.
_____	_____	e. Auto workers lobby for domestic content legislation stipulating that at least 90 percent of each car sold in the U.S. be constructed from U.S.-made parts.
_____	_____	f. To become Certified Public Accountants, candidates must pass an industry-administered exam that over three-fourths of all applicants fail.

LEARNING THE MECHANICS – MULTIPLE CHOICE

1. Which of the following factors will substantially *improve* the ability of a union to raise the wages of its workers?
   a. A tax increase on firms that employ the union labor
   b. An inelastic demand for the product produced by union labor
   c. A reduction in tariffs on the type of products the union workers produce
   d. Passage of a right-to-work law in the state where the union operates

2. Wages of unionized workers are usually estimated to be how much higher than they would have been under nonunion conditions?
   a. 90-110 percent
   b. 50-70 percent
   c. 12-16 percent
   d. 40-45 percent

3. A monopsony is
   a. another word for a monopoly.
   b. the existence of a single buyer in a market.
   c. the existence of several sellers in a market.
   d. the existence of a single seller in a market.

4. If a craft union was able to reduce the supply of workers into the craft, it would most likely *not*
   a. increase wages.
   b. reduce employment.
   c. increase the wages of all workers in the economy.
   d. increase wages without the need for hard bargaining.

5. Unions are not likely to obtain large wage increases for their workers when
    a. the demand for the product is inelastic.
    b. the supply of substitute inputs in highly inelastic.
    c. the demand for the product the workers produce is elastic, and machines can easily be substituted for labor.
    d. the demand for the product is rapidly increasing.

6. "Marginal factor cost is to a monopsonist as marginal revenue is to a monopolist." Which of the following is true?
    a. The quotation is inherently incorrect.
    b. The quotation is basically correct.
    c. The quotation is partially correct, but the comparison should be to marginal revenue for a perfectly competitive firm.
    d. The quotation is partially correct, but the comparison should be to average revenue for a monopolist.

7. Use statements I and II to answer this question. **(I)** During the past 20 years, the number of worker-hours of work time lost as a result of strikes has been less than three-tenths of 1 percent of the total — far less than the work time lost due to absenteeism. **(II)** A strike often imposes substantial costs on secondary parties (wholesalers, consumers, and other manufacturers, for example) who are not involved in the labor-management collective bargaining.
    a. I is true, II is false.
    b. I is false, II is true.
    c. Both I and II are true.
    d. Both I and II are false.

8. A union shop provision means that a worker
    a. cannot be employed until he has joined the union.
    b. must agree when he is hired never to join a union.
    c. must join the union within a specified length of time after he is hired.
    d. has the freedom to join the union at any time, should he wish to do so.

9. The data on the distribution of income among individuals and families in the United States
    a. indicate that the power of labor unions is the major determinant of income inequality.
    b. indicate that unions have no impact on the incomes of members.
    c. indicate that substantial inequality in annual income emanates from differences in education, age, hours worked, and family size.
    d. indicate that differences in annual income emanating from ownership of capital assets are the major source of economic inequality.

10. In winning concessions from employers, a labor union has as its most important tool
    a. the strike.
    b. the lockout.
    c. monopsony power.
    d. the injunction.

Questions 11-13 are based on the following material:

"Rap Rapture," a small cloth manufacturer, can sell all the cloth it can produce at $1.00 per yard on the national cloth market. In the local market for cloth laborers (their only factor of production), they are a monopsonist. Their production and cost schedules for various numbers of workers hired are:

Number of workers	Wage ($/hour)	Total cloth produced (yards/hour)
1	3.00	10
2	3.50	20
3	4.00	29
4	4.50	37
5	5.00	44
6	5.50	50
7	6.00	55

11. Given the above information, Rap Rapture will hire
   a. 2 workers.
   b. 3 workers.
   c. 4 workers.
   d. 6 workers.

12. The firm's profits (per hour) are
   a. $44.00.
   b. $25.00.
   c. $19.00.
   d. $17.00.

13. The cloth workers organize, and the company accepts a minimum wage of $6.00 per hour. As a result, the firm now hires
   a. 3 workers.
   b. 4 workers.
   c. 6 workers.
   d. 7 workers.

THE ECONOMIC WAY OF THINKING – MULTIPLE CHOICE

1. As the baseball season approaches, the likelihood of a player strike would
   a. give neither party much incentive to bargain seriously.
   b. give only management incentive to bargain seriously.
   c. give only players incentive to bargain seriously.
   d. give both players and management incentive to bargain seriously.

2. Suppose that during a ten-year period the number of coal miners declined from 400,000 to 300,000. The hourly wages of the mine workers doubled during this same period because of the strength of the United Mine Workers. Which of the following set of economic factors is most consistent with the wage and employment data of the mining industry?
   a. The supply of miners was highly inelastic, and therefore a small reduction in the demand for mining labor led to a small reduction in employment.
   b. Even though the demand for mining labor was inelastic, as wages increased, the number of miners employed declined significantly.
   c. While the supply of miners was increasing, the demand was increasing more rapidly, leading to higher wages.
   d. The demand for mining labor was elastic, and the supply of miners was reduced, leading to higher wages.

3. Over the last four decades, the share of national income going to labor, including self-employed workers, has
   a. remained nearly constant at slightly more than 80 percent of national income.
   b. fluctuated between 50 and 75 percent of total national income.
   c. increased, as union members became a larger percent of the total work force.
   d. decreased from nearly 75 percent to its current level, approximately 50 percent of national income.

4. The empirical evidence strongly suggests that unions have increased
   a. wages of industrial workers more than those of craft employees.
   b. the share of national income going to labor by 25 percent.
   c. the average wage of union members, but have had little impact on the share of income going to labor.
   d. the wages of most union members by at least 35 percent.

5. Regarding union strength, the "importance of being unimportant" refers to
   a. a lack of political clout on the part of the union.
   b. the union's having organized only a small share of workers in its trade.
   c. the union's wage bill being small, compared to the costs the management would incur if operations were shut down because of a strike.
   d. the union leadership's desire to avoid headlines.

6. As a result of union strength, nonunion workers might suffer if
   a. inflation were an indirect result of the attempts of macro planners to offset cutbacks in employment caused by union wage increases.
   b. supply restrictions in unionized areas increased the supply of workers in nonunion markets, causing nonunion wage rates to decline.
   c. union wage increases in competitive industries were passed on to consumers in the form of higher prices.
   d. All of the above are likely to harm nonunion workers.

7. In which case below are both union strategies listed likely to have similar effects on wages and employment?
   a. Supply restriction and demand increase
   b. Bargaining power in a monopsony situation and supply restriction
   c. Bargaining power in a monopsony situation and demand increase
   d. None of the above

8. Because the demand for a broadly defined product line (automobiles, for example) is less elastic than the demand for a more narrow product category (Fords, for example), a union will be better able to raise wages without large unemployment effects when
   a. it has organized an entire industry, rather than only one firm.
   b. it organizes only a few firms in each industry.
   c. it bargains with all firms in a narrow product line, but ignores the rest of the industry.
   d. only a small part of the industry that makes the broadly defined product is unionized.

9. By raising wages, unions typically have
   a. increased total productivity, which must rise proportionally with the wage rate.
   b. encouraged employers to find a substitute for the union labor.
   c. raised the wages of nonunion workers.
   d. caused much of the inflation experienced in the United States.

10. Some advocates of unions argue that higher union wages induce greater work effort, so both employees *and* employers end up better off. Which of the following indicates an inconsistency with this line of reasoning?
    a. Employers would not pay higher wages even if higher wages increased work effort and labor productivity.
    b. Employers would not resist higher wages if they were more than offset by productivity increases.
    c. Unions are unable to raise the wages of their members.
    d. Nonunion workers have higher productivity than union workers.

11. The addition of a player's union to the originally monopsonistic baseball industry is likely to
    a. decrease the number of players hired.
    b. increase the average wage of the players.
    c. decrease the average wage of the players but allow more players to be hired.
    d. have little impact on the average wage of the players but allow more players to be hired.

12. According to recent figures, the percentage of nonfarm-working time lost due to strikes is the lowest it has been in the last forty years. This decrease can be attributed in part to the fact that
    a. union membership as a proportion of nonfarm employment has been increasing at only approximately 1% a year.
    b. unions have increased the wages of all workers, both union and nonunion, higher than they would have been otherwise, so strikes are less necessary.
    c. both a and b.
    d. neither a nor b.

THE ECONOMIC WAY OF THINKING – DISCUSSION QUESTIONS

1. Consider the following contrasting opinions about strikes:

   Opinion 1: "The right to strike is a basic right of all workers. Without strikes, unions would be powerless against industrial interests when bargaining for the employee."

   Opinion 2: "The threat of a strike is a form of economic blackmail. The right to strike grants unions the power to collect bribes for not interfering with what is actually a perfectly legitimate economic function – the productive process."

   a. Are workers "powerless against industrial interests" without strikes? Why or why not?
   b. Are strikes "economic blackmail"? Are they more painful for employers than employees? Why or why not?
   c. On balance, which opinion do you find more persuasive? Explain.

2. "The wages of union workers are higher than the wages of nonunion workers." Which of the following can we conclude from this observation? Explain your decision in each case.
   a. Unions raise the wage rates of union members.
   b. Unions are effective in organizing low-wage workers.
   c. Higher union wages put upward pressure on the wages of all employees.

3. For each pair of situations below, decide which condition is more conducive to the ability of unions to raise the wages of their members. Explain your reasoning in each case.
   a. A union shop versus an open shop.
   b. A union in an oligopoly industry versus a union in a competitive industry.
   c. An industry in which each firm has its own union versus an industry with a single union for all the industry employees.
   d. A union whose workers produce an internationally traded good versus a union whose workers produce a good protected from international competition.
   e. A union in the public sector versus a union in the private sector.

4. Business decision-makers can sometimes argue that they cannot make a profit because of the excessive wage demands of unions. Suppose that a strong union in a highly competitive industry obtains for its members a 15 percent increase in wages.
   a. Will the higher wage rates reduce the industry's rate of profit in the short run? In the long run?
   b. Who will actually shoulder the burden of the higher wage rates?

5. "Every union knows that an airline is more vulnerable to strikes than most other businesses. Airlines have high fixed costs regardless of whether their planes are flying. They can neither stockpile seats during a strike nor sell from inventory afterward. Strike losses cannot be recovered. The strong impulse is to avoid a strike, even if that means settling on an unsatisfactory basis." [From an airline newsletter.]
   a. Do you think the airline industry is particularly vulnerable to union demands? Why or why not?
   b. If the airlines are vulnerable, who would pay for an "unsatisfactory" labor settlement in the short run? In the long run? Explain.
   c. Many economists have concluded that, in the absence of regulation, barriers to entry are pretty low in the airline industry. How does this affect your answer to part a?
   d. Do you think unions would favor or oppose a return to government regulation of airlines? Why or why not?

27

Inequality, Income Mobility, and the Battle Against Poverty

TRUE OR FALSE

T F

☐ ☐ 1. Differences in hours worked are an important source of income inequality among households in the United States.

☐ ☐ 2. Official poverty figures indicate that more than 11 percent of U.S. families lived in poverty in 1989.

☐ ☐ 3. The wealthiest 5 percent of all income recipients in the United States receive approximately 40 percent of all income.

☐ ☐ 4. Income is distributed more unequally in the United States than in most other countries in the world.

☐ ☐ 5. In general, income is distributed more equally in Sweden and England than in the United States.

☐ ☐ 6. One way to help the social security system solve its future financial problems would be to decrease the normal eligibility age from 65 to 62.

☐ ☐ 7. Households headed by females are overrepresented among the poor.

☐ ☐ 8. Of all children born to parents in the top fifth of the income distribution, more than three-fourths maintain that high-income status.

☐ ☐ 9. U.S. income inequality remained relatively unchanged from 1950 through 1970 but income inequality increased somewhat during the 1970s and 1980s.

☐ ☐ 10. Official poverty figures fail to recognize transfers in kind.

PROBLEMS AND PROJECTS

1. Susan Smith is an orthodontist. Jane Jones is a part-time clerk in a small store, where she earns $3.50 per hour. Jane would like Dr. Smith to straighten the teeth of Brenda Jones, Jane's daughter. Jane is willing to work an extra part-time job (at the same pay) to meet this expense, even though it is not a medical necessity. Dr. Smith would be willing to take on this extra work if she were paid $700.

   a. In the absence of taxes, how many hours does Jane have to work in order to pay for her daughter's treatment?

   b. If Dr. Smith was in the 50 percent tax bracket, and Jane received transfer payments (for example, food stamps, housing subsidies, AFDC) that put her in the 65 percent *implicit* tax bracket (see Exhibit 11 in Chapter 27 of the text), how many hours must Jane work to enable Dr. Smith to earn the same $700 in exchange for the treatment? (*Hint*: Hours x $3.50 x 0.35 x 0.5 = $700.)

   c. If Dr. Smith paid no taxes, but Jane was in the 65 percent implicit tax bracket, how many hours must Jane work to earn the $700?

   d. If Dr. Smith paid 70 percent of her income in taxes, and Jane paid none at all, how many hours would Jane have to work for Dr. Smith to take home $700?

   e. Considering your answer to part d, would you say that high taxes on productive, highly-paid people hurt low-income people?

   f. Considering your answer to part c, would you say that taxes on productive lower-paid people hurt higher-income recipients?

   g. Would Jane (and Brenda) Jones be better off without the transfer program that puts Jane in the implicit 65 percent tax bracket? Why?

2. Suppose that the government passed a negative income tax that involved a $4000 government subsidy to a family of four if zero income was earned. Assume a 50 percent marginal tax rate on earned income; that is, for every $1000 earned, the subsidy is reduced by 50 percent of the $1000. Using this NIT plan, fill in the columns labeled government subsidy and total income in Exhibit 1. Do you think this is a good plan for achieving a more equal income distribution? Why or why not?

Exhibit 1

Earned income	Government subsidy	Total income
$ 0	$4000	_____
2000	_____	_____
3000	_____	_____
4000	_____	_____
5000	_____	_____
6000	_____	_____
7000	_____	_____
8000	_____	_____

3. Robert Reckman is currently unemployed and qualifies for unemployment compensation of $138.00 per week. He has been offered a new job paying $200.00 per week, subject to income taxes of 33 percent and social security taxes of 7 percent.

   a. From society's point of view, is it desirable that Reckman accept the job? Why?

   b. Is it to Reckman's financial advantage to accept the job? Why?

   c. Calculate Reckman's marginal tax rate (including both explicit and implicit taxes) if he accepted the job.

   d. If Reckman's unemployment benefits had been subject to an income tax of 20 percent, would it have been in his financial interest to accept the job? Why?

4. The more income mobility there is, the less serious the poverty problem.
    a. The income mobility information from Exhibit 5 of Chapter 27 of the text is summarized below:

	Family Income Position, 1984		
Family Income Position, 1980	*Top 20%*	*Middle 60%*	*Bottom 20%*
Top 20%	62%	36%	2%
Middle 60%	12%	77%	11%
Bottom 20%	1%	34%	65%

Which occurs more frequently, falling from the top, or rising from the bottom?

    b. Consider the country of Static discussed in the text. Complete the table below to reflect the complete absence of income mobility in Static:

	Family Income Position, 1984		
Family Income Position, 1980	*Top 20%*	*Middle 60%*	*Bottom 20%*
Top 20%	_____	_____	_____
Middle 60%	_____	_____	_____
Bottom 20%	_____	_____	_____

    c. Now consider the country of Dynamic discussed in the text. Complete the table below to reflect perfect income mobility:

	Family Income Position, 1984		
Family Income Position, 1980	*Top 20%*	*Middle 60%*	*Bottom 20%*
Top 20%	_____	_____	_____
Middle 60%	_____	_____	_____
Bottom 20%	_____	_____	_____

5. A handy way to compare income distributions is to rank each country's households from poor to rich (usually by quintile), and compute a running total of the percentage of the country's households and their percentage share of total household income. The information from Exhibit 1 of Chapter 27 of the text can be used for these comparisons.

   a. Before we can use the information, we must convert it slightly. To do so, fill in the missing information below (the first two cases are completed as examples):

	Percentage Share of Household Income Received by:		
Country Line 1:	Lowest 20%	Middle 60%	Top 20%
Line 2:	Lowest 20%	Lower 80%	All 100%
(1) Perfect Equality	20.0%	60.0%	20.0%
	20.0%	80.0%	100.0%
(2) Brazil	2.4	35.0	62.6
	2.4	36.4	100.0
(3) Japan	8.7	53.8	37.5
	___	___	___
(4) United States	4.6	50.8	44.6
	___	___	___
(5) Sweden	7.4	50.9	41.7
	___	___	___

   b. The diagram in Exhibit 2 plots the cumulative household and household income information from the table above. The result is called a Lorenz Curve. The Lorenz Curve for Brazil has already been plotted. Plot the Lorenz Curves for Perfect Equality, Japan, and the United States.

Exhibit 2

   c. Plot the Lorenz Curve for Sweden. Is Sweden's income distribution more or less equal than Brazil's? Than Japan's? Why is it difficult to compare the income distributions of Sweden and the United States?

LEARNING THE MECHANICS – MULTIPLE CHOICE

1. As of 1989, the poorest 20 percent of all U.S. families received what percentage of the total income?
    a. Approximately 2 percent
    b. Approximately 5 percent
    c. Between 11 and 12 percent
    d. Between 18 and 20 percent

2. The distribution of income in which of the following countries is more equal than that of the United States?
    a. Malaysia
    b. Japan
    c. Brazil
    d. Mexico

3. Under the negative income tax concept, an additional dollar of earnings would cause the disposable income of
    a. a high-income taxpayer to increase by an additional dollar.
    b. a low-income recipient to increase by more than a dollar.
    c. a low-income recipient to increase, but by less than a dollar.
    d. a high-income taxpayer to decrease by some positive tax, and that of a low-income recipient to remain unchanged.

4. From 1976 to 1989, the percentage of poor families that were headed by an elderly person
    a. fell steadily.
    b. rose steadily.
    c. remained virtually unchanged.
    d. fell steadily until President Reagan took office.

5. In the last 20 years or so, it appears that family incomes have
    a. become less equal.
    b. become more equal.
    c. maintained the same level of inequality.
    d. declined substantially.

6. Compared to high-income families, low-income families tend to have
    a. fewer workers.
    b. more workers.
    c. fewer youthful or retired members.
    d. about the same level of education.

7. Which of the following is false about data on the inequality of annual family (or household) incomes?
    a. The degree of inequality is reduced when transfers and taxes are considered.
    b. The inequality in annual income data actually understates the degree of inequality in lifetime income.
    c. Differences in age and family characteristics contribute to the degree of inequality.
    d. The difference between the after-tax and transfer income per hour worked between high- and low-income recipients is much smaller than the difference in annual income.

8. The official definition of poverty in the United States does not account for
   a. social security income.
   b. cash income transfers.
   c. income earned by workers other than the head of a household.
   d. in-kind transfers.

9. The negative income tax, a scheme that would have the Internal Revenue Service pay money directly to individuals with low incomes, is closely identified with
   a. Milton Friedman.
   b. Adam Smith.
   c. Arthur Okun.
   d. Alan Blinder.

10. By the year 2025, when some of you may be retiring, it is estimated that the number of workers per social security beneficiary will be
    a. ten.
    b. five.
    c. four.
    d. two.

11. Which of the following contributed to the increase in income inequality in the U.S. over the last two decades?
    a. Poor people have become more and more lazy.
    b. The proportion of dual-parent, single-earner families has increased during the last two decades.
    c. As marginal tax rates were reduced during the 1980s, the observed incomes of high-income Americans increased sharply.
    d. Earnings differentials between skilled and less-skilled workers have decreased during the last two decades.

THE ECONOMIC WAY OF THINKING – MULTIPLE CHOICE

1. In a market system, each individual chooses how to employ his or her own resources. One who chooses not to employ his or her resources is held responsible by
   a. the high prices of goods.
   b. laws against vagrancy.
   c. welfare case workers.
   d. the opportunity cost of leisure.

2. **(I)** High implicit marginal tax rates reduce the incentive of the poor to earn. **(II)** The transfer program unwittingly encourages activities that lead to poverty.
   a. Both I and II are true.
   b. Both I and II are false.
   c. I is true, II is false.
   d. II is true, I is false.

3. With a few exceptions, it is generally true in most countries that the share of income going to the wealthiest people is greater in
   a. more developed countries.
   b. less developed countries.
   c. countries with a homogeneous population.
   d. industrialized countries.

4. Even if lifetime incomes were equal, there still might be substantial inequality in annual income data because
   a. wage rates might differ substantially.
   b. some might have inherited their wealth.
   c. some might have retired, while others are prime-age earners.
   d. educational levels might differ substantially.

5. The poverty threshold income level is calculated and adjusted in such a way that, for a given family, it would rise 10 percent in one year if
   a. the family's income rose 10 percent.
   b. the family's income fell 10 percent.
   c. the price of all consumer items rose 10 percent.
   d. national income rose 10 percent.

6. Of all poverty families, approximately one-half are headed by
   a. a female.
   b. a female who does not work.
   c. a male who does not work.
   d. a male working full time.

7. Placing a dollar value on in-kind transfers to the poor is problematic because
   a. no market price is available for many of the items.
   b. the taxpayer cost of the items is usually unrelated to their market price.
   c. the market price of many of the items is a poor measure of actual production cost.
   d. the value of the items to the poor is often less than the market price of the items.

8. The advantages of a negative income tax system include which of the following?
   a. Some of the degradation and despair associated with our current transfer system would be avoided.
   b. The costs of our redistribution system would almost surely fall.
   c. An individual would never have an implicit marginal tax rate greater than 100%.
   d. All of the above.

9. (I) In 1989, almost 70 percent of all poor people were white. (II) In 1989, blacks were overrepresented in the poverty population.
   a. Both I and II are true.
   b. I is true, II is false.
   c. I is false, II is true.
   d. Both I and II are false.

10. (I) Our tax transfer system frequently adds thousands of dollars to the income of the poor families, in the form of cash as well as in-kind transfers. (II) A poor family receiving welfare payments and in-kind benefits will generally be able to take home a larger share of a $1000-per-year increase in its earnings than would a family earning $20,000 per year and receiving no transfers.
    a. I and II are true.
    b. I is true, II is false.
    c. I is false, II is true.
    d. I and II are false.

11. Imagine two cities, Engelgrad and Legreeville, that have identical average annual incomes. In the city of Engelgrad, the poorest families one year almost always end up as the richest families the next year and become middle-income families the year after that. In the city of Legreeville, however, poor remain poor and rich remain rich. Which of the following is true about the two cities?

   a. The distribution of income in any given year is more equitable in Engelgrad than it is in Legreeville.

   b. The distribution of income in any given year is more equitable in Legreeville than it is in Engelgrad.

   c. The dynamic distribution of income over time is more equitable in Engelgrad than it is in Legreeville.

   d. The dynamic distribution of income over time is more equitable in Legreeville than it is in Engelgrad.

THE ECONOMIC WAY OF THINKING – DISCUSSION QUESTIONS

1. What happened to income inequality in the United States from the 1950s to the 1990s? What happened to the amount of poverty in the United States from the 1950s to the 1990s. How, if at all, could the level of poverty change without the amount of income inequality changing at the same time?

2. What are some of the problems with annual income data at a given time as a measure of one's economic well-being? Do you think that, across individuals, lifetime earnings are more or less unequal than annual earnings? Explain.

3. What are some of the social costs of having nearly 13 percent of the U.S. population living in poverty? Could the United States eliminate its poverty? If so, how? What would be some of the social costs of your anti-poverty proposal?

4.   a. Do you think a free-market economy results in a socially optimal distribution of income? Why or why not?

   b. Economist Milton Friedman has argued that a perfectly equal income distribution would thoroughly undermine our incentives to be productive. Do you agree or disagree?

   c. Friedman was also one of the first advocates of a negative income tax. Do you favor a negative income tax? If so, why? If not, why not? What would you recommend, if anything to make the income distribution of a free-market economy fairer?

5. Many economists, including Marxists, suggest that people born into low-income families in market economies have little chance to escape their low-income positions, whereas those born to rich parents will remain wealthy. What does the empirical evidence indicate concerning the amount of income mobility that actually exists? Do you think the evidence supports the view that there is in fact little income mobility?

6. How does income distribution in the United States compare with that of other developed nations? Of less developed nations?

7. Do you think the official poverty statistics in the United States are misleading? If so, in what ways? How would you change the way poverty is measured?

8. "All this worry about marginal tax rates is silly. Anyone who thinks a poor person will remain poor just to collect welfare payments has never had to live on those meager payments." Comment.

3. Which of the following approaches to values and costs should be used when dealing with natural resources?
   a. Opportunity costs
   b. Marginal values
   c. Both a and b
   d. Neither a nor b

4. Use statements I and II to answer this question. (**I**) The demand for energy products is considerably less elastic in the short run than is true for the long run. (**II**) As the result of the lengthy time period between exploratory activities and the refining of a petroleum product, the supply of petroleum is generally more elastic in the short run than in the long run.
   a. Both I and II are true.
   b. Both I and II are false.
   c. I is true, II is false.
   d. I is false, II is true.

5. Between 1950 and 1980, proved inventories of copper, iron, lead, and aluminum
   a. increased substantially, because new ores had been discovered and the cost of processing lower-grade ores had fallen.
   b. increased slightly, because conservation efforts cut down our use of these ores.
   c. decreased slightly, because new discoveries were swamped by increased usage of these ores.
   d. decreased substantially, because no amount of discoveries or conservation will keep us from running out of nonrenewable resources like these ores.

6. Proved reserves of petroleum are
   a. the only reserves likely to be available in the future.
   b. refined products waiting to be shipped to market.
   c. the oil industry's equivalent to raw material inventories.
   d. the same thing as absolute reserves.

7. Over the last twenty-five years, the amount of metal required per beverage can has
   a. increased slightly.
   b. decreased slightly.
   c. decreased to only one-half of the former amount.
   d. decreased to only one-fifth of the former amount.

8. When the demand for whale oil increased sharply during the mid-1800s, the price of whale oil rose sharply. As a result
   a. many people were unable to afford to light their homes until electricity was developed.
   b. the supply of whale oil increased rapidly, as entrepreneurs developed a new technique for breeding whales.
   c. consumers turned to substitute energy sources, which eventually provided much cheaper heating and lighting than could be supplied with whale oil.
   d. the government imposed rigid price controls and rationed whale oil in order to mitigate the energy crisis.

9. "Doomsday" predictions about the imminent depletion of one or more of our vital natural resources usually are
   a. correct but are not reflected by relative price changes within our market economy.
   b. incorrect because of arithmetic calculation mistakes.
   c. incorrect because they disregard human responses to relative price changes.
   d. incorrect because they disregard the ever-decreasing availability of substitutes for such natural resources.

10. The classic study of Barnett and Morse found that
    a. resource costs have been rising at a rate that implies that within 50 years, we will have impossibly high prices for natural resources.
    b. the ever-increasing availability of substitutes has outrun our ability to use up scarce natural resources.
    c. resource costs have been rising for a long period, but predictions of a coming "doomsday" are unlikely to be correct.
    d. the currently proven reserves of most minerals are becoming perilously low.

11. The demand for energy products is
    a. perfectly inelastic, since energy is needed to produce everything we consume.
    b. quite inelastic in the short run, but considerably more elastic in the long run.
    c. quite elastic in the short run, but considerably more inelastic in the long run.
    d. highly elastic in both the short and long runs.

12. Proved reserves are
    a. the total reserve supply of a resource that will be available for future consumption.
    b. the total reserve supply of a resource that is recoverable, assuming that energy prices and technology continue to increase at current rates.
    c. the total amount of reserves in existence.
    d. the current holdings of verified reserves that we can expect to recover at current energy prices and technology.

THE ECONOMIC WAY OF THINKING – MULTIPLE CHOICE

1. "Our timberlands are being depleted by short-sighted profiteers who are clear-cutting whole forests without planting replacements or even worrying about erosion." The situation described in this statement is a good example of the problems that occur when owners of forestland
   a. maximize profits without regard to environmental impact.
   b. do not maximize long-run profits or are not held accountable for some of the costs of their actions.
   c. worry too much about the environmental impact of their decisions.
   d. use benefit-cost analysis to make decisions.

2. One flaw in the argument that the environment can be helped by private ownership of land and other non-renewable resources is that
   a. since short-run profits are the goal of the private owners, they will ignore the long-run implications of their decisions.
   b. even if long-run profits are the goal of the private owners, they still will ignore the social costs of their decisions.
   c. private owners will only look at superficial business issues when making decisions and have no incentive to investigate future pollution costs or similar problems.
   d. the private owner may attempt to conceal any pollution caused in order to avoid the loss of profits.

3. Opportunity cost is used in determining the most valued use of a resource like land or capital; when deciding how to use natural resources, opportunity cost is
   a. not applicable because natural resources are not replaceable.
   b. just as applicable.
   c. only as applicable in cases where wildlife is not involved.
   d. only applicable in cases where cost-benefit analysis is involved.

4. Cost-benefit analysis sometimes does a poor job of separating the efficient from the inefficient because
   a. assigning a dollar amount to the costs and benefits of a project can be difficult.
   b. an inappropriate rate of interest may be used when calculating the present value of the benefits and costs.
   c. political decision-makers often listen to special interest groups.
   d. all of the above.

Questions 5-8 refer to the following material:

The Chicago Board of Trade recently proposed the opening of the first national market in air-pollution allotments for sulfur dioxide, the prime component of acid rain. Under mechanisms created by the 1990 amendment to the federal Clean Air Act, polluters will be prohibited from emitting sulfur dioxide beyond certain specific allotments (based on their current needs and EPA clean-air goals). Polluters will be free to choose between polluting up to their allotment or investing in cleaner technology and thus have allotments available for sale.

5. This new program probably
   a. won't work because some rich polluters will be able to buy up allotments and keep polluting.
   b. won't work because the EPA is sending a signal that profits are more important than the environment.
   c. will work because some firms will be able to pay for the purchase of sulfur-dioxide reducing technologies through the sale of allotments.
   d. will work because the allotment payments will provide income that the EPA can use to do a better job of enforcing sulfur-dioxide regulations.

6. For the new program to be most effective, the allotment prices should be
   a. set as low as possible, so as to encourage trading.
   b. set as high as possible so as to discourage pollution.
   c. set by the EPA, the agency that best understands the costs involved with sulfur-dioxide pollution.
   d. set by supply and demand, working through the Board of Trade market.

7. As we learned in the text, many economists and other market-oriented environmentalists think that a greater reliance on property rights will help improve the environment. How are these pro-property-rights individuals likely to react to the proposed Board of Trade allotment program?
   a. They are likely to approve, since the allotment proposal is a variant of the property rights proposal.
   b. They are likely to approve, but only because the allotment proposal is better than the current regulations and therefore is "the lesser of two evils."
   c. They are likely to disapprove, because the allotment proposal establishes no property rights.
   d. They are likely to disapprove, because the allotment proposal is likely to encourage firms to act exactly opposite the way they would act under a property rights mechanism.

8. If the Chicago Board of Trade allows the price of sulfur-dioxide pollution allotments to move freely in an open market, we'd expect the price per ton eventually (perhaps after a few years) to
   a. be approximately equal (on average) to the cost of society of one ton of sulfur-dioxide pollution.
   b. be approximately equal (on average) to the expected cost of avoiding one ton of sulfur-dioxide pollution.
   c. be approximately equal (on average) to the expected cost of cleaning up the acid rain caused by one ton of sulfur-dioxide pollution.
   d. randomly fluctuate up and down, having no meaningful average approximate value.

9. Given the past relationship between conservation in the capitalist nations and conservation in socialist nations, the recent move towards market economies of the former Soviet Union and other previously communist nations seems likely to
   a. improve conservation in the newly market-oriented economies immediately.
   b. worsen conservation in the newly market-oriented economies immediately.
   c. improve conservation in the newly market-oriented economies in the long run.
   d. worsen conservation in the newly market-oriented economies in the long run.

10. The irreversibility effect makes decision-making about natural resource preservation especially difficult because
   a. a natural resource, once ruined, is ruined irreversibly.
   b. a delay in taking advantage of an economically sound use of a natural resource can postpone benefits in a way that loses a portion of them irreversibly.
   c. both of the above.
   d. neither of the above.

11. Formerly, the U.S. Army Corps of Engineers used a discount rate of zero when conducting benefit-cost analyses of proposed waterway transportation projects. Since costs tend to precede benefits in these projects, the zero discount rate tended to result in
   a. excessive approval rates for proposed waterway projects.
   b. excessive denial rates of proposed waterway projects.
   c. no impact on the approval rates of proposed waterway project.
   d. an uncertain impact on the approval rates for proposed waterway projects.

THE ECONOMIC WAY OF THINKING – DISCUSSION QUESTIONS

1. What are some of the instances of price responsiveness cited in the text? Why do you think they might surprise many people? Why should they be less surprising to students of microeconomics? Can you think of some other cases of price responsiveness in resource markets?

2. Diesel fuel can be rationed by price, by waiting in line, or by government allocation. Rank these three rationing methods according to the amount of each of the following activities they generate by diesel fuel users such as trucking firms and farmers: (a) conservation efforts, (b) rent-seeking efforts, and (c) time diverted from output activities. Rank the three rationing methods with regard to their impact on the future supply of diesel fuel.

3. Suppose that the government installed in your family car a monitor that measured the pollutants in the car's exhaust. Further suppose that you received a monthly bill of $1.00 for every pound your car polluted the air. How fair would this be? Would you change the amount of your driving because of it? If you were charged only for those pollutants that were emitted during smog alerts, would you change the times of your driving?

4. What was the whale oil crisis of the early 1800s? What lessons, if any, does it have for us now?

5. What are the social costs of massive substitution of nuclear power for fossil fuel power? What are the social benefits? How should society go about choosing between these alternatives?

6. Suppose that an African nation unfriendly to the United States has a huge oil strike, and sells to anyone *except* the United States. How will this affect oil supplies reaching the United States? How much could the United States gain by making political concessions to the oil-rich country in order to buy the oil? Use a supply-demand diagram for the world oil market in writing an explanation of why the United States might gain nothing from such concessions, so long as a worldwide market for oil exists.

PERSPECTIVES IN ECONOMICS

Disposable vs. Cloth Diapers
"Which Are Best for the Environment?"
By The Consumers Union

Disposable diapers have come to symbolize all things one throws away heedlessly. Like other disposable products, they take up space in landfills at a time when many landfills are just about full and others are getting there fast.

Far from cutting back on waste, Americans are putting out more – four pounds per person per day, up from less than three pounds 20 years ago, says the U.S. Environmental Protection Agency. As old landfills have closed, few have replaced them, because of rising land costs, stricter standards, and people's reluctance to have a landfill as a neighbor.

The disposable diaper is often seen as the pariah of America's dumps. Myriad books on environmental themes have recommended cloth diapers, and legislators in at least 20 states are considering proposals to tax or ban disposables or otherwise restrict their use.

Actually, though, disposable diapers make up only 1.7 percent, by weight, of the solid waste that is landfilled or burned. (By volume, according to the EPA, they make up about 3.3 percent.) That's the same share that paper bags have. Plenty of materials account for a greater portion: Paper as a whole heads the list, with a 40 to 50 percent share; plastics, metals, and yard waste each account for a sizable part. Still, 1.7 percent is high for a single product used by a relatively small fraction of the populace.

Cloth would be the clear choice for parents concerned about the environment if overstuffed landfills were the planet's only problem. But they're not. When you look at cloth and disposable diapers at every stage of their existence, in what's called a life-cycle analysis, you'll see that each has a variety of environmental drawbacks.

In the beginning, when the cotton for cloth diapers is grown, for example, pesticides are used, water is consumed, and soil can erode. When disposable are made, trees are cut and the wood is turned into pulp through a process that can result in air and water pollution. The plastic parts of the diaper come from petroleum, whose extraction and refining also pollute air and water.

Energy is used in manufacturing both cloth and disposable diapers, and the trucks and cars that transport them to stores and homes use fuel and pollute the air.

At home, when you load the washing machine and dryer to launder cloth diapers, you're using a lot of water and energy. Human wastes from cloth diapers leave the house in wastewater, along with plenty of detergent and bleach. With disposable diapers, wastes usually go to a landfill.

At the end of the line, it's obvious that disposables contribute much more than cloth diapers to solid-waste problems. A child will wear 6000 or so disposable diapers before being toilet-trained, whereas a child wearing cloth will go through about 50 diapers.

Several organizations have already performed this kind of "cradle-to-grave" study on diapers. What have they concluded about environmental effects? That depends on which analysis you look at. In March 1990, Arthur D. Little Inc. released the results of a study commissioned by Proctor & Gamble, which makes disposable diapers. Not surprisingly, the report concluded that disposables were no worse than cloth diapers, environmentally speaking.

Four months later, Franklin Associates Ltd. unveiled a report sponsored by the American Paper Institute. It came to much the same conclusion as the Arthur D. Little study: It didn't flatly recommend either type of diaper.

Last January, the National Association of Diaper Services released a study it had assigned to consultants Lehrburger, Mullen, and Jones. No surprises there, either. It favored cloth.

Comparing these analyses is a bit like comparing strained apples and orange juice. There is no standard method for conducting life-cycle analyses, so each study was free to make its own – often divergent – assumptions. For instance, for the number of diapers a baby uses each day, the Arthur D. Little study assumed 6.4 disposables or 12.1 cloth; Franklin Associates assumed 5.4 disposables or 9.7 cloth; Lehrburger et al. omitted this factor and simply compared the environmental impacts per 1000 changed.

All three studies also oversimplified complex comparisons. How is a consumer to compare a ton of solid waste produced by throwing away disposables with, say, a million gallons of wastewater produced by washing cloth diapers? Which is worse: 10 pounds of nitrogen oxides or 1500 parts per million of hydrocarbons?

The life-cycle analyses are far better at raising questions than they are at providing answers, but one thing is clear: Consumers won't make a big contribution to the health of the environment by choosing one type of diaper over another. They may, however, make a small contribution to the well-being of their region. If you live in an area where the solid-waste problem has become acute, as it has in many parts of the Northeast and Midwest, consider using cloth diapers. If water is at a premium in your town or city, as it is in California and much of the Southwest, disposables might be the better choice for the environment.

Discussion

1. Everyone knows that using disposable diapers causes pollution. How does Consumers Union visualize a circumstance in which disposable diapers are best for the environment?

2. Think about the landfill, energy, and water situations where you live. Given the life-cycle analysis in the article, do you think that disposable diapers or cloth diapers are best for your area? Why?

3. To what other kinds of environmental decisions might life-cycle analysis be applied? Explain how you might go about applying life-cycle analysis to one of those decisions. What information would you need? What value judgements, if any, would you have to make?

29
Problem Areas for the Market

TRUE OR FALSE

☐ ☐ 1. Voluntary exchange is proof of expected mutual gain.

☐ ☐ 2. Private interest and ideal economic efficiency sometimes conflict, even for a smoothly functioning, competitive price system.

☐ ☐ 3. Poor information on the part of buyers is very seldom a factor in real-world markets.

☐ ☐ 4. Spillover, or neighborhood, effects are the same thing as externalities.

☐ ☐ 5. When externalities are present, some parties must be trying to harm others.

☐ ☐ 6. Social costs include those accruing to consenting *and* secondary parties.

☐ ☐ 7. Prohibition is often less desirable than acceptance by society of activities that generate externalities.

☐ ☐ 8. When external costs are low, markets are unlikely to handle externalities in a socially desirable manner.

☐ ☐ 9. When large numbers of people are involved, external costs are usually low.

☐ ☐ 10. Poorly defined property rights increase external costs.

☐ ☐ 11. Taxing polluters according to the damage they do is administratively simple, but makes no sense economically.

☐ ☐ 12. When externalities are present, secondary effects are always negative, not positive.

☐ ☐ 13. Public goods are a special case of spillover benefits to secondary parties.

☐ ☐ 14. The free-rider problem occurs when an activity benefits people who are not forced to pay for their benefits.

☐ ☐ 15. An advantage of the zero-price solution to the public goods problem is that extra information is made available about consumer valuation of the goods.

PROBLEMS AND PROJECTS

Exhibit 1

Output (per month)	Supply: producer's marginal cost	Demand: consumer's valuation	External cost (for alternative levels of supply)	Marginal social cost
70	65¢	110¢	0¢	65¢
80	70	95	5	75
90	75	85	10	85
100	80	80	15	95
110	90	75	20	_____
120	100	70	30	_____

1. Exhibit 1 presents data on the producer's cost and consumer's valuation of paper pulp, a competitively produced product. Since production of the pulp generates an undesirable odor, the market supply curve does not accurately reflect the marginal social cost. The estimated external costs at alternative output levels are so presented in Exhibit 1.
   a. At what price and output would the quantity supplied equal the quantity demanded?
   b. Fill in the marginal social cost data for alternative output levels. How does the marginal social cost compare with the consumer's valuation of paper pulp at the competitive equilibrium price?
   c. What would be the ideal output level, considering the costs that are external to the producer?

2. You have just been hired to be on the staff of a member of the U.S. House of Representatives from a coastal state. An electric utility is trying to build a power plant near the mouth of a river in the state and wants the right to use water from the river in its cooling towers. Agricultural interests own the water rights, however, and law forbids their transfer to industrial users. The utility points out that water rights among farmers trade for about $10 per unit, whereas the utility would pay $80. You are told to spend the night writing a short paper briefing the representative on (a) whether or not the private property rights system is working efficiently in this case, (b) the true value of the water in dispute, and (c) the distribution of benefits (who would thank the representative) and costs (who would complain to the representative) if Congress overruled state law and gave the utility the right to bid for the water in this specific case. As you write this short, clear paper, remember the basic principles of economics concerning marginal valuation and the opportunity cost. (Would your analysis differ if the power plant location were 200 miles inland, where much of each farm's irrigation water returned to the river and was reused?)

3. Exhibit 2 shows the actual estimated costs of pollution reduction (measured in percentages) for a beet sugar refining firm and a petroleum refining firm, both of which initially emit identical amounts of pollution.

Exhibit 2

| Amount of pollution reduction (percent) | Marginal cost of reduction | |
| | Beet refining | Petroleum refining |
	(cents/pound)	
10	0.5	3.0
20	0.5	3.0
30	0.5	3.5
40	0.5	4.0
50	1.0	5.0
60	2.0	6.0
70	3.0	14.0
80	4.5	15.0
90	6.0	21.0

Source: Based on data in Allen V. Kneese and Charles Schultze, Pollution, Prices and Public Policy, (Washington, D.C.: Brookings Institution, 1975).

a. Suppose the government instituted a maximum emission standard that required each firm to reduce its pollution by 60 percent. What would be the marginal cost of reduction for the beet refiner? For the petroleum refiner?

b. If instead government instituted a pollution tax of 4.5 cents per pound of pollution emitted, by what percent would the beet refiner reduce pollution? The petroleum refiner?

c. Explain briefly why the second approach is more economical (efficient) than the first.

4. Dan Vencill is a likable fellow who hates yardwork, partly because he dislikes the activity and partly because he doesn't mind a somewhat unkept yard. However, his neighbors all love to work on their yards and are extremely fastidious about them. Exhibit 3 shows Vencill's estimate of his marginal cost of yardwork (per hour) along with his estimate of the marginal value (to him) of his yardwork (per hour). Also shown is Vencill's neighbors' estimate of the value to them of Vencill's work on his yard, a benefit which has nothing to do with Vencill's private decision about how much time to spend working on his yard.

Exhibit 3

Quantity of Vencill's yardwork (hours/week)	Vencill's marginal cost of yardwork (dollars/hour)	Vencill's marginal value of yardwork (dollars/hour)	Vencill's neighbors' marginal value of Vencill's yardwork (dollars/hour)	Social marginal value of Vencill's yardwork (dollars/hour)
1	1.00	3.00	18.00	21.00
2	2.00	2.00	16.00	18.00
3	3.00	1.00	13.00	_____
4	4.00	0	10.00	_____
5	5.00	0	8.00	_____
6	6.00	0	6.00	_____
7	7.00	0	4.00	_____

a. Fill in the missing information in the tale.
b. Considering only Vencill's benefits and costs of yardwork, how many hours per week will he spend working on his yard?
c. Calculate the *total net* benefit (to Vencill alone) of this many hours per week. How much do Vencill's neighbors benefit from this amount of work?
d. Considering all costs and benefits of Vencill's yardwork, what is the socially ideal (efficient) number of hours for Vencill to work on his yard? How much would Vencill's neighbors benefit if he spent this much time working? What is the total *social* net benefit of this many hours?
e. Suppose that Vencill's neighbors told him that if he spent 6 hours per week working on his yard, they would pay him $30.00. Based solely on the information in the exhibit, would Vencill accept this offer? Is the offer an economically sensible one from the neighbors' point of view? Explain.
f. Suggest some reasons why the solution above would probably not work as a general solution to this sort of problem (*Hint*: Remember the free-rider problem.)

5. In the diagrams in Exhibit 4, the two left-hand panels depict the water pollution attributable to two industries, paper producers and beer producers. The right-hand panel depicts the total water pollution of the two industries and the marginal external damage cost of the water pollution:

Exhibit 4

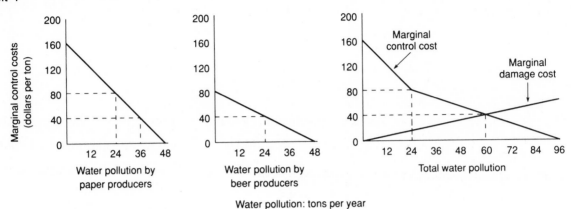

Water pollution: tons per year

a. In the absence of any policy to control water pollution, what is the amount of
    i. water pollution by paper producers? _____
    ii. water pollution by beer producers? _____
    iii. total water pollution? _____
b. What is the socially efficient amount of water pollution? Why isn't a pollution level of zero preferable?
c. Suppose the government mandates that both industries reduce their water pollution 30 tons per year. At the new levels of pollution, what is the marginal pollution control cost for
    i. paper producers? _____
    ii. beer producers? _____
    Why is this inefficient?
d. Suppose instead that the government achieves the same pollution reduction by levying an effluent charge. How large should the effluent charge be?
e. With the effluent charge policy, what is the amount of water pollution by
    i. paper producers? _____
    ii. beer producers? _____
f. Comparing the effluent charge to the reduction in part c,
    i. does paper producer pollution rise or fall? _____
    ii. does beer producer pollution rise or fall? _____
    iii. does social efficiency rise or fall? (Why?) _____

LEARNING THE MECHANICS – MULTIPLE CHOICE

1. Production and distribution of which of the following is more likely to impose significant externalities in the absence of government intervention?
    a. Ice cream
    b. Household maid service
    c. Paper pulp
    d. Soap

2. If there are no spillover effects, voluntary exchange results in
   a. expected net gain for each participant.
   b. expected social benefits that exceed the expected social costs.
   c. both a and b.
   d. neither a nor b.

3. If important social benefits (externalities) are associated with consumption of a product, it can be said that
   a. the supply curve for the product lies too far to the right to provide an efficient allocation of resources.
   b. the demand curve understates the relative importance of the product; therefore, resources are underallocated to its production.
   c. special excise taxes should be levied on producers of the product.
   d. government should enact legislation to prohibit the production of the commodity.

4. Which of the following activities is most likely to result in substantial costs that are external to the decision-maker?
   a. Consumption of an ice cream cone
   b. Production of a handcrafted billfold
   c. Consumption of a supersonic air flight from New York to Los Angeles
   d. A firing of a high-powered rifle in the desert lands of Nevada

5. The major distinction between pure private and pure public goods is that
   a. private goods generate external effects, whereas public goods do not.
   b. the government can produce public goods, but not private goods.
   c. public goods must be consumed jointly, since supplying the goods to one person simultaneously makes them available to others.
   d. public goods are free, whereas private goods have a cost.

6. When costs are incurred that are external to the decision-maker, a firm is likely to be producing more of a good than is socially desirable
   a. because it is not required to fully consider external costs when its price and output decisions are made.
   b. because the firm will not pay attention to buyers' wishes in such a case.
   c. because the firm is a free rider.
   d. because communal property rights are absent.

7. Producers are more likely to be concerned with customer satisfaction when
   a. they are largely dependent on repeat customers.
   b. it is difficult for the customer to evaluate product quality accurately.
   c. they are dependent on tourism for their sales.
   d. the demand for the products of the producer is inelastic.

8. Even if one assumes a purely competitive market, the pricing mechanism can be (and is) criticized because it
   a. encourages firms to seek profits by neglecting the preferences of consumers.
   b. fails to register fully the benefits and costs resulting from externalities.
   c. encourages workers to unionize because of the low wages that will prevail in a market economy.
   d. fails to provide an incentive for firms to minimize their per unit dollar costs of production.

9. Emission charges increase the cost of
   a. catering to the preferences of repeat customers more than to tourists.
   b. producing pollution-intensive goods.
   c. using production methods that result in less pollution.
   d. using pollution control devices.

10. The Montagnais Indians were
    a. not willing to use any type of private property rights.
    b. successful at using private property rights to preserve buffalo populations.
    c. successful at using private property rights to preserve beaver populations.
    d. a tribe that was nearly responsible for the extinction of the plains buffalo.

11. When property rights to a farm are held by an individual, the individual
    a. has an incentive to see that the resource is put to the use of its highest valuation.
    b. has no incentive to use the resource such that others can benefit.
    c. has no choice but to use the resource wisely.
    d. cannot benefit *personally* when the resource is not used such that society benefits.

12. Which of the following is the least costly way to achieve the efficient output of an easily monitored pollutant?
    a. Ban the pollutant.
    b. Issue marketable discharge permits for the pollutants.
    c. Issue nonmarketable discharge permits for the pollutant.
    d. Rely on unrestricted private markets.

THE ECONOMIC WAY OF THINKING – MULTIPLE CHOICE

1. Fish in the sea are "owned" communally. No individual, group of individuals, or firm has the right to buy, sell, and/or trade the fish of the sea. A leading consequence of this lack of ownership is
   a. monopoly power in commercial fishing because of the ease of restricting entry.
   b. that individual fishermen have almost no incentive to practice conservation.
   c. full economies of scale cannot be attained with respect to the size of individual fishing boats.
   d. that fishermen inevitably earn lower wages than persons in other activities.

2. One major advantage of the market is that it allows consumers to select freely among commodities. Yet, buyers of automobiles in America are forced by law to pay for additional safety equipment that many (perhaps the majority) would not freely choose to buy under an optional marketing arrangement. This procedure may be justified on efficiency grounds for which of the following reasons?
   a. The per unit cost of the safety equipment will fall whenever all buyers are forced to purchase it.
   b. The private demand for safety is low.
   c. External costs are associated with automobile accidents.
   d. Buyers who would choose safety equipment under the optional arrangement are likely to be those drivers who need the equipment least.

3. Courts have consistently held that people ("receptors") have a right to clean air (a property right); therefore, if a polluter begins to foul the air and cause problems for receptors, the receptors can collect all damages proved to be caused by the polluter. Yet, the market system recognizably fails to handle the pollution problem adequately. This is because
   a. receptors have no property rights regarding pollution.
   b. no one knows whether damage truly results from air pollution ("proof" does not exist).
   c. polluters are monopolists.
   d. receptors have property rights, but since it is difficult to *prove* damages, causation, and a specific culprit, *enforcement* of the rights is often very costly.

4. A pure market economy is unlikely to provide a sufficient amount of public good like national defense because
   a. the consumers are poorly informed as to the value of national defense.
   b. it is generally impossible to withhold national defense from a nonpaying customer.
   c. national defense does not yield a benefit to individuals.
   d. private firms will be less efficient than public firms when producing a public good such as national defense.

5. Control of air and water pollution is likely to be an important economic issue in the foreseeable future. Using economic efficiency as our criterion, which of the following general approaches to pollution control would be best?
   a. Reduce the role of economic growth, which is the major cause of pollution.
   b. Prohibit all economic activities that cause pollution.
   c. Use our existing resources to eliminate all damage to our environment that results from pollution.
   d. Eliminate a pollution-causing activity only when the marginal damage costs of the action exceed the marginal social benefits associated with the use of the resource in a manner that leads to pollution.

6. Which of the following activities is most likely to generate a positive externality – an external benefit – that will result in a free-market output level that is less than the socially desirable amount?
   a. The production of crude oil and its by-product, natural gas
   b. Research on a new diet and exercise program that will reduce the likelihood of cancer
   c. The delivery of orange juice by milkmen, reducing the net cost to the consumer
   d. The development and patent of a new automatic clutch designed to improve the efficiency of the automobile

7. Suppose that on the outskirts of Orlando, Florida, a city of about 100,000 people, an orange grove were bought by the city and turned into Orange Grove Park, where the care, upkeep, and orange consumption will be handled by all city individuals on a volunteer basis, "not for the benefit of one greedy individual." The result of this institutional change, the elimination of *private* property rights, would most likely include
   a. more resources devoted to the orchard's upkeep, since roughly 100,000 people would have a stake in the orchard's production.
   b. many oranges to be picked before optimal ripeness, since for any individual, waiting for those particular oranges to ripen completely might mean only one chance in 100,000 that he or she would be the one to benefit from waiting.
   c. less wasting of oranges from the grove, since every picker would realize the social value of oranges.
   d. more fertilizer being purchased by volunteer individuals and applied at appropriate times.

8. In many countries, cigarettes are sold by a government monopoly. If cigarette smoking generates external costs, then having a monopoly carry out cigarette sales
   a. reduces cigarette consumption below the efficient level.
   b. increases cigarette consumption above the efficient level.
   c. results in the efficient level of cigarette consumption.
   d. could result in too much, too little, or just the right amount of cigarette consumption.

9. Compared to the maximum emission standard method of control, the emission charge method will produce a given reduction in pollution with
   a. a larger impact on the product's social cost, since the polluter pays money in addition to control costs.
   b. a higher social cost, since many firms will continue to pollute.
   c. a lower social cost, since the most economical reductions in pollution will be made first.
   d. a lower social cost, since virtually all pollution will cease if it really costs firms money to pollute.

10. New products provide a classic case of the consumer information problem. However, in some cases consumers partially solve the problem by trusting the "brand name" of the producer of the new product. Since firms spend millions of dollars advertising and maintaining their brand names, the likelihood of a "brand name" firm's intentionally selling a dangerous or shoddy new product is
    a. high, because big firms are always after a quick dollar.
    b. high, because their brand name is a communal property right.
    c. low, because big firms do not make mistakes.
    d. low, because the firm with a brand name has a lot to lose if word spreads about bad consumer experiences.

Questions 11-14 relate to the following material:

Fishermen who use nets to catch tuna also sometimes net dolphins, which, because they are mammals, drown before they can be released. Currently, the price and quantity of tuna determined by the market does not take into account the cost to society of killing the dolphins (marginal external cost). Listed below are market demand and supply schedules for tuna as well as the marginal external social costs associated with dolphins killed in the process of catching the tuna. All costs and valuations are listed in terms of dollars per pound of tuna.

Quantity of tuna (thousands)	Consumers' valuation (of tuna)	Marginal private costs (of tuna)	Marginal external costs (of dolphins)
1,000	$3.50	$1.70	$0.90
2,000	3.00	1.80	1.20
3,000	2.50	1.90	1.50
4,000	2.00	2.00	1.80
5,000	1.50	2.10	2.10
6,000	1.00	2.20	2.40
7,000	0.50	2.30	2.70

11. The current price per pound of tuna is
    a. $2.00.
    b. $2.10.
    c. $3.00.
    d. undefined, but somewhere between $1.50 and $2.00.

12. The socially optimal quantity of tuna (in thousands of pounds) is
    a. 2,000.
    b. 3,000.
    c. 4,000.
    d. 5,000.

13. In order to attain the socially optimal equilibrium, the government would have to impose a per-pound tax on suppliers of
    a. $1.00.
    b. $1.20.
    c. $1.80.
    d. $3.00.

14. Of this tax, consumers would end up paying, per pound,
    a. $0.20.
    b. $0.65.
    c. $1.00.
    d. $1.20.

THE ECONOMIC WAY OF THINKING – DISCUSSION QUESTIONS

1. Do you think charity is a public good? A pure public good? Why might individuals be more willing to contribute $25 to the local community charity drive if they could be assured that others would do so? How does the raising of money for charitable purposes illustrate the free-rider problem?

2. Jones gets a real bargain on 100 acres of land because it is near an airport. He decides to use the land to breed his prize-winning race horses. One year after buying the land, Jones sues the airport because his horses, disrupted by the noise of jet planes, are not breeding.
    a. If you were the judge, how would you decide Jones's case? Why?
    b. Would you have decided any differently if Jones had owned the land before anyone considered building an airport nearby? Why?

3. With a system of emissions charges, some polluters would find it cheaper to pay some emissions charges than to stop polluting entirely, even when the pollution is damaging to the public's health. Does this mean that emissions charges are useless policies? Why or why not?

4. What do you consider to be the main advantages and disadvantages of each of the following anti-pollution policies?
    a. effluent charges
    b. marketable discharge permits
    c. maximum emission standards

    Could any of these policies result in too little pollution, from a social point of view? Explain.

5. For each of the following pairs of firms, decide which, if either, has the greater incentive to provide customer satisfaction regarding price and quality control:
    a. A large franchised hamburger stand versus a single stand operation, both located at a busy interstate freeway exit.
    b. A major brand-name whiskey distiller versus a regional distiller with no plans to expand nationwide.

6. "The unregulated private economy will always provide consumers with what they want at the lowest possible cost to society. As long as consumers are willing to pay the cost of an item, the free market will provide it for them." Evaluate this statement. Do you agree? Do you disagree? Explain your reasoning.

7. In general, we have argued that private sector markets will allocate too few resources to public goods like national defense. Do you think the public sector allocates too few, too many, or just the right amount of resources to such goods? What is your evidence? How should we go about determining the socially optimal amount of public goods to produce?

8. A good topic for a group discussion is the economics of pollution. Be sure to discuss
    a. why air and water pollution are problems.
    b. the ideal amount of pollution from society's point of view.
    c. who gains (and loses) from failure to force polluters to pay for the use of valuable resources, such as clean air and water.
    d. alternative strategies for pollution control.

30
Public Choice: Understanding Government and Government Failure

TRUE OR FALSE

T F

☐ ☐ 1. Market failure enhances the argument for, and likelihood of, government intervention and its success in overcoming particular shortcomings of the market.

☐ ☐ 2. A politician can be viewed as a political entrepreneur or supplier.

☐ ☐ 3. Voting, like other decisions, is carried out with imperfect information.

☐ ☐ 4. Most voters are chiefly concerned with just a few of the many issues decided legislatively.

☐ ☐ 5. With collective action, an individual can usually be sure that she will not pay for something she does not want.

☐ ☐ 6. The efficiency of the political process would be enhanced if the primary beneficiaries of government activities were clearly identified small groups of voters.

☐ ☐ 7. The "public good" quality of antipoverty efforts will, according to economic analysis, encourage collective action for redistribution of income.

☐ ☐ 8. Government failure strengthens the case for use of the market system.

☐ ☐ 9. An individual voter has a strong economic incentive to fight special interest legislation with his or her own time and money, because such legislation is costly to all members of society.

☐ ☐ 10. Passage of special interest legislation is not always inefficient.

☐ ☐ 11. Voters are more likely to be short sighted on a complex issue than a simple one.

☐ ☐ 12. Public sector decision-makers have a strong incentive to be efficient, since most of the people they deal with are their employers.

☐ ☐ 13. When exercising their voting rights, voters usually must choose among complex bundles of goods, services, and costs.

PROBLEMS AND PROJECTS

Exhibit 1

	Actual net dollar benefits (+) or costs (−) for the voter			Political entrepreneur's estimate of the voter's perceived net dollar benefits (+) or costs (−)		
Voter	Proposal A	Proposal B	Proposal C	Proposal A	Proposal B	Proposal C
1	$5	$10	$10	$5	$10	$10
2	5	4	−4	5	4	−4
3	5	3	−2	5	3	−2
4	3	1	−1	3	0	0
5	3	1	−1	3	0	0
6	3	1	−1	3	0	0
7	1	−8	−1	1	−8	0
8	1	−4	−1	1	−4	0
9	−2	−3	−1	−2	−3	0
10	−2	−3	−1	−2	−3	0

1. Exhibit 1 presented data on the actual and perceived benefits of voters resulting from the passage of three different legislative proposals.
    a. Calculate the actual benefit/cost ratio for each of the three proposals.
    b. Which of the three proposals do you think will be favored (opposed) by the political entrepreneur? Why?
    c. Given that proposal B exerts only a small impact on voters 4, 5, and 6, why might it be sensible for them to ignore proposal B?

2. Assume that price supports for dairy products are in the interests of U.S. dairy product producers but not in the interests of U.S. dairy product consumers.
    a. Use the concepts and analysis of this chapter to indicate why dairy farmers might be successful in organizing to persuade Congress to adopt price supports.
    b. Conduct a similar analysis to show why consumers might be unsuccessful in attempting to organize to persuade Congress not to adopt price supports.

3. Match the letters on right with the numbers on the left.

_____ (1) Special interest groups	a.	It explains why the market has trouble allocating public goods efficiently.
_____ (2) Externalities	b.	It results because information is costly, and voters do not expect their vote to be decisive.
_____ (3) The free-rider problem	c.	They are a good potential source of campaign contributions for political entrepreneurs.
_____ (4) The rational ignorance effect	d.	It would reduce the power of special interest groups.
_____ (5) The short-sightedness effect	e.	They strengthen the case for government intervention.
_____ (6) Referendum decision-makers	f.	It explains why macropolicy is likely to be excessively expansionary 12-18 months before a major election.

4. Some activities, such as prostitution and the marketing of certain recreational drugs, involve voluntary transactions between buyers and sellers and have therefore been classified as victimless crimes. However, the activities appear to generate external costs by morally offending many nonparticipants. Consider the example of a recreational drug presented in Exhibit 2. (Quantities are in millions of grams, and values are in dollars per gram.):
   a. Complete the last two columns of the table.

Exhibit 2

Quantity of drug use	Users		Nonusers		Society	
	Marginal benefit	Marginal cost	Marginal benefit	Marginal cost	Marginal benefit	Marginal cost
10	150	30	0	20	150	50
20	120	30	0	40	___	___
30	90	30	0	60	___	___
40	60	30	0	80	___	___
50	30	30	0	100	___	___
60	0	30	0	120	___	___

Suppose that 5 percent of the total adult U.S. population would be users of this drug in an unrestricted market. These several million potential users are widely dispersed and unable to effectively organize for political purposes.
   b. Determine the quantity of drug use that would
       i. be socially efficient: _____
       ii. occur in an unrestricted private market: _____
       iii. tend to result from the political process: _____
   c. Your text covered what might be called the "tyranny of special interests." Explain why the problem here illustrates a possible "tyranny of the majority."

5. Consider each of the following quotes:

   Following the example set by the ending of Prohibition, we should legalize marijuana, cocaine, and certain other drugs we have failed to control. Excise taxes and punishments could hold drug use to tolerable levels and discourage their use prior to engaging in activities that might harm others. (Gary Becker, economist)

   Drug use is out of control in our society. Making it legal would only reinforce the erroneous perception that drugs such as marijuana and cocaine can be used without consequences. (Lee I. Dogoloff, Executive Director, American Council for Drug Education)

Assume that you are the vice-president of the United States and have to cast a vote to break a tie in the Senate on the issue of the legalization of marijuana and cocaine. In a single paragraph, state your decision, and carefully and clearly support your position. Be sure to address both points of view expressed above.

LEARNING THE MECHANICS – MULTIPLE CHOICE

Ideal public sector action can potentially improve economic efficiency

1.   a.   because goods can be provided free by the public sector.
     b.   when market inefficiency results because of spillover effects.
     c.   if prices can be fixed below the equilibrium level, thereby limiting the power of greedy businesses.
     d.   because political decision-makers generally place the public interest above the pursuit of personal gain.

2.   With economic efficiency as the criterion, which of the following is the best justification for the government's providing some economic goods and services, rather than relying on the market?
     a.   Government provision of goods eliminates misallocation that results from the power of special interest groups.
     b.   It is important that political goods and services be provided free of charge.
     c.   There is often no way to sell public goods in a private market, because the benefits cannot be limited to persons who pay for them.
     d.   It would be unethical and unreasonable to allow private individuals to make a profit by providing education, police protection, and similar services.

3.   The political roles of legislators and voters
     a.   are analogous to those of producers and consumers in the market.
     b.   have no relation to the actions of market participants.
     c.   can serve to express collective preferences, but not individual preferences.
     d.   are effective for expressing preferences only by voting.

4.   In explaining public sector choices, economic theory
     a.   is perfectly appropriate, since money prices are used in the public sector in the same way as in the private sector.
     b.   is inappropriate, since individuals act in the public interest, not out of self-interest, when doing the public's business.
     c.   is useful because individuals, including those who participate in the political process, will respond in a predictable way to changes in personal costs and benefits.
     d.   is useful only if political entrepreneurs are highly selfish.

5.   In general, voters are concerned
     a.   with most issues, since information on most issues is cost free.
     b.   with most issues, since each issue will have some impact, however slight, on each citizen.
     c.   with the views of a particular political candidate on all issues.
     d.   with a few specific issues – those that directly affect them in a substantial way.

6.   Which of the following groups is likely to have the greatest influence on legislative collective decision-making? (*Hint*: Remember special interest issues.)
     a.   Nonunion employees
     b.   Consumers
     c.   Taxpayers
     d.   Business interests and labor unions

7. A characteristic of the public sector is that individuals, in selecting their legislative representatives
    a. have no influence over political decision-makers.
    b. can normally use their voting power on an issue-by-issue basis.
    c. cannot effectively vote for politicians on an issue-by-issue basis, but must accept all the views of a candidate as a package.
    d. can usually find a representative who reflects the individual's views on all significant issues.

8. Governmental allocation will more likely be preferred to market allocation when
    a. consumers are well informed.
    b. the shortsightedness effect dominates.
    c. the rational ignorance effect dominates.
    d. high external costs are associated with market decision-making.

9. Economic theory suggests that it is often rational for a vote-maximizing politician to support special interest groups at the expense of other unorganized, widely dispersed groups (for example, taxpayers or consumers)
    a. when the gains that accrue to the special interest groups are much smaller than the costs imposed on others.
    b. when the non-special interest voter is unconcerned or uninformed, and campaign funds are readily available from the special interest.
    c. if, and only if, government action is socially efficient.
    d. if the government action would reduce the monopoly power of business or labor.

10. The impact of a special interest group will be stronger if the issue is
    a. simple and easily understood by the voter.
    b. complex and difficult for the average voter to comprehend.
    c. decided by a referendum vote.
    d. one that promotes economic inefficiency.

11. Operational efficiency in the public sector tends to be low because the individual government employee
    a. is usually able, in a dishonest manner, to take home the money that would be called profit in the private sector.
    b. is unable to profit directly from the extra care and effort that efficiency requires.
    c. is usually not as competent as the private sector employee.
    d. usually is a victim of rent seeking.

THE ECONOMIC WAY OF THINKING – MULTIPLE CHOICE

1. (I) In the public sector, unlike the private sector, personal gain is usually not the stated goal of entrepreneurial decision-makers. (II) In the public sector, as in the private sector, we can expect individuals, including political entrepreneurs to be motivated by self-interest most of the time.
    a. Both I and II are true.
    b. I is true, II is false.
    c. I is false, II is true.
    d. Both I and II are false.

2. Economic theory leads us to expect that the typical voter will be uninformed on many issues because
   a. most issues are so complex that voters will be unable to understand them.
   b. even though information is free, most voters do not care what politicians are doing.
   c. information is costly, and the individual voter casting a well-informed vote can expect negligible personal benefit.
   d. citizen apathy about political matters is inevitable, except when decisions are made by referendum.

3. In a market system, individuals normally pay for what they get. With public sector operation
   a. the individual consumer often does not pay, although someone else must.
   b. the individual often does not pay, nor does anyone else, since production is not for profit.
   c. an individual's tax bill will approximate the value to him or her of government's service.
   d. payment is avoided since costs are irrelevant in the public sector.

4. Economic theory suggests that laws against crimes such as murder, arson, and robbery are
   a. the result of our moral code, even though they promote economic inefficiency.
   b. examples of government actions that improve resource allocation by discouraging activities that generate external costs and violate our moral code.
   c. impossible to understand from a strictly economic viewpoint.
   d. examples of government action that stem from the power of special interest groups.

5. Public choice theory suggests that political entrepreneurs will be most likely to favor redistribution of income from
   a. the rich to the poor.
   b. disorganized individuals to well-organized special interest groups.
   c. middle-income taxpayers to both the rich and the poor.
   d. well-organized business and labor groups to consumers.

6. According to economic theory, each voter supports the candidate
   a. who offers the greatest number of programs.
   b. who offers to make the greatest aggregate decrease in taxes, other things constant.
   c. who offers the greatest personal gain, with no consideration of effects on others.
   d. who offers the greatest *net* benefits, including utility that might be derived as the result of improvement in the economic welfare of others.

7. "The ideal public policy, from the viewpoint of a political entrepreneur, is one that provides widespread benefits to the voting populace, even if it means that a small number of voters will *individually* bear substantial cost." This statement is probably
   a. correct, because voters will be well informed when they are the beneficiaries of a political action.
   b. incorrect, because most of the beneficiaries are likely to be rationally uninformed, whereas the special interest group that bears the cost will tend to oppose strenuously politicians who follow such a course.
   c. correct, since the political process dilutes the influence of special interests because each has only one vote.
   d. incorrect, because the well-informed voter will oppose policies that conflict with the views of small groups of people.

8. "Special interests will no longer have special influence, once we throw the rascals out of office and elect people who are basically honest." The facts of life bias representative government against this view because
   a. special interest group members are richer and can buy more votes than other people.
   b. all politicians are basically honest.
   c. even perfect and costless information for voters could not reduce special interest groups' influence by much.
   d. even honest politicians have a strong incentive to support special interest positions.

9. Suppose that macroeconomic policy increases output and employment between 6 and 18 months before it causes an acceleration in the rate of inflation. According to the shortsightedness effect, expansionary macroeconomic policy would be
   a. highly attractive to political entrepreneurs before each election.
   b. highly attractive to political entrepreneurs after an election.
   c. attractive to political entrepreneurs only if such a policy would help to stabilize the economy.
   d. unattractive to political entrepreneurs because of the future inflation it might cause.

10. Which of the following political positions does the special interest effect make more attractive to a vote-maximizing political entrepreneur?
    a. Abolition of the present tax credit for industry X
    b. Abolition of tenure for college professors
    c. 15 percent increase in social security benefits
    d. 50 percent reduction in import taxes on foreign-produced automobiles

11. Garbage-removal services are provided in different cities by different kinds of organizations. If a newly developed truck has just come on the market, and managers in all garbage-removal organizations are analyzing the net benefits of buying the new type of truck, which of the following should expect to undertake the most serious, painstaking examinations?
    a. Managers of city-owned garbage agencies
    b. Managers of large, profitable corporations in little danger of sinking below the normal level of profits
    c. Owner-managers of medium-sized private firms
    d. Big-city mayors

12. When a federal agency requests funds to build a dam to subsidize irrigation of farmland used to grow potatoes near a river in Idaho, we would expect the *least* active support from
    a. farmers with land near the proposed dam.
    b. the construction unions whose members would work on the project.
    c. the chamber of commerce in a city located near the project.
    d. consumers of potatoes nationally.

13. Several economists have argued that when the government imposes import quotas, the import permits should be auctioned off to the highest bidder rather than given away. Auctioning off the permits would
    a. reduce the economic rents earned by importing firms.
    b. make it easier to see the economic costs of the quotas.
    c. reduce the government budget deficit.
    d. have all of the above effects.

14. One problem contributing to government failure is the short-sightedness of politicians. Stockholders of business firms are
    a. also likely to be short-sighted since they won't own their stock forever.
    b. less likely to be short-sighted because a dollar in the future is worth more than a dollar today.
    c. less likely to be short-sighted because short-sighted policies reduce the resale value of stocks.
    d. also short-sighted since they generally hire business executives to make day-to-day decisions, and the business executives eventually retire.

15. Assume that you're a member of the U.S. House of Representatives from your home state and district. Which of the following best explains why you have a strong incentive to force the Federal Government to finance pork barrel projects in your district?
    a. Most of the benefits of pork barrel projects within your district will accrue to your constituents, while most of the costs will be imposed on voters from other districts.
    b. Most of the costs of pork barrel projects within your district will be imposed on your constituents, while most of the benefits will accrue to voters from other districts.
    c. Pork producers are a powerful political lobby that will influence the actions of legislators in all districts.
    d. This is a trick question; in a representative democracy, there is little incentive for legislators to support pork barrel projects.

THE ECONOMIC WAY OF THINKING – DISCUSSION QUESTIONS

1. Do you think real-world politicians consider how their positions on issues will affect their election prospects? For each of the following pairs of states and constituents, what type of special-interest legislation can you think of that was almost certainly favored by the politicians in the indicated state?

State	Constituents
a. Michigan	autoworkers
b. Florida	retirees
c. Texas	oil producers
d. Name-a-state	defense contractors

2. "We may always have death and taxes, but we will never see a government agency go bankrupt."
   a. Under what circumstances should a government agency discontinue a current function?
   b. Is the absence of the bankruptcy criterion a strength or a weakness of the public sector?

3. Which of the following do you think are special interest issues?
   a. Tariffs on imports of television sets.
   b. Tax-free interest income from municipal bonds
   c. Tenure for college professors
   d. Below-cost tuition for college students
   e. Rent controls for your local community
   f. Interest-free educational loans for college students

   Are you in favor of some special interest issues? Which ones?

4. "Government bureaucrats are only as important as the size of their departments, so they always will spend their entire budget allocation so as to avoid having their budgets cut in the next year."
   a.   Do you agree with this quote? Why or why not?
   b.   If bureaucrats act this way, are they profit maximizers? Are they cost minimizers?
   c.   If they aren't maximizing profit, what are they maximizing?

5. What are the major factors that contribute to market failure? What are the major factors that contribute to government failure? Which type of failure do you think is more common? More costly?

6. Explain how the theory of public choice, laid out by James Buchanan, Anthony Downs, Gordon Tullock, and others, accounts for:
   a.   rational ignorance.
   b.   low voter turnouts.
   c.   the disproportionate strength of special interest groups.
   d.   the prevalence of biased and misleading information.
   e.   a cynical attitude toward politicians.

7. Would you favor or oppose each of the following?
   a.   A ban on lobbying and campaign contributions.
   b.   A federal law requiring that state and local governments auction off their restrictive occupational licenses instead of giving them away.
   c.   A requirement that legislators set a budget constraint.

   Support your position in each case.

CURRENT DEBATES IN ECONOMICS

Debate Number Five: Should We Have a Capitalist/Market Economy?

Yes, We Should Have a Capitalist/Market Economy:

Return of the Invisible Hand
By Geoffrey Sampson

[Adapted, with permission, from the August 1985 issue of *Reason* magazine.
Copyright ©1985 by the Reason Foundation,
2716 Ocean Park Blvd., Suite 1062, Santa Monica, CA 90405.]

In any human society there must be *some* means — perhaps efficient or perhaps inefficient, perhaps morally admirable or perhaps abominable — by which the activities of its members are coordinated. By this means, the various choices that individuals might be disposed to make in isolation are resolved into a set of decisions that are compatible taken as a whole, so that nobody is processing or consuming anything that does not exist because it has not been produced.

There are two contrasting principles by which this coordination can be achieved. The principle that, arguably, seems most natural is the principle of *planning and command*. The task of finding an efficient and fair solution to the coordination problem is an immensely complex task, so a competently staffed organ of state is charged to work out a satisfactory solution, and the state delegates to this body the authority to impose its solution on individuals in their roles as producers and consumers.

The opposite principle is that of the *market*. Under this principle, the state claims no authority to dispose of the various resources within society, each of which is controlled instead by some particular individual or voluntarily established institution. No overall plan of coordination is formulated, and instead a pattern of coordination emerges spontaneously as individuals attempt to satisfy their wants as consumers by engaging with others in voluntary exchanges of the resources under their respective control (including their labor).

Surely, if the problem of coordinating millions or tens of millions of individuals' lives is as difficult as I have suggested, the natural thing is to suppose that a satisfactory solution requires a great deal of careful and well-informed thought. Perhaps plans can never be better than just sitting back and leaving everything to the accidents of billions of decisions made by millions of independent individuals, few of whom know, or care, very much about the implications of their decisions for society in general. Any wise man tries to plan his own affairs, rather than just drifting at the mercy of every momentary gust and current in life. Surely we owe it to ourselves and to one another to arrange for society's affairs to be organized at least as carefully as we organize our own?

Not until 200 years ago was the remarkable idea first propounded that the market system is actually better than the command system at achieving the very goals — the beneficial coordination of individuals' decisions — that motivates the command system's idealistic supporters. The classic statement of the virtues of the market was Adam Smith's *Wealth of Nations*, published in 1776. As Smith put it, in a market system based on private property, each participant "neither intends to promote the public interest, nor knows how much he is promoting it . . . he intends only his own gain, and he is in this . . . led by an invisible hand to promote an end which was no part of his intention. . . . By pursuing his own interest he frequently promotes that of the society more effectually than when he really intends to promote it."

Smith's "invisible hand" is for liberals a key concept in understanding the functioning of society. Any attempt to invoke state power to modify society's workings, liberals argue, is likely to lead to results that are the opposite of those intended. Society is a delicately balanced self-regulating machine, and if we find that things are going amiss in some areas of society, the liberal's reaction is to look for a cause in terms of unnecessary state regulation of some activity or failure to parcel out some collectively held resource into a set of private property rights.

When decisions about how to allocate resources are made politically, public life becomes a sea of individuals and groups all constantly asking, with various degrees of urbanity or shrillness, for more resources. Only a finite quantity of resources is available, so decisions get made almost accidentally, in terms of which pressure group can best publicize its case, who knows how to get access to the relevant decision makers, which minister is felt to deserve a success, and the like — all of which has very little connection with satisfying people's real needs.

Running an economy is a job so massively complex that, as Adam Smith put in *The Wealth of Nations*, "no human wisdom or knowledge could ever be sufficient." We need to leave it to the market because its system of transmitting information and motivation via prices is subtler than any human alternative.

One virtue of the market is that, since individuals as consumers exert control over production decisions, resources are diverted to those users where they can yield most real benefit. Another virtue is that it maximizes the *quantity* of benefit derived from each resource and minimizes waste. By treating each resource as the private property of some individual, it gives that individual a motive to husband the resource so that it yields the most good.

The point can be illustrated by a trivial example. In my university department, two electric typewriters are housed in neighboring rooms. One is in the departmental secretary's office; legally she is not its owner, but in practice it is controlled by her, and no one else touches it without her permission. The machine next door is available for any member of the teaching staff to use. The secretary's typewriter is beautifully looked after; it has given many years of good service, and if

any problem arises its "owner" has it seen to without delay. The "public" machine, by contrast, is mistreated badly. Users rarely replace the dustcover and sometimes even leave the motor running overnight; the typeheads fill with dirt, faults are left to cure themselves, the work done by the machine deteriorates and fairly soon it will be a write-off.

Taking good care of an electric typewriter requires a certain amount of effort — it is quicker not to bother to replace the dustcover after use, for instance. To the secretary, it is worth making this effort because it is repaid in terms of easier and more satisfying work with the machine in the future. But many of the individual users of the "public" machine no doubt calculate, consciously or unconsciously, that it is pointless for them to do their share of looking after the machine, since they cannot force other users to be equally careful; so the machine is neglected.

This example is on a very small scale, but what is true on a small scale is true in the large. Consider, for instance, how stocks of some species of fish have been virtually eliminated by overfishing in the North Sea and elsewhere. Fish in the sea are a public resource, so no one fishing enterprise has a motive to restrain its catches. It cannot prevent others from taking the fish that it does not, so for each enterprise it is rational to take as much as it can while stocks last. If it were technically feasible, a liberal would prefer the world's oceans to be divided up into privately owned sectors separated by underwater fences impermeable to fish; then it would be in the interests of each owner to take each year only as many fish as enabled the stock to keep up its numbers.

Replacement of the market by the command system of social organization is objectionable because it robs consumers of their power to influence producers and because it leads to wasteful, destructive uses of society's resources. Perhaps worst of all, though, it creates a class of people with a direct interest in further increasing state power and in misusing the resources that come under the control of the state: namely, state employees.

What is distinctive about a "welfare" state is that it provides the citizen with goods and services whose production and distribution can without difficulty be controlled by private market interactions. But what about the core of state activities that are necessarily performed by the state because the market is inherently incapable of providing them? The two obvious examples are defense of the realm and a judicial system that enforces private contracts and punishes force and fraud. More generally, there is a range of what economists call "public goods" (some economists prefer the term "collective goods").

A "public good," to an economist, is something that, if provided at all, cannot be provided exclusively to those who choose to pay for it — which makes it difficult or impossible to provide it through the mechanism of the market. The example commonly cited is the lighthouse: there is no way to stop sailors who have not subscribed to a private-enterprise lighthouse service from seeing its beams and acting on their warning, so it would seem to be impossible to run private-enterprise lighthouses profitably. (As it happens, the example is less straightforward than it seems; private enterprise did play an important role in the development of British lighthouses.) Defense might be regarded as a particularly central example of a public good.

Liberals accept that states are needed to produce public goods and also to limit the production of "public bads" such as air pollution. But liberals would add that the categories of public good and bad must be defined narrowly, since the extension of state power needed to produce extra public goods or control extra public bads is itself a major public bad – as Milton Friedman puts it, "Every government measure bears, as it were, a smokestack on its back."

Defense, the judiciary, and the financing of public goods were for Adam Smith the three proper fields of state activity. Friedman, and many other contemporary liberals, would add to Adam Smith's agenda the duty of guarding the interests of individuals who cannot provide for themselves, such as children and lunatics. Most children are provided for by their parents; but if a child has unusually cruel or feckless parents, or is an orphan, he cannot fend for himself, and Friedman would argue that the state should look after him rather than leaving this task to private charity.

Again, however, any liberal would want to draw a tight boundary around the class of people who are regarded as nonparticipants in the market system because of youth or infirmity. One of the liberal's objections to the welfare state is that it effectively broadens this category to include masses of ordinary able-bodied adults in command of their mental facilities.

Since state activities in a liberal society are few, taxation is low, so that questions about the precise system of taxation lose their urgency. But it is worth examining why liberals reject the idea of redistribution from richer to poorer, since, obviously,this concept lies at the heart of welfare-state ideology.

In the first place, even if morality were thought to require either equality of incomes or at least some closer approximation to equality than the market yields, there is no way that state action could achieve that result. If decisions are made politically rather than in the market, individuals do not stop striving to better their lot; they simply redirect their efforts toward the new source of benefits. If increased money incomes are robbed of their value to the individual by steeply progressive taxation, then people will strive to secure other kinds of benefit – money is only a device for getting real goods, after all.

Our state provides extensive subsidies for the arts – picture galleries, opera, and so forth. These are not in the economist's sense "public goods" (there is no *technical* difficulty in charging for admission), and it seems implausible that most of the poor people on whose behalf the welfare state is supposed to spend perceive a strong need for these things; but the upper-middle-class types who know how to influence the state like them, so the state gives them the opportunity of visits to the opera subsidized heavily by ordinary blokes out in the sticks who prefer relaxing in front of video recorders that they have to buy themselves out of after-tax income.

Inequality is inevitable, whether in a market or a command system. The difference is that, in a market system, the individual's urge to a better life is harnessed to the satisfaction of others' wants; in a command system, one person's success is bought at others' expense. To put the point very personally: the welfare state, looked at objectively rather than through rose-tinted ideological spectacles, is largely an enormously costly device for subsidizing people like me, with our "civilized," middle-class tastes. I cannot believe that people like me are a proper object of public charity.

Liberals go further and argue that there is no moral justification for redistribution. In a free market, if one individual's contributions to society are 10 times as lucrative as another's, then the first individual has given 10 times as much value and is entitled to 10 times the return. The state has no resources of its own; it can make the poor less poor only by making the rich less rich. For liberals, then, progressive taxation is not merely inexpedient (because, for instance, it reduces the incentive for possessors of highly valuable skills to work long hours) but actually immoral: it is a device by which society exploits its more prosperous members by taking their productive contributions and then depriving them of their fair return.

Particularly objectionable from a liberal point of view are taxes on capital, such as capital-gains tax or death duties, since these are blatantly unrelated to any notion of payment in exchange for services rendered. Collectivists often justify capital taxes by suggesting that even a self-made man cannot be seen as having created his wealth independently: we are all dependent in all aspects of our lives on the society we inhabit, so our society has every right to decide how to dispose ultimately of the accumulation of wealth that rich men are allowed to use temporarily.

What is likely is that the patterns of activity that emerged in a liberal society would differ quite a lot from the patterns of activity promoted by a command system. Command systems always tend to favor what is orthodox, what is seen as morally uplifting or in accordance with traditional values, rather than what is experimental or offbeat. Partly, no doubt, this is because people who attain positions of responsibility in a political structure tend to be . . . men with traditional tastes, and partly it is because traditional values are perceived as supporting state power while "underground" movements may threaten it.

The consequence is that, although the world of business is often seen as hostile to iconoclastic, experimental styles of living, in reality just the reverse is the case. Probably many men in the record industry find the various waves of modern music as unpleasant as I do, bit if it is what the kids want, then to a businessman his personal tastes are irrelevant – he produces the records, because there is a market for them. In a thoroughgoing command economy such as those of Eastern Europe, on the other hand, pop music is scarcely obtainable. The state asserts by implication that its tastes are the real, "proper" tastes, and conflicting tastes (however real for those who hold them) are somehow improper and not to be taken into account.

It is ironic that so many partisans of this or that brand of "alternative society" believe that in some vague way socialism is on their side. The reality is that thoroughgoing socialism would be likely to kill stone dead almost all of their various attempts to create the good life. However, as Samuel Brittan, assistant editor of the *Financial Times* and a leading British advocate of classical liberalism, pointed out in his 1973 book, *Capitalism and the Permissive Society*:

> The values of competitive capitalism have a great deal in common with . . . contemporary radical attitudes. Above all they share a similar stress on allowing people to do . . . what they feel inclined to do rather than conform to the wishes of authority, custom, or convention. Under a competitive system, the businessman will

PROBLEMS AND PROJECTS

1. Use Exhibit 1 when answering the following.

Exhibit 1 The Production Possibilities of Rhineland and Nepal

	Rhineland			Nepal	
	Food	Clothing		Food	Clothing
A	0	900	A	0	500
B	100	750	B	100	450
C	200	600	C	200	400
D	300	400	D	300	300
E	400	200	E	400	150
F	500	0	F	500	0

a. What is the per unit opportunity cost of expanding food production from 200 to 300 in Rhineland? In Nepal?

b. In the absence of trade, the people of Rhineland will choose to produce at point D. The people of Nepal will choose point B. Given their preferences for food and clothing, could the nations gain from trade? How can you tell? How would trade flow between the two countries?

c. Suppose that both countries produced at point C and that Rhineland traded 100 units of its domestically produced clothing for 100 units of food produced in Nepal. Compared to the no-trade point B alternative, how would this transaction affect the goods available to the people of Nepal? What would happen to the joint output of the two countries?

d. Suppose that Rhineland produced at point B and Nepal at point D. If Rhineland traded 225 units of clothing for 200 units of Nepal's food, how much would each country gain, relative to the no-trade chosen combination of part b? What would happen to their joint output, relative to their mutual production at point C?

e. If Rhineland expanded its clothing production still farther, to 900, what would be its per unit opportunity cost of producing clothing in this range? What would be Nepal's per unit opportunity cost of producing clothing in this range? What would be Nepal's per unit opportunity cost of the first 300 units of clothing domestically? Once Rhineland is producing at point B and Nepal at point D, can joint output be expanded by additional specialization? Are *additional* mutual gains from the trade possible? Explain.

2. The country of Arcadia produces and consumes unique computers. Exhibit 2 shows Arcadia's demand and supply curves for their computers along with the demand for Arcadian computers from the rest of the world (ROW).

Exhibit 2

Price (dollars/ unit)	Arcadia's quantity supplied	Arcadia's quantity demanded	ROW's quantity demanded	Total quantity demanded
$2400	1200	750	280	1030
2200	1100	800	300	_____
2000	1000	850	320	_____
1800	900	900	340	_____
1600	800	950	360	_____
1400	700	1000	380	_____
1200	600	1050	400	_____
1000	500	1100	420	_____

a. Fill in the missing information in the table.
b. If Arcadia has no trade with the rest of the world, what will be the equilibrium price of computers in Arcadia? What will be the equilibrium quantity demanded and supplied?
c. What will be the equilibrium price of computers if Arcadia trades with the ROW? Compare this price to the equilibrium price of part b. Why is it higher?
d. With trade, what is Arcadia's equilibrium quantity of computers supplied? Compare this with the quantity without trade. What must have happened to Arcadia's production of other goods and services as a result of international trade?
e. With trade, what is Arcadia's quantity of computers demanded? Compare the quantity of computers demanded in Arcadia without trade. In what way can this difference be of benefit generally to Arcadia consumers?
f. What quantity of computers is exported by Arcadia? Do Arcadia's computer producers clearly benefit by unrestricted international trade in computers?
g. As a result of Arcadia's exports, what do you suppose has happened to the price of computers in the ROW? How would you feel about this if you were an ROW computer "producer," either worker or entrepreneur? And if you were an ROW computer buyer, how would you react?

3. Suppose that the United States can purchase motorcycles from abroad for $3,000 each, and that this price does not vary with the quantity the U.S. purchases. Alternatively, the U.S. can produce its own motorcycles according to the supply schedule given in Exhibit 3, which also shows the U.S.'s demand for motorcycles.

Exhibit 3

Price (dollars/unit)	Domestic quantity supplied	Domestic quantity demanded
		(thousands/year)
$4500	1000	700
4000	900	900
3500	800	1100
3000	700	1300
2500	600	1500
2000	500	1700

a. In the absence of international trade what would be the price of motorcycles in the U.S.? What quantities would be demanded and supplied?

b. Suppose that motorcycles can be imported into the U.S. without restriction. What will be the price of motorcycles in the U.S.? What will be the quantities demanded and produced domestically? What will be the quantity of imports? By how much will domestic production decline relative to the no-trade amount?

c. Suppose that workers and management lobby Congress for a tariff on imports on the grounds that they need temporary protection from imports in order to maintain domestic markets while they "retool" to incorporate the latest and most efficient techniques of motorcycle production (a version of the "infant" industry argument). If government grants domestic producers a tariff on imports of $500 per cycle, what will be the domestic price of motorcycles? By how much will domestic production increase? (This is called the "protective effect" of a tariff.) By how much will U.S. purchases of motorcycles fall? By how much will imports fall?

d. Suppose that *instead* of the tariff of part c, government imposed a quota on imports of 300 motorcycles per year. In this case, what would happen to the price of motorcycles as compared to the unrestricted ("free") trade price? (*Hint*: locate a price at which the domestic quantity supplied plus 300 equals the domestic quantity demanded at the price.) What will be the protective effect (increase in domestic quantity produced) of the quota?

e. Judging from your answers to c and d above, what is the basic difference between a tariff and a quota?

4. Consider the following hypothetical information about the United States and South Korea:

	Output per worker per day	
	United States	*South Korea*
Tons of steel	8	4
Bushels of wheat	80	8

a. Which country has the
absolute advantage in steel production? _____
absolute advantage in wheat production? _____
comparative advantage in steel production? _____
comparative advantage in wheat production? _____

b. If these countries trade steel and wheat with each other, which country will export steel and import wheat?

c. Suppose that the United States and South Korea agree to a daily trade of 10 tons of steel for 50 bushels of wheat. One worker in the United States then switches from steel production to wheat production. Complete the following table to show that both countries end up with more steel and more wheat then they had initially:

United States	*Tons of steel*	*Bushels of wheat*
Change in production:	−8	+80
Trade:	_____	_____
Change in consumption:	_____	_____

South Korea	*Tons of steel*	*Bushels of wheat*
Change in production:	_____	_____
Trade:	_____	_____
Change in consumption:	_____	_____

5. The diagram in Exhibit 4 reflects the approximate impact on the domestic heavyweight motorcycle market of the motorcycle tariffs recently imposed by the United States (*Pf* denotes the free trade price, and *Pt* denotes the price with the tariff):

Exhibit 4

a. Use the figures from the diagram to compute the following values:
   Consumers' cost of the tariff: _____
   Domestic producers' gain from the tariff: _____
   Tariff revenue: _____
   Net social cost of the tariff: _____
b. It has been estimated that the tariff on heavyweight motorcycles created 700 jobs in the domestic motorcycle industry. How much did each of these jobs "cost" U.S. consumers?
c. What size quota on heavyweight motorcycles would have achieved the same impact as the indicated tariff?

LEARNING THE MECHANICS – MULTIPLE CHOICE

1. Which of the following best describes the implications of the law of comparative advantage? Each trading nation can gain by
   a. selling services for which it is a high opportunity-cost producer and buying goods that it produces at a low cost.
   b. selling those services that it enjoys, while buying goods for which it is a low opportunity-cost producer.
   c. selling services for which it is a low opportunity-cost producer and buying those things for which it is a high opportunity-cost producer.
   d. selling those services that it dislikes, while buying those that it finds most enjoyable to produce.

2. A trade policy that limits the entry of foreign goods to the U.S. market will
   a. benefit consumers at the expense of producers.
   b. increase the nation's real income by protecting domestic jobs from foreign competition.
   c. reduce the demand for U.S. export goods, since foreigners will be less able to purchase our goods if they cannot sell to us.
   d. enhance economic efficiency by permitting domestic resources to be fully utilized.

3. The national defense argument for high tariffs on a commodity
    a. is stronger if large supplies of the commodity can be stored cheaply.
    b. is stronger if storage of the commodity is costly.
    c. is based on the economic principle of comparative advantage.
    d. is based on the economic principle of absolute advantage.

4. A higher tariff on foreign-produced steel would be most likely to benefit
    a. domestic consumers of products that contain steel.
    b. producers in export industries.
    c. producers and workers in the steel industry.
    d. producers and workers in all industries except steel.

5. A nation will benefit from international trade when it
    a. imports more than it exports.
    b. exports more than it imports.
    c. imports goods for which it is a high opportunity-cost producer, while exporting goods for which it is a low opportunity-cost producer.
    d. exports goods for which it is a high opportunity-cost producer, while importing those goods for which it is a low opportunity-cost producer.

Use the following information to answer the next *three* questions. Exhibit 5 outlines the production possibilities of Italia and Slavia for food and clothing.

Exhibit 5

Italia		Slavia	
Food	*Clothing*	*Food*	*Clothing*
0	8	0	20
4	6	2	15
8	4	4	10
12	2	6	5
16	0	8	0

6. What is the opportunity cost of producing one unit of food in Italia?
    a. One-quarter of a unit of clothing
    b. One-half of a unit of clothing
    c. Two units of clothing
    d. Five units of clothing

7. Which of the following is true?
    a. Slavia has a comparative advantage in the production of both goods.
    b. Italia has a comparative advantage in the production of food.
    c. Slavia is the low opportunity-cost producer of food.
    d. None of the above.

8. The law of comparative advantage suggests that
    a. neither country would gain from trade even if the transportation costs for the products were zero.
    b. Slavia would not gain from trade because it has an absolute advantage in the production of both goods.
    c. both countries could gain if Italia traded food for Slavia clothing.
    d. both countries could gain if Slavia traded food for Italia clothing.

9. The law of comparative advantage
   a. is applicable to both domestic and international production and trade.
   b. applies only in domestic situations, such as occur when doctors who are good typists hire secretaries to do medical typing.
   c. applies only when one nation is absolutely more efficient in the production of the first good and another nation is absolutely more efficient at the production of the second.
   d. is only theoretical; it does not work in the real world.

10. The infant-industry argument about tariffs states that
    a. it is unfair to place tariffs on items intended for use by infants.
    b. tariffs should be placed on items produced by new domestic industries only in the short run.
    c. tariffs should be placed on items intended by new domestic industries in the short or long run.
    d. tariffs should be placed on items produced by new domestic industries in the short or long run.

11. Which of the following is a true statement about trade liberalization?
    a. Trade liberalization reduces efficiency since it reduces competition in industries affected by the trade.
    b. Trade liberalization tends to increase the rate of inflation since it pushes the prices of exports upward.
    c. Trade liberalization improves consumer welfare by increasing product variety.
    d. All of the above are results of trade liberalization.

12. Exhibit 6 compares the production possibilities of the country of Brenton for wine and bread before specialization and trade (point O) with a number of post-trade consumption possibilities. International trade (based on comparative advantage) which resulted in the export of wine and the import of bread will move Brenton from point O to point

Exhibit 6

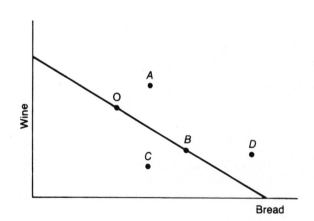

    a. A.
    b. B.
    c. C.
    d. D.

THE ECONOMIC WAY OF THINKING – MULTIPLE CHOICE

1. Suppose that the United States eliminated its tariff on automobiles, granting foreign-produced automobiles, granting foreign-produced automobiles free entry into the U.S. market. Which of the following would be most likely to occur?
   a. The price of automobiles to U.S. consumers would decline, and the demand for U.S. export products would increase.
   b. The price of automobiles to U.S. consumers would increase, and the demand for U.S. export products would decline.
   c. The price of automobiles to U.S. consumers would decline, and the demand for U.S. export products would decline.
   d. The price of automobiles to U.S. consumers would increase, and the demand for U.S. export products would decline.

2. Economic incentives suggest that the union leaders of workers in a protected "infant industry" will support tariff protection for the industry
   a. if, and only if, they believe that the industry is still immature.
   b. unless they believe that the tariff is harming the consumers of the industry's product.
   c. if management is opposed to the protection.
   d. regardless of how mature the industry may be at the time.

3. If a country had a comparative disadvantage in the production of watches, a tariff on imported watches set just high enough to offset this disadvantage in the retail market
   a. would help the entire economy by increasing employment.
   b. would help watch consumers as a group, by giving them a real choice between foreign and domestic brands.
   c. would help workers in the watch industry by increasing the demand for their services.
   d. would help watch producers at the expense of the workers in the domestic watch industry.

The following quotation from a U.S. textile industry executive applies to the next *two* questions.

> What bothers our manufacturers is that it is not really a matter of Japanese competitiveness, but a maze of impenetrable supports and subsidies. Our people feel that whatever they do, the Japanese will just lower their prices.

Assume that the Japanese government does, in fact, continually subsidize their textile industry so that they can undersell other textile exporters.

4. A textile-importing nation would best take advantage of the Japanese subsidization policy by
   a. setting a tariff high enough to keep cheap foreign competitors out of its own potential textile industry.
   b. setting a declining quota on the import of Japanese textiles such that its own textile industry could continue growing at the same rate as the rest of the economy.
   c. gladly accepting the subsidy of the Japanese government to textile users, making whatever adjustment assistance seems appropriate to the temporarily displaced resources in the domestic textile industry.
   d. setting a tariff just to equalize Japanese and domestic textile prices to the consumer.

5. We would expect that domestic textile industry executives and textile union leaders would
   a. gladly accept the reduced burden of having to produce ever-increasing amounts of textile goods domestically.
   b. fight for tariffs and quotas on imported Japanese textiles "to protect the American economy."
   c. argue that comparative advantage should prevail, so that domestic producers would be forced to meet the price of textiles that prevails in the world market if they were to survive.
   d. disagree among themselves, with the industry executives demanding protection, whereas union leaders would favor a tariff reduction that would benefit the worker-consumers.

6. Relative to a no-trade situation, what effect will importing a good from foreign nations have on the domestic market for the good?
   a. Equilibrium price will rise and total domestic output will fall.
   b. Equilibrium price will rise and total domestic output will rise.
   c. Equilibrium price will fall and total domestic output will fall.
   d. Equilibrium price will fall and total domestic output will rise.

7. Economic theory suggests that the popularity of tariffs among politicians is
   a. surprising, since tariffs generally lower a nation's level of real income.
   b. not surprising, since tariff protection for an industry is generally a special interest issue.
   c. surprising, since numerous consumers are generally harmed in order to help a few industrial and labor interests.
   d. not surprising, since tariffs generally help domestic investors, workers, and consumers at the expense of foreigners who cannot vote.

8. Economics suggests that some of the political popularity of tariffs stems from the fact that "jobs lost" due to an expansion of imports are easily identified
   a. whereas "jobs created" by an increase in foreign spending on domestic exports can seldom be traced back to the reduction in tariffs.
   b. whereas the gains associated with holding larger amounts of foreign currencies are elusive, even though they are real gains.
   c. and they cannot be replaced by an expansion in other industries.
   d. and they cannot be replaced without a trade policy to restrict competition with cheap foreign labor.

9. If all tariffs (and quotas) between countries on the North American continent were eliminated
   a. small Central American countries would be hurt, since they would be unable to compete with larger nations.
   b. the United States would gain at the expense of the less-developed North American countries.
   d. the combined wealth of the countries would increase, since the elimination of trade restrictions would permit greater gains from specialization.
   d. wage rates in the United States would decline to the average for the North American continent.

10. Relative to a no-trade situation, what effect will exporting a good to foreign nations have on the domestic market for the product?
    a. Equilibrium price will rise and total domestic output will fall.
    b. Equilibrium price will rise and total domestic output will rise.
    c. Equilibrium price will fall and total domestic output will fall.
    d. Equilibrium price will fall and total domestic output will rise.

Questions 11-14 refer to Exhibit 7, which contains hypothetical data on the market for shoes (per month) in the United States and in the entire world (including the U.S.).

Exhibit 7

Price per pair	World Market (including the U.S.)		Domestic Market (U.S. only)	
	Q supplied	Q demanded	Q supplied	Q demanded
$10	5900	6100	250	400
$20	6000	6000	275	375
$30	6100	5900	300	350
$40	6200	5800	325	325
$50	6300	5700	350	300
$60	6400	5600	375	275
$70	6500	5500	400	250

11. Under a regime of free international trade, the U.S. would
    a. import 50 pairs of shoes per month.
    b. import 100 pairs of shoes per month.
    c. export 100 pairs of shoes per month.
    d. purchase a total of 325 pairs of shoes per month.

12. Suppose that the domestic shoe industry is in long-run equilibrium under international free trade but that then the U.S. imposes a $10/pair tariff on shoes. What would be the most likely result?
    a. The price of shoes in the U.S. would increase by $10 per pair.
    b. The price of shoes in the U.S. would increase, but by less than $10 per pair.
    c. The U.S. supply curve of shoes would shift to the right (increase) in the short run.
    d. The U.S. demand curve for shoes would shift to the left.

13. Given the tariff described in question #12 above,
    a. the tariff revenues of $500 outweigh U.S. social deadweight loss, so overall producer plus consumer surplus increases.
    b. tariff revenues of something less than $500 outweigh U.S. social deadweight loss, so overall producer plus consumer surplus increases.
    c. tariff revenues do not compensate for U.S. social deadweight loss, so overall producer plus consumer surplus decreases.
    d. there is a redistribution of surplus between producers and consumers, but the overall magnitude of the producer plus consumer surplus is constant.

14. The same U.S. price and quantity of shoes purchased under the tariff described in question #12 above could have resulted from the imposition of a quota of
    a. 50 pairs of shoes per month.
    b. between 50 and 100 pairs of shoes per month.
    c. 100 pairs of shoes per month.
    d. more than 100 pairs of shoes per month.

THE ECONOMIC WAY OF THINKING – DISCUSSION QUESTIONS

1. "We are not opposed to competition when it does not destroy jobs. But last year, while many American auto workers were idle, we exported a million jobs to foreigners by importing automobiles that could have been produced by domestic workers. An increase in the tariff on automobiles would strengthen our economy, provide jobs, and improve our standard of living." [Auto Workers' Union official]
    a. Do you agree that higher automobile tariffs would "provide jobs"? Why or why not?
    b. Do you agree that higher automobile tariffs would "improve out standard of living"? Why or why not?
    c. Prior to the 1970s, the United Auto Workers was an advocate of free trade. What do you think accounts for the reversal in their position?

2. Why would you expect the management of U.S. Steel and the president of the United Steel Workers' Union to fight strongly together for tariffs on imported steel "for the good of the nation," when they disagree on so many other matters of public concern? Would you expect both to oppose lower tariffs on copper, aluminum, or other steel substitutes? Why or why not?

3. Nations have become increasingly interdependent since the Second World War.
    a. What are the advantages of self-sufficiency? The disadvantages?
    b. From a political perspective, do you think nations should endeavor to become more or less interdependent?
    c. Why do you think international trade as a percentage of GNP is 54 percent for the Netherlands but only 9 percent for the United States?

4. a. Montana encourages a local liquor-bottling industry by taxing bulk imports into the state at lower rates than bottled liquors. Does this make economic sense? Why or why not?
    b. Should Connecticut ban imports of bananas to promote a local banana industry? Explain.
    c. Should state governments adopt trade restrictions to target specific industries for promotion? If not, why not? If so, why, and under what circumstances?

5. In the United States, the price of labor is relatively high and the price of capital is relatively low. In developing countries, the reverse is true.
    a. Based on these resource market conditions, what types of products would you expect the United States to import from developing countries? To export to them?
    b. Most U.S. trade is with other industrial high-wage nations. In light of the law of comparative advantage, is this surprising? If not, why not? If so, why, and how can you account for this aspect of U.S. trade?

6. Suppose that Brazil, the world's leading coffee producer, decides to levy an export tax on coffee.
    a. Use a demand and supply curve for Brazilian coffee to determine whether each of the following will rise, fall, or change in an uncertain direction: (i) the world price of coffee; (ii) world expenditures on Brazilian coffee; and (iii) the receipts of Brazilian coffee growers.
    b. Decide whether you think each of the following would favor or oppose the export tax: (i) Brazilian coffee growers; (ii) U.S. coffee drinkers; (iii) U.S. tea drinkers; and (iv) Colombian coffee growers.

CURRENT DEBATES IN ECONOMICS

Debate Number Six: Should We Adopt Free International Trade?

Yes, We Should Adopt Free International Trade:

The Economic Case for Free Trade
By Milton and Rose Friedman

[Reprinted with permission from Chapter 2 of *Free to Choose*
(New York: Harcourt Brace Jovanovich, 1980.) Abridged.]

Today, as always, there is much support for tariffs — euphemistically labeled "protection," a good label for a bad cause. Producers of steel and steelworkers' unions press for restrictions on steel imports from Japan. Producers of TV sets and their workers lobby for "voluntary agreements" to limit imports of TV sets or components from Japan, Taiwan, or Hong Kong. Producers of textiles, shoes, cattle, sugar — they and myriad others complain about "unfair" competition from abroad and demand that government do something to "protect" them. Of course, no group makes its claim on the basis of naked self-interest. Every group speaks of the "general interest," of the need to preserve jobs or to promote national security.

One voice that is hardly ever raised is the consumer's. The individual consumer's voice is drowned out in the cacophony of the "interested sophistry of merchants and manufacturers" and their employees. The result is a serious distortion of the issue. For example, the supporters of tariffs treat it as self-evident that the creation of jobs is a desirable end, in and of itself, regardless of what the persons employed do. That is clearly wrong. If all we want are jobs, we can create any number — for example, have people dig holes and then fill them up again, or perform other useless tasks. Work is sometimes its own reward. Mostly, however, it is the price we pay to get the things we want. Our real objective is not just jobs but productive jobs — jobs that will mean more goods and services to consume.

Another fallacy seldom contradicted is that exports are good, imports bad. The truth is very different. We cannot eat, wear, or enjoy the goods we send abroad. We eat bananas from Central America, wear Italian shoes, drive German automobiles, and enjoy programs we see on our Japanese TV sets. Our gain from foreign trade is what we import. Exports are the price we pay to get imports. As Adam Smith saw so clearly, the citizens of a nation benefit from getting as large a volume of imports as possible in return for its exports, or equivalently, form exporting as little as possible to pay for its imports.

The misleading terminology we use reflects these erroneous ideas. "Protection" really means exploiting the consumer. A "favorable balance of trade" really means exporting more than we import, sending abroad goods of greater total value than the goods we get from abroad. In your private household, you would surely prefer to pay less for more rather than the other way around, yet that would be termed an "unfavorable balance of payments" in foreign trade.

The argument in favor of tariffs that has the greatest emotional appeal to the public at large is the alleged need to protect the high standard of living of American workers from the "unfair" competition of workers in Japan or Korea or Hong Kong who are willing to work for a much lower wage. What is wrong with this argument? Don't we want to protect the high standard of living of our people?

The fallacy in this argument is the loose use of the terms "high" wage and "low" wage. What do high and low wages mean? American workers are paid in dollars; Japanese workers are paid in yen. How do we compare wages in dollars with wages in yen? How many yen equal a dollar? What determines that exchange rate?

It is simply not true that high-wage American workers are, as a group, threatened by "unfair" competition from low-wage foreign workers. Of course, particular workers may be harmed if a new or improved product is developed abroad, or if foreign producers become able to produce such products more cheaply. But that is no different from the effect on a particular group of workers of other American firms' developing new or improved products or discovering how to produce at lower costs. That is simply market competition in practice, the major source of the high standard of life of the American worker. If we want to benefit from a vital, dynamic, innovative economic system, we must accept the need for mobility and adjustment. It may be desirable to ease these adjustments, and we have adopted many arrangements, such as unemployment insurance, to do so, but we should try to achieve that objective without destroying the flexibility of the system — that would be to kill the goose that has been laying the golden eggs. In any even, whatever we do should be evenhanded with respect to foreign and domestic trade.

What determines the items it pays us to import and to export? An American worker is currently more productive than a Japanese worker. It is hard to determine just how much more productive — estimates differ. But suppose he is one and a half times as productive. Then, on average, the American's wages would buy about one and a half times as much as a Japanese worker's wages. It is wasteful to use American workers to do anything at which they are less than one and a half times as efficient as their Japanese counterparts. In the economic jargon coined more than 150 years ago, that is the *principle of comparative advantage*. Even if we were more efficient than the Japanese at producing everything, it would not pay us to produce everything. We should concentrate on doing those things we do best, those things where our superiority is the greatest.

Another source of "unfair competition" is said to be subsidies by foreign governments to their producers that enable them to sell in the United States below cost.

Suppose a foreign government gives such subsidies, as no doubt some do. Who is hurt and who benefits? To pay for the subsidies the foreign government must tax its citizens. They are the ones who pay for the subsidies. U.S. consumers benefit. They get cheap TV sets or automobiles or whatever it is that is subsidized. Should we complain about such a program of reverse foreign aid? Was it noble of the United States to send goods and services as gifts to other countries in the form of Marshall Plan aid or, later, foreign aid, but ignoble for foreign countries to send us gifts in the indirect form of goods and services sold to us below cost? The citizens of the foreign government might well complain. They must suffer a lower standard of living for the benefit of American consumers and of some of their fellow citizens who own or work in the industries that are subsidized. No doubt, if such subsidies are introduced suddenly or erratically, that will adversely affect owners and workers in U.S. industries producing the same products. However, that is one of the ordinary risks of doing business. Enterprises never complain about unusual or accidental events that confer windfall gains. The free enterprise system is a *profit* and *loss* system. As already noted, any measures to ease the adjustment to sudden changes should be applied evenhandedly to domestic and foreign trade.

We are a great nation, the leader of the free world. It ill behooves us to require Hong Kong and Taiwan to impose export quotas on textiles to "protect" our textile industry at the expense of U.S consumers and of Chinese workers in Hong Kong and Taiwan. We speak glowingly of the virtues of free trade, while we use our political and economic power to induce Japan to restrict exports of steel and TV sets. We should move unilaterally to free trade, not instantaneously, but over a period of, say, five years, at a pace announced in advance.

Few measures that we could take would do more to promote the cause of freedom at home and abroad than complete free trade. Instead of making grants to foreign governments in the name of economic aid – thereby promoting socialism – while at the same time imposing restrictions on the products they produce – thereby hindering free enterprise – we could assume a consistent and principled stance. We could say to the rest of the world: we believe in freedom and intend to practice it. We cannot force you to be free. But we can offer full cooperation on equal terms to all. Our market is open to you without tariffs or other restrictions. Sell here what you can and wish to. Buy whatever you can and wish to. In that way cooperation among individuals can be worldwide and free.

No, We Should Not Adopt Free International Trade:

"Free Trade" Is Impoverishing the West
By John M. Culbertson

[Reprinted from *The New York Times*, July 28, 1985.
©1985 by The New York Times Company. Reprinted by permission.]

For most of this century, United States trade policy has been based on the belief that unregulated international trade, or "free trade," fits a theoretical pattern that automatically makes it beneficial to the nations involved. Thus, "barriers to trade" and "protectionism" are harmful. The difficulty with this elegantly simple theory is that it bears little relation to reality.

The evidence shows that not all trade is the same – different patterns of foreign trade exist, and they have different effects. Some are very damaging. The pattern of foreign trade that has caused the extraordinary shift of industries from the United States in recent years is of the destructive kind.

The stereotype within which economists have viewed international trade was developed by Adam Smith, in the 18th century. It depicts each nation as specializing in products to which it is peculiarly suited, in which it has low relative costs or a *comparative advantage*. Thus, a nation rich in iron ore might trade with a nation that produces steel efficiently. Both would gain by the trade.

In this "comparative-advantage rule," the gain in efficiency from international specialization benefits both nations. Further, the trade is assumed to be in balance, so there is no general shift of industries from one nation to another – with the chain of serious consequences it can bring.

The error in the theory gained new importance in the modern ear, when changes in technology, transportation and communications began to break down the conventional economic barriers between countries. Today, most United States trade is not based on comparative advantage and is not efficient. There is no gain in efficiency from shifting factories that are producing goods for the domestic market from the United States to Asia or Latin America. There is little comparative advantage in today's manufacturing industries, since they produce the same goods the same ways in all parts of the world. Why, then, is industry after industry moving out of the United States?

These industry shifts are based on the transfer of industries and jobs to countries with low standards of living, and low wage rates. American factories are closed because foreign-made goods are cheaper. These goods are cheaper because the workers who make them earn wages one-half, one-fifth and even one-tenth as high as those of American workers. This trade is not comparative-advantage trade, but "wage-cutting trade."

Wage-cutting trade does not offer the benefits arising from comparative-advantage trade. It does not increase economic efficiency; often it reduces efficiency by adding transportation costs. Thus, it cannot possibly make both nations, and the world, better off. If wage-cutting trade benefits one nation, it does so by damaging the other one. In an immediate sense, such trade commonly benefits the low-wage nation that is gaining industries and jobs and damages the high-wage nation that is losing them. In the long run, it may be damaging all around, dragging all nations down to a low standard of living. There are signs that even Japan is becoming concerned with this trend.

The debilitating, long-run effects of wage-cutting trade derive from its out-of-balance character. The high-wage nation cannot go on forever losing industries and jobs, importing more than it exports and running up its foreign debt. It is forced by rising unemployment and burgeoning foreign debt to "become competitive," which it must do by accepting declining wage rates – as the United States has begun to do.

How much does the high-income nation's standard of living have to decline to make it "competitive" under "free trade?" That depends entirely on the circumstances of the case. With cheap transportation, instant communications, multinational corporations to shift technology and management around the world, low-wage and unemployed people now numbering in the billions and population rising very rapidly in some already populous nations, the economic decline suffered by the United States and Europe under "free trade" could be a shattering one.

More broadly, "free trade" in an increasingly overpopulated world would cause wage-cutting trade to pull all nations down to a lowest-common-denominator level. It would put all nations into a shared "population trap" in which no accomplishments would permit a nation to improve its lot. Thus, a nation that perfected a particular industrial process would not be enriched. It would simply lose its industry to a lower-wage nation. In this respect, "free trade" has the same effects as "free migration."

The implications for the United States of comparative-advantage trade and of wage-cutting trade are as different as day and night. When the facts are considered, it is impossible to deny that recent economic developments in the United States have been dominated by wage-cutting trade. To argue for a policy of "free trade" – and to terminate the import quota on Japanese automobiles, and seek further reductions in tariffs and quotas – on the basis of comparative advantage is not just erroneous but dangerously misleading.

Past economic progress has occurred through an evolutionary process in which one nation finds a way to put together a more effective economy. Other nations advance by copying the success. This pattern requires that nations have the economic independence to experiment, to create constructive patterns – rather than being helpless within a worldwide commune forced by "free trade."

A reasonable trade policy in today's world, then, must encourage mutually beneficial, comparative-advantage trade by curbing destructive wage-cutting trade and other destructive patterns of foreign trade. The starting point for a realistic interpretation of trade is the recognition that different patterns have different effects, and some are destructive.

To curb wage-cutting trade requires balancing arrangements. Balance in trade prevents excessive imports from low-wage nations from undercutting the standard of living of high-wage nations. Balanced trade thus provides the framework within which mutually beneficial trade between nations can develop. Actions to limit a nation's imports, and mutual agreements between nations to prevent damaging trade developments, have been common. We need to use such policies more coherently and cooperatively, with a new understanding of the patterns of trade that are to be encouraged or curbed.

The recent trade policy of the United States has encouraged the wage-cutting foreign trade that has been draining away the nation's industries and jobs and created an enormous trade deficit. Given this staring point, the economic state of the nation can be radically improved simply by adopting realistic policies that limit imports so as to bring the nation's foreign trade into balance.

Holding a Debate

Many students will enjoy participating in a debate on this topic either in class or in an informal study group. After completing both readings and possibly doing some additional research (for example, see pages 790-799 of the text), get three to four volunteers for each side of the debate, choose a moderator if your instructor is not available, and devote about a half an hour to opening statements, rebuttals, and summaries.

Discussion

1. If you read both articles, what did you conclude? When a Senator speaks out in favor of protectionism against imports, how do you react? Is this debate a question of economic theory against political reality, or are there political and economic arguments on both sides? Explain.

2. As you read the Friedman article, you were probably impressed with the superb logic and internal consistency with which the Friedmans write. If you were going to attempt to refute their arguments, where would you start? Are there any major assumptions you could question? Are there any secondary effects that they neglect to analyze? Explain.

3. If you read the Culbertson article, how did you react to his statement that "'free trade' has the same effects as 'free migration'"? Under what circumstances would Culbertson be right? Can you think of a situation in which free trade would be substantially different in impact from free migration? Explain your answer.

32
International Finance and the Foreign Exchange Market

TRUE OR FALSE

T F

☐ ☐ 1. Foreign exchange markets enable an individual to exchange the currency of one nation for units of currency of another nation.

☐ ☐ 2. A nation's exports generate a demand for the currency of the exporting nation on the foreign exchange market.

☐ ☐ 3. Under a system of fixed exchange rates, a balance-of-trade equilibrium is automatic.

☐ ☐ 4. Under a system of flexible exchange rates, the government must use monetary policy to ensure balance-of-payments equilibrium.

☐ ☐ 5. The economic analysis of foreign trade is unique in that supply-and-demand relationships do not usually determine equilibrium.

☐ ☐ 6. One problem with a system of flexible exchange rates is that black markets in foreign currencies are more likely to develop than with controlled rates of exchange.

☐ ☐ 7. A country's balance of trade has no bearing on its balance of payments on current account.

☐ ☐ 8. The United States would invariably import more than it exports if foreigners were willing to accumulate ever larger amounts of dollars.

☐ ☐ 9. If imports consistently exceeded exports, U.S. consumers would be hurt as a result of an unfavorable balance of trade implied by such a situation.

☐ ☐ 10. If Israel sold U.S. dollars to France, the U.S. balance of payments would be unaffected.

☐ ☐ 11. A rapid U.S. monetary expansion would tend to make the price of German marks rise, in dollar terms, other things constant.

☐ ☐ 12. Domestic macropolicy-makers can effectively disregard the foreign exchange markets when making a choice between alternative policies.

PROBLEMS AND PROJECTS

1. Match the letters on the right with the numbers on the left.

_____ (1) balance-of-payments deficit-fixed exchange rates

_____ (2) will cause the domestic currency to appreciate

_____ (3) will cause the domestic currency to depreciate

_____ (4) flexible exchange rates

_____ (5) fixed exchange rates

_____ (6) gold standard

a. an increase in the nation's exports

b. will cause a depreciation of the nation's currency when it is experiencing a balance-of-payments deficit

c. international monetary system in effect before World War I

d. excess supply of the nation's currency on the exchange market

e. higher interest rates abroad

f. reduce the flexibility of macropolicy

2. Each of the diagrams below represents the U.S. demand for and supply of foreign exchange (English pounds). For each of the events described below, diagram how the demand and/or supply of pounds changes (use a +, −, or 0 to show no change); and then fill in the blanks to the right of the diagram, indicating in the last blank whether the dollar has appreciated, depreciated, or undergone an indeterminate change as a result of the event(s). (The first question has been answered as an example). (*Hint*: P = dollars per pound.)

Events	Diagrams	D	S	Change

a. As a result of recovering from a depression, U.S. incomes rise significantly.

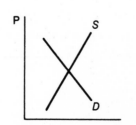

+   0   depreciated

b. The United Kingdom experiences a serious recession causing a decline in income.

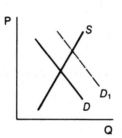

___ ___ _____

c. Restrictive monetary policy in the U.S. causes U.S. interest rates to rise relative to United Kingdom rates.

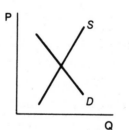

___ ___ _____

Events	Diagrams	D	S	Change

d. The Chairman of the Fed is quoted as saying, "If the high value of the dollar is not soon corrected by market forces, the Fed will take corrective action."

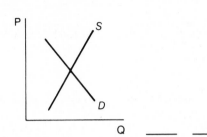

_____ _____ _____

e. While the U.S. experiences stable prices, prices in the United Kingdom rise by 15 percent.

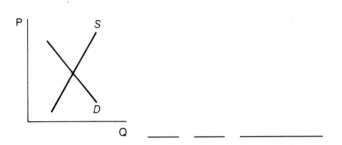

_____ _____ _____

f. In an effort to stimulate the economy, the U.S. embarks on an expansionary fiscal policy.

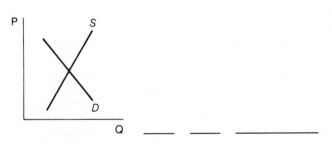

_____ _____ _____

g. Both the U.S. and the U.K. experience inflation rates of 20 percent.

_____ _____ _____

3.   Exhibit 1 presents balance-of-payments data for the United States for 1980.

Exhibit 1

Debit		Credit	
	(billions of dollars)		
Current account			
Merchandise imports	249.3	Merchandise exports	224.0
Service imports	84.6	Service exports	120.7
Net unilateral transfers	7.1		
Capital account			
U.S. investment abroad	18.5	Foreign investment in the U.S.	10.9
Loans to foreigners	58.1	Loans from foreigners	70.2

a.   Use the data of Exhibit 1 to calculate the balance on (1) merchandise trade account, (2) services account, (3) current account, (4) capital account, and (5) current-and-capital account.

b.   Compare these balances to the ones for 1989 in Exhibit 6 in the text. What happened to U.S. international balances between those years? Why do you think this occurred?

LEARNING THE MECHANICS – MULTIPLE CHOICE

1.   Since each nation has its own currency
   a.   transactions across national borders normally require the conversion of one currency into another.
   b.   gold must be used as the international medium of exchange.
   c.   direct exchange of goods, through brokers, is the normal means of exchange.
   d.   one dominant currency (currently the English pound) is used in more than 95 percent of all international transactions.

2.   An appreciation in the value of the U.S. dollar would
   a.   encourage foreigners to make more investments in the United States.
   b.   encourage U.S. consumers to purchase more foreign-produced goods.
   c.   increase the number of dollars that could be purchased with the Mexican peso.
   d.   discourage U.S. consumers from traveling abroad.

3.   The balance of payments is an annual accounting statement of a nation's
   a.   exports and imports.
   b.   balance due on imports and exports.
   c.   holdings of gold and foreign currencies.
   d.   international trade and financial transactions.

4.   A nation that has a balance-of-payments surplus is
   a.   importing more goods and services than it is exporting.
   b.   selling more goods, services, and financial assets abroad than it is purchasing from foreigners.
   c.   exporting more tangible goods than it is importing from foreigners.
   d.   exporting more tangible goods than intangible services and financial assets.

5. Which of the following would *not* be likely to cause a nation's currency to depreciate?
    a. An increase in the nation's exports
    b. More rapid domestic rate of inflation than that of the nation's trading partners
    c. Lower domestic interest rates
    d. Higher foreign interest rates

6. Under a system of flexible exchange rates, transactions that supply the nation's currency to the foreign-exchange market will cause the nation's
    a. currency to depreciate in value.
    b. balance-of-payments surplus to increase.
    c. balance-of-payments deficit to fall.
    d. products to increase in price in terms of foreign currencies.

7. A system of fixed, rather than floating, exchange rates
    a. eliminates problems that arise from changing prices or comparative advantage in international trade.
    b. forces traders to bear the risk involved in making manufacturing or farming commitments well in advance of retail market sales.
    c. ensures that those who benefit most by buying or selling in international markets bear the cost of any uncertainty associated with such trade.
    d. grants international traders some protection from uncertainty at the expense of a reduction in the nation's freedom to follow an independent course in other areas of economic policy.

8. If, to correct a balance-of-payments deficit, U.S. authorities increased import tariffs in order to cut imports, we should also expect
    a. foreign demand for U.S. exports to increase.
    b. U.S. consumers to benefit.
    c. decreased exports as well as decreased imports.
    d. strong opposition from U.S. industries now forced to supply goods formerly imported.

9. With fixed exchange rates, a balance-of-payments surplus would probably be lessened by
    a. restrictive monetary policy, keeping prices down and real interest rates up.
    b. expansionary monetary policy, pushing prices up and real interest rates down.
    c. a decrease in foreign-aid grants.
    d. an increase in income from investments abroad.

10. Which of the following is *not* a debit item in the U.S. balance of trade?
    a. A U.S. import of a German car
    b. A U.S. purchase of insurance from Lloyds of London
    c. A trip to Japan by an American student
    d. A short-term loan to a U.S. resident from a South American

11. With time, a depreciation in the value of the nation's currency in the foreign market will cause the nation's
    a. imports to increase and exports to decline.
    b. exports to increase and imports to decline.
    c. both imports and exports to decline.
    d. both imports and exports to rise.

12. The tendency of a nation's current account deficit to react to a depreciation by worsening in the short run and improving in the long run is called
    a. a double change in the 10-currency index.
    b. a hyper-reactive deficit.
    c. the J-curve.
    d. a capital account outflow problem.

13. All of the following are likely impacts on the U.S. of an unanticipated expansion in the U.S. monetary policy except:
    a. a depreciation in the exchange rate.
    b. a decline in the real interest rate.
    c. an outflow of capital.
    d. an increase in the size of a current account deficit.

THE ECONOMIC WAY OF THINKING – MULTIPLE CHOICE

1. "Wine experts are discovering that California wines of several varieties and vintages are comparable to many of the best French wines. The result is an increased demand, here and abroad, for California wines." With regard to the U.S. balance on current account, this trend will
    a. increase the U.S. deficit, because of the rise in the price of California wine.
    b. decrease the U.S. deficit, because of increased shipments of California wines abroad.
    c. decrease the demand for U.S. dollars.
    d. increase the U.S. demand for French francs.

2. In a world of fixed exchange rates, if a country cut its foreign-aid grants by 50 percent, and if the aid had been "tied" so that 75 percent of the grant had to be spent in the granting country for exports to the recipient, we would expect the change to
    a. increase any existing balance-of-payments deficit existing in the granting nation, since its exports would fall.
    b. decrease any existing balance-of-payments deficit existing in the granting nation by the amount of the cut in foreign aid.
    c. decrease any existing balance-of-payments deficit by less than the cut in foreign aid.
    d. have no impact on the granting nation's balance-of-payments.

3. If the United States could, with fixed exchange rates, run a perpetual balance-of-trade deficit so that other countries held ever increasing stocks of dollars, Americans would, compared to a no-trade deficit situation, be
    a. better off, since consumption could be perpetually higher.
    b. worse off, since the balance of payments would always be unfavorable.
    c. better off, since exports would have to be higher.
    d. worse off, since imports would have to be lower.

4. A fad that made a particular brand of cross-country skis, imported from Norway, extremely popular in the United States would tend to
    a. increase any existing balance-of-trade surplus for the United States.
    b. decrease any existing balance-of-trade deficit in the United States.
    c. decrease any existing U.S. balance-of-trade surplus.
    d. affect the U.S. balance of payments, but not the balance of trade.

33
Economic Development and the Growth of Income

TRUE OR FALSE

T F

1. The most obvious characteristic of a less-developed nation is low per capita income.

2. More than half of the world's population lives in countries with per capita incomes of less than $500 a year.

3. The exchange-rate conversion method of comparing GNPs is a good indicator of differences in the purchasing power of currencies for goods and services that are not exchanged on international markets.

4. A nation may experience extensive economic growth, even though output per person is not rising.

5. Monetary instability discourages investment and therefore hurts economic growth.

6. The evidence since the Second World War suggests that one policy option for governments that want to promote prosperity is to follow macroeconomic policies consistent with relatively stable prices.

7. Technological advance, defined as the invention of – but not adoption of – new techniques, enables workers to produce additional output with the same amount of resources.

8. The concept of the vicious circle of underdevelopment states that living standards barely above the subsistence level make it difficult for a nation to generate the investment and human capital necessary to foster future economic development.

9. Economic growth over the last century has created an enormous gulf between developed and less developed countries.

10. Capital market restrictions such as interest rate controls tend to keep interest rates low enough to stimulate investment and therefore help economic growth.

11. The annual per capita growth rate of real GNP for Taiwan, Hong Kong, and South Korea exceeds the growth rate of most industrial nations, including the United States.

PROBLEMS AND PROJECTS

1. The text specifies four key sources of economic growth:
    (1) Investment in human and physical capital
    (2) Technological progress
    (3) Efficient allocation of resources
    (4) Investment in infrastructure

    Each item below is an impediment to one of the key conditions for economic development listed above. Match each impediment with the relevant development condition.

    _____   a.   Much of the labor-saving research and development that occurs in advanced countries is not very useful to developing countries where labor is abundant and capital is scarce.

    _____   b.   Instead of exploiting their comparative advantage, many developing countries have tried to become self-sufficient through import-substitution policies.

    _____   c.   Because of the debt crisis, foreign loans and direct investments in most developing countries have dropped sharply since 1982.

    _____   d.   In response to the debt crisis, many developing country governments have curtailed spending on transportation and communication systems in order to reduce their budget deficits.

2. Exhibit 1 is a compound interest table in which each entry shows the amount to which $1.00 will accumulate at various rates of interest after n years. For example, if $10.00 were to grow at 2% interest for 5 years, it would grow to a value of $11.04 = $10.00 x 1.104.

Exhibit 1

| | Rate of interest or growth | | | | | |
Years	2%	3%	4%	5%	6%	7%
5	1.104	1.159	1.217	1.276	1.338	1.403
10	1.219	1.344	1.480	1.629	1.791	1.967
15	1.346	1.558	1.801	2.079	2.397	2.759
20	1.486	1.806	2.191	2.653	3.207	3.870
25	1.641	2.094	2.666	3.386	4.292	5.427
30	1.811	2.427	3.243	4.330	5.743	7.612
35	2.000	2.814	3.946	5.516	7.686	10.677
40	2.208	3.262	4.801	7.040	10.286	14.974
45	2.438	3.781	5.841	8.985	13.765	21.002

a.   Suppose the mythical economy of Gromangro has in 1950 a real GNP of &20 billion and a population of 100 million. (& is the symbol for "mango," the national currency of Gromangro). What is the real GNP per capita of Gromangro in 1950?

b.   In 1950, the U.S.'s real GNP per capita was $6,330. If in 1950 the exchange rate between the dollar and the mango was &1 = $2, what was Gromangro's 1950 GNP per capita in dollars? What was the difference in dollars between the per capita GNPs of the two?

c.   Suppose that Gromangro's GNP grows at 7% from 1950 to 1990 while her population grows at 3%. Use Exhibit 1 to calculate the value (in mangos) of Gromangro's GNP and her population in 1990. What is Gromangro's per capita GNP in 1990?

d.   Suppose the U.S.'s per capita GNP grows at 2% from 1950 to 1990. What is its value in 1990?

e. If the dollar/mango exchange rate remains the same as in part b, what is Gromangro's 1990 per capita GNP in dollars? What is the dollar difference between the two countries' per capita GNPs in 1990?

f. Gromangro grew at a faster *rate* than the U.S. What happened to the *absolute* difference in per capita income?

3. One way of analyzing economic growth is through simple equilibrium GNP models. Consider a hypothetical economy in which

$$
\begin{aligned}
Y &= C + I + G \\
C &= 200 + 0.9Y_D \\
Y_D &= Y - T
\end{aligned}
$$

investment is constant at 50, government expenditure is 300, and taxation is 250. Verify that equilibrium GNP is 3250. One problem with this economic model is that it is for a closed economy. How could you change it to incorporate international trade? (*Hint:* Remember that our definition of GNP also includes net exports.) How could an economy incapable of borrowing from abroad or from the public increase equilibrium GNP? Try a few alternatives to see what could be done; as you will quickly realize, without capital of some sort, it is very difficult to generate sustained economic growth.

4. One handy device to help get a good feel for what various growth rates mean is the "Simple 70" rule. The rule is just a formula for closely approximating how long it takes a growing value to double in size:

Doubling time = 70 / percentage growth rate

a. The Simple 70 rule works quite well. Try it with the following hypothetical GNP growth rates:

Annual growth rate of GNP	Actual	Simple 70 rule estimate
2.0	35.0	____
3.5	20.1	____
7.0	10.2	____

Years required for GNP to double:

b. Use the Simple 70 rule to contrast the estimated per capita GNP doubling times each of the following countries:

	Annual growth of GNP per capita 1965-1986	Years required for GNP per capita to double
India	1.8	_____
Brazil	4.3	_____
China	5.1	_____
South Korea	6.7	_____
Japan	4.3	_____
United States	1.6	_____

c. Many observers are concerned about the impact of population growth on development prospects, since per capita GNP growth % is approximately equal to GNP growth minus population growth %. For the countries in Exhibit 2, compute the current per capita GNP doubling times and then compute the per capita GNP doubling times if population growth could be reduced to 1.0 percent, the current rate in the United States.

Exhibit 2

Annual growth rate, 1965-86:	India	China	Brazil
GNP:	4.1	7.0	6.6
Population:	2.3	1.9	2.3
GNP per capita:	1.8	5.1	4.3
GNP per capita with 1.0% pop. growth:	_____	_____	_____
Years required for GNP per capita to double:			
Presently:	_____	_____	_____
With 1% pop. growth:	_____	_____	_____

LEARNING THE MECHANICS – MULTIPLE CHOICE

1. Which of the following is *not* a typical characteristic of most less-developed countries?
    a. Low per capita income
    b. Rapid population growth
    c. A large agricultural sector
    d. Fairly equal (but low) income distribution

2. Which of the following is a true statement about the percentages of the world's population and the level of per capita income in the countries in which they lived in 1986?
    a. Over 85 percent of the world's population lives in nations with annual per capita incomes under $500.
    b. Over 50 percent of the world's population lives in nations with per capita incomes under $500.
    c. Over 25 percent of the world's population lives in nations with annual per capita incomes over $7000.
    d. Over 40 percent of the world's population lives in nations with annual per capita incomes over $3000.

3. The poorest countries in the world (those with annual per capita output of $2200 or less) contain about three-fourths of the world's population and produce approximately what proportion of the world's output?
    a. one-third.
    b. one-fourth
    c. one-sixth
    d. one-ninth

4. In the United States, 2 percent of the work force is employed in the agricultural sector. In the less-developed countries of South America, Africa, and Asia, what percentage of the work force is generally employed in agriculture?
    a. Less than 5 percent
    b. 10-15 percent
    c. 25-30 percent
    d. More than 50 percent

5. The exchange-rate conversion method is
   a. a method of converting per capita income from one nation into another nation's currency through exchange rates.
   b. a method of converting exchange rates between countries to allow for differences between levels of per capita income.
   c. a method of converting exchange rates to allow for purchasing-power parity.
   d. a method of converting per capita income from one nation into another nation's currency through purchasing-power parity.

6. Although it has become increasingly popular to define economic growth in terms of the rate of change in real GNP, economic development is now widely perceived
   a. as a normative concept that ignores growth and concentrates on distribution and structural changes in the economy.
   b. as a normative concept encompassing not only growth, but a general improvement in the standard of living of the masses of the population.
   c. as a positive concept that quantifies the net economic welfare of the masses of the population.
   d. as a normative concept concentrating on the distribution of income, since economic welfare is only marginally related to income level.

7. When real GNP is expanding
   a. economic growth is extensive, but not necessarily intensive.
   b. economic growth is intensive, but not necessarily extensive.
   c. economic growth is both extensive and intensive.
   d. economic growth is neither extensive nor intensive.

8. A highly negative real interest rate would seem to encourage borrowing, investing, and (therefore) high economic growth rates
   a. but it doesn't, because negative real interest rates are impossible.
   b. but it doesn't, mainly because a highly negative real interest rate guarantees rampant hyperinflation, which tends to discourage investing.
   c. but it doesn't, mainly because the highly negative real interest rate stimulates a large capital outflow.
   d. and it does.

9. A 3 percent growth rate in GNP will bring about a doubling of GNP in about how many years?
   a. 3
   b. 12
   c. 24
   d. 48

10. If the results of a recent study are to be believed, a high level of marginal tax rates appear to be associated with low growth rates of per capita income in developing countries. One possible reason for this observation is that
    a. countries that are growing slowly have greater fiscal needs than countries that are growing quickly, and so tax rates are higher.
    b. high tax rates can potentially discourage productive activity.
    c. both a and b.
    d. neither a nor b.

11. The *simplest* method for comparing income levels between nations is the
    a. exchange-rate conversion method.
    b. dependency ratio method.
    c. purchasing-power parity method.
    d. price distortion comparison method.

12. The most *accurate* method for comparing income levels between nations is the
    a. exchange-rate conversion method.
    b. dependency ratio method.
    c. purchasing-power parity method.
    d. trickle-down method.

THE ECONOMIC WAY OF THINKING – MULTIPLE CHOICE

When answering the next two questions, use the information in Exhibit 3:

Exhibit 3

	Per capita GNP (dollars)	GNP growth rate (percent)	Rate of population growth (percent)
Egypt	710	5.3	2.7
Cameroun	910	5.2	1.0
United States	18,430	3.0	1.0

1. In which country is the level of economic development (not growth) the highest?
   a. Egypt
   b. Cameroun
   c. United States
   d. It is impossible to tell because of the problems of comparing GNPs from different countries and the lack of information about items other than per capita GNP.

2. In which country is the *growth rate* of per capita GNP the highest?
   a. Egypt
   b. Cameroun
   c. United States
   d. It is impossible to tell because adequate information is not given.

3. Which of the following best characterizes the relationship between the developed nations and the less-developed nations?
   a. The developed nations are growing and the less-developed nations are stagnating.
   b. The less-developed nations are growing, but the developed nations are growing even faster.
   c. Population is growing faster in developed nations.
   d. It is an oversimplification to divide the world into the growing, developed nations and the stagnating, less-developed nations.

4. Which of the following is *not* a good reason for using indices other than per capita GNP to measure economic development?
   a. Per capita GNP does not take income distribution into account.
   b. Per capita GNP is overly influenced by changes in population.
   c. Per capita GNP does not take nonmarket transactions into account.
   d. Per capita GNP does not take externalities, such as pollution, into account.

5. Which of the following is most likely to meet our definition of a less-developed nation?
   a. A country with a small agricultural sector, low rate of population growth, and low per capita GNP
   b. A country with a high population growth rate, a high per capita GNP growth rate, and an unequal distribution of income
   c. A country with inadequate health care, poor educational facilities, and low per capita GNP
   d. A country with low per capita GNP, a large population, and a small agricultural sector

6. If annual per capita GNP in the United States is $16,000 and in Great Britain is £6,000, then under which of the following exchange rates would Great Britain have a larger GNP than the United States?
   a. £1 = $2
   b. £1 = $3
   c. £3 = $1
   d. £2 = $1

7. The difference between extensive and intensive economic growth is about the same as the difference between the growth rate of
   a. total GNP and per capita GNP.
   b. total GNP and total net economic welfare.
   c. per capita GNP and per capita net economic welfare.
   d. real per capita GNP and per capita net economic welfare.

8. What is the difference between economic growth and economic development?
   a. Growth has to do with the area of a country, while development has to do with the maturity of a country.
   b. Growth has to do with the rate of change of GNP, while development has to do with the improvement of the overall standard of living.
   c. Growth can be extensive or intensive, while development can only be extensive.
   d. When you come right down to it, both growth and development can only be measured with per capita GNP, so there is *no* difference.

9. Which of the following would be most likely to improve the rate of growth of a less-developed nation?
   a. Development of strong labor unions
   b. An increase in foreign investment attracted by the expectation of economic and political stability
   c. An increase in the dependency ratio
   d. Foreign aid to construct a steel plant

10. According to Alvin Rabushka, a country with low marginal tax rates (or high thresholds for medium and high-rate tax schedules) is likely to:
    a. grow rapidly, because the low rates will give businesses and entrepreneurs an incentive to expand economic activity.
    b. grow rapidly, because the low rates will allow the government to afford to improve the educational system, eventually improving economic growth.
    c. grow slowly, because the low rates will make it difficult for the government to improve the infrastructure.
    d. grow slowly, because the low rates will encourage the rich to move elsewhere.

11. Which of the following "absurd" suggestions is the best government policy in terms of improving economic growth?
    a. Cut all tax rates to zero, since it has been shown that low taxes encourage rapid growth.
    b. Cut all tariff rates to zero, since it has been shown that high tariffs discourage rapid growth.
    c. Cut all real interest rates to zero, since it has been shown that high interest rates hurt rapid growth.
    d. Cut government expenditures to zero, since it has been shown that state ownership of enterprises hinders rapid growth.

Exhibit 4

	Mexico		United States	
	1975	*1985*	*1975*	*1985*
Gross national product (billions of units of domestic currency):	1,100.1	45,588.5	1,697.5	3,957.0
Population (millions):	60.1	78.5	216.0	239.3
Pesos per dollar:	12.5	256.9	–	–

The next two questions can be answered using the information in Exhibit 4.

12. In 1985, GNP per capita in Mexico was
    a. about 14 percent as large as GNP per capita in the United States.
    b. about 4 percent as large as GNP per capita in the United States.
    c. about 19 percent as large as GNP per capita in the United States.
    d. about 5 percent as large as GNP per capita in the United States.

13. Comparing the changes between 1975 and 1985 in GNP and GNP per capita in Mexico as proportions of GNP and GNP per capita in the United States,
    a. both proportions rose.
    b. GNP in Mexico rose relative to GNP in the United States, but GNP per capita fell relative to GNP per capita in the United States.
    c. GNP in Mexico fell relative to GNP in the United States, but GNP per capita rose relative to GNP per capita in the United States.
    d. both proportions fell.

THE ECONOMIC WAY OF THINKING – DISCUSSION QUESTIONS

1. What are the major conditions for economic growth? The major obstacles? Can you think of a country that has experienced rapid economic growth without a strong natural resource base? Without a slowing in the rate of population growth? Without a high rate of investment? Without substantial upgrading of literacy?

2. Why do you think the purchasing power parity method of comparing living standards yields smaller gaps across countries than the exchange rate conversion method? Which method do you think is more accurate? Which is easier to compute? Explain.

3. How do you think the less-developed countries can best help themselves attain more rapid growth rates? How do you think the developed countries can best help them?

4. In this chapter, it is implicitly assumed that most countries *want* to become developed. What arguments can you think of that might lead a country to want to stall its development?

5. Some argue that most households below the poverty line in the United States are not poor when compared to typical households of less-developed countries. Do you think such a comparison is valid? Why or why not? Who should we help most, the poor at home or those abroad who are even poorer?

6. More than half of the world's population lives in countries where average annual per capita income is less than $500. Plan a budget and try to figure out how you might get through a year with only $500. How much is that per month? Suppose that you could live for free (on the floor) with some relatives. Would you then have enough to pay for food, clothes, or school?

PERSPECTIVES IN ECONOMICS

Third World Facts and Fictions
by Charles Wolf Jr.

[Reprinted with permission of Charles Wolf Jr. from the *Los Angeles Times*, January 27, 1981.]

Secretary of State Alexander Haig Jr. has observed that the Third World ("A misleading term if ever there was one") is a myth.

"Recent American foreign policy," Haig said, "has suffered from the misperception which lumps together nations as diverse as Brazil and Libya, Indonesia and South Yemen, Cuba and Kuwait . . . (The) failure to tailor policy to the individual circumstances of developing nations has frequently aggravated the very internal stresses which Western policy should seek instead to diminish"

Following Haig's lead, it may be timely to try to separate myths from realities, because the conventional wisdom about the so-called Third World is more conventional than wise.

Myth: The "Third World," consisting of some 130 less-developed nations, is a reasonably cohesive entity, unified by similar interests and ideologies that enable its members to act effectively and in concert.

Reality: The nations of the Third World are, in fact, divided in many more ways and by many more conflicting interests than those that unify them.

Of course, it is a fact that certain attitudes – intense nationalism, hypersensitivity to foreign condescension, a liking, perhaps waning, for socialist ideology, to name only a few – are shared by many developing nations. But more objective circumstances tend to divide them.

For example, the Third World includes oil importers (Brazil, India, Pakistan) and oil exporters (Saudi Arabia, Libya, Iraq, Mexico, Venezuela); rapidly growing economies (Korea, Brazil, Singapore) and slowly growing or stagnating ones (most of the remaining nations); centrally planned economies as well as market economies; major international debtors (Brazil, Mexico, Turkey) and major international creditors (Saudi Arabia, Libya, Kuwait); communist nations, procommunist nations and vigorously anticommunist nations (as well as many in between), and nations ruled by military governments and nations that profess the primacy of civil over military control.

The rhetoric of Third World unity is more spurious than real. The reality of the Third World is cultural, political and economic diversity.

Thus, almost any action by the Reagan administration is likely to evoke support from some Third World nations, opposition from others and indifference from many. Our policy-makers would be well advised to think about the "Third World" as a plural, not a singular, entity.

Myth: Achieving significant and sustained economic development in the Third World is an overwhelming and intractable problem, made even more difficult by the rigidity and discrimination of the present international economic order.

Reality: Achieving rapid and sustained development, with the present international economic order, is a much less formidable problem than is usually supposed. The means and methods for realizing economic development are well known, have bee widely demonstrated and are generally acknowledged even if they are not widely adopted. By and large, these recipes have been amply demonstrated by the impressive development of the small number of Third World nations (Brazil, Korea, Taiwan and Singapore) that have maintained average rates of real economic growth of 9 percent annually during the 1970s.

These nations have made economic progress possible by achieving political stability, including infrequent changes of government. In addition, such nations have provided a hospitable economic climate for market forces and market prices, have encouraged infusions of foreign capital and the selective import of foreign technology, and have avoided hyperinflation.

Orientation toward the market, while typical of these relatively successful Third World nations, does not necessarily imply private ownership, or an inactive role for government. Where government interventions occur, they usually are selective and limited in number.

As to the rigidity and adverse effects of the present economic international order, and the sometimes shrill call for a "new international economic order," again the reality departs sharply from the myth. In fact, the "old" order has been remarkably flexible, rather than rigid, and hospitable rather than resistant to development in the Third World.

For example, the drastic shift from a regime of fixed exchange rates to fluctuating ones, the recycling of several hundred billion petrodollars over the last half dozen years, and the transfer of technology are all indications of the adaptability of the present international economic setup to changing needs and forces.

Myth: Economic development is essential for political stability and democratization in the Third World.

Reality: There is no significant relationship between economic development and either political stability or democratization. Nations such as South Korea have developed dramatically without significant progress toward democracy. Nations such as India have maintained relatively democratic and stable institutions without notable success in economic development. In some nations — for example, Iran — rapid economic development has brought with it political instability. And in other nations, such as Turkey, adverse economic conditions have provided an environment in which terrorism has flourished and emerging democratic institutions have been set back.

Perhaps there is a weak relationship between economic progress and political stability. If an economy stagnates and if unemployment is high, it is probably easier for opposition to be kindled, simply because idle hands are more likely to be mischievous ones.

Myth: The primary objective of Third World nations is to modernize their economies as rapidly as they can.

Reality: On the contrary, most Third World leaders have other goals and objectives. These include achieving greater national recognition and prestige in the international community; acquiring modern and advanced military equipment; pursuing ideological preferences; and agitating for international redistribution of income, rather than domestic economic growth.

If one looks at behavior rather than rhetoric, development is among the goals and priorities of most of the nations of the Third World, but not at the top of the list.

There is a paradox in all this: If development is accorded primary emphasis among national objectives, success seems to depend on imposing limits on the scope and character of government intervention. Few Third World leaders are willing to let go of the reins of control and unleash the market forces that can help their economies grow.

Discussion

1. Do you agree with Wolf's perceptions of reality in all four cases? About which are you skeptical? Why?

2. What sort of changes in policies toward Third World nations do these new "realities" imply? How easy would it be to bring these policy changes about?

3. Can you think of other "Third World facts and fictions"? If so, what are they?

34
Comparative Economic Systems

TRUE OR FALSE

T F

☐ ☐ 1. The agricultural sector has consistently been a problem for the Soviet economy.

☐ ☐ 2. Ownership of physical capital differs between socialist and market systems, but the mechanism for allocating resources is the same.

☐ ☐ 3. Under socialism, investment decisions normally are decentralized.

☐ ☐ 4. In a market system, the price mechanism determines the distribution of income as well as the allocation of resources.

☐ ☐ 5. In reality, all modern economies are a combination of capitalist and socialist economic organization.

☐ ☐ 6. The concept of opportunity cost does not apply in a socialist system.

☐ ☐ 7. Private garden plots in the Soviet Union account for a significant share of the total agricultural output.

☐ ☐ 8. The centralized Soviet economy invests a substantially smaller share of its product annually than does the U.S. economy.

☐ ☐ 9. In recent years, observers have tended to overestimate the growth of the Soviet economy, at least in part because of insufficient allowance for the poor quality of products.

☐ ☐ 10. Under Soviet planning, resources are centrally rationed in physical terms.

☐ ☐ 11. Well-organized industry-wide unions have played a major role in promoting the rapid growth of the Japanese economy since World War II.

☐ ☐ 12. It's ironic but true that the same peaceful revolution that is causing dramatic changes in the Soviet Union may also cause political instability that will act as a deterrent to economic progress.

PROBLEMS AND PROJECTS

1. Match the letters on the right with the numbers on the left.

    _____ (1) A characteristic of a Socialist economy

    _____ (2) Gosplan

    _____ (3) Investment decisions

    _____ (4) A characteristic of a capitalist economy

    _____ (5) Investment as a share of GNP

    _____ (6) Per capita gross national product.

    a. They are market determined under capitalism, but made by central planners under socialism.

    b. Nonhuman resources are owned by individuals.

    c. Central planning agency in the Soviet Union.

    d. Physical resources are owned by the state.

    e. Nearly twice as great in the Soviet Union as in the United States

    f. Market socialism

    g. More than twice as great in the United States as in the Soviet Union

2. Use the list of distinguishing economic characteristics of economies as presented in column 1 of Exhibit 1 in the text to devise a similar exhibit describing these characteristics as they apply to the specific economies of Japan and Yugoslavia rather than to the general categories of "capitalism" and "socialism."

3. Match each of the countries below that were discussed in this chapter with the identifying characteristic listed in the right-hand column.

    _____ United States
    _____ Soviet Union
    _____ Japan
    _____ Sweden
    _____ Hong Kong
    _____ China

    a. Most market-oriented economy
    b. Highest GNP per capita
    c. Allocates highest proportion of GNP to national defense
    d. Most equal income distribution
    e. Highest growth rate of GNP (among large industrial nations)
    f. Economy characterized by employee-managed firms
    g. Most rapid growth of output of the agricultural sector in the 1980s.

LEARNING THE MECHANICS – MULTIPLE CHOICE

1. The business firms in a socialist economy
    a. are guided by boards of directors that perform functions similar to those of boards of directors of U.S. corporations.
    b. typically confront a strong labor union.
    c. are guided by central planners who use a reward-penalty system to affect the decisions of plant managers and workers.
    d. operate outside of the central planning apparatus.

2. At least four basic economic concepts apply to all economic systems. These four include all of the following except
   a. diminishing marginal returns.
   b. comparative advantage and efficiency.
   c. opportunity cost.
   d. private property rights.

3. The gross national product in the Soviet Union is
   a. less than one-fourth the size of the U.S. GNP.
   b. approximately one-half the size of the U.S. GNP.
   c. approximately three-fourths the size of the U.S. GNP.
   d. approximately nine-tenths the size of the U.S. GNP.

4. Which of the following is not a characteristic of a socialist economy?
   a. Detailed central planning
   b. Government ownership of physical capital
   c. Government ownership of human capital
   d. Wages and prices are fixed by government edict

5. The choice between production of capital goods and consumer goods in the Soviet Union
   a. is made by consumers and business enterprises.
   b. results in a rate of investment that is similar to the rate of investment in the United States.
   c. is made by the central planners, who apparently have assigned a low priority to consumption goods.
   d. is made by planners who, in the past, have assigned a high priority to consumer goods.

6. Which of the following nations would best be described as a centrally planned socialist economy?
   a. Yugoslavia
   b. Sweden
   c. United Kingdom
   d. Soviet Union

7. The economy of Hong Kong can best be described as
   a. one of the world's best working models of pure socialism.
   b. one of the world's best working models of pure capitalism.
   c. one of the world's best working models of a combination of pure capitalism and pure socialism.
   d. an interesting exception to the idea that economies incorporate pure capitalism and pure socialism to various degrees.

8. All but one of the following have contributed to the rapid rate of growth of the Japanese economy. Which has *not* been a significant source of economic growth in Japan?
   a. High rate of capital formation
   b. Persistent tax cuts
   c. Adoption of modern technology borrowed from other industrial Western nations
   d. A strong national federation of unions that has established a uniform national wage scale in most major industries

9. Suppose that a centrally planned country changes the way it specifies goals for bread production from the number of loaves of bread produced to the number of pounds of bread produced. All else equal, we'd expect the average size of a loaf of bread in this country to
   a. decrease.
   b. increase.
   c. remain unchanged.
   d. increase, decrease, or remain unchanged, depending on the most efficient size of a loaf of bread.

10. Labor unions in Japan are
    a. strongly centralized national unions.
    b. influential in setting wage differentials.
    c. seldom company unions.
    d. important primarily for blue-collar workers.

11. **(I)** The Japanese tax structure is progressive. **(II)** In Japan, individuals can partially avoid paying taxes by saving or investing in specified industries.
    a. Both I and II are true.
    b. I is true, II is false.
    c. I is false, II is true.
    d. Both I and II are false.

THE ECONOMIC WAY OF THINKING – MULTIPLE CHOICE

1. Which of the following is *not* a characteristic of socialist economic organization?
   a. Centralized economic planning
   b. Workers are employed by government or by government-controlled cooperatives.
   c. The rate of return of human capital is determined by market forces.
   d. Investment in nonhuman capital is determined by political factors.

2. If socialist planners wanted to allocate resources efficiently, they would
   a. attempt to have each product produced by the low opportunity-cost producer.
   b. expand the use of a resource as long as its marginal product were positive.
   c. expand the production of a good as long as consumers received some positive marginal utility from it.
   d. not need to utilize such capitalist concepts as opportunity cost and comparative advantage.

3. Suppose that producers of cut-glass jewelry were rewarded according to the weight of the glass used in producing the jewelry. As a result, necklaces made with very thick glass would be produced. If the rules were changed to piecemeal production – that is, the managers were rewarded by the number of necklaces made – and the quantity of output increased, it could be concluded that
   a. the cost of production of the latter method is lower.
   b. the latter method implies increased production, higher rates of growth, and thus good management on the part of the central planning authority.
   c. the jewelry makers' behavior implies that incentives count in any economy.
   d. the enterprises increased output only for the purpose of amplifying their level of achievement.

4. If the black market price of a good is higher than the price of that good as determined by a centrally planned government,
    a. consumers probably want more of that good than is currently being produced.
    b. consumers probably want less of that good than is currently being produced.
    c. consumers probably are unhappy with the quality of the good being offered on the black market.
    d. consumers must be happy with the quality of the good being offered on the black market.

5. The material balance method
    a. uses a planning agency to keep track of and allocate resources.
    b. uses a planning agency to keep a balance between keeping track of and allocating resources.
    c. uses a hypothetical market to keep a balance between the supply of and the demand for material resources.
    d. uses a hypothetical market to keep a balance between the needs of various state enterprises which are in need of material resources.

6. If a centrally planned economy fixes the quantity of blue jeans produced and also fixes the price of blue jeans below the equilibrium price for that quantity,
    a. blue jeans shortages will develop and lines will form.
    b. the black market price of blue jeans will be higher than the fixed price.
    c. tourists will have an incentive to bring an extra pair of blue jeans into the country to trade for local goods.
    d. all of the above.

7. According to the text (which went to press in late 1991), recent reforms in the Soviet Union have included
    a. an expansion in the freedom to operate small private businesses.
    b. an increase in the number of large denomination bills (currency) in circulation.
    c. the announcement that the ruble is fully convertible to hard currencies such as the dollar, mark, and yen.
    d. a decrease in the number of business cooperatives.

8. Use statements I and II to answer this question. **(I)** "Japanese workers have been more likely to accept a reduction in wages during a business slump than workers in most Western nations." **(II)** "The rate of unemployment in Japan has generally been higher than that in the United States."
    a. I is true, II is false.
    b. II is true, I is false.
    c. Both I and II are true.
    d. Both I and II are false.

9. The Soviet Union appears on the verge of attempting to move from a communistic planned economy to a socialistic market economy. Even if this move is successful in the long run, we'd expect per capita incomes in the USSR to
    a. increase in the short and long run.
    b. decrease in the short and long run.
    c. increase in the short run but then decrease in the long run.
    d. decrease in the short run but then increase in the long run.

10. If the 15 republics of the former Soviet Union were to break up into a number of different countries, each with its own tariffs, currencies, capital restrictions, and so on, it's possible that the gains in production due to moving towards a market economy could be offset by
    a. a decreased use of expansionary monetary policy.
    b. a decreased use of expansionary fiscal policy.
    c. a decreased use of comparative advantage.
    d. a decreased use of trading opportunities with the U.S.

11. Economic theory suggests that, all else equal, lifetime employment commitments tend to
    a. reduce cyclical fluctuations in price.
    b. reduce cyclical fluctuations in output.
    d. reduce fixed costs as a share of total costs.
    d. reduce the incentives of management to make the best use of a firm's employees.

THE ECONOMIC WAY OF THINKING – DISCUSSION QUESTIONS

1. How do you think capitalist and socialist economies compare with regard to
   a. variety of products available?
   b. quality of products available?
   c. innovative behavior?
   d. equality in the distribution of income?
   e. share of income allocated to investment?
   f. amount of cyclical unemployment?
   g. efficiency in the allocation of resources?

2. How large is the market sector in the Soviet Union? What is likely to happen to the size of that sector as the current policy changes continue? What sorts of difficulties does the Soviet Union seem likely to encounter as it attempts to complete these policy changes?

3. How do the economies of the United States and the Soviet Union compare with regard to
   a. size of GNP?
   b. composition of GNP?
   c. per capita income?
   d. growth rate of GNP?

4. Why do black markets exist? Do you think the existence of a black market helps or hurts the performance of a socialist economy? Why?

5. What are the advantages of central planning compared to markets? The disadvantages? Do you think the United States does too little planning, too much, or just the right amount? Describe some specific examples of how planning could help or hurt the performance of the U.S. economy.

6. a. Compare the Japanese economy with that of the United States.
    b. Which aspects of the Japanese economy do you find attractive? Unattractive?
    c. Do you think the economy of Japan is more or less pro-business than the economy of the United States? More or less pro-labor? What examples can you think of to support your views?

PERSPECTIVES IN ECONOMICS

"From Marx to the Market"
From *The Economist*

[Reprinted with permission from
The Economist, May 11, 1991. ©1991 The Economist Newspaper Ltd.]

The task that confronts the economies of Eastern Europe is only now becoming clear. The region's political transformation, extraordinary though it has been, was just the start. A much bigger challenge lies ahead. It is not merely to build capitalism, but to build it from the wreckage of an existing, and still sort-of-functioning, economic system; to maintain support for policies that are sure to make many, if not most, people worse off, at least for a while; and, hardest of all, to disappoint hopes of a quick recovery without destroying the ambition to succeed in the years to come.

Even in eastern Germany, with all its advantages, the transition to capitalism is proving much tougher than most people expected. Since unification, output has slumped; unemployment, open and disguised, is rising fast. Even the enterprises that were the pride of the old regime, the show-piece earners of hard currency, have turned to dust. In Poland, which has undertaken the boldest reforms in the region, consumer spending fell last year (on admittedly flawed official estimates) by nearly 30% in real terms. Yet the closure of inefficient firms and the surge in unemployment that will go with it have hardly begun. The pace of reform in Hungary and Czechoslovakia has been slower. With economic restructuring there barely under way, output has already shrunk and seems certain to fall further. Except in eastern Germany, with a frowning Bundesbank thrust upon it, inflation in these countries is running at upwards of 40% a year.

The picture is not all black. Small traders have appeared from nowhere and do brisk business (which is often not captured in official figures), belying any lack of entrepreneurship. Best of all, Eastern Europe's reforming governments, unlike the paralysed leadership of the Soviet Union, seek no illusory "middle way" between communism and capitalism. Their ambition is to create market economies on the western model as quickly as possible. That is why privatisation has become their top priority.

A year ago that could not have been taken for granted. Some western advisers believed that market economies could be created merely by freeing prices, thus abandoning the most visible sign of communist central planning; private enterprise was desirable, of course, and would come, but there was no need to rush. The region's reformers knew better. They saw that you cannot have capitalism without capitalists. Freeing prices replaces the necessary ignorance of central planners with usable information: prices are signals that tell the economy how its resources can best be used.

But unless those resources – and, above all, productive assets – are privately owned, the signals will simply be ignored.

Privatisation is essential in other ways, too. When a firm's assets are owned by the state – in effect, by nobody – its managers face no financial discipline. So they borrow even though they have no efficient use for the money. Expanding credit has been a powerful engine of inflation in the region. Now the process has started to take new forms (fewer cheap loans from governments, more forced credit from other enterprises), but it is still work, fuelling inflation and adding to a hidden burden of bad debts. As the competitive squeeze on enterprises tightens, the coming debt crunch will only grow worse – unless capital is quickly transferred to owners with reason to preserve its value. Privatisation is not an optional extra for Eastern Europe; it is not a reform that can wait for better times. Without it, better times will never come.

The reformers agree; the question is how. Throughout the region governments face a contradiction. To create a market economy, there must first be private ownership. But to create private ownership, there must first be a market – otherwise how are you to value the assets to be privatised?

One answer to this riddle is that the assets of these economies cannot be valued, and must therefore be given away (to a citizenry, mind you, that is already supposed to own them). Poland and Czechoslovakia, though disagreeing strongly over details, have decided to privatise largely by distributing assets free, or at a nominal charge, across wide sections of the population. Arguments over these schemes have caused costly delay, but once agreement is reached privatisation might happen very rapidly: working market economies might be created within months. Hungary's government has preferred not to wait: it is privatising those assets for which it can find willing buyers. So far, this approach has achieved more, but it would take years to place most of the economy in private hands. Indeed, it may never succeed, because so many of Eastern Europe's enterprises are simply unsellable.

Hungary's approach is admirably pragmatic, but conviction is needed, too. Privatisation should not be mainly about raising revenues. Indeed, it would be dangerous to let the government's finances come to depend on the proceeds. The overriding aim should be to privatise as much of the economy as possible in the shortest time.

Discussion

1. The article claims that privatisation (that is, converting government owned businesses to privately owned businesses) or private property "is essential" to the creation of a market system. Do you agree? Explain your answer.

2. The problem of moving from Marx to the market applies to the Soviet Union as well as to the economies of Eastern Europe. Do you think the transition will be more or less difficult in the Soviet Union? Why? In what ways?

3. The article seems to ignore macroeconomic issues such as unemployment and inflation. How do you think these will be affected as an economy moves from Marx to the market? What factors might change your answer? Explain.

Answer Key

CHAPTER 1

True or False

The following are true: 1, 3, 5, 7, 8, 11, 13.

Problems and Projects

1. a. No
    b. Yes
    c. Yes
    d. Remaining workload
    e. No
    f. Lower
    g. Both
    h. Yes
2. b. Positively related.
    c. 15 miles; 1/15
3. b. 8/1; 4/1
4. b. Positive.
    c. $174 billion; $168 billion; $168/174 = 0.95$
    d. 0.95; no.

5. (Guideposts are listed by number)
    a. 5
    b. 6
    c. 1
    d. 2
    e. 3
    f. 7
    g. 4
6. c. Negatively related.
    d. Increase by 160 thousand tons.
7. a. (3)
    b. (2)
    c. (1)

Learning the Mechanics — Multiple Choice

1. d. It alone involves what ought to be done. (pp. 13-14)
2. c. The statement concerns what the U.S. "ought" to do. (pp. 13-14)
3. c. See the definition, p. 4.
4. c. It alone involves what "will" as opposed to "ought" to be. (p. 13)
5. a. The statement concerns what the government "ought" to do. (pp. 13-14)
6. d. The first three are listed as guideposts, but the last confuses scarcity with poverty. (pp. 6-13).
7. c. It involves prediction — a testable hypothesis; the others involve prescription. (p. 13)
8. b. Humans may *provide* freely but cannot *acquire* or produce freely. (p. 7)

9.   a.   It stresses the interdependence of economic effects. (p. 11)
10. d.   Each can be used to produce economic goods. (p. 5)
11. c.   Statement (erroneously) says what is true for one must be true for all; this is the fallacy of composition. (p. 15)
12. a.   Plotting the functions will show this. (p. 22)
13. d.   P increases by 10 while Q increases by 5. (p. 22)
14. b.   Both Y and Z have P = 50 when Q = 25. (p. 22)

The Economic Way of Thinking – Multiple Choice

1.   c.   All other answers are characteristics of *both* micro and macro. (p. 15)
2.   b.   All other answers involve costs with no gains. (pp. 7-8)
3.   d.   In the other answers, individuals act contrary to their self-interest. (pp. 8-9)
4.   c.   "Should" implies normative economic reasoning. (pp. 13-14)
5.   b.   Both positive and normative economics deal with costs, benefits, and theory. (pp. 13-14)
6.   d.   In each answer benefits and costs of action must be weighed. (pp. 7-8)
7.   a.   Incentives matter, even for "non-economic" behavior. (pp. 8-9)
8.   b.   Both high food prices and inflation may be caused by some other factor. (p. 15)
9.   d.   Neither good is freely available in amounts consumers desire. (p. 4)
10. b.   Other answers are tests, but this is usually accepted as *best*. (pp. 12-13)
11. d.   Persons often desire nonmaterial items and sometimes their actions are ill-formed or appear to be irrational to others. (pp. 7-8)
12. a.   Smith opposed *b* but had some sympathy for *c* and *d*; see pp. 16-17.
13. a.   The $3 billion is an unrecoverable cost; if remaining cost does not exceed value of $25 billion, the project is worthwhile. (pp. 9-11)
14. b.   Computing and comparing costs is an objective process. (pp. 13-14)

CHAPTER 2

True or False

The following are true: 3, 4, 7, 8, 9, 11.

Problems and Projects

1.   a.   2; 1
     b.   no; Sam makes 10 chairs, Larry makes 4 tables.
2.   a.   no
     b.   yes; 400 bushels of wheat, 150 bushels of oranges
     c.   yes; he would gain 50 bushels of oranges; total output increases by 100 bushels of oranges
     d.   yes
3.   a.   The U.S.'s opportunity cost for coffee = 3; Brazil's = 2. The U.S.'s opportunity cost for tobacco = 1/3; Brazil's = 1/2
     b.   Brazil has a comparative advantage in coffee. The U.S. has a comparative advantage in tobacco.
     c.   Brazil
     d.   Brazil

4. a. yes; yes; no.
    b. 900 million bushels; 200 million bushels.
    c. 100 million bushels; 1 bushel of wheat.
    d. 2 bushels of wheat.
5. a. $13,000
    b. $19,600
    c. The U.S. birthrate would fall.
6. a. (3)
    b. (1)
    c. (5)
    d. (4)
    e. (2)
7. a. (1) $C = 3$; $I = 5$ (2) $C = 5$; $I = 3$ (3) $C = 4$; $I = 4$
    b. The answer to all three parts of *a* would be $C = 3$, $I = 3$.

Learning the Mechanics – Multiple Choice

1. c. See the definition, p. 30.
2. c. The opportunity cost of time spent not working is the wage forgone. (pp. 30-31)
3. c. Opportunity cost always refers to values of *alternatives*. (p. 30)
4. a. Comparative advantage ensures efficiency which raises available output. (p. 42)
5. a. Since *each* trader can gain, exchange will arise voluntarily. (p. 45)
6. c. See the discussion, pp. 45-46.
7. b. If misuse of property is not enforced, there is no incentive to consider the wishes of others. (pp. 35-36)
8. d. Two units of food must be sacrificed for eight units of clothing; $2/8 = 1/4$. (pp. 30 and 41-42)
9. d. Italia's opportunity cost of food $= 1$; Slavia's $= 4$. (pp. 41-42)
10. c. Gains arise when countries export their low opportunity cost goods. (p. 42)
11. c. Curve represents output possibilities when resources are fully utilized. (p. 37)
12. d. See the definition, p. 36.
13. c. See the definition, p. 32.
14. b. "Middlemen" specialize in providing information and arranging trades so you will not have to. (p. 33)
15. c. See the definition on p. 34.

The Economic Way of Thinking – Multiple Choice

1. b. Failure to realize specialization gains means inefficient resource use. (pp. 37-38)
2. c. Crusoe's opportunity cost of good $y = 1/2$; Friday's $= 1$. (pp. 30 and 41-42)
3. b. See Exhibit 2, p. 37
4. b. Going to school means sacrificing the alternative of working and earning income. (p. 31)
5. a. Specilization raises efficiency and reduces costs (time) of production. (pp. 40-42)
6. b. The alternative to the date is to have $10 and play tennis. (p. 30)
7. b. Higher investment means greater production possibilities in the future. (pp. 38-39)
8. d. The extra money cost of driving is $(3 \times \$80) - \$50 = \$190$. (p. 31)
9. b. Because production according to comparative advantage concentrates on minimizing opportunity cost. (p. 42)
10. a. Most (not all) wealth was built through voluntary (non-exploitative) trade. (p. 45)

11. d. Considering the wishes of others will help maximize income. (pp. 34-35)
12. c. This is a part of the "worker alienation" that can accompany specialization. (p. 44)
13. a. The last soybean produced (at A) causes rice production to decrease by much more than the first (at D). (pp. 30-31)
14. a. The production possibilities frontier shifts in. (p. 37)
15. c. Productivity improves for soybeans but not rice. (p. 38)

CHAPTER 3

True or False

The following are true: 1, 2, 3, 5, 7, 8, 9.

Problems and Projects

1. b. $12
   d. $15
2. a. $4; 10
   b. $7; 12
   c. Higher soybean prices will shift the demand for wheat to the right.
3. a. Decrease, increase
   b. decreased demand for steel, increased demand for aluminum
   c. increase
   d. increased unemployment
   e. increase
   f. increase, increase
   g. increase
   h. increase
   i. increase
   j. decrease
   k. remain the same
   l. increase
4. b. $0, -, +, -$
   c. $-, 0, -, -$
   d. $+, +, ?, +$
   e. $-, +, -, ?$
5. b. increase
   d. The below equilibrium rental price reduces the incentive of sellers to expand the future supply of rental housing.
   e. no; landlords will favor friends and discriminate against groups they don't like
6. a. $P = \$2.20$; $Q = 3.3$
   b. $Qs = 3.7$; $Qd = 3.1$; Q stockpiled $= 0.6$
   c. Receipts $= \$9.25$ billion; Consumer spending $= \$7.75$ billion; Taxpayer cost $= \$1.5$ billion
   d. Market price $= \$1.60$. Deficiency payment $= \$.90$
   e. i. remain the same; ii. rise. Target price option is better because overall cost is the same but corn consumption is higher.
7. Correct: "risk of driving many dairy farm families out of business." Incorrect: "higher milk prices."

Learning the Mechanics – Multiple Choice

1. d. A below-equilibrium price results in an excess of quantity demanded relative to quantity supplied. (p. 60)
2. b. If soybean prices rise, demand for wheat rises (demand curve shifts right). (pp. 53, 62)
3. c. The demand curve shows how quantity responds to *changes* in price. (p. 62)
4. a. When cigar prices rise, smokers will substitute cigarettes for cigars. (p. 53)
5. d. Sellers will want to supply more and buyers will demand less, resulting in a surplus. (p. 71)
6. a. Assuming Bud is a substitute for Miller. (p. 53)
7. a. This reflects the law of demand; see the definition, p. 53
8. a. Travelers will substitute bus, train and air travel for auto travel. (pp. 53, 62)
9. a. The price mechanism rations goods to their most highly valued use. (p. 52)
10. b. This is necessary to eliminate excess supply; see Exhibit 4, p. 59.
11. b. Demand for U.S. cars (a substitute) increases; higher price raises quantity supplied. (pp. 62, 64-65)
12. b. This is "abstract" as opposed to "historical" time. (pp. 58-61)
13. d. See the definition on p. 61
14. d. While markets are not always (necessarily) in harmony with the general welfare, they are generally so. (pp. 76-77)

The Economic Way of Thinking – Multiple Choice

1. b. Increased price raises quantity supplied and reduces quantity demanded. (pp. 59, 69)
2. c. The tax raises price causing *quantity demanded* (not demand) to fall. (pp. 62-64)
3. a. Driving smaller cars is one way of economizing on higher priced gas. (p. 68)
4. b. With lower prices, landlords attempt to maintain profits by cutting costs. (pp. 72-73)
5. c. A price ceiling above equilibrium has no effect. (p. 70)
6. d. The drought reduced supply; the millers' expectations of higher future prices raised current demand. (pp. 62, 68)
7. a. Florida's demand is not affected; if California's supply rises, price falls. (pp. 62, 68)
8. c. All other answers involve "interferences" with the price mechanism. (pp. 73-74)
9. b. This lowers auto *demand*, which changes *quantity supplied*, not supply. (pp. 64-68)
10. c. Response *a* would lower price; *b* lowers quantity; *d* sharply raises quantity. (pp. 62-68)
11. c. Supply of nannies will shift left and up. (p. 66)
12. d. All others shift the demand for nannies. (p. 65)
13. d. Demand for day care will shift right and up. (p. 62)
14. b. At $120, quantity demanded exceeds quantity supplied. (p. 70)

CHAPTER 4

True or False

The following are true: 1, 2, 4, 5, 6, 7, 8, 11.

Problems and Projects

1.	a.	B
	b.	B
	c.	PG
	d.	P
	e.	B

f. P
g. P
h. B
i. PG
j. B

2. a. (2)
   b. (3)
   c. (1)
   d. (3)
3. a. $10, 100 billion
   b. $1000 billion
   c. $15; $1200 billion
   d. Consumer valuation of the last barrel is $15, which is greater than the producer valuation of $5, so this is inefficient.
4. a. P = $120, Q = 4,000 tons/year
   b. P = $130, Q = 3,000 tons/year (*Hint*: Add $20 to each price and graph new supply curve with the old quantity supplied and the new prices. Find the new equilibrium point.)
5. a. P = 50; Q = 26
   b. 32
   c. A subsidy.
   d. The supply and demand for public sector action.

Learning the Mechanics — Multiple Choice

1. d. Lower quantity supplied leaves some mutual gains unrealized; see Exhibit 1, p. 83.
2. a. Answers *c* and *d* assume no "spillover effects" (externalities). (pp. 84-87)
3. c. The other responses may lead government to *reduce* efficiency. (pp. 92-94)
4. c. Such exchange reduces efficiency and may or may not lead to political action. (pp. 85-87, 88)
5. b. Public goods are characterized by non-rivalry in consumption. (pp. 87-88)
6. c. External costs are not included in private production decisions; see Exhibit 3. (pp. 86-87)
7. b. Inefficiency may result from the special interest or shortsightedness effects. (pp. 96-97)
8. b. Element of compulsion may prevent public use of price mechanism. (p. 91)
9. a. Defining the ideal income distribution is a perplexing matter. (pp. 93-94)
10. d. The personal benefits of casting an informed vote may be less than the costs of being informed. (pp. 94-96)
11. d. This reflects the "no free lunch" guide to economic thinking. (p. 91)
12. d. Response *a* confers external benefits; *b* external costs; *c* external benefits. (pp. 85-86)
13. b. Rent-seeking is an action aimed at restructuring public policy to redistribute income to a group or industry. (p. 94).

The Economic Way of Thinking — Multiple Choice

1. a. Spillover effects are unconsidered impacts of your actions on others. (pp. 85-86)
2. c. Public goods break the individual consumption-payment link. (p. 87)

3. d. With no individual consumption-payment link, there may be insufficient private demand. (pp. 90-91)
4. a. If either is violated, some mutual gains will be unrealized; see Exhibit 1. (pp. 82-83)
5. c. The *individual* consumption-payment link may be absent. (pp. 90-91)
6. d. If individual costs are small it is rational for others to be ignorant. (pp. 94-96)
7. c. Costs of organizing "influence" are justified by large potential gains. (p. 96)
8. b. Each of the others has *some* public good aspect, but clean air has more. (pp. 87-88)
9. c. One may *favor* an action (altruistically) without personally gaining. (p. 82)
10. a. Those who do not gain from voluntary exchange do not participate. (pp. 82-84)
11. d. Gains to special interest groups justify the costs to them of influencing politicians. (p. 96)
12. a. This appears to be an effective way of getting votes. (pp. 96-97)
13. a. Both buyers and sellers overlook the external costs. (pp. 86-87)

CHAPTER 5

True or False

The following are true: 1, 2, 3, 6, 9,12.

Problems and Projects

1. a. 0.10 ($20,000) + 0.20 ($10,000) = $4,000
   b. $11,000
   c. progressive
   d. Add 10% to each income level, keeping tax rates the same.
2. a. 14.7%, 29.6%; progressive
   b. 19.6%, 44.0%; greater than
   c. no; yes; bracket creep
3. a. $150, $180, $200, $210, $210, $200
   b. Laffer curve
4. a. canned peas; cigarettes
   b. cigarettes; equilibrium quantity falls less.
   c. Cigarette smoking imposes external costs.
5. a. 67%   22%   15%
      22%   22%   20%
      13%   22%   25%
   b. Option 1: regressive; option 2: proportional; Option 3: progressive

Learning the Mechanics – Multiple Choice

1. c. See Exhibit 13, p. 124.
2. a. See Exhibit 13, p. 124.
3. b. See the definition, p. 113.
4. b. See Exhibit 7, p. 113.
5. b. See the definition, p. 108.
6. d. Divide the increase in taxes ($200) by the increase in income ($1000). (p. 109)
7. c. The underground economy is used to avoid or reduce taxes. (p. 114)
8. a. See Exhibit 6, p. 108.

9. d. See Exhibit 2, p. 103.
10. b. See Exhibit 13, p. 124.
11. d. By taking the same *number* of dollars, a low-income individual will pay a larger percentage of her income than will a high-income recipient. (p. 109)
12. c. With equal consumption, all will pay equal taxes, so tax bill as a share of income falls as income rises. (pp. 109-110)

The Economic Way of Thinking – Multiple Choice

1. a. The average tax rate would be greater for high-income families. (pp. 108-109)
2. d. See Exhibit 8, p. 114.
3. c. The revenues that businesses use to pay taxes come from consumers, stockholders, or employees. (p. 123)
4. d. Such a special-interest group would oppose tax revision most of all.
5. d. Price would rise by 2 cents only if demand were completely vertical. (p. 113)
6. c. An increase in rates will tend to shrink the tax base, thus the tax revenues increase less than proportionally. (p. 116)
7. d. See the definition, p. 112.
8. d. One's *constant purchasing power* tax liability would remain the same. (p. 118)
9. a. The marginal rate determines after-tax value of *additional* income. (p. 109)
10. b. Either case means equilibrium price rises by full amount of tax. (p. 113)
11. c. Laffer popularized, but did not discover, the principle involved. (p. 116)
12. c. The tax equals "S + tax" minus S; at Q=80, this can be seen to be $0.50. (pp. 112-113)
13. b. 80 times $0.50 equals $40.00. (pp. 112-113)
14. b. See Exhibit 7 on page 113.

CHAPTER 6

True or False

The following are true: 1, 2, 5, 6, 11.

Problems and Projects

1. a. 5463; 4887
   b. 5463; 4887
2. 2419; 3188; 4154
3. 230; 190. The expenditure approach must be used because not enough information is given to use the resource allocation approach. (Profits and Proprietor's Income must equal 10.)
4. a. +   g. +   l. −
   b. −   h. −   m. 0
   c. −   i. +   n. +
   d. 0   j. 0   o. +
   e. 0   k. +   p. 0
   f. +
5. a. CPI = 150.0; GNP deflator = 140.0
   b. 50%; 40%

6. a. $4887 billion
    b. $4417 billion
    c. $4645 billion
    d. $3945 billion

Learning the Mechanics – Multiple Choice

1. c. Real GNP is what GNP is "really" worth, that is, adjusted for price changes. (pp. 140-41)
2. b. RealGNP90 = MoneyGNP90 x (GNPdeflator80/GNPdeflator90) = 2500 x 1/2. (p. 141)
3. c. Producers pay resource costs (incomes) which sum to GNP; see Exhibit 5, p. 140.
4. b. See the definition, p. 141.
5. a. If prices rise, moneyGNP90 must be adjusted downward; see answer 2 above. (p. 141)
6. c. The others represent current production of a final good. (pp. 131-33)
7. a. See Exhibit 5, p. 140.
8. d. Answer *a* is Net National Product (NNP); see the discussion, pp. 136-38.
9. c. NNP = Emp.Comp + Prop.Inc. + Rents + Corp.Prof + Interest + Ind.Bus.Tax&Tran. (p. 139)
10. c. See Exhibit 11, p.151; Personal Income = NNP – Ind.Bus.Tax&Tran. – Corp.Prof. + Soc.Sec.Contr. + Div. + Govt.Tran.Pay., NetInt.Paid&Bus.Tran.
11. b. Disposable Income = Personal Income – Personal Taxes. (p. 151)
12. d. GNP = NNP + Depreciation. (pp. 139 and 151)

The Economic Way of Thinking – Multiple Choice

1. b. "Cleaning up" represents currently produced final goods and/or services. (p. 148)
2. c. It is often difficult to obtain dollar prices for these transactions. (pp. 142-43)
3. d. Measurements of the "production of the economy" should not reflect price changes. (pp. 141-42)
4. b. This would involve double counting of intermediate production stages. (pp. 131-33)
5. b. See the definition, p. 141.
6. d. If real GNP had not changed, prices would have risen by 3 percent. (pp. 140-41)
7. c. GNP overstates net output since some of the capital stock depreciates. (p. 139)
8. b. See the definition, p. 141.
9. d. Real GNP is adjusted for price level changes but not for the other changes. (pp. 142-43 and 146-48)
10. a. See the definition, p. 149.
11. c. Nominal wage rose from $2.65 to 3.35; real wage fell from $1.46 to $0.98. (pp. 141-42)
12. b. Answer *a* gives national income; *c* overlooks net exports. (pp. 137 and 151)

CHAPTER 7

True or False

The following are true: 1, 3, 4, 6.

Problems and Projects

1. a. R
    b. R
    c. E
    d. E
    e. R
    f. E
2. (1) a; (2) a; (3) b; (4) a; (5) c; (6) b; (7) c.
4. For 1964: 5.1; 5.2; 59.4; 58.7
    For 1974: 5.5; 5.7; 61.7; 61.3
    For 1984: 7.4; 7.5; 64.7; 64.3

5. a) N; b) E; c) N; d) U; e) N.
6. a. $-$ (8.98/3.404 < 8.76/3.284)
    b. $-$ (9.4 $-$ 3.7 < 9.0 $-$ 1.9)
    c. 0 (21,134/3.404 = 20,380/3.284)
    d. $-$ [(21,134 $-$ 3,049)/3.404
        < (20,380 $-$ 2,438)/3.284]

Learning the Mechanics – Multiple Choice

1. d. See the definition, pp. 163-64.
2. d. See the definition, p. 159.
3. c. Allowance must be made for "normal" unemployment. (p. 168)
4. b. Inflation refers to a *process* of *general* rising prices. (p. 172)
5. a. This is the definition of the natural rate. (p. 168)
6. b. Inflation = i = [(CPI90 $-$ CPI89)/CPI89] x 100 = [15/150] x 100 = 10. (p. 172)
7. b. See the definition on p. 160 and Exhibit 3, p. 161.
8. c. Lenders would not have included price changes in terms of loan contracts. (p. 174)
9. b. Other answers do not result in an increase in the *general* price level. (p. 172)
10. c. Other answers refer to cyclical conditions; see the definition, p. 166.
11. c. See Exhibit 1 and the discussion, pp. 157-58.
12. b. See the definition and Exhibit 9, pp. 170-71.

The Economic Way of Thinking – Multiple Choice

1. a. This is an example of "search" unemployment; the other answers are incorrect. (pp. 163-64)
2. a. If only one of the two is unemployed there is still *some* family income. (pp. 161-63)
3. c. The principal cause of frictional unemployment is imperfect information. (pp. 163-64)
4. a. Idle plants and manpower allow increased output (supply) as demand grows. (pp. 158-59)
5. c. The Myopian lender and the Pessimismian borrower will both be worse off. (p. 174)
6. a. There are other economic goals, all of which must be balanced against noneconomic ones, such as environmental goals. (p. 157)
7. b. Public policy must often anticipate changes in economic conditions. (p. 166)
8. a. Lenders would not have included price changes in terms of loan contracts. (p. 174)
9. b. See the definition, p. 176; male deer weight gain is called stagobesity.
10. b. Money value of the loan would fall faster than interest accumulated. (pp. 174-75)
11. c. Economist think both caused an increase in the natural rate for the 1970's. (p. 168)
12. b. This is a part of frictional unemployment. (pp. 164 and 168)
13. b. As inflation rises, real value of the fixed mortgage payments will fall. (p. 174)
14. c. The numerator of the unemployment rate falls by a greater percentage than the denominator; employment rate is constant. (p. 159)

CHAPTER 8

True or False

The following are true: 1, 5, 6, 7, 9, 11, 12.

Problems and Projects

1. b. 1933
   c. 1969
   d. 1988
2. a. 5%; real interest rate = nominal interest rate − rate of inflation.
   b. In the short run, the real rate of interest will be negative.
   c. In the long run, when inflation is anticipated, the real interest rate will move back up to 5% (nominal interest rate = 11%).
3. a. 1.4%; 8.8%; 6.0%; 5.0%; rising and then falling
   b. between 1979 and 1982; increased willingness to loan
      betwen 1982 and 1985: increased willingness to borrow
      between 1985 and 1988: increased willingness to borrow
4. a. Real GNP = 300; P = 130
   b. 390
   d. A recession; output is below full employment level.
   e. 150; overestimated.
   f. High real wages depress profits and reduce output.
5. b. Surplus of labor; shortage of loanable funds; shortage of goods and services.

Learning the Mechanics – Multiple Choice

1. b. Choice *a* represents part of the aggregate demand curve, *c* represents part of the resource market, and *d*, the price variable in the aggregate goods and services market. (pp. 183-84)
2. c. A constant money supply and lower prices will increase the purchasing power of those holding money balances. (p. 186)
3. a. See the definition and the discussion on p. 197.
4. c. It represents an economy that is operating at its maximum sustainable rate of output. (p. 192)
5. c. Current output takes place where AD = SRAS. (pp. 190, 193)
6. d. The house is included in "goods and services." (p. 195)
7. a. See the discussion, p. 196.
8. d. Money interest rate (10) − infla. premium (6) = real interest rate (4). (p. 198)
9. c. The inflationary premium reflects the expected rate of inflation. (pp. 197-98)
10. d. People will buy now at the lower prices before their purchasing power declines. (p. 186)
11. d. The price of loanable funds is the interest rate. (pp. 184, 196-97)
12. a. The other three will decrease aggregate supply in the short run. (pp. 188-90)

The Economic Way of Thinking – Multiple Choice

1. a. This is the real balances effect. (p. 186)

2. b. A backward shift of aggregate demand will cause lower prices; choices *c* and *d* will shift aggregate demand forward. (pp. 185-87)
3. b. Producers will increase output only at a higher price level. (p. 188)
4. a. See the discussion, pp. 188-190.
5. d. The aggregate supply curve will become vertical. (pp. 189-90)
6. d. Producers will increase output; the increase may lead to above- or below-capacity output levels. (pp. 188-89)
7. c. See the discussion, pp. 200-01.
8. a. AD must equal AS for short and long run equilibrium, but also in the long run, the current level of prices must equal the expected price level. (pp. 190-92)
9. c. Resources are being underutilized. (pp. 200-01)
10. a. This is the definition of long-run equilibrium. (p. 192)
11. a. See the discussion, pp. 188-89.
12. a. Escalator clauses make resource prices adjust faster. (pp. 188-89)
13. a. In the long run, our capacity for real output is a function of our resource base and technological capabilities. (pp. 189-190)

CHAPTER 9

True or False

The following are true: 2, 4, 5, 8, 9, 10.

Problems and Projects

1. a. +, 0, 0, +, +
   b. 0, +, +, −, +
   c. −, 0, 0, −, −
   d. +, −, 0, +, ?
   e. 0, +, +, −, +
2. c. Resource prices adjusted slowly in the downward direction due to long-term contracts, uncertainty, and unwillingness of workers to accept lower nominal wages.
3. a. −, ?, ?
   b. −, −, +
   c. 0, 0, 0; without a strike, no change.
   d. −, −, +
   e. −, −, +
4. a. T
   b. T
   c. F (If individuals develop inflationary expectations, SRAS will shift.)
   d. F
   e. F
   f. T
   g. F
   h. F
5. a. −, −, +
      −, 0, 0,
   b. +, +, −
      +, 0, 0

Learning the Mechanics – Multiple Choice

1. c. See the Thumbnail Sketch on p. 208.
2. c. An increase in the LRAS means a *higher* rate of sustainable output. (p. 209)
3. d. People will wait to buy goods and services when prices are lower. (p. 207)
4. a. Increased labor increases the economy's short and long term production possibilities. (See the Thumbnail Sketch, p. 211)
5. a. U.S. goods will cost foreigners less, stimulating net exports. (p. 211)
6. b. The SRAS will shift to the right. (pp. 216-17)
7. c. The market will adjust wages and prices to either stimulate or slow the economy to where unemployment equals the natural rate. (pp. 219-21)
8. d. People will wait to make purchases, shifting AD back. (pp. 207, 215-16)
9. c. A favorable supply shock will shift SRAS to the right. (pp. 211, 216)
10. d. The aggregate demand curve shifts back. (pp. 215-16)
11. c. The SRAS curve shifts back. (pp. 217-18)
12. a. See the discussion, pp. 219-21.
13. a. See the discussion, pp. 216-17.
14. c. If we're producing beyond capacity, prices will go up. (p. 214)

The Economic Way of Thinking – Multiple Choice

1. c. This is a favorable supply shock. (p. 216)
2. b. People will save more, shifting AD back. (pp. 205-06)
3. a. Optimism stimulates current investment and goods and services purchases. (p. 206)
4. c. Increased productivity increases short- and long-term production possibilities. (p. 210)
5. b. A shortage of resources will cause costs and prices to rise, shifting SRAS back. (pp. 220-21)
6. b. People will use their savings to maintain their consumption level and decrease the supply of loanable funds. (p. 218)
7. d. All others change long-run aggregate supply incentives. (p. 211)
8. a. See the discussion, pp. 215-16.
9. d. A favorable supply shock – the SRAS shifts to the right. (pp. 211, 216)
10. c. In the short run, real GNP will decrease, prices will fall, and the unemployment rate will rise. (pp. 215-16)
11. a. Price changes will not shift aggregate demand. See Thumbnail sketches, pp. 208, 211.
12. b. The oil price increase is a resource price increase, shifting aggregate supply left. (pp. 217-18)
13. a. SRAS shifts up in the short run and back down in the long run. (pp. 210-11)

CHAPTER 10

True or False

The following are true: 3, 4, 5, 6, 9, 11, 13.

Problems and Projects

1. a. 2/3
    b. 1/1.5 = 2/3
    c. 1
    d. (4 − 1)/4 = 3/4
2. a. 3
    b. 3
    c. infinity
    d. 4
3. a. 1.2
    b. 120; from savings
    c. Round 1: 100   120
        Round 2: 120   144
        Round 3: 144   172.8
    d. No; income rises at an increasing rate instead of a decreasing rate
4. a. Round 2:   100   50
        Round 3:   50   25
        Round 4:   25   12.5
        Round 5:   12.5   6.25
        Subtotal: 387.5   193.75
        Grand total: 400   200

5. a. 600 + 3 (50) = $750 billion
    b. 800 − 4 (100) = $400 billion
    c. Y = 3/4 (Y − 300) + 100 + 300 = $700 billion
    d. Y = 200 ÷ 4/5 (Y − 500) + 150 + 600 = $2750 billion
6. a.
	Savit		Spendit	
Round 2:	12.5	6.25	22.5	20.25
Round 3:	6.25	3.13	20.25	18.23
Round 4:	3.13	1.56	18.23	16.40
Round 5:	1.56	0.78	15.40	14.76
All Others:	1.56	0.78	147.6	132.9
Total:	50.0	25.0	250.0	225.0

    b. Spendit
    c. 1/2; 9/10
7. a. Increase by $20 trillion

Learning the Mechanics – Multiple Choice

1. c. See the definition, p. 241.
2. b. Keynes rejected Say's Law. (pp. 229-30)
3. b. The multiplier effect of the investment increase raises incomes and, hence, sales. (pp. 241-42)
4. d. This is the basic Keynesian equilibrium condition. (p. 234)
5. c. See the definition, p. 234.
6. b. Remember (from Ch. 8) that the resource costs of production are also incomes. (p. 228)
7. a. The multiplier = $1/(1 − MPC) = 1/(1 − 3/4) = 4$. (p. 243)
8. b. The notion "supply creates its own demand" is Say's Law which Keynes attacked. (pp. 228-30)
9. b. The others do affect consumption, but this is the *primary* determinant. (p. 231)
10. c. It raises expected profits; others (including *b*) might *lower* investment. (pp. 232-33)
11. d. The higher the MPC, the more income there is to spend in the next round. (p. 243)
12. c. See the definition. p. 231.
13. b. Part of increased income is spent, the remainder is saved, i.e., MPC < 1. (pp. 231, 242)

The Economic Way of Thinking – Multiple Choice

1. c. MPC = additional consumption/additional income = 200/300. (p. 242)
2. c. This was one of Keynes' major challenges to classical thinking. (p. 229)

3. b. It may lead to increased borrowing or less saving currently. (p. 231)
4. b. This was one of Keynes' major objections to Say's Law. (pp. 228-29)
5. d. The quote is a description of the multiplier process. (pp. 241-42)
6. d. This is a major conclusion of Keynesian economics. (p. 230)
7. b. The multiplier applies: $(1/(1-0.75))$ ($12 mil.) = $48 million. (p. 243)
8. c. A greater MPC raises the multiplier, which equals $1/(1-MPC)$. (p. 243)
9. d. See the discussion, p. 228-31.
10. a. Multiplier is 5, so if autonomous spending rises by 80, real output will rise by 400. (p. 243)
11. c. See the discussion, p. 239-41.
12. b. Aggregate demand (900) > aggregate supply (800), hence supply (GNP) increases. (pp. 234-36)
13. c. The Keynesian model, not the AD/AS model, has been the center of macroeconomics for four decades. (p. 228)

CHAPTER 11

True or False

The following are true: 2, 4, 8, 9, 10, 11, 13, 14.

Problems and Projects

1. a. K
   b. C
   c. NC
   d. K
   e. C
   f. SS
   g. NC
   h. SS
2. a. AS
   b. AS
   c. both

   d. AD
   e. AS
   f. both
   g. AD
   h. both
4. a. 3
   b. 270; crowding out due to interest rate and price effects.
   c. 60; they save 1/3 of the tax cut.
   d. 180
   e. True

Learning the Mechanics — Multiple Choice

1. c. Government expenditure and taxation policy constitute fiscal policy. (p. 254)
2. a. Increase in government spending = $300 billion/multiplier(3) = $100 billion. (p. 243)
3. d. See the definition, p. 254.
4. d. See "Applications in Economics," p. 264.
5. b. A shortage of resources and labor cause higher prices and wages. (Ch. 10 and p. 256)
6. c. See the definition, p. 258.
7. b. Inflation implies that the price level continually increases. (p. 172)
8. a. The public will have to pay higher taxes later to pay for current government expenditures. (p. 260)
9. d. Investment expenditures are not automatic and actually add to the unstable, cyclical nature of the economy. (p. 266)

10. b. Countercyclical policy to ensure general economic conditions replaced the concept of the annual balanced budget. (p. 257)
11. b. See the definition, p. 258.
12. a. Taxpayers expect higher future taxes. (pp. 259-61)

The Economic Way of Thinking – Multiple Choice

1. b. This is a result of the multiplier effect. (Ch. 10)
2. c. This is the third part of the modern synthesis. (p. 273)
3. a. The multiplier effect increases aggregate demand even more. (pp. 242, 256)
4. b. Choices *a* and *d* will offset inflation, choice *c* combines expansionary and contractionary policy. (pp. 255-58)
5. d. Increased disposable income will increase consumption. (p. 231)
6. a. Refer to the introduction and first section of Chapter 10. (pp. 228-30)
7. a. The higher the marginal tax rates, the greater the benefits from tax-exempt income and tax-deductions. (p. 264)
8. b. This question is a bit controversial, but all answers except b are clearly wrong. (p. 271)
9. c. Fiscal policy lags can cause more problems than remedies. (pp. 264-66)
10. c. It calls for deficits during recessions and surpluses during "peaks." (p. 257)
11. b. See Thumbnail Sketch, p. 271.
12. c. See the discussion, pp. 272-73.
13. a. New classicists would expect a deficit to cause higher savings to allow inheritances to offset future tax liability. (p. 260)
14. a. Imperfect information and a "world of dynamic change" cause fiscal policy often to become a source of economic instability. (p. 273 and Exhibit 5, p. 265)

CHAPTER 12

True or False

The following are true: 3, 6, 8, 11.

Problems and Projects

1. a. 5
   b. 5
   c. 5
   d. 2.5
2. $575 billion
3. purchase $5 billion worth
4. a. — 0
   b. 0 +
   c. + +
   d. 0 0

5. a. Raise the money supply
    b. Round 1:   10,000   2,000   500   7,500
        Round 2:   7,500   1,500   375   5,625
        Round 3:   5,625   1,125   281   4,219
        Round 4:   4,219   844   211   3,164
        Subtotal: 27,344   5,469   1,367   20,508
        Total: 40,000   8,000   2,000   30,000
6. a. $20,000; $0
    b. Reserves: $40,000; Loans: $80,000; Demand Deposits: $120,000; The money supply
        increased by $20,000.
    c. Continental –
        Reserves: $20,000; Loans: $80,000; Demand Deposits: $100,000
        Acme –
        Reserves: $30,000; Loans: $40,000; Demand Deposits: $70,000
        The money supply remained the same.
    d. $0; $16,000
        Continental –
        Reserves: $36,000; Loans: $80,000; Demand Deposits: $116,000
        Acme –
        Reserves: $14,000; Loans: $56,000; Demand Deposits: $70,000
        The money supply increased by $16,000
    e. $20,000 x 1/.20 = $100,000

Learning the Mechanics – Multiple Choice

1. d. It lowers banks' cost of funds, raising expected profits on loans. (pp. 293-94)
2. d. The shift makes M2 a more stable predictor of spending, etc. (pp. 281-82)
3. c. Usually it will perform its three basic functions no matter how much circulates. (pp. 278-79)
4. c. Legislative bodies such as Congress levy taxes, not the Fed. (Exhibit 11, p. 295)
5. d. To pay for the bonds the public gives up $5 million in money (demand deposits). (p. 292)
6. b. The contraction multiplier = 1/.10 = 10; 10 x $5 mill. = $50 mil. (p. 286)
7. a. The Fed has substantial autonomy in carrying out this responsibility. (pp. 287-89)
8. c. Potential money deposit multiplier = 1/reserve ration = 1/.10 = 10. (p. 286)
9. a. Required reserves = reserve ration x demand deposits; 1000 = reserve ratio x 5000. (pp. 290-91)
10. c. See the definition, p. 278.
11. d. The meaning of expansionary monetary policy is that the rate of growth of the money supply is rapid. (p. 295)
12. b. They are the most flexible hence the most often used. (p. 292)
13. a. The act lifted many of the restrictions from the latter that distinguished them from commercial banks. (p. 300)
14. c. See the definition, p. 291.

The Economic Way of Thinking – Multiple Choice

1. b. Fiscal policy is *budget policy:* higher spending, lower taxes in this case. (Ch. 11 and pp. 296-97)

2. a. Choices *c* and *d* reduce the money supply; the Treasury is a budgetary agency. (Exhibit 11, p. 295)
3. c. Open market operations affect the *volume* of bank reserves, not reserve *ratio*. (pp. 291-92)
4. b. Early goldsmiths practiced fractional reserve banking. (pp. 283-84)
5. c. Public writes checks for securities; Fed collects from banks, lowering reserves. (p. 292)
6. b. Potential deposit multiplier = 1/reserve ration. (p. 286)
7. d. See the discussion, p. 300.
8. d. Each action here reduces the money supply. (Exhibit 11, p. 295)
9. a. Idle excess reserves do not enter the deposit expansion process. (p. 287)
10. d. This is *fiscal* policy. (Exhibit 11, p. 295, and p. 296)
11. c. Open market policy is the responsibility of the Open Market Committee. (p. 292)
12. d. Checking accounts become more attractive relative to *all* alternatives. (p. 281)
13. b. They now account for one-third of the money supply. (p. 281)
14. b. The money supply would only increase if the Fed purchased the government securities as part of its open market operations. (pp. 296-97)

CHAPTER 13

True or False

The following are true: 2, 3, 6, 7, 8, 10, 11, 12.

Problems and Projects

1. Unanticipated (Long run): aggregate demand remains at the higher level; real interest rates, aggregate output, and unemployment unchanged.
    Anticipated (Short run): aggregate demand increases; all else unchanged
    Anticipated (Long run): same as Unanticipated (Long run)
2. a. Nominal GNP: 4013, 4231, 4514, 4872, 5201, 5465
        Velocity: 6.5, 5.8, 6.0, 6.2, 6.5, 6.6
    b. No; higher interest rates raise the opportunity cost of holding money and therefore tend to raise velocity, and vice versa.
    c. Against; variable velocity breaks the direct link between money and nominal GNP.
    d. More stable; in general (but not always) dividing by a more stable number should create a more stable velocity calculation.
4. a. Higher real GNP and a higher price level.
    b. No
    c. Continued price level increases (sustained inflation).
6. b. Rise; transaction
    c. Fall
    d. Investment and interest-sensitive consumption.

Learning the Mechanics – Multiple Choice

1. b. See the discussion, pp. 307-308.
2. d. Both types of policy can affect unemployment, inflation and the volume of government bonds bought or sold. (p. 182)

3. b. The economy needs an expansionary policy. (pp. 312-15)
4. d. See Exhibit 3, p. 314.
5. a. The impact is not permanent. (pp. 314-15)
6. b. Decision-makers expect a slower growth rate of money and will react accordingly. (pp. 321-22)
7. a. See the definition, p. 310.
8. c. See the definition, p. 307 and Exhibit 1, p. 309.
9. d. See the discussion, pp. 312-14.
10. d. Inflation will be anticipated and money interest rates will rise, p. 321 and Thumbnail Sketch, p. 325.
11. c. It can affect both through two different channels. (Exhibit 2, p. 313, and Exhibit 3, p. 314)
12. c. Open market operations are one of the ways to increase the money supply. (pp. 289-95)
13. d. M1 increased and M2 stayed the same; velocity decreased. (pp. 281-82 and equation, p. 310)

The Economic Way of Thinking – Multiple Choice

1. b. Excess money supply causes lower interest rates and increased spending. (Exhibit 2, p. 313, and p. 314)
2. d. The government spending is expansionary; restrictive tax and monetary policies will offset it. (See Thumbnail Sketch, p. 325)
3. a. See the discussion, pp. 309-310.
4. c. Nominal interest rates and wages could adjust so real interest rates and income remain unchanged. (pp. 311-12)
5. c. This is the primary belief of monetarists. (pp. 311-12)
6. b. Higher interest rates will affect interest-sensitive sectors more than others. (pp. 315-17)
7. d. See the discussion, pp. 330-32.
8. d. Below the full employment output, producers will increase output, not prices, until convinced increased demand is permanent. (pp. 314-15)
9. a. Choices *b*, *c* and *d* list the ways the Fed can implement expansionary policy. (Ch. 12 and p. 308)
10. b. Higher income will raise the transactions demand for money. (pp. 307-308)
11. d. Government spending recirculates the money received from security sales. (pp. 296-97)
12. b. See the Thumbnail Sketch, p. 325.
13. c. Real interest rate (4) + inflationary premium (6) = nominal interest rate (10). (pp. 197-98 and p. 321)
14. b. Each action is restrictive. (Ch. 11 and Exhibit 11, p. 295)
15. d. The shift of importance from M1 to M2 made monetary policy during this period hard to track accurately. (p. 281)

CHAPTER 14

True or False

The following are true: 3, 4, 5, 13.

Problems and Projects

2. a. 10%
    b. 3%
    c. 9%
    d. unhappy
3. a. Point B corresponds to 3% unemployment and 5% inflation.
    b. Point C corresponds to 6% unemployment and 5% inflation.
4. a. Point B corresponds to 6% unemployment and 10% inflation.
    b. no
5. a. $1.00
        1.46
        .98
    b. 0, −, 0, +, −
6. b. 3%   0
        3   −1
        2   +2
        8   0
        8   −1
        7   +2
    c. No; yes
    d. 5%
    e. Adaptive

Learning the Mechanics – Multiple Choice

1. a. Adjustments for anticipated inflation result in higher prices and no change in umemployment. (pp. 349-51)
2. b. Reduced aggregate demand initially lowers production and employment. (Ch. 11, Ch. 13, and p. 349)
3. c. Decision-makers began to expect higher rates of inflation. (pp. 350-51)
4. a. Older workers are more stable (less likely to change jobs). (pp. 357-58)
5. b. Temporarily higher anticipated profits will stimulate the economy. (Exhibit 7, p. 350)
6. c. See the discussion, pp. 339-40.
7. b. The macroacceleration will catch decision-makers by surprise. (pp. 338-39 and 346)
8. c. Monetary acceleration may be unanticipated in the short term, but in the long term (if it is persistent) it will be expected. (pp. 338-40)
9. c. See the discussion, pp. 338-39.
10. b. The result will be the same as an unanticipated expansionary policy. (p. 349)
11. a. Prices will adjust to a higher level without an increase in output. (pp. 345-48)
12. c. Workers wages will lag behind prices. (p. 349)

The Economic Way of Thinking – Multiple Choice

1. c. An expansionary fiscal and/or monetary policy is wanted. (pp. 342-44 and p. 347)
2. c. See the discussion, pp. 349-50; the Phillips curve shifts out.
3. a. On the new Phillips curve, a lower rate of inflation initially means higher unemployment than before. (Exhibit 5, p. 346)
4. a. Expected inflation will exceed actual inflation. (p. 349 and Exhibit 7, p. 350)
5. c. See the definition, p. 340.

6. c. Choices *a* and *b* increase unemployment; *d* increases inflation.
7. b. If wages can fall, unemployment can be avoided. (p. 352)
8. b. The opportunity cost of job search is less. (p. 355)
9. b. The rate of return on saving would rise.
10. c. Younger people and retirees are more likely to dissave.
11. b. The cost of hiring youthful workers is reduced. (pp. 356-57)
12. a. Expectations help us understand the past but make prediction difficult. (pp. 353-55)
13. a. People will anticipate inflation more quickly than policymakers will expect, and AD will shift right, causing more inflation. (p. 349)

CHAPTER 15

True or False

The following are true: 1, 2, 3, 5, 7, 9, 10, 11.

Problems and Projects

1. a. Trash pickup plan
    b. More government buildings, Big dam, Acid rain remover, Trash pickup plan
    c. Lightly used highway and more government buildings (the programs with the highest District's %).
2. a. Expansionary fiscal policy; activist
    b. Expansionary fiscal and monetary policy; activist
    c. Expansionary fiscal policy; nonactivist
    d. Expansionary monetary policy; activist
    e. Expansionary monetary policy; nonactivist
4. a. +
    b. +
    c. 0
    d. −
    e. −

Learning the Mechanics – Multiple Choice

1. c. See the definition, p. 364.
2. a. See the definition, p. 366.
3. d. All three are discretionary expansionary policy actions. (p. 365)
4. d. Nonactivists emphasize that discretionary actions do more harm than good. (p. 366)
5. b. See the discussion, pp. 368-69.
6. b. It takes time for macropolicy to work, so policy-makers must anticipate economic changes. (p. 367)
7. b. See the discussion, pp. 373-74.
8. b. This is the rational expectations view. (p. 377)
9. c. He proposed the most widely advocated nonactivist monetary policy, the constant money growth rule. (p. 378)
10. d. The nonactivists only have a "general strategy," not a practical, workable policy solution. (p. 382)
11. b. This is the policy ineffectiveness theorem. (p. 366)

12. c. Lags, political objectives, and the policy ineffectiveness theorem are problems with discretionary action. (p. 366)

The Economic Way of Thinking – Multiple Choice

1. a. This is an essentially Keynesian policy, but the monetarists would agree on the impact. (pp. 364-66)
2. c. See the discussion, pp. 364-66.
3. c. Choices *a* and *b* are restrictive activist stabilization policies. (p. 365)
4. c. This means the Fed conducts an open market purchase. (Ch. 12 and p. 365)
5. c. A primary argument for nonactivist policies is uncertainty about the future. (p. 374)
6. b. This is the policy ineffectiveness theorem. (p. 377)
7. a. Nonactivists' fiscal goal of a balanced budget requires actions inconsistent with their pursuit of stable policies. (pp. 381-82)
8. a. These tools serves as an early warning system, allowing time for the lags before the impact of the policy change needs to be felt. (pp. 372-73)
9. c. Time lags and political versus stabilization objectives are two of the problems nonactivists find with activists' policies. (pp. 374-377)
10. a. See the discussion, p. 367.
11. a. See the discussion, pp. 372-74.
12. c. Monetary rule does not allow any discretionary actions for severe changes in the economy. (pp. 378-80)
13. c. Recognition lag is probably the same for both but administrative and impact lags differ. (pp. 373-74)

CHAPTER 16

True or False

The following are true: 2, 4, 6, 7, 8.

Problems and Projects

1.

500	600
3.3%	3.0%
166.7	193.5
500	500
166.7	161.3

The real per capita deficit fell; the press will report an increase in the budget deficit.

2. a. 1989: 3.0%, 56.25%
        1990; 150, 2850, 5136, 2.9%. 55.5%
    b. The deficit rose more slowly than GNP.

3.

3%	13%
30	130
30	30
0	100
1,000	1,100
0	100

1,000	1,000
0	0
2,100	2,100
2,100	2,310
0	4.3%
47.6%	47.6%

4.   Case I; both appear the same; Nominal debt/nominal GNP: it is not distorted by inflation because inflation has offsetting effects on both the numerator and denominator.

Learning the Mechanics – Multiple Choice

1. b.   The debt is a running total of periodic deficits. (p. 388)
2. a.   See the definition, p. 389.
3. d.   See Exhibit 3 on p. 390.
4. a.   Government-held debt is omitted from net debt because the interest payments on it are offset by interest receipts. (p. 390)
5. d.   Much debt is in the form of real estate and stocks; loans are generally at fixed rates and always denominated in dollars. (pp. 395-96)
6. b.   Policies of the Reagan administration helped this shift. (p. 388)
7. d.   Inflation gets built into nominal interest rates and reduces the purchasing power of dollar-denominated values. (pp. 399-401)
8. c.   See Exhibit 3, p. 390, and Exhibit 6, p. 397.
9. a.   As long as the government can raise huge tax revenues, lenders can be sure money, plus interest, will be repaid when due. (pp. 396-97)
10. b.   See the discussion, p. 392.

The Economic Way of Thinking – Multiple Choice

1. c.   Future taxes are offset by future receipts; opportunity costs cannot be shifted, but inefficiency can result. (p. 391)
2. a.   Wealth effect raises consumption; higher interest rates reduce investment and appreciate the dollar. (p. 392)
3. a.   This would be the traditional view of the reverse scenario of the early 1980's. (pp. 393-95)
4. c.   This is expansionary fiscal *and* monetary policy. (pp. 291-92 and 388)
5. d.   The real value of bonds falls with inflation, but prices of physical assets tend to keep pace.
6. d.   When capital investments grow rapidly expenditures exceed depreciation, so deficits are overstated; vice versa if capital investments grow slowly. (pp. 398-99)
7. b.   Excess of receipts over interest payments reduces deficit except in the year of actual expenditure. (p. 254)
8. d.   Public choice economists feel that some constitutional constraint is necessary. (pp. 405-406)
9. a.   Countercyclical policies make deficits larger during recessions and surpluses smaller during booms. (Ch. 11 and pp. 406-407)
10. c.   Spending during recession can put otherwise idle resources to work. (p. 391)
11. d.   This is expansionary fiscal *and* monetary policy. (pp. 291-92 and 388)

Macrocross

```
C P I           M         R E S E R V E S
    M U L T I P L I E R           E     P
    I               N         R E A L   O   E
G N P     L I Q U I D I T Y             O   C
    F           U   M           A P C       U
    L           N A T U R A L           I   L
M A R K E T     N       M         B     T   A
T               T       W     M O N E Y     T
I         N O M I N A L       N             I
O               T       G     F D I C       V
U N E M P L O Y M E N T       E             E
        P                 D E M A N D
C I R C U L A R F L O W
```

CHAPTER 17

True or False

The following are true: 1, 3, 4, 8, 9, 12, 14, 15.

Problems and Projects

1. Gasoline and air travel are substitutes; gasoline and auto tires and gasoline and Yellowstone tourism are complements.
2. a. 1500, 1400, 1650; elastic, inelastic
   b. Price elasticity between \$1 and \$2 = (800/1100)/(1/1.5) = (−) 1.09
      Price elasticity between \$2 and \$3 = (150/625)/(1/2.5) = (−) 0.60
3. a.
Food:	30,	25,	20,	15,	10,	5
Clothing:	10,	7,	5,	4,	2,	1
Housing:	35,	30,	20,	15,	10,	8
   b. 3/2; 1; 35/30; food
   c. 3 food, 1 clothing, 2 housing
   d. 2 units of food are purchased when P = \$30; 4 units of food are purchased when P = \$15.
   e. Food consumption would increase from 3 to 5 units, clothing would increase from 1 to 3 units, and housing from 2 to 4 units.
4. a. 4 cups
   b. \$1.75 + 0.75 + 0.25 = \$2.75
   c. \$2.75 + (−0.15) + (−0.20) + (−0.25) = \$2.15; it is less.
   d. 5 cups; \$3.35; \$3.20, it is less
5. down; up; none; up; 1.0; up

6. a. b. c. d.

a	b	c	d
D	S	S	D
+	+	+	+
+	−	−	+
+	+	+	+
D	S	S	S
+	+	+	+
+	−	−	−
+	−	−	−
D	S	D	D
−	+	+	+
−	−	+	+
−	0	+	+
D	D	D	D
−	−	+	+
−	−	+	+
−	−	+	+

7. a.

Q_d	TE	Elasticity
27	486	
36	540	1.57
45	540	1.00
54	486	0.64

  b. Falls
  c. inelastic; elastic; unit elastic
  d. $P = 12$; $Q = 45$

Learning the Mechanics – Multiple Choice

1. b. Demand is *elastic* (elasticity $= 30\%/15\%\% = 2$); when P rises, spending falls. (pp. 425 and 429-30)

2. c. This causes a *movement along* the demand curve for green peas. (Thumbnail Sketch, p. 422)

3. c. This reflects the basic postulate of economizing behavior. (pp. 53-55 and 413-14)

4. b. See the definition, p. 418.

5. d. When income rises, purchases fall (negative change); see the definition, p. 431.

6. a. Consumers substitute oranges for grapefruit at any given price of oranges. (pp. 420-21)

7. d. "Demand" refers to the entire demand curve which shifts to the right. (pp. 62-64 and Thumbnail Sketch, p. 422)

8. a. For inferior goods, changes in income and demand are inversely related. (pp. 430-31)

9. c. Each alternative answer suggests a change in the *quantity* of milk *demanded*. (p. 413 and Thumbnail Sketch, p. 414)

10. d. The large quantity of rock music caused a low *marginal* utility. (p. 414)

11. c. If beef is normal; also, other answers suggest a decrease in demand for beef. (pp. 420-21)

12. a. A change in price of pork chops results in a movement along the demand curve. (pp. 420-21 and Thumbnail Sketch, p. 422)

13. d. Demand is inelastic (elasticity $= 10\%/50\% = .2$); when P rises, spending rises. (pp. 425 and 429-30)

The Economic Way of Thinking – Multiple Choice

1. d. The new information shifted (decreased) the demand for cigarettes. (p. 421)
2. c. A decrease in quantity sold is expected to raise both price and spending. (pp. 429-30)
3. c. Equilibrium is at Q = 30, so price = G. (p. 418-19)
4. c. Surplus will almost surely increase, but not because ACG is greater than TKF. (pp. 418-19)
5. d. Choices *a* and *b* increase demand; *c* decreases *quantity demanded*. (pp. 420-22)
6. c. "Snob" goods do not conform to the usual law of demand. (p. 423)
7. c. Reduced quantity and spending with an increased price implies elastic demand. (pp. 429-30)
8. c. Elastic implies that lower price increases revenues; costs are constant. (pp. 429-30)
9. c. Color set demand will decrease; elasticity of demand for b&w sets is unknown (pp. 420-21 and 429-30)
10. a. Both (I) and (II) are basic assumptions of consumer choice theory. (pp. 413-14)
11. a. See Exhibit 7, p. 427.
12. d. The owners expect an increase in price to lower quantity but raise revenues. (pp. 429-30)
13. b. Revenue moved in the same direction as price (both rose) (pp. 429-30)
14. c. If quantity demanded rises, consumer surplus will rise by more than $2.00; change in spending depends on the price elasticity of demand. (pp. 418-19 and 429-30)

CHAPTER 18

True or False

The following are true: 1, 2, 3, 4, 5, 7, 8, 9, 10, 12.

Problems and Projects

1. a. $9,000
   b. Owner's labor services and interest income forgone on Joe's equity capital.
   c. $48,000 + 0.10 (30,000) + 10,000 = $61,000
   d. $4,000 loss
2. a. TVC: 50, 90, 127, 166, 215, 274, 349, 446
   ATC: 100, 70, 59, 54, 53, 54, 57, 62
   AVC: 50, 45, 42.3, 41.5, 43, 45.7, 49.9, 55.75
   MC: 100, 40, 37, 39, 49, 59, 75, 97
   b. 5
   c. beyond 3
3. a. Auto A = 32 cents per mile; Auto B = 31 cents per mile; Auto B is cheaper.
   b. Auto A = 25 cents per mile; Auto B = 25.5 cents per mile; Auto A is cheaper.
   c. They decline primarily because average fixed cost is falling as the miles driven increases from 10,000 to 20,000.
4. a. Marginal product: 20, 15, 10, 5
   Marginal cost: 2.50, 3.33, 5.00, 10.00
   Total cost: 250, 300, 350, 400, 450
   b. yes

5.   360   210 150   60
      600   450 150   100

6.   a.   0; 0; −
      b.   Economies of scale; ATC falls as Q rises.
      c. $70,000; yes, since extra revenue exceeds extra cost.

Learning the Mechanics – Multiple Choice

1.   c.   See pp. 455-57.
2.   d.   Use of variable inputs expands relative to fixed inputs so productivity falls. (pp. 457-59)
3.   a.   It involves no actual money payments; it is income sacrificed. (p. 451)
4.   c.   Demand informs firms; resources are scarce because they have alternative uses. (pp. 450-51)
5.   c.   Usually the case since labor is normally variable in the short run. (p. 455)
6.   b.   See the definition, p. 468.
7.   b.   One of the major reasons for the popularity of this legal structure. (p. 448)
8.   c.   As output rises, average fixed cost declines. (Exhibit 6, p. 461)
9.   a.   A shift in demand will not cause the cost curves to shift. (p. 467)
10. d.   When MC > ATC, ATC must rise and vice-versa; see p. 459 and Exhibit 6, p. 461.
11. d.   Implicit costs are included in economic, but not in accounting, profits. (pp. 451-54)
12. a.   Carefully study the definition, p. 457.
13. a.   AFC = ATC − AVC, or 12 minus 8 = 4. (p. 456)
14. d.   Total fixed costs remain constant. (p. 455)
15. a.   Marginal cost (returns) rises from Q = 6 on. (p. 459)

The Economic Way of Thinking – Multiple Choice

1.   a.   Answer *d* would mean higher price; answers *b* and *c* are nonsense. (pp. 466-67)
2.   d.   Usually plant is fixed in the short run; the other inputs are variable. (pp. 455 and 461)
3.   d.   Relaxing these physical constraints offsets short-run diminishing returns. (Ch. 19, p. 491)
4.   a.   Efficient (ideal) plant size is an output where long-run unit cost is minimized. (pp. 464-66)
5.   d.   The car will last more than one year; implicit interest is an opportunity cost. (pp. 451 and 454)
6.   b.   The $300 mortgage payment is a sunk cost; local service charges are avoidable. (pp. 468-69)
7.   c.   All marginal concepts relate to *changes* such as additions. (p. 458)
8.   c.   Sacrificed rental value is an implicit cost included in economic profit. (pp. 451 and 454)
9.   c.   Both product spoilage and change in market conditions are valid reasons. (p. 469)
10. c.   Increased output would significantly reduce *average* fixed cost and ATC. (pp. 455-57)
11. d.   Higher demand for orange-growing inputs raises their prices and hence, the price of grapefruit. (p. 467)
12. c.   Harvester productivity is raised, lowering harvester cost per unit produced. (p. 467)
13. b.   Including normal return on investment as a cost unambiguously reduces economic profits. (pp. 451 and 454)
14. c.   At any Q, area under MC equals TVC, as does Q x AVC. (p. 456)

CHAPTER 19

True or False

The following are true: 1, 3, 4, 5, 6, 9, 10, 11.

Problems and Projects

1. a. ATC and AVC: 25, 25, 23, 21, 20, 19.8, 20, 21
        MC: 25, 25, 19, 15, 16, 19, 21, 28
    b. 6; $1 per month
    c. 7; $35 per month
2. a. FC: 40000
        VC: 0, 20000, 40000, 60000, 80000, 102000, 128000, 158000, 192000, 230000, 275000
        ATC: −, 60000, 40000, 33333, 30000, 28400, 28000, 28286, 29000, 30000, 31500
        AFC: −, 40000, 20000, 13333, 10000, 8000, 6667, 5714,5000, 4444, 4000
        AVC: −, 20000, 20000, 20000, 20000, 20400, 21333, 22571, 24000, 25556, 27500
        MC: −, 20000, 20000, 20000, 20000, 22000, 26000, 30000, 34000, 38000, 45000
    b. 6; $9,000 per month
    c. 7; $26,000 per month
    d. 5; $17,000 per month loss; 4; $36,000 per month loss; yes, in the short run, but not in the long run.
3. a. Q_s: 400, 500, 600, 700, 800, 900, 1000
        Price: 20000, 22000, 26000, 30000, 34000, 38000, 45000
    b. $29,000
    c. Each firm is making profits of $6,000 per month; yes.
    d. It will fall as new profit-seeking firms enter the market.
4. a. 1000; 8000; 8; 0
    b. yes
    c. no change
    d. go out of business – but the firm's expectation that market conditions will remain the same is probably incorrect because the market price will rise as some of the firms in the industry go out of business.
5. c. yes; no
6. a. 80
    b. 20
    c. 60
    d. 70
7. a. 30 +; 20 −; 25 0; 0 −
    b. Average profits over all 4 seasons must be non-negative.

Learning the Mechanics – Multiple Choice

1. c. All of the firm's inputs are variable in the long run, hence all costs are, too. (pp. 461 and 491)
2. d. They will seek better profit opportunities in alternative industries. (pp. 487-88)
3. b. If P > ATC, firms earn economic (excess) profits which attract new entrants. (pp. 486-87)

4. a. *b* should read "average *total* cost"; *c* "total *variable* cost"; *d*, "average *variable* cost." (pp. 478, 481-84, and 485)
5. c. Costs (hence prices) would be lower; other answers raise demand (hence price). (pp. 420-21, 467)
6. d. Firms exit alternative industries where profit opportunities are less attractive. (pp. 485-87)
7. b. Entry and expansion require that all resources be variable (the long run). (pp. 491-92)
8. c. The *market* refers to the aggregate supply decisions of all suppliers. (p. 484)
9. c. See the discussion, pp. 477-78.
10. c. AFC = (Fixed Cost/Output) must decline as output rises. (p. 492)
11. b. Some inputs are fixed, hence output responds less to changes in price. (p. 491)
12. d. See "Applications in Economics," pp. 482-83.
13. c. At P = OF, ATC is at a minimum. (pp. 494-95)
14. d. The firm will make a profit until supply shifts out, lowering the equilibrium price to OF. (pp. 485-86)

The Economic Way of Thinking — Multiple Choice

1. d. During long-run adjustment some firms would exit and price would rise. (pp. 484-85)
2. a. Price nearly tripled suggesting increased demand and inelastic supply. (pp. 486-87 and 491-92)
3. d. The cost of the inputs, grains, rose for each of these outputs. (p. 467)
4. a. Price will initially exceed ATC causing entry and expansion in the wheat market. (p. 484)
5. c. Both supply and demand would increase (curves shift to the right). (p. 66)
6. b. Firms want more than zero profits, but free entry prevents this outcome. (pp. 477 and 485)
7. b. Short-run supply is less elastic than long-run supply. (pp. 491-92)
8. d. Peak-period quantity demanded would be reduced.
9. b. At prices below average variable cost, the firm would shut down. (p. 484)
10. a. The producer should sell out since she expects only losses in the long run. (pp. 481-84)
11. c. Knowing "how to do well" (maximizing profit) implies the ability to compete. (pp. 479-80)
12. b. One more unit would *add* more to cost (MC) than it would to revenue (MR). (pp. 478-79)
13. b. From Q_0 to Q_1, MR exceeds MC, so profits rise. (p. 478)
14. d. Profits equal zero at A and C and exceed zero at B. (pp. 488-90)
15. b. Most firms can react in the long run but not in the short run. (p. 489)

CHAPTER 20

True or False

The following are true: 1, 2, 5, 7, 9, 10, 11, 12, 14.

Problems and Projects

1. a. TR: 60, 110, 150, 180, 200, 210
      MR: 60, 50, 40, 30, 20, 10
      TC: 90, 110, 136, 166, 206, 256
   b. reduce the price to $45
   c. $14
2. a. Since the LRATC curve decreases over the range of quantities which are demanded, a single firm would be the lowest-cost producer.
   e. Probably not; new competitors would have very high production costs if they started out small and would be unable to make high profits (if any).
3. a. TR: 6400, 7000, 7800, 8400, 8800, 9000, 9000
      MR: −, 600, 800, 600, 400, 200, 0
      MC: −, 400, 400, 500, 700, 1000, 1200
   b. $1.20
   c. yes; $1,100 per month
   d. $1.00
   e. Approximately $13,200 or the present value of the expected economic profit; the university would then reap the monopoly benefits.
4. a. P_4
   b. P_2
   c. P_3; profit
5. a. 1
   b. 1
   c. 2
   d. 2
6. a. 8   4   32   32   0   32   0
   b. 4   ·8   32   16   16   8   8
   c. 6   6   36   24   12   18   2
7. a. c. (table):

1.10	1.10	1.00	1.00
2.00	.90	1.90	.90
2.70	.70	2.70	.80
3.20	.50	3.40	.70
3.50	.30	4.00	.60
3.60	.10	4.50	.50
3.50	−.10	5.00	.50
3.20	−.30	5.50	.50

   b. P = $.80; Q = 4; Profit = $1.20
   d. Q = 7 (or 6); Profit = $1.50
   e. Yes; profits are higher.

Learning the Mechanics – Multiple Choice

1. a. See the definition, p. 500.
2. a. Usually in monopoly P > MC, leading to allocative inefficiency. (pp. 508-509)
3. a. The profit-maximizing behavior is restriction of output to raise price. (Exhibit 6, p. 508 and pp. 508-509)
4. a. MR should = MC for maximum profit, which may not occur if (II) is achieved (pp. 503-506)

5. b. Each firm would operate at an inefficient small level of output. (pp. 514-15)
6. d. Output should always be raised if MR > MC and lowered if MR < MC. (pp. 503-506)
7. d. This may be a *result* of monopoly, but it is not a source of monopoly. (pp. 501-502)
8. d. A competitive firm produces an output at which P = MC. (pp. 504-505)
9. b. A monopolized firm produces an output at which P > MC. (pp. 508-509)
10. d. Each serves to restrain price increases by the monopolist. (p. 521)
11. a. These barriers are probably as old as government itself. (p. 501)
12. c. Product development may depend on statically inefficient monopoly profits. (pp. 501-502 and 522-23)

The Economic Way of Thinking — Multiple Choice

1. d. This is a potential outcome of the special interest effect. (p. 519)
2. a. Total revenue will rise and total cost will fall. (pp. 502-504)
3. a. The profit-maximizing behavior is to raise profits at the expense of consumers. (pp. 508-509)
4. a. For inelastic demand, higher prices reduce sales, raise total revenues, and lower total costs. (p. 503 and Exhibit 2, p. 504)
5. d. See the discussion, pp. 516-19.
6. c. The benefits of efficiency are widely dispersed over the consumers of the product. (pp. 517-18)
7. c. The others compete with producers of several (if not many) close substitutes. (pp. 500-501)
8. c. Firm will set MR = MC to maximize profit; you want MR = 0 to maximize total revenue. (pp. 503-505)
9. d. DuPont's control over price depends on how closely other wraps can be substituted (pp. 500, 521, and 524)
10. c. ATC is somewhere between $6 and $0. (pp. 503-505)
11. d. The monopolist will produce at MC = MR. (pp. 503-504)
12. b. At Q = 48, MC will shift from $6 to $8, but MR = MC at less than $8 but more than $6. (pp. 467, 503-504)
13. b. MR = MC at P = $8. (pp. 503 and 516)
14. c. At P = $9, MC intersects the demand curve. (p. 508)

CHAPTER 21

True or False

The following are true: 1, 2, 5, 6, 7, 10, 12.

Problems and Projects

1. a. TR (market: 750,000; 1,000,000; 1,350,000; 1,600,000 2,400,000; 3,000,000; 3,200,000; 3,500,000; 3,600,000; 3,500,000; 3,200,000
        TR (firm): 187,500; 250,000; 337,500; 400,000; 600,000; 750,000; 800,000; 875,000; 900,000; 875,000; 800,000
    b. $150; 24,000; 6,000
    c. $400; $300; $250

    d. $250

    e. A certain amount of collusion is likely since there are only four firms with equal cost conditions and equal output.

2. a. His plan will work if demand for the firm's tricycles is elastic and if other firms don't follow his move.

    b. By 5000 units to a total of 25,000 tricycles.
[TR − TC = profits → \$9 (Q) − (120,000 + \$4 (Q)) = 5000 → Q = 25,000]

    c. Price elasticity = [(5000/22500)/(1/9.5)] = 2.11

3. a. Demand when industry price varies:
        TR: 270, 280, 250, 180, 70, 0, 0
        MR: 50, 10, −30, −70, −110, −70, 0
      Demand when only SC's price varies:
        TR: 240, 280, 300, 300, 280, 240, 180, 100
        MR: 60, 40, 20, 0, −20, −40, −60, −80

    b. $70; $240

    c. 5; $60; $250; profit has increased

    d. no

4. no; after-tax profits as a percentage of corporate sales or stockholder equity

5. a. 51

    b. Loose oligopoly; 12.5 percent

6. a. −

    b. +

    c. +

    d. +

    e. −; If the firms were colluding, they would raise prices to increase total revenue.

    f. +; Entry induced by above normal profit increases supply and lowers prices.

Learning the Mechanics — Multiple Choice

1. a. Entry increases competition which drives down market price and eliminates profits. (pp. 542-543)

2. c. Better products at the same price from competitors limits price increases. (p. 542)

3. a. P > MC due to product differentiation; P = AC due to low entry barriers. (pp. 532-34)

4. d. Stable, fairly certain information makes agreement easier to reach and enforce. (pp. 538-39 and 541-44)

5. a. Oligopolies control competition to some extent, but less than monopolists can. (pp. 539-41)

6. c. Both a and b are false. (p. 532)

7. c. See Exhibit 8, p. 545

8. b. Firms would pay Amy premium wages up to the value of her extra efficiency. (p. 535)

9. a. The more producers, the more difficult it is to collude. (p. 542)

10. b. The ratio gives us an indication of industry structure but not firm behavior. (pp. 544-45)

11. c. Long-run normal profits are a result of low entry barriers. (pp. 532-33)

12. c. Since entry barriers are low, economic profits will attract new entrants. (p. 533)

13. a. Evidence shows no strong relation between concentration and profit. (p. 547)

14. c. If there are hundreds of small competitors, at least 60%; if only 1-4, 100%. (Ch. 21, p. 544)

The Economic Way of Thinking – Multiple Choice

1. d. A better product at the same price is equivalent to a price cut (competition). (p. 542)
2. b. Reduction in supply as some firms exit raises price and restores normal profits. (p. 533)
3. d. Buyers are willing to pay a premium for such stocks; the "early bird . . ." (pp. 547-49)
4. a. This is a basic similarity between pure and monopolistic competition. (p. 535)
5. a. Since profits are higher, it would pay more to protect them.
6. c. This would limit entry allowing higher prices and some economic profits. (pp. 542-43)
7. d. The innovative spirit might be dulled but certainly not eliminated. (p. 542)
8. c. Return to zero-profit equilibrium causes price to rise as much as costs. (pp. 532-34)
9. d. Successful collusion + little entry = successful price control. (pp. 541-43)
10. b. Price competition might be used in an attempt to restore sales. (p. 542)
11. c. Competition equates long-run profits to zero in both cities. (p. 533)
12. d. The license fee is a sunk cost. (Ch. 18, p. 468)
13. d. This also helps to explain the success of McDonald's. (pp. 530-31)

CHAPTER 22

True or False

The following are true: 1, 3, 8, 11.

Problems and Projects

1. a.

Q	AFC	ATC
50	.20	.26
60	.17	.23
70	.14	.20

  b. At each output level, there is a $10 million loss (the total fixed cost), after rounding.
  c. At each output level, there is no profit and no loss; total revenue = total cost
  d. See the discussion of the regulation of natural monopoly, pp. 505-508.
2. (Second item listed is the actual winner of the given case):
  a. Sherman Section 2; United States
  b. Clayton Section 7; United States
  c. Sherman Section 1; Major League Baseball
  d. Sherman Section 2; United States
  e. Clayton Section 3; United States
3. a. + +
      − +
  b. yes; no

Learning the Mechanics – Multiple Choice

1. c. Price below competitor or below ATC can make economic sense, but price below MC does not. (p. 559)

2. c. See the definition, p. 571.
3. d. Such tax improvements do not enhance economic productivity. (p. 566)
4. c. See Exhibit 3, p. 557.
5. d. See the Thumbnail Sketch, p. 561.
6. d. Each of the others inhibits competition by raising the cost of entry. (Thumbnail Sketch, p. 561 and pp. 571-72)
7. c. (I) political machines work slowly; (II) a result of special interest effects. (pp. 568-70)
8. c. Apparently the income elasticity of demand for these services is high. (p. 554)
9. c. This tends to promote rather than restrict competition. (p. 561)
10. a. See the definition. (p. 562)
11. b. Rivalry to promote divisional interests; cooperation to promote GM's interest. (pp. 556-57)
12. c. Social regulations can be seen as taxes on productive activity; see Exhibit 5. (pp. 574-75)

The Economic Way of Thinking – Multiple Choice

1. a. As it is a license to earn excess profits, it is worth some effort to acquire. (pp. 568-69)
2. a. Cost minimization is an aspect of profit maximization (pp. 564-65)
3. b. Efficiency requires reliance on lowest (opportunity) cost sources of output.
4. b. Other proposals promote entry which tends to defeat the aim of the proposal. (p. 569)
5. c. The political mechanism does not always yield consistent public policies. (pp. 571-74)
6. d. It is tough to stay on top in a competitive struggle; see discussion. (p. 558)
7. d. Government and service sectors have been growing more rapidly than manufacturing. (p. 554)
8. b. This increases the number of relevant competitors for the industry in question. (Ch. 21, pp. 533-35)
9. b. Such regulation has much the same impact as a production tax; see Exhibit 5. (p. 575)
10. b. Income fell from $40,000 to $28,000. (pp. 574-75)
11. c. 80 births at $100 each. (pp. 574-75)
12. b. Drawing a diagram will help get the answer. (p. 112)
13. d. The analysis in #11 omitted the 20 births now handled by doctors. (pp. 568-69)

CHAPTER 23

True or False

The following are true: 1, 2, 3, 5, 8, 9, 10, 11, 13, 14.

Problems and Projects

1. a. MPP: 5, 4, 3, 2, 1
      TR: 500, 900, 1200, 1400, 1500
      MRP: 500, 400, 300, 200, 100
   b. 4

c. 3
d. employment level = 4; TR = $2100; profit = $900 less capital costs
e. yes
2. a. MPP: −, 5, 7, 6, 3.5, 2.5, 1
        TR: 0, 500, 1200, 1800, 2150, 2400, 2500
        MRP: −, 500, 700, 600, 350, 250, 100
    b. Quantity demanded: 1, 2, 3, 4, 5, 6
        Wage (per week): 500, 700, 600, 350, 250, 100
    c. 5
    d. 4
3. a. 0, −, +, −
    b. +, 0, +, +
    c. 0, +, −, +
    d. −, 0, −, −
    e. +, −, +, ?
4. a. No, MP of Vitacorn/P of Vitacorn = 200/800 < 400/1200 = MP of Cornpower/P of Cornpower.
    b. The farmer could produce the same output for $400 less.
    c. Yes, the decrease in the MP of Cornpower as its usage increases will cause the ratio of the MP of Cornpower to its price to decrease, eventually fulfilling the condition for cost minimization: MP of Vitacorn/P of Vitacorn = MP of Cornpower/P of Cornpower.
5. a. short-run: (10/190)/(5/35) = 0.37; long-run: (50/150)/(5/35) = 2.33
6. a.

500	500
912	412
1242	330
1496	254
1680	184
1800	120
1911	111
1976	65
1998	22
1980	−18

    b. L = 7; Q = 49; profit = 1111; ATC = 16.33
    c. 4 x 39 = 156; no

Learning the Mechanics – Multiple Choice

1. c. There will be many workers with these skills (many close substitutes). (p. 597)
2. b. The demand for resources is *derived from* the demand for the product. (p. 586)
3. a. The "marginal revenue product" is the value of the labor services to the firm. (p. 591)
4. c. A small change in resource price raises product cost and reduces sales greatly. (pp. 589-90)
5. b. Additional employment would *add* more to revenue than it would *add* to cost. (pp. 591 and 594)
6. a. The greater the demand for the product, the greater the demand for the resources. (p. 586)
7. a. Products which use the resource intensively will become more expensive. (p. 586)
8. b. It takes time to develop substitutes for the skills of carpenters. (pp. 588-89)

9. b. Since $P = MR$, marginal revenue product = value of marginal product. (p. 591)
10. d. It would use the cheaper resource intensively, driving down its marginal product. (p. 594)
11. a. If, e.g., $MPP_L/P_L > MPP_K/P_K$, diverting \$1 from buying K to buying L raises output. (p. 594)
12. d. This causes a *movement along* the demand curve (change in quantity demanded). (pp. 589-91)
13. b. The increased demand for law services will raise the clerks' MRP. (p. 591)
14. b. Wages will fall because of the lack of competition. [This question anticipates the topic of monopsony in Chapter 26.] (pp. 662-63)
15. b. Capital is more productive and costs less. (p. 594)

The Economic Way of Thinking – Multiple Choice

1. a. The other three have more easily available substitutes. (p. 597)
2. c. Price and quantity usually decrease when demand decreases.
3. b. The large short-run wage increase will encourage acquisition of engineering skills. (pp. 598-99)
4. c. This requires few acquired skills, hence there are many substitutes. (p. 597)
5. d. The aid would attract more students, increasing supply. (p. 598)
6. b. Economists are choosing alternative employments. (pp. 596-99)
7. d. Both would tend to offset the decrease in quantity demanded caused by higher prices. (pp. 586-87)
8. c. In most "capitalist" countries, but trading physical capital is illegal in some countries. (p. 586)
9. b. Lower cost resources would be substituted; less intensive use raises marginal product. (p. 594)
10. a. Aluminum bats and canoes are artificially under-priced. (pp. 586-87 and 591)
11. c. If machines have human sensibilities we are unaware of them. (p. 586)
12. c. This would make supply very inelastic in the (one year) short run. (pp. 597-99)
13. b. Employers will not be willing to pay more for workers with college degrees; competition will equalize wages. (p. 580)

CHAPTER 24

True or False

The following are true: 1, 2, 7, 9, 10, 12,13.

Problems and Projects

1. a. $Q = 3,000$; $P = \$300$
   b. $Q = 4,000$; $P = \$200$
   c. Employment rises from 120 to 128.
   d. See "Myths of Economics," pp. 600-601.
2. a. L_o
   b. $L_o \times .90$
   c. $+; 0; +; ?; -$
   d. Employers would substitute unskilled workers for machinery.

3. a. B1
   b. B2
   c. A3
   d. A2
   e. C2
   f. A1
4. a. 2 times as high; 10 times as high; 5 times as high.
   b. Brazil; Canada; neither
   c. False; Canadian workers can still compete because of their greater productivity.

Learning the Mechanics – Multiple Choice

1. a. A result of traditional work specialization patterns within the family. (pp. 612-15)
2. d. Real wages are principally determined by productivity. (p. 619)
3. d. By assumption the question eliminates other reasons for earnings differentials. (Thumbnail Sketch, p. 610)
4. c. Elasticity measures responsiveness between wage changes and employment changes. (pp. 624-25)
5. a. Believe it or not, your marginal productivity is rising as you read these words. (pp. 606-608)
6. c. When required to pay more, firms will reduce employment of the least skilled. (p. 624)
7. a. Security of income attracts more workers (increases supply) and lowers wages. (pp. 608-609)
8. d. See the definition, p. 608.
9. b. See The Economic Way of Thinking – Discussion Questions, problem 7.
10. a. Profit-minded producers are usually interested in keeping costs low. (See the definition, p. 620)
11. a. 60 men are hired at $120, while only 33 women are hired at $70. (pp. 610-11)
12. c. Employers are paying men $120 to do what a women could do for only slightly more than $70. (p. 611)
13. d. The wage will be $120 for both males and females. (pp. 624-25)
14. c. The wage would fall to $100. (pp. 610-11)

The Economic Way of Thinking – Multiple Choice

1. a. Services of more productive workers are worth more; undesirable jobs would pay more. (pp. 606-608 and 608-609)
2. c. There would be excess supply of these workers' services. (pp. 624-26)
3. d. These are some of the problems with mandated benefits (pp. 618-19)
4. c. They could earn more than the average wage by working in the private sector. (pp. 606-608)
5. b. The exemption would increase employment of black teenagers. (pp. 624-27)
6. c. See the discussion, pp. 612-15.
7. c. True, although automation can harm *specific* individuals or groups. (pp. 620-21)
8. c. The extension would encourage automation in the car wash industry. (pp. 620-21 and 624-25)
9. d. Technological progress raises labor productivity which raises real wages. (pp. 619-20)

10. b.   Is that a "discouraging word?" (pp. 608-609)
11. b.   Only the most productive bricklayers would find employment at the high wage. (pp. 624-25)
12. b.   Training (human capital formation) is often acquired on the job. (p. 608)
13. b.   Customers will be willing to pay higher prices to the discriminating firm. (pp. 610-11)

CHAPTER 25

True or False

The following are true: 1, 3, 5, 6, 7, 9, 12.

Problems and Projects

1. a. $2000(0.5066) = $1013.20 = value of broker A option
         $1000(0.6806) + $1000(0.4632) = $1143.80 = value of broker B option
    b. $1000(0.5674) + $1000(0.3220) = $889.40
    c.   14% = 12% + 2% inflationary premium
2. Price would have to exceed $1 per board foot. [$334/0.0334 = $10,000, so $334 now = $10,000 in 30 years = $1 per board foot for 10,000 board feet]
3. $12,502 + $11,158 + $9,968 + $8,904 = $42,532
4. a. $12,500
    b. $4,761,900
    c. $15,000
5. The present value of the cost of the course is $6,000 + 6($1,250) = $13,500. The present value of the income stream of $2,000 a year at an interest rate of 8% is $13,420 (from Exhibit 3 in the text), so you should *not* make this investment in your "human capital" for income reasons alone. If the course (or the skills it provides you with) is worth $81 or more in personal enjoyment, then you should take it.
6. a.   248.68; same
    b.   Buy the new refrigerator; the present value of the electricity savings (486.84 x 1.5 = $730.26) plus the resale value ($51.32) = $781.58; this exceeds the $700 cost of the refrigerator.

Learning the Mechanics – Multiple Choice

1. c.   Constructing capital equipment uses resources that could produce consumption goods. (p. 632)
2. c.   More resources would be used for present consumption leaving less for investment. (pp. 633-35)
3. c.   To offset the decline in the real value of a given nominal amount invested. (p. 635)
4. d.   Net Present Value = $100 / (1 + i). (p. 637)
5. a.   Net Present Value = $100 /(1.06) = $94.34. (p. 637)
6. c.   "Pure" interest is yielded regardless of the risk premium. (p. 636)
7. c.   NPV after 1 year = $100 /(1 + i); NPV after two years = $100 /(1 + i)^2. (pp. 637-38)
8. b.   Discounting applies to *any* investment decision; do machines have feelings? (pp. 637-42)
9. c.   As the legal right to monopoly profit, the patent itself is valuable.

10. a.   See the definition, p. 636.
11. b.   He perceived entrepreneurs as the major dynamic force of capitalism. (p. 644)
12. b.   4% plus 3%. (p. 636 and Exhibit 2, p. 637)
13. b.   With risk, the interest rate should be 9%, and $10,000/(1.09) = $9,174. (p. 636)
14. c. $9,900/(1.10) = $9,000. (pp. 637 and 639)

The Economic Way of Thinking – Multiple Choice

1. b.   A change in profit expectations will *shift* the demand for loanable funds out. (pp. 633-35)
2. c.   Interest could be paid in corn or fish or any other item of value. (pp. 633-34)
3. c.   Grasshoppers have high time preference, ants have low (remember the fable?). (p. 633)
4. d.   A below-equilibrium interest rate means excess demand for loanable funds. (p. 634)
5. c.   Dollar price falls so fixed dollar return yields a higher nominal *rate* of return. (p. 635)
6. b.   Heavy investment raises the supply of cattle, reducing return to cattle ranching. (p. 634)
7. c.   The owner could benefit from high risk premiums. (p. 636)
8. d.   Bond prices fall so their fixed returns may yield higher nominal rates of return. (p. 635)
9. c.   Current value of investments reflects current expectations of future profits. (pp. 644-45)
10. a.   See the discussion, pp. 646-49.
11. a.   Luck, efficiency and protection from competition can yield economic profit. (pp. 642-45)
12. b.   Guaranteed higher prices raise the value of crops produced on the farmland. (pp. 648-49)
13. d.   Higher interest rates mean heavier discounting; earlier retirement means shorter benefit period; higher high school grad wage means smaller wage premium for college degree. (pp. 641-42)

Microcross

CHAPTER 26

True or False

The following are true: 3, 5, 8, 9.

Problems and Projects

2. a. $7
    b. $8
    c. employment will decrease by 200 and total income will fall by $900 from $4,900 to $4,000 per hour
    d. (200/1) / (15/200) = (−) 2.5
3. a. Total labor cost: 6000, 8800, 12000, 15600
        Marginal labor cost: 24, 28, 32, 36
    c. 250; $19
    d. more, 300
4. a. 8   12
    b. 14   6
    c. 10   10
    d. 12   8
5. b. 1   −
    c. 3   +
    d. 2   −
    e. 3   +
    f. 1   −

Learning the Mechanics – Multiple Choice

1. b. Making the demand for union labor relatively inelastic increasing union strength. (pp. 665-66)
2. c. See the data, pp. 667-68.
3. b. See the definition, p. 662.
4. c. To the contrary, increased supplies in other areas might reduce other wages. (pp. 669-71)
5. c. Higher product prices would cause layoffs; machines would replace lost jobs. (pp. 664-67)
6. b. Just as MFC > resource price, so MR < product price. (pp. 662-63)
7. c. See Exhibit 3 and pp. 658-59.
8. c. See the definition, p. 656.
9. c. These factors largely determine income. (a preview from Ch. 27!)
10. a. Strikes can be extremely costly to employers. (p. 658)
11. c. The fifth worker produces and costs an extra $7.00/hour. (p. 591)
12. c. $44 minus $25 equals $19. (p. 591)
13. c. The 7th worker produces only an extra $5 and will not be hired. (p. 591)

The Economic Way of Thinking – Multiple Choice

1. d. A strike would be extremely costly to both. (p. 658)

2. b. Arc elasticity of demand = (100,000/700,000) / 1.00 = 0.14   1. (pp. 664-65)
3. a. See the "Myth," pp. 670-71.
4. c. See the data, pp. 667-68.
5. c. Management would be more likely to grant wage increases. (pp. 666-67)
6. d. All would reduce the real wages of nonunion workers. (pp. 660-61, 665-66, 670-72)
7. c. Both can raise both wage level and quantity employed. (pp. 661-64)
8. a. The more inelastic the product demand, the more powerful the union. (pp. 665-66)
9. b. A specific result of the general phenomenon of "economizing behavior." (pp. 665 and 667)
10. b. Employers would favor higher wages that raise profits.
11. b. Monopoly power may successfully bargain with monopsony power. (pp. 662-64)
12. d. Union membership has been declining; there is no evidence that unions raise the wages of all workers. (Exhibit 1, p. 655 and pp. 670-71)

CHAPTER 27

True or False

The following are true: 1, 5, 7, 9, 10

Problems and Projects

1. a. 200 hours
   b. 1143 hours
   c. 571 hours
   d. 667 hours
   g. Probably not; presumably, Jane could drop out of the transfer program if she wished.
2. Government subsidy: 3000, 2500, 2000, 1500, 1000, 500, 0
   Total income: 4000, 5000, 5500, 6000, 6500, 7000, 7500, 8000
3. a. Yes; society's tax burden is reduced by $58 each week that Reckman works.
   b. No, he will lose $18 a week by taking the job.
   c. Marginal tax rate = 109%
   d. Yes, his net income from the job would be greater than his net unemployment compensation.
4. a. Falling from the top.
   b.

100	0	0
0	100	0
0	0	100

   c.

20	60	20
20	60	20
20	60	20

5. a.

(3) 8.7	62.5	100.0
(4) 4.6	55.4	100.0
(5) 7.4	58.3	100.0

   c. more; less; Lorenz Curves cross

Learning the Mechanics – Multiple Choice

1. b. See Exhibit 1, p. 680.
2. b. See Exhibit 4, p. 685.
3. c. Some of the recipient's transfer income would be reduced. (p. 698)
4. a. See Exhibit 7 and pp. 690-91.
5. a. See Exhibit 1. (p. 680)
6. a. See Exhibit 2, p. 681.
7. b. Lifetime income inequality is overstated by annual income data. (pp. 680-82)
8. d. See the discussion, p. 689.
9. a. That's right, a "conservative." (p. 698)
10. d. See Exhibit 13, p. 701.
11. c. Tax rate cuts did help high-income Americans. (pp. 684-85)

The Economic Way of Thinking – Multiple Choice

1. d. Which equals the return the individual would have earned on employed resources.
2. a. We have created a system that actually makes it more difficult to escape poverty. (pp. 694-96)
3. b. See Exhibit 4, p. 685.
4. c. Annual incomes for the retired are less than their lifetime average; vice versa for prime-age earners. (pp. 680-82)
5. c. The threshold income level is measured in "real" (inflation adjusted) terms. (p. 689)
6. a. See the discussion, p. 690.
7. d. People generally prefer money to specific goods. (p. 689)
8. d. All three have been suggested as reasons for a negative income tax system. (pp. 698-99)
9. a. See Exhibit 7, p. 691.
10. b. Increased earnings usually mean decreased welfare benefits, often equally. (pp. 695-96)
11. c. Income mobility and time are important in determining income inequality. (pp. 686-87)

CHAPTER 28

True or False

The following are true: 2, 3, 4, 7, 9, 10.

Problems and Projects

1. a. $1.30
   b. $1.38; 95 million gallons per day
   c. long run

2. b. C   C
   c. D   C
   d. D   D
   e. C   D

3. a. 45, 60, 75, 90, 105
   b. zero
   c. profits will increase to $675; 0.47
   d. 40, 65, 90, 115
   e. $225; profits are lower in the long run; 1.00

4. a. $15; 45 MBD; no
   b. $30; 25 MBD; yes; 70 TBD
   c. $15; 45 MBD; no; 50 TBD
      (answers approximate)

Learning the Mechanics – Multiple Choice

1. b.   Changes in energy prices would not affect either quantity demanded or supplied. (p. 711)
2. c.   In the long run, changes can be made more easily. (pp. 704-10 and 712)
3. a.   Marginal values are used, but opportunity costs *should* be used. (pp. 713-16)
4. c.   It takes time to adjust consumption; lengthy time period means inelastic short run. (pp. 709-712)
5. a.   See the data. (p. 713)
6. c.   See the definition and discussion, p. 712.
7. d.   See Exhibit 5 on page 723.
8. c.   An economic response based on the principle of economizing behavior. (See **Myths of Economics**, p. 720)
9. c.   As items become scarce, we use more alternatives. (pp. 720-21)
10. b.   See "**Myths of Economics**, pp. 720-21.
11. b.   The development of substitutes (energy saving technology) requires time. (pp. 709-710)
12. d.   See the definition, p. 712.

The Economic Way of Thinking – Multiple Choice

1. b.   Such profiteers may maximize short-run profits, but they are ignoring the long-run situation. (pp. 718-19)
2. b.   Social costs are very difficult to evaluate and incorporate into profit-maximizing behavior. (pp. 718-19 and 723-24)
3. b.   Natural resources should be used in their most valued use. (pp. 714-15)
4. d.   See the discussion, pp. 716-18.
5. c.   The goal of the program is to reduce pollution efficiently, not to eliminate all pollution. (pp. 740-41)
6. d.   An EPA official stated that determining prices for the allotments "can best be done in the private sector."
7. a.   The underlying principles are similar. (p. 722)
8. b.   Polluters should decline to pay a higher allotment price. (pp. 722-23)
9. c.   There should be long-run gains, although short-run losses are certainly possible. (pp. 718-722)
10. c.   See the discussion, p. 717.
11. a.   Not discounting future benefits raises apparent net benefits. (p. 717)

CHAPTER 29

True or False

The following are true: 1, 2, 4, 6, 7, 10, 13, 14.

Problems and Projects

1. a. 80 cents, 100 per month
    b. 110, 130 (marginal social cost = producer's marginal cost + external cost)
    c. 90 per month
3. a. 2.0 cents per pound for the beet refiner and 6.0 cents per pound for the petroleum refiner.
    b. beet refiner: 80%; petroleum refiner: 45%
    c. See the discussion, pp. 722-24.
4. a. 14.00, 10.00, 8.00, 6.00, 4.00
    b. 2
    c. $5.00 − $3.00 = $2.00; $34.00
    d. 6; $71.00; $56.00
    e. yes; yes
    f. People have a strong incentive to become free-riders and enjoy external benefits (like a nice looking neighborhood) without paying part of the costs.
5. a. 48; 48; 96
    b. 60; at zero pollution, control costs exceed damage costs.
    c. 60; 30
    d. $40 per ton
    e. 36; 24
    f. rise; fall; rise

Learning the Mechanics – Multiple Choice

1. c. There are significant external costs of production; both air and water pollution. (pp. 729-30)
2. c. No net gains means no participation; sum of individual net gains = net social gain. (p. 729)
3. b. Demand curve includes only private benefits, not the external social benefits. (pp. 733 and 736)
4. c. This generates both noise and air pollution, which are external costs. (p. 729)
5. c. See the discussion, p. 743.
6. a. External costs are external to (not included in) private price and output decisions. (pp. 730-31)
7. a. Unsatisfied customers may not return. (p. 746)
8. b. Externalities are not part of the decisions of competitive decision makers. (p. 729)
9. b. Since they add significantly to the costs of producing pollution-intensive goods. (pp. 737-38)
10. c. See the discussion, p. 734.
11. a. The socially highest-valued use is also of the highest value to the individual. (p. 732)
12. b. A ban or no policy won't reach the target; discharge permits can reach the target but are more efficient if marketable. (pp. 740-41)

The Economic Way of Thinking – Multiple Choice

1. b. What one individual does not catch (conserve), another most likely will. (pp. 732-33 and 735)
2. c. One individual's misuse of an automobile causes injury to other individuals. (p. 730)

3. d. Courts have given receptors property rights, but enforcement costs can be high. (pp. 732-33 and 741-42)
4. b. This is an instance of the "free rider" problem. (p. 743)
5. d. Economizing behavior means acting only when benefits exceed costs at the margin. (p. 739)
6. b. Such information is easily available and subject to the free rider problem. (p. 743)
7. b. Overutilization is one of the problems associated with common property rights (pp. 732-33)
8. d. Monopolies restrict output, which can raise efficiency if the good has external costs, but the result depends on how much output falls. (Ch. 20 and pp. 730-32)
9. c. Only reductions costing less than the emission charge will be undertaken. (pp. 737-40)
10. d. The firm may lose sales of *all* its various products, not just the new one. (p. 747)
11. a. At Q = 4000. (p. 730)
12. a. P = $3.00 includes private and external costs. (p. 730-31)
13. b. $1.20 plus the $1.80 marginal cost. (p. 731)
14. c. $3.00 minus $2.00 (pp. 112-13)

CHAPTER 30

True or False

The following are true: 1, 2, 3, 4, 7, 8, 10, 11, 13.

Problems and Projects

1. a. 26/4, 20/18, 10/13.
   b. Proposal A will be attractive to the political entrepreneur. B will be unattractive. Proposal C will be attractive since the perceived benefit/cost ratio is 10/6 = 1.67, and the voters would favor it.
   c. The costs of obtaining information about Proposal B might be higher than the benefits of the proposal for these voters.
3. (1) c; (2) e; (3) a; (4) b; (5) f; (6) d.
4. a.
120	70
90	90
60	110
30	130
0	150
   b. 30; 50; 0

Learning the Mechanics — Multiple Choice

1. b. Public sector action may correct the inefficiency of the market. (pp. 756-57)
2. c. If some persons benefit without paying, private demand is inefficiently low. (pp. 756-57)
3. a. Legislators and voters are self-interested as well as socially-interested (pp. 754-56)
4. c. These persons are guided by self-interest as well as public interest. (pp. 754-56)
5. d. Information costs may be worthwhile only if there are direct personal benefits. (pp. 759-61)

6. d. These groups are less costly to organize and gain substantially from lobbying. (pp. 759-60)
7. c. The collective process only imprecisely reflects individual preferences. (pp. 754-55)
8. d. Government allocation can efficiently correct this market failure. (pp. 756-57)
9. b. This minimizes vote loss and maximizes vote gain for the politician. (pp. 759-60)
10. b. Information costs are high and personal benefits low. (p. 760)
11. b. In fact, savings due to extra efficiency may *reduce* the agency's budget. (pp. 765-68)

The Economic Way of Thinking – Multiple Choice

1. a. Pursuit of gain is a strong motivator in both sectors, regardless of whether decision-makers admit it . (pp. 755-56)
2. c. This is the rational ignorance effect. (p. 754)
3. a. There's no free lunch for society, but individuals may take a "free ride." (Ch. 4 and p. 770)
4. b. Private market demand for this enforcement is low due to free rider effects. (pp. 756-57)
5. b. This is likely to maximize political entrepreneurs' votes. (pp. 759-61)
6. d. This is consistent with maximum self-interest for the voter. (pp. 754-55)
7. b. This is consistent with maximum self-interest for the voters. (pp. 758-61)
8. d. This is consistent with vote maximization for the politician. (pp. 755-56)
9. a. Voters perceive only benefits before election, maximizing politicians' chances. (p. 765)
10. c. Low organization costs would produce strong opposition from the other groups. (p. 760)
11. c. They stand to benefit directly from cost reductions; the others do not. (pp. 765-68)
12. d. Each consumer benefits little while the others reap substantial individual benefits. (p. 760)
13. d. Auctioning permits removes rents, makes costs explicit and raises government revenue. (pp. 761-62)
14. c. The present value of the expected benefits from smart moves is captured in stock prices. (pp. 763-64)
15. a. See the discussion, p. 762.

CHAPTER 31

True or False

The following are true: 1, 3, 4, 6, 8, 12.

Problems and Projects

1. a. 2 units of clothing; 1 unit of clothing
   b. Mutual gains would result if Rhineland traded clothing for Nepal's food.
   c. 100 *additional* units of clothing are available to Rhineland; 50 *additional* units of clothing are available to Nepal; join output has increased.
   d. 125 *additional* units of clothing are available to Rhineland; 75 *additional* units of clothing are available to Nepal; join output has increased.
   e. 2/3 of a unit of food; 2/3 of a unit of food; no; no; additional gains are not possible because the opportunity costs of production have been equalized in the two countries.

2. a. 1100, 1170, 1240, 1310, 1380, 1450, 1520.
   b. $1800; 900
   c. $2200
   d. 1100
   e. 800
   f. 300
   g. price has decreased; I would be unhappy about receiving a lower price for my product; I would increase my quantity demanded.

3. a. $4000; 900
   b. $3000; 1300; 700; 600; 200
   c. $3500; 100; 200; 300
   d. rise to $3500; 100
   e. The only difference is that with a tariff the government gets the $500 per motorcycle, and with the quota the motorcycle importers receive the $500 difference (per imported motorcycle) between the import price of $3000 and the domestic motorcycle price of $3500.

4. a. US; US; SK; US
   b. South Korea
   c. $+10$ -50
      $+ 2$ $+30$
      $+16$ -32
      -10 $+50$
      $+ 6$ $+18$

5. a. $105 million; $67.5 million; $15 million; $22.5 million
   b. $150,000
   c. 25,000

Learning the Mechanics – Multiple Choice

1. c. Having a comparative advantage means being a low-opportunity-cost producer. (pp. 784-86)
2. c. Foreign exports (our imports) provide foreign buying power for our exports. (p. 788)
3. b. Otherwise we should buy and store cheap imports. (p. 794)
4. c. Such a tariff protects them from foreign competition. (p. 792)
5. c. Buy goods abroad when they are cheaper than alternative domestic products. (p. 782)
6. b. 2 units of clothing must be sacrificed to obtain 4 units of food; $2/4 = 1/2$. (p. 784)
7. b. Slavia's opportunity cost of food $= 5/3$ clothing $> 1/2 =$ Italia's opportunity cost. (pp. 784-87)
8. c. Each country should export its low-opportunity-cost product. (p. 786)
9. a. Iowa exports corn both to the other states and to the rest of the world. (p. 782)
10. b. To help them "mature" (become efficient) in the long run. (p. 794)
11. c. Both a and b are opposite the correct statements. (pp. 796-97)
12. d. Total consumption increases and less wine is consumed in order to trade it for more bread. (pp. 784-85)

The Economic Way of Thinking – Multiple Choice

1. a. Increased competition lowers price; increased foreign sales raise their incomes. (pp. 790-91)

2. d.   Reduced foreign competition from the tariff benefits workers in the industry. (p. 794)
3. c.   Increased price of foreign watches causes increased demand for domestic watches. (p. 791)
4. c.   Consumers gain through low prices; producers at worst do not lose. (pp. 790-92)
5. b.   Arguments for restrictions usually appeal (wrongly?) to the "national interest." (pp. 790-92)
6. c.   Foreign competition lowers price which lowers domestic quantity supplied. (p. 789)
7. b.   Special interest groups have a disproportionate influence on politicians. (p. 797)
8. a.   Try, for example, to trace increased farm employment to reduced auto tariffs. (pp. 796-97)
9. c.   This is the *basic* lesson of comparative advantage. (p. 782)
10. b.   Foreign demand raises price which increases domestic quantity supplied. (p. 788)
11. b.   World equilibrium is at P = $20. (pp. 788-89)
12. b.   The U.S. tariff will have a small but measurable effect on the world market. (pp. 790-91 and Exhibit 10, p. 792)
13. c.   The tariff creates deadweight loss. (See Exhibit 10, p. 792)
14. b.   The amount needed to get the same result as #12 above. (p. 792)

CHAPTER 32

True or False

The following are true: 1, 2, 8, 10, 11.

Problems and Projects

1. (1). d; (2) a; (3) e; (4) b; (5); f; (6) c.
2. b. 0, −, depreciate
   c. −, +, appreciate
   d. +, −, depreciate
   e. −, +, appreciate
   f. +, +, indeterminate
   g. 0, 0, no change
3. a. (1) − 25.3; (2) 36.1; (3) 3.7; (4) 4.5; (5) 8.2
   b. See the discussion, pp. 796-97.

Learning the Mechanics – Multiple Choice

1. a.   Residents usually want payment in their own national currency. (p. 803)
2. b.   Cheaper foreign currency means cheaper foreign goods and services. (pp. 804-805)
3. d.   The statement includes *all* the international economic transactions. (p. 813)
4. b.   Excess sales mean excess receipts (a surplus) of payments. (p. 813)
5. a.   More exports mean greater demand for nation's currency causing *appreciation*. (pp. 807-810)
6. a.   An increase in supply (of *anything*) tends to decrease price (cause depreciation). (p. 805)
7. d.   Exchange rates do not fluctuate but monetary policy is committed to fixing them. (pp. 826-28)
8. c.   Foreign ability to buy from us depends (partly) on the amount we buy from them. (pp. 788-89 and pp. 813-14)
9. b.   High prices promote imports; low interest rates promote financial asset exports. (pp. 812-13)

10. d. This creates a foreign (South American) demand for U.S. currency (to be loaned). (p. 814)
11. b. Depreciation makes foreign goods more expensive and domestic goods cheaper. (pp. 805-806)
12. c. See the definition, p. 823.
13. d. The exchange rate depreciation more than offsets the effect on imports of any increase in GNP. (pp. 818-20)

The Economic Way of Thinking — Multiple Choice

1. b. Increased sales increase U.S. receipts and reduce the deficit. (p. 814)
2. c. Unilateral transfers abroad decrease; exports decrease but by a lesser amount. (p. 816)
3. a. U.S. receives more goods to consume and gives up only pieces of paper. (pp. 812-14)
4. c. Increased imports mean increased payments to foreigners. (p. 814)
5. a. Higher real interest rates promote financial asset exports. (p. 813)
6. c. Dollars are spent to acquire the pesos to buy the mine. (pp. 814-16)
7. b. Higher prices raise demand for foreign exchange (imports) and lower supply (exports). (pp. 808-810)
8. c. Monetary policy is freed to pursue other goals such as price stability. (p. 820)
9. c. See the definitions, pp. 805 and 812.
10. b. It raises dollar price of foreign currency, raising dollar price of foreign goods. (p. 805)
11. c. It is making excess payments on current account transactions. (pp. 814-16)
12. a. Inelastic means *quantities* imported and exported respond little to price changes. (pp. 822-23)
13. c. Higher prices and output cause depreciation, while higher interest rates cause appreciation, but all induce a deficit in the current account. (pp. 814-16 and 819)
14. d. The deficit in the capital account exceeds the surplus in the current account, thereby draining official reserves. (pp. 813-18)
15. d. The lower rate will cause a capital outflow, depreciating the currency and causing a current account surplus. (p. 820)

CHAPTER 33

True or False

The following are true: 1, 2, 4, 5, 6, 8, 9, 11.

Problems and Projects

1. a. (2)
   b. (3)
   c. (1)
   d. (4)
2. a. &200
   b. $400; difference = $5930
   c. &299.5 billion; 326.2 million; &918.15.
   d. $13,976.64.

e. $1,836.30; $12,140.34; even though Gromangro grew at a faster rate than the U.S., the amount that its per capita GNP was lagging behind that of the U.S. more than doubled.
4.   a.   35; 20; 10
     b.   38.9; 16.3; 13.7; 10.4; 16.3; 48.8
     c.   3.1   6.0   5.6
          38.9   13.7   16.3
          22.6   11.7   12.5

Learning the Mechanics – Multiple Choice

1.   d.   Poor countries usually have more unequally distributed incomes than rich ones. (pp. 833-35)
2.   b.   See Exhibit 2, p. 835
3.   d.   See Exhibit 2, p. 835.
4.   d.   See the discussion, p. 834.
5.   a.   See the definition, p. 836.
6.   b.   This definition is economically meaningful to the wide body of the population. (pp. 838-39)
7.   a.   Population may be growing more rapidly than real GNP. (p. 839)
8.   c.   The negative interest rate causes capital fight. (pp. 845-46)
9.   c.   See Problems and Projects, Exhibit 1.
10. c.   See the discussion, pp. 846-47.
11. a.   It uses readily available data. (p. 836)
12. c.   It attempts to measure the actual consumption bundles available. (pp. 836-38)

The Economic Way of Thinking – Multiple Choice

1.   c.   U.S. per capita GNP is 26 times the per capita GNP of Egypt. (pp. 838-39)
2.   b.   % per capita GNP growth = % GNP growth – % population growth. (p. 839)
3.   d.   There is a wide variety of growth experiences *within* each of these groups. (pp. 833-35)
4.   b.   The influence of population change is precisely what is meant by *per capita*. (p. 839)
5.   c.   Find in the other answers the characteristic unrelated to poverty. (pp. 833-35)
6.   b.   6000 pounds x $3 per pound = $18,000 > $16,000. (p. 803)
7.   a.   See the definitions, p. 839.
8.   b.   A rapidly growing country is not necessarily also improving the general standard of living. (pp. 838-39)
9.   b.   Low investment caused by such instability is a main obstacle to growth. (pp. 844-46)
10. a.   Rabushka feels that the improved incentives will outweigh any reduced spending. (pp. 846-47)
11. b.   All the others are much more "absurd." (p. 849)
12. a.   [(45,588.5/256.9)/78.5] / (3957.0/239.3) = 2,261/16,536 = 13.7%. (pp. 803 and 836)
13. d.   GNP in Mexico has fallen from 5 to 4.5 percent of U.S. GNP; GNP per capita in Mexico has fallen from 19 percent to 14 percent of U.S. GNP per capita. (pp. 803 and 836)

CHAPTER 34

True or False

The following are true: 1, 4, 5, 7, 9, 10, 12.

Problems and Projects

1. (1) d; (2) c; (3) a; (4) b; (5) e; (6) g.
3. b., c., e., d., a., g.

Learning the Mechanics – Multiple Choice

1. c. Significant guidance by central planners is a common characteristic of socialism. (pp. 857-58)
2. d. A communistic system has all these except private property rights. (pp. 856-57)
3. a. By the time you read this, the answer will probably be even lower! (See Exhibit 7, p. 869)
4. c. This would imply some form of human slavery, certainly not an aspect of socialism. (pp. 858-59)
5. c. In an attempt to generate rapid growth and industrialization. (pp. 863-64)
6. d. The others rely much more on markets for resource allocation than the U.S.S.R. does. (p. 859)
7. b. At least until 1997. (See Exhibit 2, p. 860)
8. d. See the discussion, pp. 879-81.
9. b. Loaves of bread would be as heavy as possible. (p. 863)
10. b. See the discussion, pp. 879-80.
11. a. See the discussion, p. 880.

The Economic Way of Thinking – Multiple Choice

1. c. Wage structures and training costs are strongly influenced by central planners. (pp. 858-59)
2. a. An appropriate principle of efficiency in *any* economic system. (p. 857)
3. c. Apparently the change in reward structure caused the change in behavior. (p. 857)
4. a. There is a shortage in the good at the centrally planned price. (p. 864)
5. a. See the definition, p. 861.
6. d. All three are likely to be caused by the shortage at the centrally planned price. (pp. 864-66)
7. a. Keeping up with changes in this country (commonwealth?) is as easy as throwing a feather into the wind, but as of our press date, answer a was correct. (p. 871)
8. a. This is perhaps because of little conflict between labor and management. (pp. 879-80)
9. d. Short-term difficulties stand in the way of long-run gains. (p. 871)
10. c. Trade between the former republics would seem likely to fall. (pp. 874-75)
11. b. Since lifetime employment makes labor a fixed cost, firms can't reduce costs through lay-offs and also become more hesitant to hire new workers. (pp. 879-80)